The Middle Kingdom

Erwin Wickert was born in Brandenberg in 1915, and first visited China as a student in 1936. He joined the diplomatic service at the beginning of the war, and was stationed in China and Japan from 1939 to 1945.

Returning to Germany in 1947, he established a reputation as a writer, particularly of radio plays. He went back into the diplomatic service in 1955 but continued to write, publishing two novels.

His diplomatic posts included special envoy to London and then German ambassador in Bucharest, and finally, from 1976 to 1980, ambassador of the German Federal Republic in China, where, 40 years earlier, he had started as an attaché.

THE
MIDDLE KINGDOM
Inside China Today

Erwin Wickert
Translated by J. Maxwell Brownjohn

Pan Books   London and Sydney
in association with Collins

First published in Germany as *China von innen gesehen*
by Deutsche Verlags-Anstalt GmbH, Stuttgart, 1981
© Deutsche Verlags-Anstalt GmbH, Stuttgart, 1981
First published in Great Britain 1983 by Harvill Press
This edition published 1984 by Pan Books Ltd,
Cavaye Place, London SW10 9PG
in association with William Collins Sons & Co. Ltd
9 8 7 6 5 4 3 2 1
ISBN 0 330 28371 5
Set, printed and bound in Great Britain by
Cox & Wyman Ltd, Reading

Contents

On the Spelling and Pronunciation of Chinese Words

In Chinese, every syllable used originally to be a word in its own right, and each is expressed on paper by a character. Between three and four thousand of these characters are in general use today. Although many attempts have been made to transliterate them into Roman script, all leave something to be desired.

This book employs Pinyin transliteration, a Chinese-approved system which is steadily gaining international currency. In the case of a very few personal and place names such as Peking, Canton, Tientsin, Confucius, and Chiang Kai-shek, the traditional spellings have been retained.

Readers may care to note the following peculiarities of the Pinyin system:

> **q** is pronounced **ch** (as in *ch*eap)
> **x** approximates to **sh** (as in *sh*e)
> **c** is pronounced **ts** (as in bi*ts*)
> **z** is pronounced **tz** (as in *z*ero)
> **zh** is pronounced **j** (as in *j*ug)
> **s** is pronounced **ss** (as in hi*ss*ing)
> **yan** becomes **yen**
> **i** after **c**, **ch**, **r**, **s**, **sh**, **z**, and **zh** approximates to the vowel sound in h*er*d
> **eng** is pronounced **ung** (as in l*ung*)
> **u** after **j**, **q**, **x**, and **y** is pronounced **u** (as in t*oo*)
>
> NB: In Chinese, the surname or family name precedes the given name.

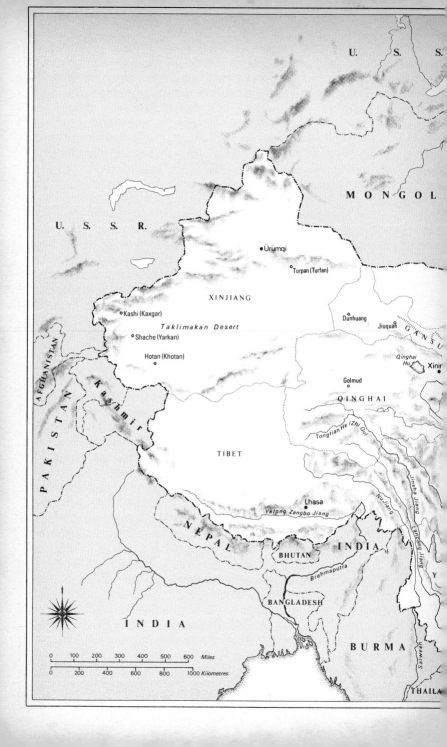

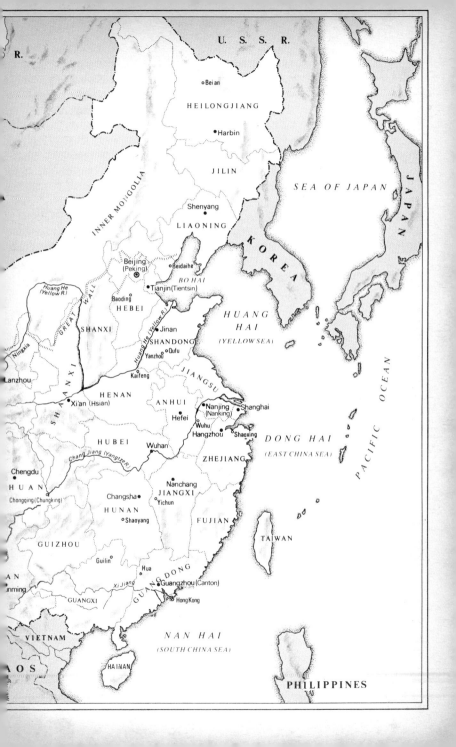

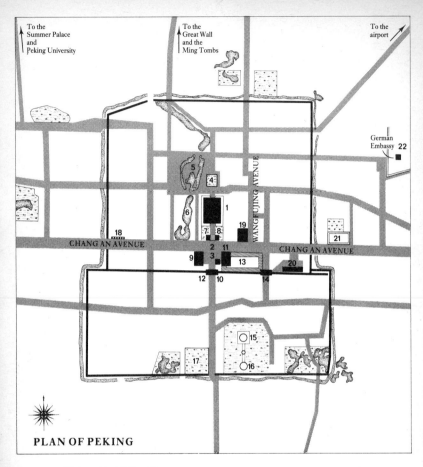

PLAN OF PEKING

1 Imperial Palace, Forbidden City
2 Tian An Men (Gate of Heavenly Peace)
3 Tian An Men Square
4 Coal Hill
5 Beihai (North Lake)
6 Zhongnanhai (Middle and South Lake),
   Party leaders' residential area
7 Sun Yat-sen Park
8 Cultural Park of the Working People
9 Great Hall of the People
10 Mao Memorial Hall
11 National Museum
12 Qian Men (formerly main south gate)
13 Former Legation Quarter
14 Hata Men (gate now demolished)

15 Temple of Heaven
16 Altar of Heaven
17 Temple of Agriculture (now built
   over)
18 'Democracy Wall'
19 Peking Hotel
20 Railroad station
21 First Diplomatic Quarter (British,
   US, and Japanese embassies)
22 Second Diplomatic Quarter (French,
   West German, East German, Swiss,
   Swedish, and other embassies)
▨▨ Extent of the former Legation Quarter
━━ Line of the old city wall,
   now demolished

Foreword

Where all condemn, one must verify.
Where all applaud, one must verify.

Confucius, *Analects* (*Lun Yü*), XV, 27.

This book recounts my experiences in China and seeks to interpret them. It does not present a formula designed to explain the country and its people. I have neither discovered such a formula nor made any great effort to do so.

I once received a visit in Peking from my friend Conrad Ahlers, the journalist. Like most people who visit China for the first time, he came armed with a ready-made theory that enabled him to understand what went on there. It took him only twenty-four hours to realize that his rule of thumb was inaccurate. The same applied to the other theories he evolved in the next few weeks, most of which he discarded just as promptly. 'I'm all mixed up,' he told me before boarding his plane. 'I know less about China now than I did when I got here.'

He had, in fact, discovered the route that leads to an understanding of China and the Chinese. Those who take it must abandon their pre-conceptions and be willing to listen with an open mind. Why? Because Chinese culture has developed in isolation from the West for thousands of years. It possesses a different system of co-ordinates as well as a different scale of values. Many visitors to China find this perplexing, if not downright perverse.

'You can't help feeling sorry for these people,' I recall a German student saying, not long after his arrival. 'They're a gifted race, sure, but hundreds of years behind the times. Technology, science, hygiene, creature comforts – those deficiencies are too glaring to mention. But as for basic human rights and liberties, personal self-fulfilment, freedom from taboos, sexual emancipation – Chinese students give me a polite hearing but seem totally uninterested in what I say. They just carry on in the same old way.'

Although plenty of modern Chinese are interested in basic human rights and democracy, the young man was right in suspecting that extreme liberalism left his fellow students cold. He continued to lecture them on the virtues of personal freedom and universal permissiveness, but not for very much longer. In preaching liberalism to the Chinese as the missionaries of the nineteenth century preached Christianity, he was flogging a dead horse.

One such missionary, the distinguished sinologist James Legge, expressed sentiments analogous to those of our student when he wrote, about a hundred years ago: 'There is hope for them if they will look away from all their ancient sages and turn to Him, who sends them, along with the dissolution of their ancient state, the knowledge of Himself, the only living and true God, and of Jesus Christ whom He hath sent.'

The Jesuits who visited China during the sixteenth, seventeenth, and eighteenth centuries penetrated more deeply into the Chinese world than the missionaries and travellers of the Victorian age. The latter, to whom everything Chinese seemed utterly 'different' and bizarre, confined themselves to passing smug and supercilious judgements on a variety of topics – Chinese music, for example, or the belief that calligraphy can be one of the supreme forms of artistic expression, or the drama of the Yüan dynasty, which has nothing dramatic to offer in the Western sense. Similar verdicts can sometimes be heard today.

The Western visitor would find many aspects of China more comprehensible if he inquired into the origins of their 'differentness', for many of them can be understood without discarding familiar criteria. Indeed, this is the only approach – the viewing of things Chinese through Western eyes and vice versa – that can lead to fruitful interaction between the two cultures. Perfervid enthusiasm for Lao-tse and the *Tao-te Ching*, meditation on the twin principles *yin* and *yang* – preferably while inhaling clouds of incense – or mystical devotion to the cryptic pronouncements of the *Yijing* (*I Ching*), on the other hand, yield nothing but misconceptions.

It is nonetheless possible to meet Western visitors who are surprised and fascinated by what comes their way in China – inquisitive souls who refrain from passing summary judgements, ask the Chinese questions, listen to their answers, and are eager to learn more. 'One of the benefits of a lengthy sojourn in Peking is that you somewhat curb your pride.' Addressed to a fellow Jesuit by Adam Schell von Bell of Cologne, these memorable words are as valid today as when he penned them in 1637.

I shall therefore try to fathom and explain certain features of China, particularly those that have emerged in recent years, from an insider's viewpoint. I would not claim to know or be capable of expounding *the* truth about China and the Chinese. There is more than one truth about this great and ancient people in whom so many traditions continue to operate, assuming different forms in every age – indeed, in every individual. I have not tried to resolve the contradictions inherent in the Chinese character – that would be impossible – but have done my best to illustrate some of those contradictions and show how the Chinese contrive to live with them.

My frequent references to Chinese history are made in defiance of Hegel's assertion that the Chinese 'really have no history at all'. The truth is that Chinese history boasts an inexhaustible wealth of dramatic figures and occurrences, notable ideas and conflicts. The Western world would profit as much from assimilating that history as it has from the study of classical antiquity, which itself is now threatened with oblivion.

I do not, however, write as a historian. I am no sinologist either, nor do I write for sinologists. This book is aimed at readers who are not content with reports on lightning tours of China – readers with an urge to understand the country and its people, learn what ideas and developments have moulded today's Chinese, and discover if their unfamiliar mental attitudes are a worthwhile object of study. This they undoubtedly are, if only because the Chinese *do* differ from ourselves.

Chinese history lacks many of the ideas that have helped to shape the Western world. The Chinese have no abstract notion of transcendence or intrinsic goodness, nor have they evolved our strict conception of property. They have taken no interest in metaphysics, logic, and epistemology. They have devoted as little thought to the concepts of space and time as to that of freedom, whether in the philosophical sense or in the realm of practical politics. It has never spontaneously occurred to them to count votes and accept majority decisions. Their thoughts have centred all the more on humanity, civilization, and education, on human relationships, on social obligations (not rights), and on the functions of government – in short, on many of the problems that currently beset our own society.

Although this book describes my tour of duty in Peking, which spanned the years 1976–80, it is not a complete, coherent, or chronological account of China's development during that period. Some political topics are discussed, others of equal importance are not. I have had to be selective. What follows is neither a textbook nor a reference book, but an aid to understanding the country and its inhabitants. It is a motley collection of anecdotes, personal encounters, observations, and descriptions – as random as the incidents I witnessed and recorded in my diary. In this I jotted down whatever seemed worthy of note, frequently varying my 'camera angle' and sometimes giving a glimpse of what goes on inside an ambassador's office.

While basing the text on a selection of diary entries, I have often expanded these by alluding to earlier experiences or inserting background material of a historical, political, and cultural nature. Different entries on the same subject have sometimes been amalgamated, for example in my accounts of Democracy Wall or the personality of Deng Xiaoping. In citing Chinese and German politicians I have kept strictly to notes made either during or immediately after our talks together. If I am reticent about their views on current political topics, it is because our discussions and the events to which they referred are still too recent.

I am indebted to those from whom I learned so much about China – colleagues, aides, and associates too numerous for me to mention them all by name. First and foremost, however, my understanding of the country was enhanced by Chinese friends and acquaintances whose contact with foreigners was not always viewed with official favour, even during the brief phase when China seemed to be flinging wide her gates to the West. I thank them for their faith in me.

Though aware that I would pass their opinions on, they were remarkably frank. For this reason, and not because they made it a condition of their candour, many of them appear in these pages with their identities disguised or their names changed. It is better so.

1976

1976

Goodbye to Hong Kong

I wished the train would put on speed. 'It stops at every last little station,' I grumbled. 'At this rate we'll take two hours to reach the frontier.' Franz rummaged in her bag for a handkerchief and mopped her brow.

It was hot and humid, and all the carriage windows were open. The other seats were occupied by students of both sexes. Right at the back, a Chinese couple presided over innumerable pieces of baggage. The woman was wearing a sleeveless dress and the man a garish sports shirt spilling over his slacks. The woman's hair was neatly permed. Their appearance stamped them as Overseas Chinese or residents of Hong Kong, and their baggage – I guessed – would be bulging with gifts for relatives in the People's Republic of China. There wasn't a 'New Man' in sight.

'If you come across a New Man,' Milovan Djilas had told me on my last visit to Belgrade, 'be sure to write me. I'm curious. Marxism-Leninism's cardinal error consists in not being tailored to man as he actually is. I'm told the Chinese have come up with a remarkable idea. Instead of tailoring communism to fit the human being, they're doing the opposite.'

'It doesn't seem to be a new idea,' I told him, '—not in China. They have a saying there: "If your shoes don't fit, cut your toes off." Anyway, how will I know a New Man if I see one?'

'That's easy. He'll look like a socialist hero on a poster: proud, strong, resolute, courageous, confident of victory, blissfully intent on the future. Socialism is his one and only thought. He has no personal needs and can survive without food. He doesn't know the meaning of envy, wants no power or privileges for himself, loves no one but the Party and the Chairman. He hates the enemies of socialism, especially Soviet hegemonists and social imperialists.'

'I'll write you as soon as I see one. All the same,' I added, 'I'd hate to think the Old Man of China was extinct.'

We were passing some eight- or ten-storeyed apartment houses. They had once been white. Now, like decaying organisms, their walls were hideously mottled with grey and black stains. Draped over bamboo poles protruding from the windows were shirts and trousers, sheets and women's dresses. They were hanging in the sun as an antidote to the mildew that lurked in their owners' hot and steamy rooms.

Huts now stood on what had once been paddy-fields. Many of them looked more than usually ramshackle because the tar-paper had been stripped off their roofs by last week's typhoon. The train pulled up alongside an open platform. Beyond it sprawled a shanty town built of timber, corrugated iron, hardboard, and sheet metal garnered from old gasoline cans. Half-naked children were playing on the paths between the hundreds of shacks. It was a spectacle wholly devoid of beauty.

We crawled on and halted, crawled on and halted again. I wondered how much longer we would take to reach the frontier post. On our right, a hill projected from the plain. The spiral road encircling it was still unpaved and looked as if it had been incised into the red mound by a milling machine. The summit had undergone partial amputation. Some of it was still intact, but the rest had been sawn off flat. No, not sawn – eaten away. Closer inspection revealed that a dozen-odd excavators and bulldozers were busy gnawing the summit level. Half-way up the hill one could visualize tennis courts and parking lots and apartment houses taking shape on a ferro-concrete plateau. They would have a view of lush green paddy-fields stretching away to the bay and the sea beyond, not of the railroad track, the shanty town, and its neighbouring dump for wrecked cars.

The spiral red wound would soon heal. Trees and shrubs, which grew quickly in this climate, were being planted on either side of it. A couple of thousand people – those who could afford to – would move here from Hong Kong, but their exodus would be imperceptible because Hong Kong's population would since have grown by several tens of thousands. 'And God blessed them, and God said unto them, Be fruitful, and multiply, and replenish the earth . . .' Although the divine commandment was addressed to Adam and Eve, one got the impression that Hong Kong had more than fulfilled it.

At the foot of the hill was a big depot crammed with concrete mixers, cranes, and stacks of building materials. Whether or not the handful of figures staring up at the hill were prospective residents admiring the site of their future home, they put me in mind of Breughel's *Tower of Babel*. The king, bottom left, has come to check on the progress made by his architect and masons. Looming above the clouds stands the celebrated tower with its spiral road. Although confidence still reigns, we cannot help recalling the end of the story. One day, with regrettable consequences known to us all, the tower collapses.

The train had slowed again. The students shut their books and bags and stood up. Beyond a long white wall enclosing well-tended lawns fringed with trees and flowering shrubs stood some spacious white buildings. No ugly stains marred their spotless exterior, no tin shacks flanked the gravel paths, no half-naked children scuffled on the grass. We had stopped at one of Hong Kong's universities. The students got out.

We were now alone in the carriage with the Chinese couple. They began to reorganize their belongings as soon as the train pulled out. The man opened a suitcase. Producing a package from her bag, his wife secreted it under several layers of clothing. Then they both turned to see if we'd been watching them.

The flow of traffic and pedestrians on the road beside the railway track had dwindled. I fell to musing.

Some remarkable things had happened in China this year. At 3 p.m. on 8 March, a meteor had plunged into the earth's atmosphere, streaked across the sky over Jilin Province in northern China, and exploded near the provincial capital. Fragments of it rained down on an area measuring two hundred square miles. One of them weighed 1.7 tons – the largest meteorite ever found, or so it was claimed by Chinese newspapers.

On 29 May, Yünnan Province had been shaken by two earthquakes. Fatal casualties were few, but a month later, on 28 July, another quake had destroyed the city of Tangshan, some hundred miles east of Peking. The dead were estimated at over half a million, making the Tangshan earthquake the most lethal ever recorded apart from the one that wiped out 830,000 inhabitants of Shaanxi Province in 1556. Many buildings also collapsed in Tientsin and Peking, where Chinese Foreign Ministry personnel continued working under canvas in the ministry courtyard. Embassy staff, with the exception of small emergency teams, were evacuated to Canton or Hong Kong. Now, a month later, they were being permitted to return.

A week ago, when I was saying goodbye to Paul Frank, the Undersecretary of State in Bonn, he'd asked me why I was in such a hurry to get to China. 'It's all these meteors and earthquakes,' I told him. 'The Chinese have always thought they portended the end of a dynasty – or an emperor's death. Great Chairmen fall into the same category, wouldn't you say?'

He stared at me for a moment. Then he said, 'You genuinely believe that?'

'The Chinese do.'

'Even today?'

'Seems so, or their newspapers wouldn't be publishing articles condemning such superstitions. I doubt if it'll do much good, though. The Chinese have long memories, historically speaking, and rational explanations conflict with their experiences over the years. The First Emperor launched a campaign against the same superstitition over two thousand years ago. It didn't do him any good either. Maybe that's why I ought to get a move on.'

Paul Frank eyed me keenly over the top of his glasses, trying to decide how serious I was. I left him still wondering.

The train slowed down as it entered the zone of tranquillity common to many frontiers. The Chinese couple stood up. I counted our bags and Franz did likewise. Franz's real name isn't Franz at all, but the family have always called her that. She'd been Franz, not Franziska or Frances, even when she travelled out east with me thirty-six years ago, a brand-new wife on her first trip to the other side of the world. Franz is a man's name, of course, but she accepted it with good grace, if only because it also happens to be the conventional nickname for a navigator in a German plane. She always was a good navigator, and she still is.

There were six bags in all, and two raincoats. I asked Franz, for the third time, if she had our passports. She nodded.

'Better make sure.'

She double-checked. The passports were there. I said, 'Mind you don't leave your bag behind.'

I can't pretend I felt nothing as we crossed the frontier. It wasn't an everyday frontier crossing or an everyday journey. I was bound for my last foreign posting – bound for the country I'd first set eyes on as a student forty years earlier. The attaché who had embarked on his diplomatic career in China thirty-six years ago was returning there as an ambassador. The wheel had come full circle. I remembered little of the language I'd begun to learn in those days. Would any of it come back to me?

'You won't get a chance to speak Chinese to the Chinese,' Foreign Minister Macovescu had told me at my farewell dinner in Bucharest. 'You'll only meet Chinese officials at official functions, and then you'll only converse through interpreters. No Chinese would dare to discuss anything personal and private with you, let alone come visiting – the sentries on the embassy gate wouldn't let him through. Peking isn't like Bucharest, where our Romanian artists and writers waltz in and out of your embassy as they please. All you can see at the theatre are the eight model operas. As for Western books, nobody translates them. Wouldn't

I be right in saying,' he added with a faintly mocking smile, 'that conditions in our country are freer?'

The train pulled into the little station of Shun Chun. A porter appeared at the door. He piled our six bags on a handcart, together with those of the Chinese couple, and bustled off. We soon lost sight of him in the crowd and could hardly wait to see our belongings again, though there was nothing we could have done. The third-class carriages were jampacked. More and more Chinese were emerging laden with cardboard boxes, basketwork suitcases, and voluminous bundles. These they carried on their backs or transported by means of a shoulder-pole. We negotiated the Lowu Bridge, which our train was not permitted to cross, by skirting the railroad track. The river below us marked the frontier between the People's Republic of China and the British Crown Colony of Hong Kong. On our side flew the Union Jack, on the other the Red Flag adorned with five yellow stars. At the end of the bridge, complete with rifle and bayonet, stood a Chinese sentry in the green uniform of the People's Liberation Army. He stared straight through us. Was *he* a New Man?

An Untouched World?

Our new train had air-conditioned carriages. After the tropical heat outside, I was reminded of a cold store or the sound-proof booth maintained by my American opposite number in Bucharest. Anyone with confidential matters to discuss there in summer was well advised to wear a heavy sweater.

The temperature inside our new carriage was hardly conducive to emotional warmth, and the longer we remained at the frontier post the cooler my relations with the People's Republic became. A scattering of Africans and Indians were already installed in the open saloon. The Chinese couple turned up last of all. I'd caught a glimpse of them while waiting to board the train, arguing with a customs officer who had spread the entire contents of their luggage across a counter. Now they hurried in, stowed their belongings on the rack, and slumped into their seats, panting and perspiring.

My mood did not improve when the train pulled out. Simultaneously, our ears were assailed by canned music played at disco volume. It was the anthem *The East Is Red*, performed by a massed choir. A Hong Kong acquaintance had charitably informed me that the loudspeaker in every compartment could be silenced by means of a knob beneath the folding table on the window side. The choir sang numerous verses while I groped for it, but I groped in vain: there was no knob beneath the folding table because ours was an open saloon. The only volume control was on the end wall. The Africans and Indians stared idly out as we emerged from the station, clearly undisturbed by the din. The exhausted Chinese couple were past listening or caring.

Next came an even more potent anthem in which the massed choir was joined by a massed band. The only words I picked out – *Mao Zhuxi*, or Chairman Mao – occurred in the higher reaches of the melody, which dwelt on them lovingly; the rest defeated me. Confronted by yet another patriotic song and the prospect of listening to these effusions in an ice-cold carriage for the remainder of our three-hour trip to Canton, I began to feel more and more disgruntled. Just how naïve did they think we were? Did they seriously hope to make Maoist converts with the aid of mawkish patriotic songs?

'Did you see that village square on the right as we left the station,' I asked Franz, '—the one where all the bicycles were parked? During the Cultural Revolution, visitors had to parade there before boarding the train and listen to speeches condemning imperialist crimes and extolling the revolutionary course adopted by the People's Republic, and well-rehearsed detachments of villagers would cheer like mad and wave their Little Red Books. I've always wondered what made the Chinese stage those charades – missionary zeal, or a wish to display their own determination? I'm wondering the same right now. What on earth do they hope to achieve by bombarding us with music for hours on end?'

Franz made soothing noises and changed the subject. 'Just look at that pretty farmhouse with the weeping willows beside it! What fun those children are having!'

'It may look like a farmhouse,' I said sourly. 'I'm sure it used to be one, too, but nowadays it's probably occupied by heaven knows how many families belonging to the brigade production group of a people's commune. It may look idyllic from the window of a train, but you can bet there's a loudspeaker in the farmyard belting out the same music from reveille at dawn to lights-out at dusk.'

A blue-uniformed conductress appeared, plaits jutting sideways from under her peaked cap. She poured hot water from a vacuum flask into the china cups on our folding table and gave us some tea bags. I asked her very, very politely – and no one, I thought, could have gathered from my tone of voice that I had an aversion to choral singing – whether it might be possible to turn the music down a little.

After my experiences in the Soviet Union, I expected a reprimand to the effect that such songs were composed in praise of socialism and the Great Helmsman, that everyone should listen to them with joy, gratitude, and reverence – indeed, that they just couldn't be played loud enough to do them justice.

The conductress filled my china cup to the brim and dabbed at a drop of water on the little lace tablecloth. Then she turned to me with her head on one side. 'Or would you prefer me,' she said, 'to turn it off?'

That really threw me. I felt ashamed of having done the Chinese railroad authorities an injustice and misinterpreted their motives. They had not been dispensing propaganda, merely trying to entertain us. Anxious to repay courtesy with courtesy, I suppressed my natural inclination to accept her offer on the spot. 'No,' I said, 'there's no need to turn it off, but perhaps you could turn it down low.'

'Very low,' said Franz.

'If you prefer, I can turn it off altogether.'

'No,' we chorused, 'very low – that'll do fine.'

The music subsided to an almost inaudible murmur. We hoped our fellow passengers would be able to endure the silence all the way to Canton. They were still staring out of the windows. None of them took any notice, even when the music finally ceased altogether.

I wondered why the conductress had complied so readily, and came to the conclusion that she was under orders to turn off the music on request, rather than provoke altercations with ignorant or rebellious foreign passengers lacking in political maturity. In the light of subsequent experience, I suspect that this was not the only reason, and that she had not yet made the crucial transition to the New Man's world – in short, that she herself was sick of anthems.

My spirits had improved. We were used to the temperature by now, and even the countryside gliding past our window seemed friendlier. It was flat land punctuated at long intervals by low hills. Trees had been planted on either side of the embankment, several rows deep. They were unattractive trees with straight, spindly trunks and very little foliage. I judged them to be only ten or fifteen years old.

Whenever our view was not obscured by trees we could see long lines of men and women at work in the fields, weeding them with hoes. Others made their way along farm tracks in single file, each balancing a shoulder-pole. The loads they carried were substantial, and the bamboo poles whipped up and down at every step. Water buffaloes were ploughing the paddy-fields. Some of the cyclists bumping along the farm tracks had baskets, sacks, or big bales of straw secured to their carriers. The only motor vehicle we saw was a bus.

No one here would have dreamed of demolishing a mountain with machines. There were no corrugated iron huts, no car dumps, no Towers of Babel. There was no industry to pollute the environment. The inhabitants planted trees, sowed and reaped. They ploughed as their forefathers had ploughed in ancient times, with water buffaloes, some guided by children perched astride their broad backs. It was an untouched, unspoiled world.

Untouched? I sternly called myself to order: an untouched world, perhaps, but only when seen from afar. I recalled Jacob Burckhardt's observations on happiness and unhappiness in human history. We tend to imagine that happiness resides in beautiful surroundings, he wrote, or in a particular house – as, for instance, when smoke rising at dusk from the chimney of some distant cottage conjures up visions of warmth and intimacy among its occupants. But that, he went on, is often an illusion.

I decided to reserve judgement on the world that was passing our window.

Canton

A small delegation bore down on us when we descended from the train. It comprised two gentlemen from the Protocol Section of the Foreign Affairs Bureau of the Revolutionary Committee, Guangdong Province; a German-speaking woman interpreter; and a porter of surprisingly frail physique. The two gentlemen from the Protocol Section bade us welcome on behalf of Guangdong Province and invited us to take tea in a small waiting-room reserved for official guests. Courtesies and expressions of friendship were exchanged. The Protocol Section would see to it that we flew on to Peking the next day by the midday plane. Meanwhile, Mr Qing of the Official Travel Bureau would escort us everywhere. We had nothing to worry about – Mr Qing spoke German fluently.

'No, no,' protested Mr Qing, 'very badly. I regret I only speak your language very badly.'

So Mr Qing wasn't a porter after all. He was our guide and interpreter, and his German was excellent.

A taxi had been placed at our disposal by the Protocol Section. The muscular, thickset driver opened the boot and stood aside, lifting not a finger as Mr Qing struggled to stow our baggage inside. We gave the poor little man a helping hand. The driver slammed the boot shut and drove us to the Dongfang Hotel, a concrete box designed by Soviet architects in the heyday of the Great Friendship. Neither our driver nor the numerous hotel employees stationed at the entrance made any move to help us unload or carry our baggage. They obviously had a very precise idea of their duties. We were surprised. Once upon a time, cab drivers and hotel staff would have snatched the bags out of our hands if we had even tried to deprive them of a tip by carrying them ourselves. Nowadays, accepting tips is considered undignified.

The Park of Culture

An early dinner left us disinclined to spend our first evening in the People's Republic of China closeted in a hotel room, but Mr Qing informed us that there were no plays or operas to be seen. No acrobats either.

What about films?

Mr Qing was unprepared for such a request from foreign visitors. Anyway, he said, there weren't any tickets to be had. We asked him why not.

'We should have applied in advance,' he said. 'Tickets aren't on sale at the box office.'

'Why not?' we asked again. 'How *do* you get hold of cinema tickets in Canton?'

Tickets, he explained, were distributed by the 'units' at places of work.

Very well, what else could we do – take a stroll through the old quarter of the city? Mr Qing was alarmed by this proposal, which appealed to him not at all. He quickly steered us in another direction. The most he could suggest was a visit to the Park of Culture – except that it would be so crowded. We might easily get lost.

One pavilion in the Park of Culture housed an exhibition of modern calligraphy. Covering the whole of the wall beside the entrance was a poem by Mao Zedong, written in the Chairman's tense, impatient, rapidly executed cursive – a blend of the forceful and the erratic. We were soon to see specimens of his handwriting in many other places. Educated Chinese praised it for its derivation from an ancient school of calligraphy.

Franz asked if it was an original. Mr Qing assured her that it was. A photographic enlargement? Naturally, said Mr Qing. So not actually written by the Chairman himself? But of course, protested Mr Qing. So great is the difference between our own conception of an original and the Chinese that even the most reputable museums exhibit copies without labelling them as such. After all, they can't be distinguished from the real thing.

An esoteric art not readily accessible to the untutored eye, calligraphy is as highly regarded by the Chinese as painting. Only those who have striven to write a satisfactory Chinese character, with all its poised, harmonious, rhythmical perfection, can begin to appreciate how long and arduous a road the calligrapher has to travel.

I had read that calligraphy had been neither taught nor practised since the Cultural Revolution, yet here were some impressive examples of the art produced by master calligraphers. But even the finest of these scrolls bore no sublime reflections on Nature, human solitude, or wind and weather. They crudely inveighed against capitalist-roaders, excoriated those who had hoisted the apricot-yellow banner of Imperial China, and attacked 'the right-deviationist wind' – in other words, Deng Xiaoping, who had been stripped of authority four months earlier, on 7 April, by Mao-inspired extremists on the far left of the Party leadership. Deng's name recurred again and again, not only in ancient seal script but in 'grass' and 'official' script.

A crowd had assembled in front of a large open-air stage with a semi-domed roof. Mr Qing was afraid he would lose us there, for all his conscientious vigilance. Once three chairs had been brought and placed in the very front row, however, he felt free to concentrate on the performance. It turned out to be a ballet–cum–opera. A troupe belonging to the Yi, a national minority some three million strong from the mountainous regions of southern China, was dancing to the music of a small orchestra.

The show had just begun. A bevy of Yi girls appeared in picturesque regional costumes, momentarily baring their legs to the knee as they pirouetted across the stage – but only once, for fear of putting irrelevant ideas into the heads of their audience.

The girls, as some of them announced in song, had gone into the mountains to gather some rare medicinal herbs. They were led by the prima ballerina, a lovely young creature who had sadly been born deaf and dumb. Because she could communicate only by gesture, we were able to follow what she told her companions. Less intelligible passages were interpreted for us by Mr Qing.

After filling their baskets with herbs, the village maidens returned to find a soldier's knapsack on the stage. They guessed – correctly, as events were to prove – that it belonged to a medical corpsman of the People's Liberation Army who had also gone in search of herbs. At the instance of the prima ballerina – and for love of the People's Liberation Army – the girls decided to put their herbs in the soldier's knapsack and fetch some more from the mountains.

They danced off left just as the soldier entered right, visibly fatigued by his unaccustomed trek through the mountains and largely unsuccessful in his quest. Then he noticed that his knapsack had become a cornucopia brimming with the rarest of herbs. Astonished, he rubbed his eyes. A good fairy? No, the enlightened revolutionary in him banished this obnoxiously feudal superstition with a resolute gesture. This, he knew, could only be the work of human hands. He peered in all directions and eventually caught sight of his benefactresses.

Realizing that they had been spotted, the girls tried to flee – in vain, needless to say. The soldier demanded an explanation. He offered to pay for the herbs, but the girls indignantly spurned this suggestion. They left it to the prima ballerina to convey, with eloquent hands and nimble feet, how grateful everyone should be to the People's Liberation Army. The herbs had been a gift to the PLA, not to the soldier himself.

The soldier accepted the girls' thanks with noble modesty, not omitting to extol the wisdom of Chairman Mao, sole author of the Chinese people's liberation. In token of his personal gratitude, he inquired the nature of the prima ballerina's disability. Her friends explained that she had been deaf and dumb from birth but was otherwise in excellent health.

The soldier did not confine himself to exploring the girl's previous medical history. He instructed her to sit down with her back against a tree trunk. Then he went to work. Producing a number of acupuncture needles from his pouch, he sterilized them with alcohol, in keeping with the dictates of modern asepsis, and inserted them at three carefully selected points in her earlobes and neck. The beautiful patient lost consciousness for a moment, but, just when anxiety was dawning on her companions' faces, she rose blithely to her feet. The soldier removed the acupuncture needles and his patient took a few deliberate steps towards the front of the stage. Then, with arms flung wide, she gave vent to her emotions. '*Mao Zhuxi wansui!*' she sang, loud and clear. 'May Chairman Mao live ten thousand years!'

The audience briefly applauded this finale. The soldiers and the maidens stepped forward and clapped likewise before dancing off in both directions. The show had clearly been enjoyed by all.

While touring the calligraphy exhibition I had asked Mr Qing what he thought of the lampoons on Deng Xiaoping. 'In addition to committing many other mistakes,' he replied, 'Deng is accused of having followed a right-deviationist course.' It would have been discourteous and futile to press him for a personal opinion. Now, when we asked him how he had liked the finale, he claimed to have heard that deaf-mutes had genuinely been cured with the aid of acupuncture.

'And the girl's first words?' I said.

Mr Qing seemed baffled by the question. 'I mean,' I said, 'did you find her tribute to Chairman Mao convincing? Wasn't it a little overdone?'

'Well, she had to sing *something* to show the audience she wasn't deaf and dumb any longer.'

Something! Didn't Mr Qing realize that gratitude to Chairman Mao, through whose hallowed agency the girl had ultimately been cured, constituted the moral of the entire performance?

I tried another tack. 'What if the girl and the soldier had taken a fancy to each other in the closing stages of the opera? Her first words might then have been, "I love you!"'

Mr Qing burst out laughing. 'That would never have done. There were so many other girls standing around – they'd all have heard. Besides, the couple had only just met.'

'What's more,' I said, 'they hadn't asked their parents' consent.'

'Quite so,' Mr Qing said firmly.

So he wasn't a New Man either.

A New Man would have replied as follows: 'Proletarian marriages are contracted by men and women without the intervention of a third party. Nowadays, in contrast to feudal times, parental wishes count for nothing. Instead, the basis of a good and lasting marriage may be said to be present when both partners possess a high degree – if possible, an equally high degree – of revolutionary consciousness.'

The Enchanted Island

I had always imagined that Shameen was an island in the Pearl or Canton River. All that separated it from the southern part of the city, I now saw, was a narrow canal spanned by two bridges.

During the early decades of the nineteenth century, Canton had been the only Chinese port in which foreigners were allowed to trade, but the Chinese authorities did not permit European and American merchants to enter the city itself. The British and French countered by developing a sandbank in the Pearl River. They enlarged it with rocks and sand, built their *hongs* or warehouses on it, and forbade any Chinese to set foot there without permission. The bridges were sealed off at night with heavy iron gates. A perpetual reminder of the humiliations to which China had once been subjected by the imperialist powers, the island of Shameen proved to be tiny – ten minutes' walk from end to end, and only half as wide.

Big old banyan trees lined the riverside promenade, and bordering the expanses of grass beyond were consulates dating from the early years of our own century. The consuls had left their luxurious quarters long ago. Bicycles and lumber could be seen on lofty balconies supported by muscular atlantes, and laundry was drying outside windows and in round-arched loggias. Any remaining venetian blinds hung awry or were only half raised. Stucco had flaked off the walls, and the masonry beneath was stained with mildew. The tree-lined streets behind the waterfront, facing the city, were almost deserted. We passed a church so dilapidated that, even had its door not been boarded up, we should have hesitated to venture inside. The locals now used it as a warehouse, Mr Qing informed us. We were not alone on Shameen. A dozen toddlers from a nursery school crossed the road under the supervision of two Chinese girls, each child clinging to the shirt of the child in front, and disappeared through a gloomy gateway like innocent little victims of the Pied Piper's revenge.

We might have been in a European ghost town that had been abandoned by its inhabitants and transported to China many years ago – a town like one of Kubin's illustrations for Edgar Allan Poe. Now it was mouldering away in the hot, steamy climate of south-east China. It was an enchanted town, enshrouding its sumptuous waterfront buildings in the cobwebs of vanished pomp and circumstance. Hidden beneath stones and rusty gratings in these overgrown gardens, I felt sure, were toads and snakes that sallied forth when darkness fell.

The Old Hundred Families

We wanted to see how the *lao bai xing* lived – 'the Old Hundred Families', or ordinary folk. The Chinese phrase has a friendly, intimate ring, expressive of the kinship that prevails among the clans and families comprising the nation as a whole.

But Mr Qing, doubtless acting on orders from above, had other plans for us. He proposed to show us the Mausoleum of the Martyrs of the Commune Insurrection of 1927. We told him we'd prefer to save that treat for another time and see something of the Old Hundred Families instead.

'Very well,' he said. 'Let's drive to the University Quarter.'

Informed that this wasn't quite what we'd meant, he had a flash of inspiration. Of course, the workers' housing estates! The only trouble was, they were rather a long way, and if we wanted to get to the airport on time . . .

We gave up and drove back to the hotel. On the way there, however, we spotted some narrow side streets running off the main thoroughfare. Asking the driver to stop, we made a rapid exit. Mr Qing did his utmost to dissuade us, for our health's sake. The streets we proposed to visit were filthy and insanitary – quite untypical, too. That was how people had lived in the old days. In any case, the buildings would soon be demolished to make room for some big new apartment houses – eight, ten, twelve storeys high.

Mr Qing looked far from happy when we politely asked him to escort us down at least one of these quite untypical side streets, if only to give us a standard against which to measure the marvels of modern Chinese architecture. He was embarrassed and reluctant to show us how poorly some of his fellow countrymen lived.

It was a familiar attitude – one we'd encountered everywhere from the Balkans to the Far East. Why photograph that gypsy caravan? Surely you don't think it typical of our transportation system in the Romanian Socialist Republic? Why should you want to visit the bazaar? Isfahan has a brand-new department store where the carpets are just as cheap. You'd like to see the Manila slums? There's nothing to see, just a few huts – and besides, we've walled them off. Why not visit our fine new Congress Hall instead?

Fully sympathizing with Mr Qing's sentiments, we said we realized that no one could modernize an entire country within a couple of decades. On the other hand, it was highly debatable whether people were happier in high-rise blocks than here, where they weren't dependent on temperamental elevators and could fetch water from the hydrant on the corner.

All the houses were timber-built, single-storeyed, and huddled close together. Living-rooms and kitchens could be seen through doors left open because of the heat. It was lunch time. Children sat perched on doorsteps – the best vantage points in the street – with bowls of rice and vegetables clamped between their knees. They were, of course, eating with chopsticks.

In a tiny shop all of two yards square sat an old man with a sparse grey beard, selling herbs and spices. The chair beside him was occupied by a tabby cat. Though free to jump to the floor or climb.on the table, it couldn't run off because one of its hind feet was tethered with string to a chair leg. It couldn't get at the pair of bamboo bird cages overhead, either. The cages looked genuinely old, and inside them hung little china plates adorned with miniature landscapes designed to give their inmates an illusion of freedom. The old man, who was eating from his rice bowl, deposited a morsel of fish on the edge of the table that doubled as a counter. After an exploratory sniff, the cat ate it. The old man took no notice of us.

I asked Mr Qing whether the herb-seller was in business for himself. No, I was told. He worked for his neighbourhood organization, so all his takings had to be handed over. He was, however, paid a wage.

'It wouldn't amount to much, I suppose?'

'No, not much, but at least he's employed and contributes to the family exchequer. He certainly earns enough to cover his food.' The old man had not been left to rot in idleness. He still inhabited the world of labour and was a productive member of society.

At the window of one house sat an adolescent boy playing the *erhu*, a two-stringed instrument with snakeskin over its resonating chamber – not any old snakeskin, of course, but a particular variety. The boy had been playing high-pitched harmonics with his eyes closed in blissful self-appreciation. When he reverted to the middle register and opened them again, he suddenly saw us. This so startled him that he darted back into the room and disappeared from view.

From another house came the strains of a Chinese opera. Cymbals and clappers were beating a crescendo – a sure sign that something exciting was about to happen on stage. Perhaps a general would come riding in, his awesome countenance heavily daubed with black greasepaint to show the audience that they were confronted by an honest and courageous warlord. He would be wearing robes of gold and silver brocade – so many layers of them that he could hardly walk – and the four flags sprouting from his shoulders would represent his armies. He would dismount from his charger, symbolically, of course, by switching his riding crop from one hand to the other, and everyone in the auditorium would know that he had done so. The horse itself was left to the imagination.

Sure enough, a bass voice issued from the loudspeaker. Then a soprano broke in with a recitative – undoubtedly a damsel in distress recounting her sad story and urgently beseeching assistance.

To most people who hear it for the first time, Chinese opera sounds like caterwauling. To us it was a reminder of the old days – of the simple pleasure derived by Chinese audiences from plots abounding in crafty villains, noble scholars, unsophisticated peasants, shrewd judges, fearless generals, and fragile ladies whose characters can be gauged at a glance from their appearance. The comic, for instance, has only to show his face for the audience to laugh at the white dots adorning his nose and forehead.

It was touching to rediscover this tradition in the New Man's China. So *that* still existed!

'No,' said Mr Qing, 'it doesn't any more. We now have the eight revolutionary model operas.'

'So what are we listening to?'

'I told you – the Quarter of the Old Hundred Families isn't typical. What you're hearing is a Peking opera.' He hesitated for a moment, then added, 'Broadcast from Hong Kong.'

The Missing Key

It was dark when we reached Peking. The road from the airport to the embassy was dead straight but not very wide.

Our chauffeur bore a striking resemblance to Buddha, at least in girth. His name was Zhou – as in Zhou Enlai – and pronounced something like 'Joe', but everyone at the embassy addressed him as Lao Zhou. Lao means 'old' and is a title that tempers familiarity with respect. Lao Zhou drove with only his parking lights on, like every other driver we passed, but the cyclists carried no lights at all. They swam out of the gloom, unseen until the last moment by anyone but Lao Zhou. On the few occasions when he briefly used his headlights, we saw rows of poplars on either side of the road. We were driving into limbo down a long, narrow, never-ending avenue. It was the stuff of which dreams – or nightmares – are made.

Nine months earlier I had told my Foreign Minister, Hans-Dietrich Genscher, that I would gladly go to Peking if the post fell vacant. Franz was less enamoured of the idea. Five years in Romania had imposed something of a strain on us, as on everyone posted there. We had become inured to constant eavesdropping and surveillance, to overtures from *agents provocateurs* and the need to discuss anything confidential while walking in the garden or the woods. Still harder to tolerate was the exposure of our Romanian friends and acquaintances to political pressure and bureaucratic tyranny, not to mention the humiliations to which all of them, even officials of senior rank, were continually subjected.

Another tour of duty in a socialist country? Macovescu had not been alone in robbing the prospect of charm. We'd heard from other sources that private conversation with Chinese citizens was impossible. Foreigners were restricted to the city limits of Peking and two short stretches of road leading to the Great Wall, the Ming Tombs, and the Western Hills. Coal

Hill, the parks and lakes adjoining the Imperial Palace, the Temple of the Azure Clouds, and the Lama and Confucius Temples were all closed to visitors, possibly because they had been vandalized during the Cultural Revolution. It was even forbidden to make the sixty-mile trip by car from Peking to Tientsin, and permission to visit the provinces was seldom granted. Had Macovescu been right to claim, in his mocking way, that Romania was a freer country than China?

I shared many of Franz's forebodings. Premier Zhou Enlai, the initiator of China's *rapprochement* with the West, had died in January. Mao was clearly a very sick man and had received no foreign visitors for several months. He had long been suffering from Parkinson's disease and was rumoured to have had a stroke. The reins of power, it seemed, had already slipped from his grasp. The political leadership was deeply divided and public life at a standstill. What would happen when Mao died – a free-for-all? There was every possibility of a lengthy power struggle, during which our own freedom of movement would be even more restricted. Whatever the outcome, however, China's entry into the post-Mao era would be a radically new departure well worth observing at close quarters. Could there be a revival of the Cultural Revolution, so many aspects of which escaped my comprehension? In short, I was curious.

Lao Zhou continued to speed along the dark avenue with his headlights off. Visibility did not improve even when we swung left on to a wider road. Another change of direction took us down a narrower one. We made out some trees, and beyond them high walls with brightly lit gateways guarded by Chinese soldiers. We had reached the Embassy Quarter.

We turned into one of the gateways, saluted by a pair of sentries. The exit and entrance of the residence were festively illuminated. The residence itself, a two-storeyed building screened by trees and shrubs, was in darkness. We received another salute as we drew up outside, this time from our German embassy guard.

The front-door key was missing. Where could it be? The guard devoted serious thought to this problem, but failed to solve it. So did my number two, Gerd Berendonck, who had turned up from the airport after greeting us there with other members of the embassy staff. I suggested that my predecessor might have borne it off to Europe in his pocket, but everyone rejected the idea – it had been there earlier in the day. We should just have to wait for Palu. Nothing could be done without Palu, long-time personal secretary to my forerunners in office.

Palu turned up in her ancient blue Volkswagen beetle. The key? Of course, she had a spare one with her. We carried our bags upstairs to the first-floor suite. Our footsteps and voices echoed round the empty rooms, which had just been redecorated in shades of pale blue and green. We passed no comment on the redecoration itself – there was nothing to be done about the colour scheme – but praised its timely completion.

Many walls had acquired cracks in the recent earthquake, some of them wide enough to accommodate a finger with ease. Other cracks had already been grouted with plaster and repainted. The bedroom contained two Chinese beds, two armchairs, two garden chairs, and a small office desk. It was the only furnished room. We should be living in it for the next three months, until our household effects arrived by sea.

A quick tour of the downstairs reception rooms revealed that the drawing-room was vast and the dining-room table long enough to seat thirty-two guests. There was also a library bare of books – a deficiency I remedied later. The reception rooms were as well appointed as our private quarters were not.

We retired to the Blue Room, a small sitting-room, and tucked into some sandwiches made by Palu on the correct assumption that we wouldn't have eaten since leaving Canton. The domestic staff had been off duty since four o'clock that afternoon, and working hours, we learned, were strictly regulated.

The night was dry and very warm. We slept soundly with our windows wide open – slept, that is, until we both sat up with a start. It wasn't the last trump that had roused us, as we momentarily suspected on waking, but something far worse. Relayed through a powerful loudspeaker and sung by massed choirs with massed-band accompaniment, *The East Is Red* rent the air in a dawn reveille. The loudspeaker, which served the musical needs of some construction workers' huts on a neighbouring site, repeated this salutation at half past five every morning – six in winter.

Politics and Poetry

2 September

Foreign Minister Qiao Guanhua had requested my presence.

The building to which Lao Zhou drove me had not been designed with an eye to architectural effect. Originally intended for employees of the Academy of Sciences whose task it was to translate and process the results of Western scientific research, it had now been occupied by the Foreign Ministry for several years. All that relieved its boxlike façade were five or six superimposed tiers of windows. A plain flight of steps led up to an equally unembellished entrance in the centre of the box. The lobby was just as bleak and bare, with corridors flanking it on either side. The reception rooms were on the right. In one of these, the Chinese Head of Protocol had instructed me two days earlier in the conventions to be observed when presenting one's credentials. It was said that no Western visitor had ever been admitted to the left-hand corridor or any of the upper floors.

The Head of Protocol greeted me outside on the steps, then ushered me across the lobby and up a few more steps to the Great Reception Hall. Even when an invisible hand opened the glass door, nothing could be seen of the interior because my view was obscured by a screen. It was not there to keep out draughts, but evil spirits, which, as every Chinese knows, are incapable of turning corners.

Foreign Minister Qiao Guanhua was standing in the middle of the big Chinese carpet. He came to meet me, a tall, slim man with the face of an intellectual – a good face. His manner, which radiated warmth, was relaxed, but his reactions were swift and sure. Later in the interview he laughed aloud several times – heartily, as if he didn't have a care in the world.

Qiao shook hands and welcomed me to Peking in German, then switched to English, displaying a fluent and accurate command of both languages. He had long been interpreter and personal secretary to Premier Zhou Enlai, who promoted him and appointed him Assistant Foreign Minister. During the Festival of Souls in April, three months after Zhou Enlai's death, the inhabitants of Peking had paid tribute to his memory. The ensuing riots were quelled by force, and the Party staged a counter-demonstration in which Qiao had taken part, marching through the streets at the head of his Foreign Ministry officials. Many observers were puzzled by this because it seemed to be a slur on the memory of the man to whom he owed everything. Other ministers with more backbone had refrained from joining the demonstration, even though it had been officially decreed by the Party.

On the far side of the reception hall, beyond the central carpet and beneath a portrait of Mao, two armchairs awaited us. More armchairs flanked them in a horseshoe. The Foreign Minister took his place on the right, beneath Mao's picture, with the Head of Protocol at his elbow. I sat on the left with my deputy, Minister Berendonck, beside me. No one else was present apart from two Chinese interpreters who hovered behind us. Had this been a major reception, other officials would have occupied both sides of the horseshoe. Our seating order was dictated by protocol, and I always sat this way from now on, except when abdicating my place to German guests of honour. There was no conference table – that largely redundant piece of furniture – so all of us were visible from head to toe.

A girl brought tea and poured it into the china bowls that stood on our side tables, together with memo pads and needle-sharp pencils. This was another invariable custom.

'I had a high regard for Herr Pauls, your predecessor,' Qiao said, speaking in Chinese. 'He was a man of integrity. I'm sure we shall work together just as well. You're no doubt wondering why I invited you here today, even though you've still to present your credentials. We Chinese don't stand on ceremony. As far as we're concerned, you can exercise all your ambassadorial functions as of now.

'Relations between the People's Republic of China and the Federal Republic of Germany are satisfactory. Our volume of trade is increasing. As to the political situation, we shall shortly be discussing that in detail, but I still don't know if we shall have an opportunity to do so prior to the forthcoming session of the UN Assembly.'

I reminded him that we should be joining the Security Council in the coming year. We should welcome Chinese support for our UN initiatives relating to the establishment of a court of human rights and an international accord on the treatment of hostage-takers. His response, as might have been expected, was non-committal.

'We must go into that more closely in due course. When did you first visit China?'

'In 1936. I was a student at the time.'

'Then we must be roughly the same age. I was studying at Tübingen in those days.'

Although I knew that he had belonged to the Faculty of Philosophy and was the author of a dissertation on the *Zhuangzi*, one of philosophical Taoism's most important texts, I steered clear of the subject. Taoism was banned nowadays, and left-wing ideologists would be bound to regard Qiao's thesis as a blot on his curriculum vitae.

He went on to ask the question that has always, from time immemorial, served to define the scope of a person's education in China. How many Chinese characters could I write?

'Very few,' I told him. 'I've forgotten most of the ones I knew, but I hope I'll be able to write more by the time I leave Peking.'

My reply was necessarily vague. Even if I had mastered all the characters in general use, courtesy would have prescribed the same answer.

I expressed the wish to travel widely in China, just as I had in the old days. Qiao approved.

'Did you ever visit any of our rural areas? You did? Good! Then do so again. Our villages are the best guide to all the changes that have taken place here.'

Quite abruptly, he changed the subject. 'Tell me,' he said, 'do translations of Chairman Mao's poems exist in Germany?'

'Yes, and I find them quite readable. How far they've been accurately construed and translated is another matter. That I couldn't say.'

'Recently,' said Qiao, 'I made a detailed study of the English translations and found numerous mistakes. It's naturally hard to capture the meaning and allusions in a Chinese poem, its adoption of poetical expressions from our classics and all its other resonances. There are limits to what any translator can achieve. Many things must be left untranslated, but I've also found some very definite errors in the English versions.

'In one poem, for instance, Chairman Mao criticizes the Red Army, but the English translator thought his criticism was directed at the army of the Kuomintang. That mistake completely perverts the sense of the poem. You see: by misunderstanding Chairman Mao's poems, anyone can infer the diametrical opposite of his intended meaning.'

I listened with mounting surprise. Had he summoned me there to tell me that people would soon be starting to misinterpret Mao, or was he thinking of other political misinterpretations – for example, the Sino-American Shanghai Communiqué of 1972, which meant different things to Washington and Peking? He surely wouldn't have invited me to the Foreign Office for a literary chat.

Still trying to fathom his intentions, I gave the conversation a political twist. 'Poetic misinterpretations are often unavoidable,' I said, 'but they seldom have serious consequences. It's different in politics. For instance, the German Democratic Republic's misinterpretation of the Quadripartite Agreement had major political repercussions.'

But Qiao declined to follow my lead and comment on the Shanghai Communiqué. He appeared to be genuinely worried that people might misread Mao and infer the contrary of what he had meant.

'The misinterpretation or mistranslation of a poem from the pen of Chairman Mao can also have major repercussions.'

I didn't dispute this, certainly where his political poems were concerned. 'But it doesn't apply to poems alone, of course. People are far too careless with words in general, and our German poets – when they refer to politics – can be worse than anyone. I don't know if I'm permitted to mention his name these days and in present company, but I've always been impressed by something Confucius said. When asked what his first step would be if he took over the business of government, he replied, "I should certainly begin by correcting appellations." ' The interpreter had trouble translating this, probably because he had never read Confucius at school.

Qiao had recognized the quotation but was careful not to take me up on it, Confucius having long been officially proscribed. 'I don't have time to discuss Confucius at length, not now. Besides, I'm not sure if any one individual should be at liberty to alter terms and appellations. I incline more to Hegel's view that . . .' And here the interpreter's German failed him. After he had made a number of attempts, Qiao broke in. 'I refer to Hegel's notions of the absolute idea.' He added, also in German, 'What I mean is, ideas are immutable. They continue to exist irrespective of whether one gives them this name or that, or whether one tries to adulterate them by misinterpretation.'

Even though Mao's ideas, which stood so high in the firmament, were sometimes obscured or distorted by misinterpretation, they would some day shine forth once more, pure and unadulterated, and show mankind the way: was that his implication? Was he worried because Mao's time for words was past – because the day was dawning when all would be able to interpret his pronouncements to suit themselves?

As if what mattered had now been said, Qiao observed Chinese custom by inquiring after the welfare of my family, children, and grandchildren. I replied in kind and thanked him for having received me so promptly.

While escorting me out, Qiao reverted to German. 'So we're roughly the same age, but your Foreign Minister is a good deal younger than either of us.'

'Quite so,' I said. 'And fatter, if I may say so without disrespect.'

Qiao guffawed and relayed my remark in Chinese to the Head of Protocol. My cable to the Foreign Office tactfully wound up with an account of his views on the interpretation and misinterpretation of Mao's poetry.

At the door, he shook hands and said, '*Auf Wiedersehen.*'

I never saw him again.

In Search of Old Peking

Very deliberately, Lao Zhou turned and gave me an inquiring, un-comprehending stare. I repeated my request. I wanted him to drive me to Hata Men, the great gate in the city's south-east wall.

'Hata Men?' He seemed about to add something. Then, after a moment's hesitation, he said, 'Very well.'

We drove along a broad avenue. Beyond a double row of trees stood some four-storeyed, barrack-like apartment houses built of grey brick. We turned off into another street, also lined with trees and grey, four-storeyed apartment houses. Similar barrack-like buildings could be seen on either side of an even broader avenue flanked by triple rows of trees. We drove along it for several miles.

The ground beneath the trees was thick with huts. People had slept in the open for the first few nights after the earthquake of 28 July. Then, when the rains came, they improvised roofs out of planks, corrugated iron, hardboard, and plastic sheeting. Now they were busy converting these shelters into huts. Minor tremors continued to make themselves felt, and rumour had it that the seismic epicentre was approaching Peking.

The buildings in the background were monotonous, but the huts provided their occupants with ample scope for all their native ingenuity and imagination. Children were toting stones from walls demolished by the earthquake, sackcloth curtains being replaced with crudely fashioned doors. Many huts were sunk into the ground to reduce their wall area.

I tried to get my bearings. This had been quite easy in the old days because Peking was laid out like a chess board, and you could always gauge your position by the wall that was visible from every major thoroughfare. The city had been dominated by its wall – one reason, perhaps, for the sense of security that reigned inside.

All the streets ran either north–south or east–west. You directed a rickshaw coolie by calling 'North!' or 'South!', not 'Left!' or 'Right!' Even at home, a houseboy would be asked to move an armchair a little to the west. Now that the wall was no longer there to aid my sense of direction, I might have been spinning like a top.

Lao Zhou pulled up just short of a large intersection. 'Here we are,' he said. 'Hata Men.'

I got out and peered in all directions. Where was it? Lao Zhou must have brought me to the wrong place – the gate was too big to be missed. Surmounting the lofty barrel-vaulted gateway and the city wall, which itself was fifty feet high, had been a multi-storeyed tower with two projecting roofs, one above the other. The rest of the towers in the wall were equipped with gongs. This one had contained a bell that was rung every evening – something to do with a pig-dragon that had been sighted there a long time ago and might have flooded the moat unless pacified. The clang of a bell did the trick, whereas gongs proved ineffective. But what had happened to the tower?

At long last, Lao Zhou deigned to enlighten me. The gate had been demolished. As for the lofty wall on which townsfolk used to stroll, all that remained of it was a wide swath of rubble and wasteland running through the city as though drawn with a ruler. It was a sad sight – not only bewildering but distressing to the eye and memory.

At least I now knew roughly where I was. I looked for the Nord-Hotel, which had belonged to a German family named Marschall. Though styling itself the Hôtel du Nord for the benefit of an international clientele, it was more comparable with the best hotel in a provincial German town. I decided that it must have been pulled down to make room for one of the three buildings opposite.

Asking Lao Zhou to park in the shade and wait, I headed north in search of the Street of Old Bowyers. On my left, or to the west, where once had been the glacis in front of the Legation Quarter – later its polo ground – were hummocks dotted with trees and bushes. They proved to be mounds of rubble from the city wall.

My last visit to Peking had been seven enchanted days spent in a city untouched by the passage of time. Grass sprouted from the temple and palace roofs, with their blue or yellow glazed tiles, and stood waist-deep in the spacious courtyards of the Forbidden City. The roof timbers of the great halls were rotten and infested with pigeons. Another few years, so one felt in the middle of the war, and Peking's inhabitants would fall asleep, their city enclosed by an impenetrable hedge of briars.

But they weren't asleep yet.

Brisk activity had reigned in the Chinese City, as the quarter outside and south of the wall was known. Separate lanes were devoted to the selling of silver and jade, ivory and porcelain, silk and paintings, and one could spend days roaming from one small shop to the next in quest of treasures or trifles. I spent whole afternoons with a carpet dealer named 'Sammy' Lee, sipping tea, inspecting his wares, learning about carpets, and haggling. Sammy owed his nickname to an expert knowledge of Samarkand carpets, as the British called carpets from Xinjiang. Camped beside the city wall were camels belonging to caravans that brought such merchandise from Khotan, Kashgar, and Yarkand. They lay there torpid with exhaustion, their brown hides matted and hanging in folds.

Kindness and good cheer were universal, even among the rickshaw coolies who waited outside hotels and the railway station. They were far from being the poorest of the poor. Their guild was tightly organized, and licences to ply for hire were hard to come by. Just as strict, if not more so, was the beggars' guild. Becoming a beggar was no easy matter in Peking.

Although poverty existed on all sides, it did not assume the dire extremes found in Shanghai and elsewhere. A rich man would have accounted it a serious loss of face if a beggar had expired on his doorstep. It was the people of Peking who helped beggars and filled their rice bowls. The authorities did nothing for them. Corruption being widespread, the Chinese had cheerfully, if short-sightedly, come to terms with it.

Peking was a city of leisure and contemplation. At daybreak in parks and open spaces outside the city walls, men could be seen at their *taiji* exercises – slow-motion callisthenics performed in a strictly prescribed sequence. Greybeards carried their song-birds into the parks on perches or in cages to give them a change of scene. Except in winter, these elderly gentlemen would install themselves on benches, their cages suspended from a nearby branch until conversation or card-play palled.

Amateur goldfish breeders used to exhibit their latest creations – no other word could describe the fantastic products of their genetic engineering – in front of the White Dagoba overlooking North Lake. From time to time the air would be filled with a sound that swelled and faded like the strains of an organ. Not angels, as one would have liked to assume, but pigeons were the source of this celestial music – pigeons with little bamboo pipes secured to their breast- or tail-feathers. Whenever a flock took wing, flew past, or settled on a roof, these aerial flutes would emit a harmonious crescendo or diminuendo.

But Peking had 'criminal' as well as musical pigeons. These were housed in Bamboo Wattle Lane. Their owners, who had taught them to steal from granaries, artificially enlarged their crops and emptied them after each foray by giving them alum to drink. The rice was then washed, dried, and sold. A man with a hundred such birds could garner fifty pounds of stolen rice a day. At night they were kept in bamboo cages to protect them from marauding cats, hence the name of the street.

Almost every building, garden, and narrow street – and some of the alleyways were barely wide enough to admit a rickshaw – had a story connected with it. The names of the gates and streets were stories in themselves. There were, for instance, the Gates of Military Might, Abiding Sincerity, Heavenly Peace, Earthly Repose, Righteous Dominion, Great Perfection, and Decorous Behaviour.

The Street of the Superior, Noble Persons, needless to say, faced the Temple of Confucius. Another street was known as New North Bridge, although no such bridge existed. Its name was intended merely to deceive a creature alleged to dwell there – a pig-dragon about whose nature and appearance I never managed to obtain any satisfactory information. In the Street of Equine Physiognomists lived the experts who could deduce a horse's vices, virtues, future, and value from its head – a lucrative art in the days before the internal combustion engine. Catch-the-Thief Street was presumably so called to deter superstitious burglars, for what Chinese criminal would have invaded a street with such an ominous name?

I continued to head north in search of the Street of Old Bowyers. It was nowhere to be found. I roamed this way and that, still searching, and came to the conclusion that it had been pulled down long ago. It was forty years since my one and only visit.

I recalled the occasion vividly. Each of the small wooden houses had a sign above the door – a bow or crossbow. The workshops inside were invisible. Some of the windows were unglazed and had transparent paper panes instead, but even the glass panes were filmed with the residue of dust-storms.

The master bowyer had been working at his window. He rose when I entered, and I saw that he was blind in one eye. 'He's the greatest living master of his craft,' a knowledgeable friend had told me, '—and the last, in all probability. Soon there won't be anyone left with a true appreciation of his art.'

The master invited me to sit down in his little workshop, which scarcely had room for a chair, and one of his apprentices began heating water for tea on a spirit stove. I was shown how bows were glued together in two sections, each comprising seven layers of bamboo. The vertex had to be absolutely central and the tensile strength of each half absolutely equal. I was also shown a bow made of buffalo horn and a variety of arrows. Some were tipped with iron, others blunt-headed so as to kill or stun an animal without injuring its hide. There were still hunters in Mongolia who preferred the bow because it was quieter than a rifle.

The three apprentices worked, ate, and slept in the workshop itself. One of them set a bowl of tea in front of me. 'By the time they complete their apprenticeship,' the master told me, 'no one will be hunting with bows any more. There'll be no work for them, but never mind. Apprentices learn more than how to make bows.'

Phylax

Thanks to my new red permit, I was able to walk right up to the plane that had just landed. It came from Bucharest. The Chinese, who probably thought I was there to greet some high-ranking politico, directed me to the forward exit, but Phylax hadn't flown first class. Phylax was a big, fair-haired fellow. He had been born in Germany and reared by us in Romania. He was a VIP in his own right – one to be reckoned with by any stranger who entered a room unannounced.

I made my way aft to the air-conditioned freight compartment. The hatch was just being opened. As soon as I whistled I heard a tail thump the side of a crate – thump and go on thumping.

Phylax was eventually released from his crate in the customs building. I led him outside to a tree, which relieved him considerably, and returned to find the customs officers poring over his health and vaccination certificates. They couldn't read Romanian.

What was the dog's name?

Phylax, I told them. It was a Greek word meaning 'sentinel'.

How did one write Phylax in Chinese? The customs officers had no idea. Nor had I, so I entered it on the form in Roman script.

What breed? Romanian?

No, I said, German. Phylax was a Hovawart, but that was even harder to write in Chinese. Perhaps it would be sufficient if they made a note of his weight. He weighed 135 pounds. They wrote that down and refrained from checking my information. Phylax started straining at the leash. '*Platz!*' I said, and he lay down. The customs officers looked impressed. One wag inquired if he also spoke Chinese.

Of course, I said. They didn't know whether or not to take me seriously, so I addressed him in Chinese. '*Ni hao?*' I said, giving him a signal known only to the two of us. He replied with a deep-chested bark which everyone interpreted as '*Hao!*' Great enthusiasm reigned over my multilingual dog. Curious onlookers crowded round, and Phylax was encouraged to show off his Chinese again and again. The customs officers reverted to the subject of his health certificate. I reminded them that we had already inquired after his health a dozen times, and each time the answer had been '*Hao!*', meaning 'Good!' In other words, we had his personal assurance that his health was excellent.

The customs officers laughed, stamped his papers, and issued him with an entry permit.

Great and Good Friends

8 September

'The Ambassador', so an *aide-mémoire* from the Foreign Ministry had informed us, 'will be collected by the Foreign Ministry's Head of Protocol in a ceremonial car flying the Chinese national flag and driven to the Great Hall of the People. Other members of the embassy staff will travel in embassy cars.' The big limousine was a Chinese-manufactured Hong Qi, or Red Flag. These are the vehicles in which senior Chinese officials customarily travel, at liberty to survey the outside world through black silk blinds that shield them from view.

It was only when we were about to leave that the Head of Protocol told us who would be accepting my credentials as acting Head of State. Marshal Zhu De, the last incumbent of this honorary post, had died two months earlier, but the Foreign Ministry had been unable to inform us who was currently performing his duties.

The Politburo was split and had failed to appoint a stand-in, still less a permanent successor. All the most senior posts would be redistributed when Mao died, so nobody wanted to jump the gun. The leadership's paralysis and incapacity was all too evident, even in the matter of protocol.

The Head of Protocol announced that I would be handing my credentials to Xü Xiangqian. Geert Ahrens, our political counsellor, quickly gave me an off-the-cuff summary of his career. One of the twenty-two Deputy Chairmen of the Standing Committee of the National People's Congress, Xü Xiangqian had been a member of the Communist Party for fifty-odd years and was among its most distinguished military leaders. He had been created a Marshal in the mid-1950s.

'That title has been abolished,' said the Head of Protocol. 'The correct form of address is "Deputy Chairman".'

The Great Hall of the People overlooked Tian An Men, the Square of Heavenly Peace. I guessed it to be a hundred yards deep and three or four hundred yards long. There was a tall, column-adorned portal on each of its four sides, and over each hung a gigantic portrait of Mao Zedong. In addition to a banqueting hall and a congress hall seating ten thousand people, the building contained thirty large reception rooms named after the provinces of China.

Dictatorships and tyrannies tend to erect massive pieces of architecture. It is their way of assuring themselves that all things are possible. The Great Hall of the People had been constructed at breakneck speed, and was ready for use within a year. I looked round, as we walked up the steps to the main entrance, to make sure that Ahrens hadn't missed his place in the convoy. He was following with my credentials at the ready. They were sandwiched between two handsome vellum covers of which the uppermost bore a Federal eagle. The document itself had been skilfully penned in copperplate by our Foreign Office calligrapher.

'Deputy Chairman, Great and Good Friend!' began the text of the missive in which the Federal President introduced me and announced that my proven qualities entitled him to expect that I would strive to earn the recognition of 'Your Excellency, my Great and Good Friend'. Standard international wording, I thought, but rather on the cautious side. The Federal President further asked that his new Ambassador be benevolently received and accorded full credence in any matter he might be called on to discuss on the President's behalf or that of the Government of the German Federal Republic. 'At the same time, I take this opportunity of expressing my best wishes for the prosperity of the People's Republic of China and Your Excellency's personal welfare.'

Awaiting us in the reception hall were old Xü Xiangqian, a Vice-Foreign Minister, and several other dignitaries. Marshal – or ex-Marshal – Xü was a tall, upstanding man in his mid-seventies. His wrinkled face, with its heavy, drooping eyelids, was impassive. I told him why I had come and proffered my credentials with both hands, as Chinese protocol demanded. He accepted them in similar fashion, then passed them to an aide as we retired to the adjoining room.

We seated ourselves in the customary order of precedence. The Deputy Chairman reciprocated my greetings from the Federal President in carefully chosen phrases. I spoke of the further development of our relations and our common interest in preserving peace.

That, said Xü, would call for active efforts on our part – it would not come about by itself. China and the Federal Republic had a common neighbour who threatened both us and the peace of the world.

I agreed that peace could not be attained by protestations and declarations alone. That was why, to defend ourselves against a potential aggressor, we had many years ago drawn the appropriate conclusions by joining NATO. I forbore to point out that we had been far quicker to draw those conclusions than the People's Republic of China.

The Deputy Chairman and ex-Marshal declared that the division of Germany was unjust. Germany, he said, must be reunited. I thanked him for his appreciation of our paramount national problem.

The old soldier sat motionless in his armchair, listening with hooded eyes – like an imperial mandarin, as one of my aides put it later. When a lull set in, he looked up and proposed that, subject to my agreement, we might defer further discussion until another time. He concluded by thanking me and wishing me success.

The interview had been brief, ceremonious, and very formal. I sensed that the Deputy Chairman's mind was not entirely on the matter in hand. Judging by the news that broke next day, he might well have been pre-occupied with the immediate future.

Moon Cookies

The same night

I was giving a dinner for some visiting German scientists from the Max-Planck-Gesellschaft and members of the Academia Sinica, or Chinese Academy of Sciences. Their Chinese interpreters persisted in referring to the *Marx*-Planck-Gesellschaft. This wasn't just a question of habit. Although the Chinese characters for Marx and Max are different, their pronunciation is identical.

Our chef, Lao Huo, had baked some moon cookies for dessert – small, round, and very sweet. The Chinese were touched by this reminder that today, the fifteenth day of the eighth month in their old lunar calendar, had once been celebrated as the Moon Festival, one of the year's most popular events, by processions bearing coloured lanterns.

'At home in the country,' said the vice-president of the Academia Sinica, 'we used to have a moon-cookie society. Poor families contributed two or three coppers every month, and the baker acted as treasurer. He was allowed the use of the capital until the Moon Festival came round. Then he had to supply all his members with moon cookies.' I asked if the festival was still celebrated in the traditional way. Our guest shook his head. 'All we have now are moon cookies.'

I didn't pursue the subject. If I had, he might have felt obliged to explain why customs observed in China's old, feudalistic society were not permitted to survive in the new.

We repaired to the terrace after dinner. The moon floated, bright and serene, above the trees and the embassy swimming pool. A momentary silence fell. The air was dry and refreshingly cool.

Our Chinese guests agreed that autumn was on the way. They sounded a little depressed.

End of an Era

An unforgettable day and date.

Like Chinese government ministries, we were still working summer hours. Our official day ended at 2 p.m. This one had passed like any other: routine morning conference, summaries of press and radio reports, discussions, visitors, return visits to government departments, telegrams to and from Bonn.

The air was still crisp and the sun blazed down from a cloudless, deep blue sky. The thermometer was nudging ninety Fahrenheit, but my urge for a swim had to remain unsatisfied. We badly needed a wardrobe for our empty suite of rooms, and Hanna Höfer, the wife of the dpa [German Press Agency] correspondent, had volunteered to help us buy one. Franz was paying an official call on the wife of the Spanish Ambassador, so I set off alone with Hanna, who came to fetch me in her car.

Her chauffeur was an expert on the second-hand shops in the southern quarter, whose old, single-storeyed, brick-built houses had suffered more from the earthquake than the modern buildings in our own north-eastern district. Many of them had been wholly or partly destroyed. Roofs hung askew, windows had fallen out, and mounds of smashed tiles lay everywhere. Rubble was still being carted out of courtyards and dumped in the streets.

In one second-hand shop we unearthed a pair of old cupboards that looked as if they'd spent decades in a stable. Acting on Hanna Höfer's advice – 'Once you've had them repaired and stripped they'll simply *make* your room!' – I bought them. You couldn't say as much for new cupboards, she went on, quite apart from the fact that they weren't to be had.

We drove down Chang An Avenue, Peking's main east–west thoroughfare. It was almost four o'clock when we passed a large ceremonial gate in the old Chinese style, all red beams and gilded ornamentation. It was open, but we couldn't see in because of the spirit-wall beyond. That, too, was dark red like the gates and columns in the nearby Forbidden City. The spirit-wall bore an inscription in Mao's handwriting. Guarding the gate with fixed bayonets were two sentries in the green uniform of the People's Liberation Army, and above them flew the five-starred Red Flag. This one was made of silk, so the colours were particularly brilliant. I asked the driver to pull up for a closer look, but he either didn't hear or didn't want to.

Could this be the entrance to the pleasure grounds west of the Forbidden City, where I had often drunk tea in the old days? Hanna laughed at my question. That, she said, was Zhongnanhai, a park no common mortal could enter. It was the *sanctum sanctorum* of the Central Committee of the Chinese Communist Party. All the most exalted Party leaders had their homes there, Mao included.

We continued to skirt the high red wall enclosing the area, then turned north into a narrower street. The shops we passed sold fruit and vegetables, bicycles and vacuum flasks, pots and pans.

All at once, Hanna froze. 'Turn on the radio!' she called to her chauffeur. 'Quick, turn it on!'

My first thought was of another earthquake, imperceptible while the car was in motion. On the radio, an announcer was reading a prepared text in measured tones. It referred to the services rendered by Mao Zedong.

'Chairman Mao is dead,' said the chauffeur.

'My God,' said Hanna, 'my husband's been hovering over the teleprinter day and night, waiting for this news, and now he's in the embassy swimming pool. The embassy, quick!'

The obituary, a long one, was followed by the national anthem and the *Internationale*.

I turned to Hanna. 'How did you guess?'

Good newsman's wife that she was, she had caught sight of someone half-masting a flag in a courtyard and jumped to the right conclusion.

A figure was hurrying to the flagpole outside the Iranian Embassy as we drove past. At our own embassy, two doors down, cheerful activity reigned in and around the swimming pool. Hans Höfer and his daughter Tina were sunbathing.

My companion hailed her husband almost before the car had stopped. 'Mao's dead!' she called.

'Good God!' said Höfer. He sprang to his feet, galvanized, and sprinted to a cubicle. Once he had scrambled into some clothes, he and Hanna drove to his office round the corner.

By now it was 4.15 p.m., or 9.15 a.m. in Bonn. I told the embassy guard to half-mast our flag.

Within minutes of my return, a messenger from the New China News Agency delivered the English version of Mao's obituary, which covered three pages. Typed without benefit of capital letters, it began:

message to the whole party, the whole army
and the people of all nationalities throughout the country

48

comrade mao tsetung, the esteemed and beloved great leader of our party, our army, and the people of all the nationalities of our country, the great teacher of the international proletariat and the oppressed nations and oppressed people, chairman of the central committee of the communist party of china . . . passed away at 00.10 hours, 9 september, 1976, in peking because of the worsening of his illness and despite all treatment, although meticulous medical treatment was given him in every way after he fell ill.

No information was released, either then or later, about the nature of his illness.

My deputy, Gerd Berendonck, and Hans-Bodo Bertram of the Political Section joined me in the Blue Room for a detailed study of the document listing Mao's services to the nation and the world. We checked the wording for clues to China's future policy, domestic and international, and to the predominance of one particular faction, radical or moderate, inside the Politburo. Nothing in it seemed to answer our questions or suggest a change of policy. The phraseology was familiar to us, being that of the left-wing radicals who controlled the press. Ahrens was struck by an allusion to Mao's campaign against left-wing as well as right-wing opportunists. Though new, this verbal refinement availed us little, because left and right could be almost identical. The Party leadership decided which was which, though its condemnation of left-deviationists tended to be milder because they were essentially well-meaning comrades who had strayed leftward in an excess of zeal.

At 5 p.m. the Foreign Office called from Bonn. It was the head of the Far East desk, asking if we could confirm the dpa report of Mao's death. Radio Luxemburg was the first radio station to telephone and inquire how we had learned the news.

The embassy's files contained no prefabricated assessment of Mao and all he had accomplished, nor had I prepared one myself. Perhaps it was just as well. Someone pointed out that the Foreign Office would be bound to want to know who was to succeed Mao.

'Confucius may be out of favour,' I said, 'but let's take his advice. The Master said, "You, shall I teach you what knowledge is? To recognize what one knows as knowledge and what one does not know as ignorance – that is knowledge." '

I told Bertram to tour the city and see how people were taking the news.

Having presented my credentials only yesterday, I was now expected to report on the death of the most important figure in modern Chinese history and assess its potential consequences. It was a tall order. Although I had kept up with developments in the Chinese People's Republic, which fell within my purview at the Foreign Office, I had neither lived there in Mao's day nor observed his influence at first hand. I was merely one of many China-watchers – long-range observers versed in names and facts, but short of personal experience.

My first full day of official accreditation had coincided with the most important event that was likely to occur throughout my tour of duty. I had listened to my aides' views on Mao's death and the current situation in China, but the report itself was my own responsibility. *Res ad triarios rediit*, as the Romans used to say when the *triarii*, or seasoned warriors, had to go into action. I retired to my office.

It was only then, while reflecting on Mao's role in our century and the history of China, that I recalled how violently the ground had trembled the night before, during our stroll on the moonlit terrace. It was as if a mountain had subsided, signalling the end of an era. No one, it seemed to me, could predict China's course now that the Great Helmsman had breathed his last.

I drafted a report and discussed it with my aides. By 8 p.m. my cable was in the radio room on the embassy's top floor. An hour later, at 2 p.m. Central European Time, it was lying decoded on a desk in Bonn.

Mao Zedong died in Peking at oo.10 hours today. He was eighty-two years old. The Chinese radio is broadcasting solemn music interspersed with the news of his death and an obituary.

Mao will undoubtedly be numbered among the greatest men in Chinese history, which abounds in distinguished and dominant figures. Few previous rulers have wrought greater changes in China than he. His objectives were sometimes utopian, for example 'The Great Leap Forward', which proved so disastrous to the Chinese economy. The Revolution, the 'purges' and the Cultural Revolution claimed innumerable victims . . .

Mao died at a time when controversy over his ideas and policies had already broken out. Conjecture will be rife as to how the struggle for succession will turn out and which groups and individuals will come to the fore. In fact, however, little more can now be said than that China contains several political forces of varying strength: the Party leadership, which is split into at least two groups; the armed forces; and, finally, the provincial authorities.

At a rally last week, doubtless in expectation of Mao's death, the Chinese leadership strove to present a picture of complete unity. It is impossible to say how long this impression can be maintained. What is certain is that the group which placed very special reliance on Mao, namely, his wife Jiang Qing and the so-called Shanghai radicals, will be particularly hard hit by his death . . .

The Square of Heavenly Peace

The moon was as bright and silvery as it had been the night before. The gigantic portrait of Mao over the central gateway was draped in black.

Lao Zhou pulled up beside the marble bridges on the north side of Tian An Men Square. Beyond these bridges, which spanned the moat enclosing the old imperial palace, stood the Forbidden City's south wall, purple and massive, and in the centre towered the palace's main entrance, with its five barrel-vaulted gateways. The tallest and innermost of these had once been reserved for the emperor's sole use. This was Tian An Men, the Gate of Heavenly Peace.

Qian Men, principal gateway in the erstwhile city wall, had not been demolished. Its dark shape loomed above the southern extremity of the square. The majestic gate towers in the north and south went ill with the colonnaded façades of the two huge modern buildings in the east and west: the Great Hall of the People and the National Museum. Few people could be seen between us and the monumental portraits of Marx and Engels, Lenin and Stalin. They seemed to be thicker on the ground at the southern end, near the Martyrs' Monument honouring the Revolution's dead.

This was where, five months ago, the people of Peking had deposited wreaths, flowers, and poems in memory of Zhou Enlai, who had died in January. Their tribute to him had developed into a spontaneous demonstration against the ultra-left-wing faction in the leadership. Pinned to the flowers were poems and slogans hostile to the political course espoused by the leadership and its supporters. Those who condemned Mao's wife, Jiang Qing, did so in true Chinese fashion by writing panegyrics on his *first* wife or lampooning other women for their political machinations – an indirect but unmistakable form of criticism. Mao himself was spared like the emperors of yore, who had always been attacked through the medium of their advisers.

The demonstrations continued for a week. More and more people crowded into the square each day until estimates of their number exceeded a million. They scuffled with the militia and destroyed a police station, but no really serious violence occurred until the authorities removed the wreaths under cover of darkness. Next day, when this sacrilege was discovered, the mood of the crowd became ugly and somebody high up in the leadership ordered the square to be cleared. About a hundred demonstrators were arrested, hustled into the Forbidden City between two cordons of militiamen, and clubbed to death. I was told this two years later by an eyewitness whose anger at the recollection of this outrage convinced me of his sincerity; but no full account of the day's events has yet been published.

We walked across the square between the monumental portraits of the Marxist classics – two hirsute Germans and two hirsute Russians – to the Martyrs' Monument. People were few and far between, even here. Whether they numbered a few hundred or a few thousand, their shadowy figures were lost in the vast expanse of the moonlit square.

Some marble steps led up to the base of the memorial column, but the soldiers guarding them peered at us suspiciously. A few dozen Chinese were converging on the south side of the monument, presumably because there was something of interest to be seen there. Borne along by the crowd, we saw that someone had laid a small bunch of red flowers – ordinary garden flowers – on the bottom-most step. The Chinese pressed forward, looking for a dedication or poem of some kind, but all that lay there was a simple bunch of flowers.

People came and went. Nothing could be heard but the shuffle of cloth soles on flagstones. No one spoke – no one even whispered. It was an eerie scene.

To a nation aware that Mao was not immortal, the subject of his death had been taboo. Anyone wishing to speak of the period thereafter had relegated it to 'a hundred years' time'. More than two millennia ago, Chinese alluding to the period after a reigning emperor's death characterized it as a time lying far in the future – one that would come 'after ten thousand years and the passage of a thousand autumns'.

The crowd stood there shoulder to shoulder, silent and uneasy. We saw no overt signs of grief. Outbursts of public lamentation, of weeping and wailing, were only to be witnessed in the ensuing days. Here, in the vastness of the moonlit square, people felt anonymous and unrecognized. All we sensed was concern, insecurity, and fear of what the future might hold in store.

We three – Franz, Ahrens, and I – were the only foreigners in sight. The expressions of the Chinese around us conveyed that our presence was unwelcome. They preferred to be alone.

We made our way back to the car. It was parked beneath Mao's portrait on Tian An Men, the Gate of Heavenly Peace.

China Mourns

We were not roused next morning by *The East Is Red*, to which we were already inured, but by the official tribute to Mao's services. Then came the national anthem, the *Internationale*, and a Chinese funeral march, all three played in the slowest possible time.

The same programme was repeated throughout that day and the days that followed. The whole of Peking was similarly bombarded, as were all China's cities, communes, and factories from the remotest corners of Yünnan and Tibet to the provinces of the far north and the oases of Xinjiang – anywhere, in fact, that had an electric power supply. The loudspeakers installed throughout Peking, even in parks and the Forbidden City, usually regaled its inhabitants with revolutionary songs and hymns to Mao. Now, their output was restricted to the obituary programme. Anyone in search of peace and quiet had to go to the zoo, whose loudspeakers had been removed when zoologists discovered that the noise upset their charges. They were particularly concerned about the giant pandas, which seemed to suffer more than most.

Lao Liu, who supervised our household staff, was wearing a black armband when he silently laid the table that morning. Xiao Wang, known as 'Little' Wang because he was only twenty and full of mischief, had also donned one, as had Lao Huo the chef and Aunt Gao. Female domestics had formerly been addressed as *amah*, South Chinese for 'aunt'; now they were known as *ayi*, Modern Standard Chinese for the same word. The traditional term was considered an unseemly hangover from the bad old days. As with those in the West who refer to rat-catchers as pest control officers, so with the Chinese!

Gao Ayi, or Aunt Gao, entered the dining-room in tears. She told us that everyone at home had wept over breakfast – her husband, herself, and her three children. She continued to lament the death of Chairman Mao while making the beds, cleaning the bathroom, and doing the ironing. Her nerves were in such a state by lunch time that we had to send her home. Mr Ma, our Chinese telephonist and interpreter, was made of sterner stuff. Ma being the spokesman and senior member of our Chinese embassy staff, I sent for him and expressed our condolences. He showed no sign of grief, merely thanked me on his own behalf and that of his Chinese fellow employees, then said he needed another three passport photos of me and my wife for insertion in our driving licences.

The Peking edition of the *People's Daily* carried a black-bordered photograph of Mao on page one, uncaptioned, and national mourning was proclaimed until 18 September. Meanwhile, Mao's body was to lie in state in the Great Hall of the People. I watched the news on colour television every evening. The monotony of the programme during the first few days could scarcely have been surpassed. A black-and-white still of Mao filled the screen while an invisible announcer read his obituary, the 'message to the whole people'. The mournful voice was superimposed on the national anthem, the *Internationale*, and the funeral march, all performed – as ever – at a snail's pace. Once the announcer had said his piece, silence fell. Mao's picture hovered on the screen for the next thirty minutes. Then the announcer launched into another reading of the same obituary to the same musical accompaniment. Such was the extent of Peking's television news.

A little variety was injected as the days went by. Other stills of Mao were shown, most of them dating from his youth. These were joined in due course by a few well-known photographs of the Long March and the years in Yenan. They were also reproduced in the press. Comparing them with photographs in books of mine, I noticed instances where figures had been touched out – that of Lin Biao, the Marshal whom Mao had appointed as his successor, who died when he tried to flee to the Soviet Union, for example. No films of Mao were shown because they also showed persons who had since become non-persons, and non-persons are difficult to delete from motion pictures.

So China followed the pattern set in other communist countries where the past was just as potentially dangerous. Back issues of *Scinteia*, the official Romanian daily, had been hidden away in Romanian libraries and were accessible only to holders of special permits. Soviet newspapers were similarly treated in Moscow libraries. Anyone wishing to consult issues of the *People's Daily* from 1965, which contained speeches by Lin Biao, had to substantiate his request in full before borrowing them from a Chinese records office, just as, prior to Mao's death, anyone delving into Shanghai newspaper archives for issues from the 1930s could well discover, often too late, that he had incurred the gravest suspicion. He might, after all, have been trying to unearth something discreditable about Jiang Qing, then a Shanghai actress noted for her Bohemian lifestyle.

The good communist, and the New Man in particular, must have no political or historical memory capable of proving that what is true today was untrue a year ago. It is enough that the Party possesses a memory. Being master and maker of history, it can rewrite the annals again and again, forever producing revised versions of what *really* happened in the past.

Several days went by before motion pictures reappeared on the screen –

interminable sequences of tearful men and women shuffling past the Chairman's bier in the Great Hall of the People. Soldiers and militiamen, who came to pay their respects to his corpse in rank and file, were likewise overcome when they saw it.

Another programme showed a grief-stricken nursery-school teacher informing her two- and three-year-old pupils that the Great and Good Chairman had died at Peking and would never, ever come back to life. At this, the toddlers broke into heart-rending sobs and the camera zoomed in on their faces. Film reports in this morbid vein would last a good half-hour, not just a minute or two, and close-ups were reserved for those who wept more spectacularly than the rest.

Embassy staff who recalled the public mourning for Zhou Enlai told me that it had been more sincere, spontaneous, and heartfelt. Zhou was the humane and kindly, dependable and approachable leader, Mao the imperious hurler of thunderbolts and author of change, a remote and challenging figure who gave his fellow countrymen not a moment's rest.

But there was no touchstone that might have tested the mourners' sincerity. Although many people must undoubtedly have lamented the loss of the man who had remoulded China into a country and the Chinese into a nation, the fierce and unbridled manifestations of grief we find so alien and histrionic have little to do with depth of feeling. Customary in many parts of the East, they begin as far west as the Balkans. The sight of the dead triggers a reflex outburst of weeping and wailing – a convention familiar to all from their earliest childhood onwards. Loud lamentation is the order of the day, not dignity and restraint. We may here be confronted by a very ancient ritual, so hallowed by tradition that it has become second nature. Though cathartic in effect, it affords no guide to the depth, duration, and sincerity of the grief expressed.

We could not decide how many Chinese were miming or theatrically overplaying sorrow in token of their political loyalty, but we probably tended to underestimate their number. Chinese society had always demanded that its members signify love for the deceased by loudly lamenting them. Anyone who did not was no true mourner. A son who failed to weep and wail over a parent's coffin – who evinced only 'dry' sorrow – was guilty of that gravest sin, lack of filial devotion. Later on, when the Chinese began to speak more freely in my presence, some of them told me how constrained they had felt to exaggerate their displays of grief under the watchful gaze of superiors who noted the intensity of their sorrow and reported it to a higher authority. Not only Party functionaries, they said, but colleagues, too, had to be universally convinced how overwhelmed they were at the loss of Chairman Mao.

The whole population, young and old, wore black arm-bands. Many wore white paper chrysanthemums as well, white being the ancient colour of mourning. Many a radiator cap was similarly adorned, and shopkeepers substituted pictures of Mao, fringed with crêpe and decorated with flowers, for the fly-blown goods or dummies in their windows.

But mourning itself could be carried too far. Before long, the Chinese authorities issued an admonitory slogan: 'Convert sorrow into strength.' This led to unwonted activity on the part of neighbourhood organizations in districts of Peking where earthquake damage had been exceptionally severe. Late into the night, men and women could be seen repairing walls, carting rubble out of courtyards into the street, or reroofing houses. Serviceable bricks were retrieved from the ruins and loaded into trucks by long human chains of adults and children. Within a few days, the streets were clear of rubble.

People became calmer and life a little more subdued. Those who had worries concealed them. Gao Ayi, whose emotional state had improved, no longer sprinkled my shirts with tears while ironing. She, too, was endeavouring to convert sorrow into strength.

Peking and Moscow

11 September

'China's conflict with the Soviet Union will last ten thousand years.' So said Mao Zedong to Anthony Crosland, then Britain's Foreign Secretary, in the spring of 1976.

'Even if you normalize your economic and interstate relations?' asked Crosland. 'In that case,' Mao replied, 'perhaps nine thousand.' Sir Murray MacLehose, Governor of Hong Kong, had told me this story when I called on him two weeks earlier.

'If we accept that ten thousand or nine thousand years means the same as "a long time",' I said, 'Mao's prediction will come true. Mind you, I called at the Indian Foreign Ministry a week ago. The head of their Planning Department is afraid the Russians and Chinese may team up again after Mao's death and re-establish a joint foreign policy.'

Sir Murray laughed. The Indians, he said, had suffered from that obsession for years.

But not the Indians alone. One of the first German political commentaries I read after Mao's death declared that, from now on, anything could happen. If the pragmatists gained control of the Chinese leadership, they would terminate their country's ideological conflict with the Soviet Union and restore the *entente* of the 1950s.

To counter such conjectures, I sent our Foreign Office a long cable seeking to show that the dispute between Moscow and Peking was more than a product of ideological controversy. It had arisen from definite conflicts of interest which not only remained in being but had intensified and would persist unless the Soviet Union undertook a radical change of policy. No one would recognize this more clearly than the pragmatists in the Chinese political leadership. Mao's successors were faced with a choice between pursuing the present policy of total confrontation with the Soviet Union and, at most, normalizing inter-state relations. The latter course would not, however, remove any fundamental conflicts of interest. No new *entente cordiale* between China and the Soviet Union would be established in the foreseeable future. Thus, because ideology had played only a secondary role in the dispute, the term 'ideological conflict' was false and misleading.

In the course of a dialogue to which much ink has been devoted, and to which I had alluded in my interview with Foreign Minister Qiao Guanhua, the pupil Zilu told Confucius, 'The Prince of Wei is proposing to entrust you with the government. What, in your view, should first be done?'

The Master replied, 'The most pressing need is to begin by correcting appellations.'

'Surely you're mistaken,' said Zilu. 'What could you hope to achieve by such a correction?'

Annoyed by this reply, the Master reprimanded him. 'Isn't that a trifle discourteous of you? The superior person reflects before speaking of things he does not understand.

'If appellations are incorrect, words fail to accord with reality. If words fail to accord with reality, the business of government cannot be carried on. If the business of government cannot be carried on, morality and harmony suffer. If morality and harmony suffer, penalties are wrongly imposed. If penalties are wrongly imposed, people don't know what to do with their hands and feet.

'That is why the superior person considers it needful that appellations be correct, and that his words be correctly translated into action. He tolerates no disorder in his words.'

So much, very freely rendered, for Confucius in the *Analects*. Anyone who describes China's conflict with the Soviet Union as purely ideological is employing false terminology. But there are other examples.

The word *détente* denotes an activity. The term 'policy of *détente*' was relevant in the days when both sides were trying, albeit not in equal measure, to mitigate the tensions of the Cold War. At that time the policy effected a certain superficial easing of tension; thereafter it eased nothing, merely pretended to defuse situations by taking action. But it took no real action at all, merely let things slide and simulated action with the aid of empty gestures and half-hearted protests.

The superior person tolerates no disorder in his words.

Vanity of Vanities

The trees were a constant source of surprise to us. They not only lined our route but bordered farm tracks, ditches, and canals. In the old days, the plain between Peking and the Fragrant Hills had been almost treeless. Nothing had punctuated the flat fields but an occasional bamboo treadmill with a man inside, running on the spot like a caged hamster as he pumped a thin trickle of water from the ditch on to his plot of land. The treadmills had gone now, like the windmills of Europe. The pumps in the ditches were motorized.

This road, which led to the Thirteen Tombs of the Ming Emperors and the Great Wall, and the road to the Fragrant or Western Hills, were the only ones available to us for excursions into the country. All that we were permitted to see outside Peking could easily be seen in a single weekend. On this occasion, Gerd Ruge, the journalist, and his wife Lois Ruge-Fisher, the author, had invited us and Otto Humin to a picnic in the precincts of a ruined imperial tomb. Otto was one of my oldest friends in China. He now lived in Hong Kong but visited Peking almost every month.

Fengshui was the science of wind and water, a highly esteemed and indispensable branch of knowledge in ancient China. No one ever built a house or bridge without consulting the geomancer, or *fengshui* expert. Other scientific authorities – astrologers, for instance, or soothsayers – could be dispensed with at a pinch. Not so the geomancer, especially when it came to finding an auspicious burial place where ancestors would be shielded from the influence of evil spirits. In gratitude for a favourable *fengshui* site, ancestors blessed their descendants with prosperity and good fortune throughout succeeding generations. An unfavourable *fengshui* site could disturb ancestors' slumbers, dog their descendants with misfortunes and afflictions of every kind – poverty and disease, for example –

and cause their wives to give birth to freaks or bear nothing but daughters, which was almost worse.

Even a layman could tell that the Ming Tombs were blessed with an excellent *fengshui* location. The towers in front of the burial mounds had numerous curving roofs and stood widely spaced in a semicircle formed by two ranges of hills facing south – where else? The emperor was the only person in China permitted to inhabit a building with a southern aspect. As for the hills themselves, they shielded the tombs against the malign influences that tended, then as now, to assail China from the north.

To the discerning eye, the jagged ridges beyond the tombs resembled two sleeping dragons lying head to head, as they so often do in carved reliefs. Far from being creatures fit only for slaughter by bloodthirsty knights, Chinese dragons were purveyors of good fortune and symbols of imperial majesty. Any burial place with a river on its left and a dragon on its right was highly prized and beyond the reach of ordinary mortals. The aforementioned pig-dragon that wrought such mischief in Peking belonged to an altogether different species – quite a rare one, even in China.

Gerd Ruge stressed that we must never leave the road under any circumstances. A few weeks ago, he said, an embassy official had been severely reprimanded by a sentry for taking his little boy down to the river on the *right* to collect some pebbles. So saying, Gerd himself swung *left* off the authorized route and drove along a farm track. After a few hundred yards he parked the car behind a wall and beside a stream. Otto observed that the *fengshui* of this spot was ideally suited to illicit parking.

There was no bridge over the stream, just a row of stepping stones, so we took off our shoes and socks and tiptoed safely to the far bank. The environs of the Ming Emperor's tomb were anything but majestic. Instead of approaching it by way of a thuja-lined avenue, we had to skirt fields and cross orchards.

A village came into view on our left. I was all for taking a closer look, but the Ruges said no – we were off-limits as it was. We could but try, I argued. After all, the Foreign Minister himself had urged me to visit some Chinese villages because they provided the best illustration of the difference between then and now.

Rather unenthusiastically, Gerd gave in.

The houses were squat, single-storeyed cottages built of sun-dried bricks rendered with mud. Despite their dirty and neglected appearance, we were later to discover on numerous occasions that mud houses can be quite snug inside.

We didn't get that far today. Though muddy, the path was dry enough in parts for us to avoid the puddles. Even before entering the village, we were enveloped in an acrid stench. It came from some open sties in which pigs could be seen, mostly sows with litters. A tousled little dog yapped fiercely at us in the village street. Women emerged from their houses and stood watching. Some children peeped at us over a wall, open-mouthed. We greeted the women cheerfully.

'*Ni hao? Ni haoma?*'

'*Ni hao?*' they replied, but their manner was subdued and unsmiling. The village looked just like the villages of forty years ago, except that then we should have been mobbed by a crowd of inquisitive children. At the point where the village street widened to form a small square stood a notice board bearing some printed and handwritten sheets of paper. We made for it, hoping to decipher them with Otto's help, but were thwarted by three men who materialized from a gateway and headed us off. We could go no further, they said – we must turn back.

It would have been pointless to insist – it always is, in China. You have to plead your case and substantiate it with a series of reasoned arguments, but arguing would have been just as pointless. The men were plainly alarmed.

So we turned back. I was disappointed at not having found out what the notices said, but Otto assured me that we hadn't missed anything. One poster would have been bound to criticize Deng Xiaoping, who was currently blamed for everything. Others would have advised the inhabitants on what to do in an earthquake, enjoined them to step up their campaign against flies and other pests, and called for a general increase in their level of revolutionary consciousness.

'But why weren't we allowed to read them?' Franz protested. 'Why weren't we allowed into the village? Even in Romania we could go wherever we liked. Is there a military installation near here – is that why they're jumpy?'

'Not at all,' said Otto. 'Maybe they think they'll lose face if foreigners see how low their living standards are. Poor sanitation, primitive agricultural implements, et cetera.'

Lois Ruge cocked an eyebrow. 'You mean the peasants think that way?'

'Not the peasants, the authorities who have orders not to let us leave the main road. On top of that, there's the universal Chinese love of secrecy.'

'But why were they scared?' asked Franz.

'Foreigners bring nothing but trouble with the authorities,' Otto told her, '—interrogations, accusations, reprimands, punishments.'

Orchards enclosed the beginnings of the processional route, with its big marble slabs. The outer burial precinct was roughly a hundred yards square, but much of the perimeter wall had been demolished. The bricks would have come in handy for building houses or pigsties in the neighbouring village.

Three old pine trees jutted into the azure sky, with their horizontal limbs outspread. Many Chinese regard the pine as the noblest of all trees. Li Liweng, 'the old man in the bamboo hat', paid tribute to it three centuries ago. Sitting in a garden filled with peach trees, willow trees, and flowers, but devoid of a pine, he wrote, is like sitting among women and children in the absence of a stern, severe paterfamilias to whom one can turn and look up.

Ancient pine trees are accounted persons in China. One venerable pine at the foot of Tai, the sacred mountain, was appointed a mandarin fifth class by the First Emperor over two thousand years ago. It still stands today – if it really is the same one – nor is it the only mandarin among the trees of China. Every Chinese painter and art-lover knows the two pines, one symbolic of welcome and the other of farewell, that stand near the Jade Pavilion, beneath the principal peak of the Yellow Mountains. Later on, Franz and I spent a night in the hut there, so as to be able to feast our eyes on the pines and mountains in the misty light of dawn – great and venerable personalities, one and all.

The pines in the outer precinct of the Emperor's tomb were also venerable but had not yet acquired names of their own. They were still too young for that, although more than three hundred and thirty years old. The last Ming Emperor had hanged himself in 1643, when Peking was occupied by an army of rebellious peasants.

The grass was knee-deep as we approached the funerary tower, and we had to be careful not to trip over fragments of marble. We passed through a small, dilapidated gateway built of glazed yellow brick, though we could just as well have walked round it, because the walls on either side had been demolished.

We were now in another funerary precinct. The wall in the background, which was still standing, rivalled a city wall in height and would not have been so easy to demolish. It was slightly recessed at the top to leave room for a terrace. This we ascended by way of some lopsided, tumbledown steps, respectfully avoiding places where the roof tiles overhung us too far. A whole heap of them lay at our feet, probably dislodged and smashed by the earthquake.

The roof timbers were rotten – mouldering away. They had been erected centuries ago by master craftsmen using neither bolts nor screws. We were amazed by the skilful jointing of the intricate structure, with its numerous load-bearing and load-transmitting beams and joists. Equally miraculous was the way in which single beams had been tailored to fit so many different blocks of stone. Some of the projecting ends were marvels of geometrical ingenuity, but they, too, were rotten and disintegrating.

Inside the tower, beneath a vaulted roof, stood the marble stele inscribed with the name of the Emperor, or, more probably, of the period spanned by his reign. Beyond the tower lay the massive mound containing his tomb. We circled this on top of the wall for ten minutes or so, then returned to the pine trees below the tower. Otto drew our attention to a *baipi sung*, a pine with silvery bark and needles in clusters of three, not two like those of other pines. This specimen was half inside the wall and projected almost horizontally into the precinct in front of the tower.

Lois Ruge had left the picnic basket on a granite table with a top at least fifteen feet long. We seated ourselves on the slab and used it to crack our hard-boiled eggs on. Only Otto remained standing. He looked curiously forlorn and irresolute.

'What's the matter?' we asked.

'Oh,' he said, 'nothing, really. It's just that you're sitting on the sacrificial slab – the Emperor's altar.'

We laughed, then thought better of it and continued our meal in the dry brown grass. Gerd poured us some lukewarm beer. It came from Tsingtao, where German brewers had introduced their art in the days when Tsingtao formed part of the German Protectorate of Kiao-chow.

Otto raised his cardboard cup of beer and turned to the funerary tower. '*Imperious Caesar, dead and turned to clay*,' he declaimed, '*might stop a hole to keep the wind away* – how does it go on?'

Gerd recited the next couplet in German, not knowing his *Hamlet* too well in English, and I thanked the Ruges for showing us this ruined tomb before either of the two that had been restored. 'It's a monument to human vanity,' I said. 'You can sense it in every rotten timber.'

'And death in every fallen stone,' someone chimed in.

'You're being un-Chinese,' said Otto, who so often thought like a native. '*Memento mori*, the Hooded Stranger, the Grim Reaper who cuts us down or drags us away from the dance of life – they're Western ideas, all of them. Out here, people have never taken themselves as seriously as we do. They're part of a family, and when they die the family lives on – that's what counts with them. They may not die gladly, but at least they die with an easier mind. Many of us find it hard to understand how a person can die for something else – his people, his country, his beliefs and convictions. We like to think there's nothing more important on earth than ourselves.'

'Do they still die as easily today?' asked Franz.

'Yes.' Otto's initial hesitation vanished. 'Yes,' he repeated firmly, 'even today. Think of the thousands of people who committed suicide during the Cultural Revolution because they declined to undergo the humiliation of a public hearing. There's an old Chinese proverb: "The spirit can be killed but not humiliated."'

'You're right,' I said. 'Impermanence is the great Chinese theme, not death. Shall I quote you an example, or would it bore you?'

'Carry on,' said Gerd. 'Is there a sandwich left?'

'Over two thousand years ago,' I said, 'Governor Yanghu made an excursion up Mount Xian, which overlooks the city then called Xiangyang, with a party of friends. High above the plain and the Han River, probably in a pavilion at the summit, they ate and drank their fill and wrote poems – pretty little pieces of verse, one suspects, and no great strain on the intellect. Then, struck by a sudden thought, Yanghu rose and addressed the festive gathering. "This mountain has been here since the world began," he said. "Many people abounding in virtue and wisdom have stood up here like us, but all are dead and forgotten. Just wait, my friends – it will not be long before we are forgotten likewise." And his eyes filled with tears.

'After Yanghu's death, his friends erected a stone on the summit in memory of the tears he had shed over human transience – but that,' I added quickly, 'isn't the end of the story.

'About a thousand years later the mountain was climbed by the poet Li Bai, or Li T'ai Po, as we generally call him in the West. While up there he wrote a poem. I can only reproduce it in prose: "Mount Xian looks down on the River Han. Its waters are blue, its banks dazzling as snow. Here on the summit stands the Monument of Tears, eaten away by wind and weather, its inscription covered with moss."

'End of story,' I said. 'Li Bai's poem wouldn't be comprehensible without the first part, but why do you think I told it at all? Because Li Bai superimposed one illustration of human insignificance on another.'

'A sort of Chinese *vanitas vanitatum*,' commented Otto.

We wondered which of the Ming emperors lay buried here. Nobody knew for sure, but Otto plumped for Xizong, the penultimate member of the dynasty. Franz asked why. Otto 'just had a hunch', probably because Xizong had married a celebrated beauty named Precious Pearl.

'She was a foundling,' said Otto. 'From orphan to Empress – ideal Hollywood material. She was more than a pearl, incidentally. She was an angel of goodness in a corrupt and loathsome imperial court dominated by eunuchs. I can imagine her lying in that mound beside her royal husband, who was a depraved and dissolute weakling. The strong man of the court was Wei, the chief eunuch.'

'Can you call a eunuch a man?' asked one of the ladies.

'Good question,' said Otto, '—needs thinking about. Anyway, it was Wei who ruled the empire, terrorized the court, and ruthlessly exterminated anyone who didn't suit his book. Once he went too far, though. He had the effrontery to mount a horse in the Emperor's presence. Xizong was so staggered and infuriated by this piece of impertinence that he had the horse beheaded on the spot. Nothing happened to Wei, of course.'

Gerd poured us some more warm beer and we drank to the memory of Empress Precious Pearl. We were convinced by now that she lay buried in the mound behind us, beside her depraved and dissolute weakling of a husband.

Lois cleared away our debris and repacked the picnic basket. We left the imperial couple in their lonely resting place beyond the ruined tower. We hadn't seen another soul in all this time.

And at night?

'At night,' said Otto, 'foxes reign in the tombs and their litters gambol around on the coffins. There's an old Chinese poem about it.'

Beside Mao's Bier

13 September

Chang An Avenue, which leads into the Square of Heavenly Peace, was closed to ordinary traffic. Men, women, and youngsters with militia arm-bands on the sleeves of their blue working tunics were posted at intervals along the white lines marking the roadway. The only traffic heading for the Great Hall of the People consisted of embassy cars travelling in convoy. Tian An Men Square was otherwise deserted. We pulled up outside the north door of the massive building. All foreign embassy staff had been invited to take leave of the late Chairman.

We climbed the great steps. Between the engaged columns above the entrance hung a large, black-bordered portrait of the dead man. Once inside the vestibule we were conducted by officials from the German section of the Foreign Ministry to a table on which lay some big sheets of rice paper. We signed our names and were then ushered into the spacious hall itself, where a number of dignitaries waited in line to receive us. They were Marshal Xü Shiyou, the Politburo member under whose protection Deng Xiaoping was then living, the Uighur Saifudin, two Deputy Premiers, and a Minister. I shook hands with each of them in turn and offered my condolences. The Minister, who could not disguise his emotion, was weeping with head averted. All that broke the silence, apart from our subdued voices, was the hum of obsolete television cameras.

We made our way into the body of the hall down an avenue of easel-like tripods on which wreaths were displayed. Another portrait of Mao bordered with black and yellow crêpe adorned the rear wall, and between it and us stood the bier. Propped against the catafalque were several more wreaths, prominent among them Jiang Qing's. All the others consisted of white chrysanthemums, carnations, yellow roses, or lilies; the dead man's wife had laid a wreath of rice ears and wild flowers. The legend on the ribbon read: 'In profound sorrow for the Great and Revered Teacher from his pupil and comrade-in-arms, Jiang Qing.' No word of affection, no reference to their marriage or their daughter Li Ming. It was a purely political wreath. Beside it stood wreaths from Mao's other children, but their names were partly obscured by flowers. There was no sign of a wreath from his second wife, He Zizhen, whom he had repudiated in 1937 in order to marry Jiang Qing, and who was said to be living under house arrest in Shanghai, certified insane.

Mao lay flat on the bier, shrouded from chest to feet in a red flag with the hammer-and-sickle emblem in the centre. He was wearing the high-necked grey jacket familiar to the world from every picture of him. His face looked unnaturally dark. The features were relaxed, the lips slightly parted. His last published photographs, taken in May, had made him look older and frailer than he did now.

We remained standing in front of the dead man for a minute before bowing and moving on. By whatever means, he had united the nation beneath the banner of his own ideas. He had gained brilliant victories and sustained crushing defeats. He had committed grave errors and squandered much of the trust reposed in him by his people. The individual mattered little to him. He had strayed far from the old Confucian, or even pre-Confucian, principle that the state's sole function is to ensure the welfare of the people. With the possible exception of Qin Shihuang, the First Emperor, few Chinese rulers had thought as he did. Mao was preoccupied, not with the people, but with revolution and a new, socialist order.

He was capable of making ideological demands whose only purpose was to galvanize the masses and keep himself in power. This he did even though the spring tide, as he once called his Cultural Revolution, devastated the country. 'Revolution is no embroidery lesson' – such was the slogan he coined to excuse the cruelties and atrocities of his era. In none of his recorded utterances can any compassion be detected for those who suffered as a result of his policies. He was, on the other hand, heard to make crude and cynical remarks.

Loyalty was not for Mao. Even his oldest comrades could be sacrificed for the sake of personal power. If it would save him, he swiftly modified his views and attitudes. He was a master of subterfuge, a connoisseur of political highways and byways, but even he could come to grief. There were times when he overplayed his hand and diminished his authority.

Mao was devoted to grand, Utopian schemes. He aspired to be the great author of change – to pull down whatever remained of the old political edifice. When the Cultural Revolution threw everything into turmoil and confusion, he delightedly proclaimed that Chinese society was a blank page waiting to be filled anew. With what? 'The newest and finest words, the newest and finest pictures,' said Mao. But what *sort* of words and pictures?

Though eager to design a new social structure, he was forced to concede, after the Great Leap Forward had failed, that he knew nothing about economics. He liked to achieve the seemingly impossible. One of his poems begins: 'I have always reached for the clouds.' When his comrades engaged in heated theoretical debate, however, he was quick to devise common-sense solutions.

One of his greatest achievements during the revolutionary struggle constituted a deviation from the Soviet line – indeed, from that laid down by Marx himself. In defiance of the Comintern and his own Party leadership, he wooed and won the peasants instead of relying on the weak Chinese industrial proletariat.

However momentous Mao's contributions to communist theory may have been, their philosophical content and reasoning are poor and often amateurish. As against this, he could define the nub of a complex problem with terse simplicity. His strength lay in converting fellow revolutionaries and large sections of the population to his ideas at a time when victory was still remote. He became the fount of authority – and, when the Revolution triumphed, a remote figure whom many regarded with quasi-religious awe. For all that, some of his recorded remarks and published letters come from the heart.

Mao was a man without whom his country would not have become what it is. He was great in his achievements, great in his errors and contradictions.

We bowed to his corpse in the knowledge that, while verdicts on him might fluctuate, Chinese history would number him among its greatest figures, and the Chinese people would bear the burden of his name and image for many years to come.

The Forbidden City

The imperial palace has been known as the Forbidden City since ancient times. It is not, in fact, a single building, but a large rectangular city within a city – Peking itself is almost square – comprising audience chambers, temples, administrative buildings, barracks, residential quarters, spacious squares, here called courtyards, and parks or pleasure grounds.

This city within a city was truly 'forbidden', as one can still see today. The palace is separated from Peking proper by a moat and a massive wall with defensible towers. Inside it dwelt the Son of Heaven, whose task was to keep heaven and earth attuned, outside it the common people.

Only those who enter the Forbidden City from the south, by the Gate of Heavenly Peace, can discern its rhythmical flow and harmonious proportions. In the centre, on the north–south axis, lie smaller courtyards enclosed by the single-storeyed houses once occupied by the emperors, their wives and concubines of varying rank, and their court officials, nearly all of whom were eunuchs. Today, nobody lives in the Forbidden City.

I walked through one of the five tunnel-like apertures in the Gate of Heavenly Peace and out into the tree-lined courtyard where the imperial guards had been quartered, then through the Gate of Decorous Behaviour – walking decorously, of course – and into the courtyard beyond. This was dominated by Wu Men, the Midday Gate. Roughly a hundred yards across, the huge gatehouse had towering, dark red walls and was flanked by projecting wings. After the space and serenity of the outer courtyard, I suddenly felt hemmed in and overlooked by an unrelieved mass of masonry.

Wu Men did not encourage further progress. Menacing and forbidding, it warned the visitor against entering in too casual and confident a mood. Luckless subjects whom the emperor had condemned to death – sometimes in the middle of an audience – had been hauled forth and summarily executed in front of this gate, overlooked by these selfsame walls.

I entered the gateway in a rather subdued frame of mind, to be greeted on the other side by a scene of unexpected splendour. Peking was basking in one of its glorious autumn days. Brilliant sunlight and a clear blue sky intensified the yellow of the glazed roofs and made the marble of the bridges spanning the courtyard's Golden Water Stream whiter than usual.

On the north side of the courtyard, above a triple balustraded terrace, also in dazzling white marble, stands the Hall of Supreme Harmony. Beyond this, visitors who have mounted the steps will find the Halls of Perfect and Protecting Harmony. These large audience chambers do not oppress or dwarf the beholder, nor do the spacious courtyards make him feel lost like the Square of Heavenly Peace, which used to be on a human scale until enlarged to make room for gigantic rallies and parades. Not to be outdone by the Russians, the Chinese have blown it up to four times the size of Red Square.

The Hall of Perfect Harmony is a little jewel, but even the larger halls are simple and unpretentious. Although their architecture does not set out to impress, it is self-assured and effective. This, undoubtedly, is because of its harmonious proportions. One would not be surprised if careful measurement disclosed that the horizontals are ever so slightly curved, as in the temples of Greece, or that the gently upswept roofs and the relationship between one roof and its superimposed twin can be reduced to mathematically simple formulae.

It is doubtful whether the architects carried their computations to such extremes, given that anyone who learns Chinese characters automatically acquires a sense of proportion and harmony. Whatever the truth, the palace was built at the beginning of the fifteenth century by an early and illustrious member of the Ming dynasty, Yongle, who transferred the imperial seat from Nanking to Peking.

Seen from my vantage point on the terrace, the roofs stretched away like successive ranges of hills, all in a brilliant imperial yellow that mirrored the sunlight. Above them in the north rose Coal Hill with its pavilions, and west of it the White Dagoba, or domed pagoda, which looked strangely alien and exotic in the midst of so much Chinese architecture.

I paid a brief visit to the residential district in the western quarter because Otto, whom I had arranged to meet on the terraces, had not yet turned up. The courtyards are small and the houses formerly occupied by the emperors and empresses single-storeyed. A bronze unicorn waits in one courtyard. In other courtyards stand very old trees or bronze cranes. Their paved surfaces must once have been bright with potted flowers which were replaced when they withered, for the Chinese do not plant flowers in beds. Despite their small dimensions, the houses and courtyards are cosy rather than cramped. 'The size of a house and that of the people who inhabit it must be mutually harmonious,' wrote a Chinese aesthete at the end of the Ming period, and he went on to say that the great halls in which dignitaries entertained should properly have been reserved for beings ten feet tall. The living-room of the last Empress Dowager, Cixi (Tsu Hsi), who ruled the destinies of China for thirty-three years, is smaller than the German Embassy's drawing-room but crowded with knick-knacks and curios. Cixi did not have the Ming emperors' love of simple, sweeping lines. Like many rulers of the Manchurian Qing dynasty, she liked to surround herself with objects ornate and elaborate, colourful and garish. It may be that, despite the Manchu emperors' efforts to be Chinese, their legacy of northern or 'barbarian' blood came out in her too.

Several days earlier I had seen some photographs of Mao's house, which stood a few hundred yards away in Zhongnanhai Park. It was an old house in the same style as these imperial living quarters. Cabbages were growing in two large beds outside the door and beans along the side of the building. Mao's study was no bigger than the office of a middle-ranking business executive, but far more modestly furnished. The armchairs, which might have come from any cheap department store, were covered with blue check. Some pictures showed the great man's dressing-gown complete with darns in the sleeves, others his worn and patched slippers. Behind the house lay his open-air swimming pool.

I returned to the terrace of the great audience chamber to find Otto waiting beside the bronze turtle. 'I've just been thinking,' he said. 'Wouldn't it sound funny to a European if his parliament building was known as "The Hall of Perfect Harmony"? Here, the only people who find it odd are those who know nothing about Chinese history – who've never heard that the emperors' divine mission was to preserve harmony between heaven and earth. They extended that harmony to their living quarters. Looking at them, you can tell how highly they regarded their office and what a modest opinion they had of themselves.'

'All of them?'

'No, of course not. A lot of them were tyrannical, capricious, and thoroughly insufferable, but you won't find many who suffered from a tendency to show off or a love of pomp and circumstance.' Otto grinned. 'I can see you're itching to contradict me. Every generalization has its exceptions – I could quote you a few myself – but I'm talking about the majority. The emperors' houses and courtyards were homely places.'

'Stop,' I said, 'I can hardly believe my ears. Forget about the minor exceptions. While you were rhapsodizing about the principle of harmony,

I was recalling the "harmonious" social conditions prevailing here during the Cultural Revolution. How many people were killed or committed suicide? How many were exterminated in the middle of the last century, during the Taiping Rebellion – twenty million, thirty? Want me to go on?'

Otto laughed. '*Touché!* Harmony was the aim. All right, so the Chinese never achieved it – they may even have lost sight of it, but it was drummed into every educated person from childhood, the emperors' sons included, and transmitted by them to the people. Or has it always been present in the Chinese people themselves? Let's discuss it again when you've toured one of their rice-growing areas.'

'Social harmony was never one of Mao's aims, that's for sure. He preached just the opposite – permanent revolution.'

'True, he didn't believe in harmony. The Confucians didn't deny the existence of conflicts, but they called on people to strive for harmony and, if possible, achieve it by resolving them. Mao was so fascinated by Hegel's habit of thinking in dialectical waltz-time that he identified conflict as the source of social progress and thought the resolution of every conflict bred further conflicts. Naturally, that ran counter to tradition and an idea that had held sway for over two thousand years.'

'But what you said just now about the imperial household being homely – it just won't wash. Those houses and courtyards look snug enough, but think what went on there in the way of intrigue and character assassination, not to mention violence and suicide and murder. You know the memoirs of Princess Der Ling, the Empress Dowager's lady-in-waiting? The atmosphere at court was stifling – heavy with fear and malice, ruled by the old woman's fads and fancies. The other day I was talking to Lobmann, the Polish journalist who spent over a decade reporting on Mao's China. He told me that the atmosphere at his court was just as oppressive and stifling as it used to be here in the Forbidden City.'

'Whenever Jiang Qing was around, sure,' said Otto, who regarded her as Old Nick's daughter. 'And if the Chairman's widow comes to power, the members of her court will look back with longing on that homely and humane old witch Cixi.'

A Cursory Farewell

We foreigners had not been invited to attend the funeral rally. Instead, we watched the Chinese take leave of Mao Zedong comfortably seated in front of a television set which reproduced the scene in excellent colour.

The sun shone brightly down on Tian An Men Square. Its vast expanse was thronged with figures dressed in blue and white, and above them flew the red flags of factory groups, neighbourhood organizations, units of the armed forces and militia. Long red banners hung from the buildings around the square.

All eyes were turned towards the Gate of Heavenly Peace, with its curving yellow roofs. It was from the terrace of Tian An Men that Mao had proclaimed the People's Republic on 1 October 1949. It was there, too, that he had accepted the homage of the masses and the Red Guards during the Cultural Revolution, when they marched past him in their serried ranks.

There was no sign of a catafalque or coffin. Nobody knew what to do with the great man's body. My aides had heard a rumour that the Politburo could not make up its collective mind. Some wanted Mao cremated and his ashes scattered like Zhou Enlai's, others wanted him embalmed like Lenin or Ho Chi Min. I doubted these rumours – wrongly, as it turned out. Jiang Qing was in favour of cremation, Hua Guofeng wanted the body preserved.

Subsequent rumours were even more macabre. It was said that the corpse had presented problems which no one would have dared to raise, or even ponder aloud, before the Chairman's death. Whence could expert embalmers be imported in a hurry? From the United States, pray, or the Soviet Union? It was further reported that the vote had gone to Vietnam. Then, when Hanoi fought shy, the authorities had decided to fall back on their own resources. The results, we heard later, had not been altogether satisfactory.

Many members of the crowd had sat down or were squatting on their heels. Then stewards appeared, and everyone rose. A few minutes before 3 p.m. the Politburo emerged from the hall that ran the full width of the gatehouse. They stepped out on to the terrace one by one, earnest of mien, and were conducted by protocol officials to their places, which naturally accorded with a rigid pecking order. Not a word or glance passed between them as they took up their stations, not a gesture of courtesy or solidarity, far less cordiality. Everyone totally ignored everyone else. Each man stood aloof, as if he were alone on the terrace. The widowed Jiang Qing, too, looked aloof and self-contained.

The camera followed each member of the Politburo to his place. Thereafter it confined itself to long shots except when occasionally picking out the four members of the Politburo's Standing Committee, or supreme executive body: Hua Guofeng, Ye Jianying, Zhang Chunqiao, and the youthful Wang Hungwen.

Hua Guofeng surveyed the crowd with an air of unruffled calm. He was standing in the centre, no one having yet managed to deprive him of the leadership. Beside him stood young Wang Hungwen, the fast-rising star from the ranks of the industrial proletariat. Wang had made 'a helicopter career', as the Chinese put it. A member of the radical faction, he now looked less radical than nervous. Ye Jianying, the elderly Marshal, stood straight as a ramrod, but we had noticed that he walked with difficulty. Zhang Chunqiao, the Shanghai intellectual and close associate of Jiang Qing, continually blinked behind his thick-lensed glasses as though dazzled by the sunlight.

Jiang Qing was correctly but not prominently placed despite her status as the Chairman's widow. She wore a black trouser-suit and a black Party cap. Draped over the cap and around her neck was a black scarf, the ends of which hung elegantly down her back – rather too elegantly, so we later heard, for the taste of the toiling masses. She stood quite still, heedless of any critical glances from the mortal throng, and gazed over their heads at something in the far distance, presumably the future. Her earnest demeanour suggested that she was willing to succeed her great teacher and comrade-in-arms and uncomplainingly shoulder the burdens of government. No one would have guessed that she had waited and worked and schemed for this day for years. Ever the actress, she preserved a lingering gaze appropriate to the final close-up. The television camera should have shot her from slightly below with the Red Flag fluttering behind her against an ethereal blue background, a look of tragic greatness in her eyes.

Wang Hungwen, the helicopter careerist, could not match her poise or composure. He was evidently suffering from stage fright and kept glancing at his watch, anxious to start on time. It was Wang's privilege to compère the funeral rally.

On the stroke of three, after checking the time yet again, he stepped to the microphone and called the crowd to attention. The dead man was to be accorded three minutes' silent remembrance. Simultaneously, all Chinese throughout the vast country likewise came to attention and paid silent tribute to the late Chairman's memory. This order of the day covered everyone in any organization, military unit, factory, school, mine, business concern, shop, people's commune, and neighbourhood committee, whether indoors or out. The only exceptions were those whose work could not be interrupted for reasons of public safety or national security.

When the three minutes were up, the band at the foot of the gatehouse played the national anthem. The Politburo remained at attention, and Jiang Qing continued to stare impassively into the future.

Wang Hungwen stepped forward again. This time he uttered a single sentence: 'I call upon Comrade Hua Guofeng to speak.'

Hua read out his address prosaically, almost casually, with no discernible emotion, as if it were any old speech. Ah, what Jiang Qing would have made of it!

Although Hua's speech contained no clue to Mao's successor, we were struck by the fact that it presented all the radicals' views and ignored those of the moderates. Did this indicate that, although they had been deprived of their powerful mainstay, the leftists were unprepared to compromise and meant to pursue their militant policy?

A leading article common to all Chinese newspapers featured the following implicit demand: 'Chairman Mao adjured us: Act in accordance with the principles laid down!' We were told by Chinese that this sentence was highly significant, but it didn't get us very far. Had Mao left a political testament? Was that the key to the problem of succession?

At one point, quite oblivious of the television cameras, Wang Hungwen peered unceremoniously over the speaker's shoulder as though eager to assure himself that Hua was reading out his draft in full. Whether or not he was looking for a reference to 'established principles', Hua made no mention of them.

He made only one appeal for unity, and then only by repeating one of Mao's oft-cited injunctions: 'Practise Marxism but not revisionism! Be open and honest, do not conspire and intrigue!' We learned a few weeks later that Mao had addressed these 'three words of doing and not-doing' to the radicals early in May and warned them against 'appearing and acting as a gang of four'. The radicals wanted this passage deleted when the obituary address was discussed in the Politburo, arguing that it was too long anyway, but had failed to get their way. Hua's speech concluded with the said admonition.

Reclaiming the microphone, Wang Hungwen called for three obeisances to the portrait of Comrade Mao surmounting Tian An Men. Everyone in the square and on the terrace over the gateway bowed three times, and the band launched into a funereal rendering of the *Internationale*.

Wang Hungwen stepped forward once more and spoke into the micro-phone. 'That,' he announced, 'concludes the memorial ceremony for Comrade Mao.'

What! Was that all? Knowing the fondness of communist leaders for interminable speeches, we checked the time. Three minutes' silence and anthems included, the ceremony had lasted precisely thirty minutes. A glance at the TV set revealed that flags were already being shouldered and detachments marching off in their wake, wheeling left and right.

The nation's farewell to Mao had been dignified enough but sur-prisingly brief. Had the Politburo found it hard to agree on a suitable obituary? Possibly – no, undoubtedly. Did they also fear the emotions of the crowd and recall the riots in the same square five months earlier? Did it occur to them that the same masses who had demonstrated then were now arrayed below, and that the terrace was occupied by the same politicians who had brutally put them down? That, too, was possible.

The authorities' eagerness to get the proceedings over quickly was just as manifest as their relief when the crowd moved off and left the square.

Foreign Devils

So these were the New Men. They were scared of us – scared to touch or speak to us.

We had gone to a pharmacy to buy a Chinese herbal cold cure. We surveyed the interior through the window. The shop assistants, who had little to do all day, were blithely chatting in a group. The arrival of some *yang guizi* – 'foreign devils' – caused consternation. They exchanged apprehensive glances and scuttled into the back room. One middle-aged man, who stood his ground, informed us that he had no foreign medicines. Only Chinese medicines were sold here. He could hardly wait to get us out of the shop, but we had no intention of leaving. I said I wanted a Chinese herbal remedy, not a foreign preparation. He suddenly found my Chinese unintelligible. Then, realizing that co-operation might be the quickest means of getting rid of us, he served me after all.

In the old days? In the old days, all the assistants would have emerged from the back room and crowded round us. Our pronunciation would have amused them – convulsed them with laughter after we'd gone – and the manager would have inquired where we came from and whether the cold was a bad one.

And today? Today when we asked people the way in the street, some of them just stared at us in alarm and walked on quickly without a word. They had no wish to be seen with foreigners. With foreigners, talk was best confined to the barest essentials. If conversation proved impossible to avoid, one parroted the leader from the *People's Daily*.

It was equally hard to converse with officials – even with children. If you asked a schoolboy what he wanted to be when he grew up, his sole response was the answer he had learned by rote: 'I shall do what the Party bids me.'

The Chinese avoided talking to us because they were frightened. They could easily incur accusations of 'worshipping foreign things', having bourgeois tendencies, or – worse still – being agents and spies. These charges were hard to rebut, and it was up to the accused to prove his innocence. I was later told by Mr Qi, a Mozart devotee, that he had emptied his home of incriminating records and destroyed them.

We found it hard to learn anything about developments inside China. Getting to know the Chinese and persuading them to talk was a problem that demanded great ingenuity. At the same time, those who studied the press aright could glean a lot from official propaganda – a source on which the Warsaw Pact Embassies were wholly dependent. The Chinese themselves were avid newspaper-readers and knew which way the wind blew. They had an ear for every new note and nuance. Foreigners could also develop this knack, but only to a limited extent.

What was still more important, however, was to bridge the gulf between ourselves and the people, not in order to spread subversive ideas or elicit state secrets, but to understand what was going on. We eventually found Chinese willing to help and enlighten us in many respects, but it was a long time before they trusted us.

Expert Opinions

21 September

Our dpa representative, Hans Höfer, was giving a farewell party for Gerd Ruge, who had been posted to Moscow. The guests, who were a mixture of East and West, included numerous journalists and China specialists from other embassies. They knew the names of Chinese politicians who meant nothing to me and quoted recent statements and articles of which I had never heard. Clearly, I still had a lot of ground to make up.

Discussion centred on who would take over as Chairman of the Party,

Zhang Chunqiao or Mao's widow, or whether Zhang, the Shanghai intellectual, was angling for the premiership. Sophisticated arguments were adduced in favour of both theories. Someone opined that Mao's widow aspired to head the Party *and* the Government, but the vast majority said this was aiming too high. Someone else recalled that, during the April disturbances, Jiang Qing had been attacked through the medium of Isabel Perón. Señora Perón had been a dancer, Mao's widow an actress, and both professions were equally reprehensible in Chinese eyes. Though others disputed this, all agreed that Hua Guofeng was just a temporary compromise – that he had been permitted to deliver his speech at the funeral rally only because he was a colourless peasant from the provinces. If it came to a power struggle, he wouldn't stand a chance against the wily old masters of intrigue and infighting at Party Headquarters.

Another guest urged us not to forget young Wang Hungwen, the vertical take-off artist. Wang must have prevailed on the Politburo to let him conduct the ceremony. Besides, Mao wouldn't have let him rise so far or so fast without good reason. He must have been convinced of Wang's intelligence, sincerity, and general efficiency.

This drew a chuckle from my friend Otto Humin. In his experience, he said, those qualities were seldom an aid to political advancement. When an old politico looked around for a successor or promoted a junior member of his inner circle, he tended to pick on someone unambitious and innocuous, loyal and useful. Qualities of leadership were more of a hindrance, because those he still possessed himself. 'Let me have men about me that are fat!'

Since everyone else was groping in the dark, Otto went on, here was his own unproven contribution to the debate: Hua Guofeng might be a colourless figure, but the impression he gave was that of a smooth operator.

Otto was pretty much alone in this view, which the experts around us dismissed. Later, while he and I were sipping a nightcap on the embassy terrace, we pursued our speculations. I rather doubted if Mao's reforms would survive him for long. All the great programmes of social reform in Chinese history, from that of the First Emperor, Qin Shihuang, to those of Wang Mang in the first century AD and Wang Anshi in the eleventh, had remained operative – at best – for as long as the reformers lived. Like Mao, Wang Mang had actually been compelled to rescind some measures during his lifetime.

'But history didn't revert to its original state,' said Otto. 'We still don't know if Mao's widow will cling to the policy of permanent revolution and introduce some even more radical ideas – which would scupper her for a certainty – or whether the moderates will steer the ship into calmer waters. We'll soon see which. But even if the leadership goes back on some of Mao's more daring advances, life and politics in this country will be influenced for decades by the changes he made.'

'Where are the great reformers in Western history?' I asked. 'I don't see any.'

Otto cited Solon and the Gracchi.

'I'll give you Solon,' I said, 'but his was only a minor reform in a little Greek city state. As for the rest, they don't bear comparison with the reforms of Shang Yang and Qin Shihuang. The whole Roman principate was rocked by crises for centuries, yet it didn't produce a single blueprint for social or economic reform worth mentioning. The Western world has only been debating the subject since the eighteenth century – since Marx, properly speaking.'

'With mixed results,' said Otto.

A Bad End for Whom?

No embassy can function successfully unless its staff know what is going on in the world, the host country, and the embassy itself. I had therefore proposed that our daily morning conference be used for a fuller exchange of information and ideas.

At 8 a.m. I tuned in to The Voice of America, whose Asian service was more informative than any other. Its detailed reports on all major developments in the Far East, down to and including typhoon warnings, were a regular accompaniment to my breakfast. This being the time when Franz not unnaturally wanted to discuss our joint programme for the day, I tended to miss important items of information from one source or the other.

Our morning conference opened at 8.30 a.m. with a summary of the reports broadcast an hour-and-a-half earlier by Deutsche Welle, our own overseas service, and the Chinese domestic network. The Chinese radio news included synopses of the principle articles and leaders printed in that day's newspapers, which seldom reached us before noon. Next, our two interpreters presented a survey of the articles, commentaries, and readers' letters in the previous day's editions of the *People's Daily* and *Guangming Ribao*. We then discussed and evaluated the English-language reports issued by Xinhua, the official Chinese news agency.

By about 9.15 a.m. we were acquainted with every major development reported by the Chinese, American, and German news media. We went on to exchange non-confidential information gleaned the previous day, either in conversation with Chinese officials at ministries, receptions, and dinners, or from fellow diplomats. The morning conference furnished material for reports and stimulated lines of inquiry and action. Since everyone had to contribute and express his or her views, it also helped our embassy staff to develop a fairly homogeneous outlook on current events.

When we returned to our offices at 9.30 a.m., we would find our desks laden with deciphered telex messages from Bonn and the night's crop of radio reports from the information service of the Federal Press Bureau.

At our morning conference on 6 October, one of our interpreters reported on a lengthy programmatic article in *Guangming*. Signed 'Liang Xiao', the pseudonym adopted by the radical 'criticism group' at Peking's two big universities, it was headed 'Always act in accordance with the established principles of Chairman Mao!' and couched in the irksomely bogus and ardent language used by the press when seeking to inspire and convince 'the masses':

> At this solemn moment, when the whole Party, the whole Army, and the masses of the people of all nationalities throughout the whole country are determined to convert sorrow into strength, comply with the testament of Chairman Mao, and pledge themselves to pursue permanent revolution under the dictatorship of the proletariat, Chairman Mao's injunction 'to act in accordance with established principles' is being studied and our fighting spirit thereby reinforced. Chairman Mao's injunction shines as bright as gold . . .

Before long, however, the article proceeded to level dark insinuations and ominous warnings at the leaders of the revisionist line, who were accused of trying to distort the late Chairman's established guidelines.

Meaning whom, precisely? Not Deng Xiaoping, or he would have been named. Could it be Hua Guofeng, whose obituary speech had failed to mention any established principles, so called?

The article went on to promise that the struggle would be continued and the people enlightened on the identity of these 'capitulators'. 'Confronted by a thus enlightened people, any revisionist ringleader who dares to pervert Chairman Mao's established principles will ultimately come to a bad end!'

This was strong meat indeed. War to the knife had been declared on an unnamed ringleader. Despite the article's many puzzling features, one thing was crystal clear: the struggle for succession had begun in earnest.

Anti-Imperialism Street

Once called Legation Street, it was now known as Fandi Lu, or Anti-Imperialism Street. It traversed the elongated rectangle of the Legation Quarter, parallel with the city wall, and could be walked from end to end in fifteen minutes. The city wall had gone. So had Hartung's photographic shop at the mouth of the street, but nearly everything else had survived. The buildings seemed to have shrunk, but everyone's perspectives change in forty years. I might have been in a small European town where time had stood still for three-quarters of a century, since 1900 and the Boxer Rebellion.

The Deutsch-Asiatische Bank on the corner, built in purest Wilhelminian style, was badly dilapidated. The earthquake in July had sent part of the roof tumbling into the forecourt and broken a number of windows, exposing the rooms inside to wind and weather. A few steps further on, the tower of the Catholic Church had also suffered. The cross on the tower hung askew, as though symbolizing the state of Christianity in China, and balks of timber were stacked outside the door. The church was obviously closed. Perhaps it served as a warehouse for the fruit and vegetable shop on the next corner.

Although the gate was open, I couldn't see into the courtyard of the former French Embassy. The spirit wall not only repelled spirits but obscured my view. Prince Sihanouk was said to have lived there at one time.

The offices of Jardine, Matheson, the British firm that had once been such a commercial power in the land, were a pathetic sight. Many of the broken windows had been repaired with cardboard, and the rest disclosed a gloomy interior shored up with lengths of timber.

Our old embassy stood next door. All that could be seen of it from the street was the high wall and central gateway. The big wooden gates were glossy with dark red paint, and the curving Chinese roof overhead was in good condition, but the pair of handsome marble lions that had flanked the entrance were there no longer. Perhaps they had returned to their original post and were guarding some temple or tomb – playing sentinel to some long-dead prince or senior dignitary.

The gates were ajar. Peering through them into the grounds, I could see that the trees and buildings had survived intact – though they, too, looked smaller than of old. The modest single-storeyed house on the left of the entrance had once been the ambassador's residence. It seemed in good repair. A sentry glared at me suspiciously. I asked who lived here now, but he didn't answer, just shut the gates tight. I learned later that the house was used for entertaining official visitors and guests of the Party.

It was forty years since I had first presented myself at these gates, a student in search of cheap lodgings. Nobody worked after lunch, the Chinese gatekeeper informed me, but it might be worth asking that gentleman over there. 'That gentleman' was loosing off arrows at a target in the grounds, using a Mongol bow. His Mongol tunic, trousers, and boots stamped him as a stickler for style. He turned out to be Counsellor Hans Bidder, an eminent authority on the history, culture, politics, and language of China. That he was kindly as well as erudite became clear when he wangled me several weeks' free lodging at the German hospital.

Several years later, during the war, I had entered the same gates as an attaché on transfer to Shanghai. Peking at that time was remote from events in the outside world – even from events in China. Chiang Kai-shek's Nationalist Government was based at Chungking, the Japanese puppet Government at Nanking, and Shanghai was the country's commercial and financial centre. Peking retained only what history had left behind in the way of things and people. 'Only' amounted to a great deal, but it was not enough to keep an embassy busy. The staff read the *Peking Chronicle* – a four-page English-language daily whose coverage was limited to releases by Domei, the Japanese news agency – visited each other's offices, whiled away the time, and waited for the end they hoped would never come.

The German hospital took a lot of finding. It had shrunk more than most things, having since been enclosed by a much larger Chinese hospital. No German doctors had worked there for years, of course, but I identified the wall I used to scale when a night on the tiles kept me out after 10 p.m. It was still standing.

In 1900, after foreign allied troops had dispersed the Boxers who were besieging the Legation Quarter, they built a wall round it and compelled the Chinese Government to recognize its extraterritorial status. It was thereafter administered by the diplomatic missions whose colonial forces were stationed there – an enclave in the heart of the Chinese capital, right next door to the imperial palace itself. No Chinese were allowed to live in the Legation Quarter. Now, the same ban applied to foreigners, and their embassies had been transferred to other parts of the city.

However easy it might be to preserve the quarter's historical character, this has never been the official intention. The Chinese regard it as a monument to the humiliations inflicted on the Middle Kingdom by its erstwhile residents, the envoys of foreign powers. But it is also a monument to the stupidity of the Empress Dowager, her court and advisers, who shut their eyes to the outside world and declined to follow the example set in 1868 by Emperor Meiji of Japan. Cixi and her court wanted no truck with reform. They prevented China from adopting the policy that transformed Japan, within a few decades, from a medieval feudal state into a modern industrialized country. The Chinese have a long way to go – a very long way – before they make up the ground they lost then.

Objects Strange and Ingenious

Li Qiang, China's Minister of Foreign Trade, seemed an amiable old gentleman. He had a habit of shaping his words – almost masticating them – before they escaped his lips. Some questions he left half answered, others he avoided altogether by straying from the subject in an abrupt but disarmingly conversational manner. At first I charitably put this down to his age, which was nearly seventy, but he never digressed without some very good reason. It would, I decided, be wiser not to underestimate him.

I remarked that, since press reports of the harvest were favourable and my own country was primarily an importer of agricultural produce, prospects for purchases in China must be good. Li Qiang countered by referring to floods in this province and drought in that. He spoke of the Tangshan earthquake and its lingering effect on communications. China's domestic demand for oil and coal was great; she could not export raw materials in any case. What it all boiled down to, however amiably put, was that the Chinese could export nothing and must solve their economic problems single-handed. I could detect no interest in expanding the country's foreign trade.

Back at the embassy, while drafting a report on my interview, I recalled the letter dispatched to King George III by Emperor Qianlong (Ch'ien Lung) after Lord Macartney had visited Peking in 1793, accompanied by a glittering entourage and laden with numerous gifts, to plead for an expansion of trade with Great Britain.

'We possess everything,' wrote the Emperor, 'and set no store by objects strange and ingenious. We have no need of your country's manufactures, for Our country possesses all things in abundance. Within Our borders We want for nothing. We thus have no need to import the produce of foreign barbarians and exchange Our own therefor. But since tea, silk, and porcelain, which the Celestial Empire produces, are indispensable to

European nations and to yourselves, We have, as a signal token of Our favour, permitted foreign merchants to settle in Canton in order to meet the requirements of their countries and enable your country, too, to share in Our beneficence.'

I reminded Li Qiang of our first meeting when I paid a farewell call on him early in 1980. He laughed at the recollection. 'I was in a difficult position,' he said. 'The Gang of Four and their supporters were accusing me of selling China out. If I imported foreign machinery, they said I was worshipping foreign goods. I must be stopped, they said. There was even a proposal to abolish my Ministry altogether.'

The Plot Thickens

10 October

Something was brewing. Late yesterday, Saturday, Geert Ahrens and Hans-Bodo Bertram had dropped in to tell me about some posters they'd sighted at various points in the capital – three-foot-high characters welcoming the Central Committee's decision to appoint Hua Guofeng Chairman of the Central Committee and the Military Commission; in other words, Mao's successor. We learned by telephone from Shanghai that similar wall-posters had appeared there too. The Central Committee's decisions were based on consensus, at least as a rule. Did this mean that all its members, the radicals included, had voted Hua more offices than Mao himself by appointing him head of the Party and the armed forces, in addition to Premier?

This morning, Ahrens and Bertram reappeared with the news that the big wall-posters had been torn down overnight and replaced with others welcoming the Central Committee's decision to publish Mao's works and build him a memorial hall. Could its two hundred members have convened unbeknown to the world at large?

Many rumours circulated, most of them conflicting. One was that Mao's widow and the three Shanghai radicals had been eliminated, but what did 'eliminated' mean? Had they been excluded from meetings of the Politburo or the Central Committee? Something was brewing beyond a doubt, but we had yet to discover what.

A Night Like Any Other

The same evening

It was a night like any other, though unpleasantly cold and wet. We wrapped up warm because the Sichuan Restaurant occupied an old Chinese house with numerous draughty courtyards, and we doubted if any form of heating would yet be in operation.

David Dean, the US Chargé d'Affaires, had invited us to a small dinner party in honour of Arthur Burns. Already in his seventies, Burns was chairman of the Federal Reserve Board and one of America's financial heavyweights. The only other guests were Nick Fenn, the British Chargé, and his wife.

Sichuan Province is noted for its spicy dishes. The restaurant had been a favourite haunt of Deng Xiaoping's, so its staff had been dismissed for political unreliability and replaced. It had also acquired a new name, the Chengdu, but patrons of long standing preferred to use the old one.

Mr Burns was an extremely taciturn gentleman. Although we would happily have spent dinner discussing China's internal politics, the new arrival showed a greater interest in economics and finance. He perked up a little when conversation turned to the special drawing rights of the International Monetary Fund.

After dinner we repaired to the armchairs at the 'south' end of the restaurant, where tea was served at small tables. Burns devoted himself to the ladies while I stood chatting with David Dean and Nick Fenn.

Dean asked what we thought of the latest news. The situation seemed obscure, I replied. What were the radicals up to? How would they react?

'Maybe they can't react at all,' said Fenn.

'Maybe, maybe not,' we said. 'That's just it. There are so many rumours flying around. Nobody knows anything for certain.'

According to Dean's information, the radicals had been stripped of power; according to mine, neutralized or 'eliminated'. That suggested exclusion from the Politburo, but Fenn's clear understanding was that they had actually been arrested.

I asked the other two if they had already transmitted this report to the State Department and the Foreign Office.

'No,' said Dean, 'I only heard the news today, and it's too good to be true.'

Fenn and I had been equally chary of passing on such sensational but unconfirmed reports; they might, after all, have emanated from the same source. One of us had obtained his information from a middle-ranking education official, the other from a junior official with contacts high in the Party hierarchy. Without mentioning his name, I cited the status of my source. Our information came from three different quarters.

'It *is* too good to be true,' Dean repeated.

We wondered if the reports had been fed to us deliberately, but decided that, if so, they would have been less nebulous. Other factors militated against this theory. Was it simply a rumour that had spread like wildfire because people *wanted* to believe it? We couldn't dismiss that possibility either.

Dean had been at the airport shortly before dinner, seeing off two US Senators, Michael Mansfield and John Glenn. Nancy Tang, Mao's veteran interpreter, had escorted them during their stay in Peking. When Dean asked her where Jiang Qing was at present, Nancy hadn't turned a hair, just stared into space and said, 'In Peking, I suppose.' That was all.

Though not entirely sure, even now, we felt surer than before. 'But it *is* too good to be true,' said Dean, who remained sceptical. On that note, we readdressed ourselves to Arthur Burns, his sadly neglected guest of honour.

Chinese restaurants serve dinner early, so we were on our way home by nine. Tonight being Gerd and Lois Ruge's last night in Peking, we had invited a dozen of their friends – journalists and diplomats – to join us at ten for a farewell party.

Everyone agreed that the situation was confused, and that all depended on the radicals' next move. Their article in *Guangming* had been a call to arms and an indication that they would not let themselves be driven into a corner so easily. They were firmly entrenched in Shanghai – and also, as someone pointed out, in Peking's next-door province, Liaoning, thanks to Mao Yuanxin, the late Chairman's nephew.

Detention, neutralization, elimination – none of these was mentioned. I inquired if anyone knew where the radicals were. One of our guests surmised that they were in Shanghai, girding themselves for the fray, and that the moderates had seized their chance to put Hua in the saddle.

Young Gerson, the British Embassy's foreign policy specialist, glanced at me and surreptitiously put his wrists together, as if handcuffed.

Rumours and Reports

11 October

My enciphered telex – priority rating: Most Urgent – went off to the Foreign Office at 11.30 a.m. Peking time, or 4.30 a.m. Central European Time. That meant it would be lying on the relevant desk in Bonn when office hours began. I reported having heard from Chinese sources that Hua had obtained his appointment as Chairman of the Central Committee, or Mao's successor, in defiance of the radical members of the Politburo, and that Mao's widow, Jiang Qing, and the three Shanghai radicals had been 'eliminated'. I added, however, that it was still hard to gauge how far this story of a *coup d'état* fitted the facts, because the Chinese themselves might have fallen prey to exaggerated reports or wishful thinking.

Next, I sent an aide to the Xinhua offices to ask for some photographs of Jiang Qing taken beside Mao's bier and during her last public appearance on 30 September, the eve of China's National Day. If he got them, it would indicate that the rumours were untrue.

Early that afternoon the Premier of Papua-New Guinea flew in on an official visit. The welcoming ceremony was attended by most of the diplomats invited to it. Nick Fenn told me he had sent London a report that the Gang of Four had been arrested, refraining from comment but attributing it to a reliable Chinese source. David Dean still felt insufficiently sure of his facts to alert the State Department.

Hua Guofeng rolled up at the airport in his big Red Flag limousine with Vice-Premier Li Xiannian. The two men paced slowly to and fro, deep in conversation, until the plane taxied to a halt. Hua was the first to greet his guest from New Guinea. Once the ceremony was over he drove back to town alone, leaving Li Xiannian to do the honours. He looked calm and composed – obviously in command of the situation.

When I got back to the embassy, the aide I'd sent to Xinhua reported that no photographs of Jiang Qing were available. I called the Foreign Office, where my telex had already been read, and owned to a growing belief that its gist was accurate. Bonn seemed disinclined to believe this. No news agency or newspaper had breathed a word on the subject, I was told, and the media would surely have picked up rumours of such a sensational development. The Quai d'Orsay knew nothing of it either. It was therefore concluded that Hua Guofeng's appointment represented 'a continuation of the compromise between the rival pressure groups within the Party, who consider it inopportune to settle their differences at this time'.

It is an old ambassadorial complaint that people back home – in the Foreign Office, Quai d'Orsay, or State Department – give greater credence to telepathic brainwaves than to reports submitted by their envoys on the spot.

Next day I was back at the airport saying goodbye to Gerd Ruge. Mr Qi of the Foreign Office Information Section turned up too. I asked him point-blank whether the rumour that Jiang Qing and the Shanghai radicals had been arrested was correct. He said he had been instructed neither to confirm nor to deny it. 'No comment,' was the authorized response.

That settled it.

Reuters, who were first in the field, had reported the rumour a short while before.

Jiang Qing Under Fire

Written in oil paint on the wall beside the entrance to Peking University were the words, 'Unless Jiang Qing is executed, we shall not rest content.'

An overseas student had given us a photograph of a wall-poster displayed in the campus area closed to foreigners. Written by members of the Department of Physics, it assailed Jiang Qing with a curious hodge-podge of vague, unproven accusations, gossip, and sheer nonsense. The following are a few excerpts from a long diatribe:

> When Chairman Mao was gravely ill, Jiang Qing showed no concern for him. Instead, she tried to rally as much support as possible, attracted others to her side, formed them into a conspiratorial group, and concocted plots and schemes. When Chairman Mao's state of health declined, she went off on vacation to Dachai, heedless of this, and indulged in riotous living there. What is unpardonable is that she insisted on getting Chairman Mao up, despite his critical condition and against his doctors' advice, in an attempt – albeit fruitless – to kill him. How is that for a proletarian attitude toward our great Leader and Chairman Mao? Her sins deserve ten thousand deaths. Even were she cut into many thousands of pieces, her guilt would not be expunged.

One Chinese source informed us that Jiang Qing had tried to blackmail Mao into naming her his successor by threatening to publicize his affairs with other women. We were also assured that she had been having an affair with the present Minister of Sport. The characters in the eight model operas were sexless, but she herself had owned a whole collection of pornographic films.

'Like what?' I asked.

'Well, *Gone with the Wind*, for instance.'

We were to hear more such rumours as time went by, all designed to make the archenemy look contemptible. It was now said, for example, that Jiang Qing had soiled her trousers when arrested – a titillating thought. In China, ridicule is worse than death.

There was nothing novel about the style of these accusations, which had often been employed during the Cultural Revolution. Many similar examples can be found in Chinese history. It is less a question of proving criminal charges than of destroying a person's good name and representing his or her conduct as ignominious.

Emperor Yongzheng (1723–35) indicted his brother Yün Si in the following terms:

> He is a traitor who has conspired against me from the first and contravened my orders ever since I ascended the throne. He recruits followers by feigning generosity, when all he wants is to disguise his parsimony. He cheaply gains a reputation at my expense, but his motives are plain enough to see . . . He uses dirty sheets of the most ordinary paper when submitting memorandums to me. When he was supposed to redecorate the pavilion adjoining the sacrificial temples, where I changed my clothes during intervals in the liturgy, the stench of fresh paint made me feel so sick that I could scarcely breathe while having my clothes changed . . .

Reflections on the Unicorn

Yongle's is the largest of the Ming Tombs. He started work on it at the very outset of his reign (1402–24), as soon as he had completed his most pressing business, which was to exterminate all the ministers who had faithfully served his predecessor, together with their families.

There was nothing dilapidated about Yongle's tomb, nor were we his only visitors. Parked outside the gate stood dozens of coaches that had conveyed sightseers from Peking and soldiers from barracks in the vicinity. Tickets had to be purchased at a kiosk, so I generously played host. The admission charge was less than the cost of one cigarette for each of us four adults, and half as much for young Tina Höfer.

We strolled through the grounds to the sacrificial hall. On either side of us stood outsize pots containing cassia bushes, a kind of cinnamon with inconspicuous but heavily scented white flowers. Though rather more pungent, the cassia's scent may best be compared to that of jasmine, and we made a practice of going back every year when it was in full bloom.

The architectural features of the sacrificial hall did not differ from those of the large audience chambers in the Forbidden City, having remained almost unchanged for a thousand years. Far from seeking to startle the eye with novel stylistic elements, imposing new columns and façades, the architects had relied on harmonious proportions to achieve the beauty they aspired to.

The ceiling of the sacrificial hall was supported by thirty-two identical columns – smooth tree-trunks painted red. They were tropical trees procured by imperial command from Yünnan, fifteen hundred miles south-west of Peking. Empty save for these columns, the hall made a spacious and majestic impression. Hans Höfer had found a stone table outside in the grounds, so we sat down there to picnic under the trees.

It was forty years since I'd first seen the building. I stopped off at Nankou station after visiting the Great Wall, and dusk was falling when I got there. The coffered ceiling was veiled in shadow by the time I entered Yongle's grove of columns. There were no cassia bushes or coachloads of tourists in those days, and grass was sprouting from the cracks between the circular tiles. I rode back to Nankou in the dark, seeing little of the dirt road or my surroundings until the moon rose.

'You rode?' Tina said admiringly. 'How romantic!'

'It wasn't romantic,' I said. 'I was riding a donkey.'

'All the same,' said Tina.

I put her straight. 'Know what a donkey does when its owner runs alongside, whacking it on the rump with a stick because he wants to get home to his supper? It jiggles you up and down like a cocktail shaker. Besides, this donkey didn't have a saddle, just a thin woollen blanket. I could hardly sit down for the next few days, and as for the way I walked – well, it wasn't exactly graceful.'

'This Emperor,' said Tina, going off at a tangent, '—his name wasn't Yongle at all. Lao Zhou called him something quite different in the car just now.'

'His posthumous name, perhaps,' I said. 'Chinese emperors' names are a headache. This one's real name was Zhudi and his imperial name Chengzu, but we usually refer to emperors by their government pro-gramme, which always sounded mighty pretty. Our Emperor's motto was Yongle, meaning "Eternal Contentment".'

'I hope his subjects felt contented,' said Hanna Höfer.

'They did once he was safely dead and buried. Yongle was a great ruler, and great rulers aren't to everyone's taste.'

'A great conqueror, you mean?' said Hanna.

'No. All he conquered was Annam – North Vietnam, in other words.'

'I see.'

'Reconquered, I should have said. The Chinese had annexed the area fifteen hundred years earlier, but they lost it again whenever the empire grew weak. Yongle did a lot more than that, though. He secured the northern border against the Mongols, repaired the Great Wall and the Grand Canal, transferred the capital from Nanking to Peking, built the Forbidden City and the Temple of Heaven, lowered taxes, and commissioned an encyclopaedia listing all that was known in his day. It came out in an edition of only three copies, but there were plenty of volumes.'

'How many?' asked Tina.

'Eleven thousand-plus.'

'Wow!' said Tina, who attended the Australian school in Peking.

'But his naval expeditions were even more impressive. He sent out six of them, some involving as many as twenty thousand men. They got as far as Arabia and Africa. One of his fleets sailed clear across the Indian Ocean from Sumatra to Mogadishu – that's a distance of four-and-a-half thousand nautical miles. The biggest ship in the fleet was four hundred and sixty feet long.'

'*Wow!*'

'In that case, the Chinese were far better navigators and shipwrights than their contemporaries in Europe,' Hans Höfer said. 'I'm surprised they didn't turn their knowledge to use in power politics.'

'I don't think they wanted to,' I said. 'Yongle's successor mounted one more expedition after his death, but that was the last. Internal opposition was too strong, especially among scholars. The War Minister, who was a prominent Confucian, had every map and chart destroyed "so as not to confuse posterity and kindle its greed". Overseas expeditions were considered un-Chinese. The Emperor's task was to promote the morality, education, and welfare of his people. Why should he bother about barbarians on the other side of the ocean? Contact with them could happily be left to merchants, and they were a breed whose indispensable but immoral role in society had been deplored by the bulk of Chinese scholars and philosophers since time immemorial.'

Hans looked puzzled. 'So why did Yongle launch his expeditions at all?'

'Plenty of Chinese must have wondered that at the time, just as historians do today. His motives can't have been military. He conquered no territory, and his fleets carried more merchandise than weapons of war. Foreign trade – that's one theory, but it seems improbable. Yongle was no businessman. A lot of Chinese think he was hunting down a prince who'd skipped the country and was trying to recruit an army in the hope of grabbing the throne for himself. Others think he simply wanted to broadcast the glories of the Middle Kingdom far and wide. That's my own bet, but it may have been plain curiosity.'

'A pretty expensive hobby!'

'Except that the expeditions brought back all kinds of things. Precious stones, lions, ostriches, antelopes, monkeys, parrots – even a unicorn.'

'A unicorn?' said Tina. 'What was it like?'

'The Chinese unicorn,' I explained, 'has a body like a deer, hoofs like a horse, and a tail like an ox. Its hide is multi-coloured, though some people claim that it's covered in scales. The unicorn is well disposed towards human beings and other animals, but it never appears unless the throne is occupied by a wise, just ruler, and when the Chinese live in harmony with themselves and Heaven. In other words, its appearances are few and far between.

'The unicorn or *jilin* brought back from Somalia by Yongle's sailors didn't quite fit the traditional description – for instance, it had two little horns instead of one big one, but that was generously overlooked. The *jilin*, which we might stupidly have mistaken for a giraffe, used to live in the Emperor's garden. It was a visible sign that Heaven looked with favour on him, his virtuous conduct and wise government.'

'Has it been sighted lately?' asked Hanna.

'Surely not,' said her husband, 'or my news agency would have reported it. But mightn't it turn up now – I mean, now that the Gang of Four have been crushed?'

'It's a timid beast,' I said. 'I suspect it remains to be convinced of the new leadership's wisdom and virtue and ability to restore public harmony. Most of all, though, it wants to be sure that harmony reigns inside the leadership itself. The Chinese won't be able to live in peace unless it does, and all their hopes will be nipped in the bud.'

Shots in the Dark

21 October

At our morning conference, a military aide claimed to have heard small-arms fire between 8 and 8.30 p.m. the previous night: single shots, estimated number a hundred, estimated source half-a-mile south-west of the embassy, possibly fired at a fleeing mob. Despite the detailed nature of this report, serious doubts were expressed. None of us civilians had heard any shooting.

The Peking correspondent of a London daily, who had apparently heard similar shots a few days ago, came to a different conclusion. He reported that confederates of the Gang of Four were being executed. Although this story was seized on by the German press, we advised Bonn that nothing in Peking pointed to any such executions.

In the afternoon, 'shots' could be heard on all sides. The pandemonium steadily mounted as darkness fell, but some visitors to the embassy set our minds at rest. Bangers, firecrackers, and other noisy fireworks were being let off in token of popular rejoicing over Party Directive No. 16, which had been read out to labour units and neighbourhood organizations from early morning on. Similar meetings held in the following two days culminated in an appeal to all present to march 'spontaneously' to Tian An Men Square.

The directive 'unmasked' the four enemies of the Party and announced that Hua had been appointed Chairman of the Central Committee, and, thus, Mao's successor. Mao, said the directive, had always been opposed to *si ren bang*, 'the Gang of Four'. This was my first encounter with the phrase, which had reputedly been coined by the late Chairman himself.

Our visitors – Germans employed by the Chinese – were in a cheerful, almost exuberant mood. They quoted from memory what the Party directive had said about Mao's admonitions to the radicals and his wife in particular. The general verdict was that things could only improve. They and their Chinese colleagues would be able to speak more freely and live under less restrictive conditions. 'At least,' they added, 'everyone at the office hopes so.'

Mao's Political Testament?

We had, in a rather mysterious way, come into possession of a document said to be circulating among Party members in Peking. It was the text of a letter allegedly written by Mao to Jiang Qing in July – a species of political testament. Although the metaphorical, aphoristic style could well have been Mao's, was it a forgery concocted by supporters of the Gang of Four? Most of us thought so, but we came to no firm conclusion. The wording was as follows:

Jiang Qing,

Man's life is limited, the Revolution boundless. I strove, during the struggle of the last ten years, to scale the summit of the Revolution, but I failed. You can attain that summit. If you fail, however, you will plunge into an unfathomable abyss, shatter your body, and smash your bones.

Why was the Kuomintang defeated? Because it relied on foreigners. The Bird and the Polar Bear [1] are crude and brutal, but there is no need to fear them. However great the price that must be paid, a remnant will survive. [2]

There may be resistance within. Collaboration with the Army must then be continued. If this is done correctly, resistance will collapse. If errors are made, partisan warfare must be waged once more. If no further progress is possible in Jinggangshan, one must march to Yenan. [3] The past ten years have convinced me that no compromises should be entered into.

Wrong has been done you. We are parting now and will dwell in two different worlds. May each of us find peace. These few words shall be my final message to you.

July 1976

Mao Zedong

The Caves of Guilin

Guilin lies deep in the heart of Guangxi Province in southern China. The Municipal Travel Bureau had assigned us a guide named Mr Wu. His only language apart from Chinese was Spanish, but that he spoke with gusto. Mr Wu proposed to drive us straight from the airport to a stalactite cave. He had mapped out our schedule for the next two days, and it included three such caves. '*Embajador*,' he urged, '*vamos!*' We had no intention of visiting any caves. Caves we could see anywhere, we told him. We wanted to tour the city and visit its ancient royal palace, which dated from the Sung dynasty. Mr Wu had never heard of any such palace. He was the least endearing tourist guide we ever came across in China.

[1] The American eagle and the Russian bear.

[2] Echo of a conversation between Mao and Nehru. When the latter remarked that a nuclear war would destroy mankind, Mao – by his own account – retorted, 'If the worst happened and half of mankind were to perish, the other half would survive. Imperialism would be swept away and the world would become socialist.'

[3] Jinggangshan, a mountainous region in central China, remained Mao's military base for several years from 1927 onwards. Under pressure from Kuomintang forces, he led his followers on the Long March (1934–5) to Yenan, in the north of Shaanxi Province.

Having found the palace despite him, we realized why we weren't supposed to see it. The teacher-training college housed within its walls was a hive of 'political unrest'. There were placards and posters everywhere. Mr Wu became very edgy when I photographed one. He tried to steer us back to the hotel, hoping to persuade us to visit a cave after all. Caves were free from wall-posters and political unrest.

After dinner I strolled into the hotel's television room, where I was offered a seat by some students from Peking's Institute of Foreign Languages. We watched the crowds celebrating Hua's appointment as Mao's successor. When the programme ended, I became the focus of attention. Someone asked me if our own students had to work on the land too. Not these days, I said, but I myself had worked on the land and dug ditches as a youngster in the *Arbeitsdienst*, or Labour Service, which had been founded as a non-political organization in the 1920s.

'What was it like?'

'Tough but unavoidable. We couldn't go to university unless we'd done six months in the Voluntary Labour Service.'

'So you *had* to volunteer for it?'

'Yes.'

They laughed, knowingly. Still, six months were a mere fleabite. A lot of their contemporaries had been assigned to work on the land for six whole years, and many of them were still at it.

'I was glad when my six months were up,' I said. 'In retrospect, though, I think the system had its merits.'

'When were you in the Labour Service?'

'Ages ago,' I said. To put my reply in its proper historical perspective, I added, 'In Hitler's time.'

An embarrassed silence fell. People were either black or white, especially politicians, and Hitler – with the possible exception of Khrushchev – was the blackest of the lot. How could I bring myself to approve of a Hitlerian institution? Everyone thought hard.

When I asked if it would be permissible to drink a glass of beer in the television room, several students jumped up to fetch me one. It was a neat way of extricating themselves from a conversation that had taken such an ominous turn.

Undaunted, one youngster sat down beside me. I asked him for his own forecast of future developments in China. 'Things will improve,' he said. 'There will be more films – operas too, perhaps.'

'But will life be freer or more restricted?'

'*Bu hao shuo*,' he replied, which might have meant either 'Hard to tell' or 'It's better not to talk about it.'

'You can trust me,' I said. 'I'll keep your answer strictly to myself.'

'It will be a great deal freer,' he said, speaking emphatically now. 'I firmly believe that.'

At that moment a Chinese woman walked in. Middle-aged, with a stern expression and an austere hair style, she headed straight for us. The student beside me sprang to his feet.

'Teacher, we watched the television programme and I explained it to this gentleman,' he said. 'He comes from West Germany.'

The students were evidently under orders to address their supervisor in English and nothing else. 'Teacher' turned to me and delivered a lengthy speech in which she made it clear that she regarded the Gang of Four as pitch-black and Chairman Hua Guofeng as whiter than white. She only came to Guilin during the vacations. The students spent their time working as tourist interpreters, and it was her job to keep them out of 'trouble'. They were all returning to Peking tomorrow morning, so my young companion must go to bed at once. As for him, he had swiftly gathered that her sole motive was to preserve him from 'trouble'. My subversive remarks had probably been relayed by one of the beer-fetchers.

'Certainly, teacher,' said the boy, who was eighteen or nineteen years old. 'By the way, I have a question.'

'Well?'

'Does one say, "I have complete confidence in you" or "I have complete faith in you"?'

'You can say either.'

I was dumbfounded by the youngster's ingenious way of conveying that he trusted me – so much so that I found it hard to keep a straight face.

He nodded to me, said, 'Goodnight and thank you, sir,' and walked out with 'Teacher' at his heels.

River Trip

Mr Wu breathed a sigh of relief when we set off on our trip down the River Li, where no wall-posters or political unrest would meet our gaze. We were the only foreigners on board the flat-bottomed craft, which was designed to negotiate the river's numerous shoals. Seating ourselves in the bow, we draped our legs over the side with our feet almost trailing in the water.

Other boats passed us laden with merchandise stowed beneath curved roofs of reed matting. We received cheerful waves from the children on board, some of whom were helping their parents to wield the stern oar. We also passed some cormorant fishermen. Three bamboo trunks lashed together formed a raft buoyant enough to support a large basket, a dozen black cormorants, and the fisherman himself, who punted his craft with a long bamboo pole.

The Li flowed through a plain as flat as a billiard table except where pinnacles of rock abruptly pierced its surface like pencils thrust through a sheet of paper from below. On the banks stood farmsteads, both isolated and in clusters. Paths ran down from them to landing places and slabs of stone on which women were laundering clothes. Some houses were shaded by huge banyan trees centuries old, others dwarfed by riverside clumps of bamboo thirty or forty feet high, their curving stems weighed down with foliage.

No one who lived here could have failed to feel secure. Had anything changed over the years? For how many centuries had these houses been occupied by the same families? Had anyone here ever heard of the Gang of Four?

The landscape was innocent of power cables and telephone lines. Peasants crossed the dikes in single file, with springy little steps, transporting their wares to the nearest village on shoulder-poles. Even bicycles were an infrequent sight.

Peering closely at the horizon, which was shrouded in a pale blue haze, we made out a whole forest of cones and pencils, some – so it seemed – with hammocks slung between them. The soft blue contours deepened and resolved themselves into individual mountains towering above the river. Though swathed in greenery from base to summit, their vertical columns of rock and limestone slabs showed through. Nature had not shrunk from creating the boldest and most *outré* shapes, some protrusively phallic and others with overhanging ledges that defied the law of gravity. Bamboo sprouting from sandbanks or small, flat headlands wove dark green curtains of diaphanous foliage.

The Li was a serene and placid river, and the mountains mirrored in its yellowish waters would have tempted any painter of the Romantic school. The sky was overcast, but sometimes the sun peeped through. All colours were harmonized by the haze. Only at one point, where cliffs and pinnacles of rock closed in on the river until we had to arch our necks to see their summits, did the landscape lose its sweet serenity. Nature struck a sterner note, pounding drums and sounding trumpets, and even the river became less tranquil. The helmsman had to alter course repeatedly to keep us in the fairway, but we felt quite safe. His eyes were on the reefs and shoals, not on the rocky heights that held us spellbound as we listened to the river's mighty voice – a welcome change of tune, without which its idyllic beauty might have grown insipid.

But Mr Wu, too, helped to preserve us from being lulled into a waking dream by pure scenic beauty. When we disembarked at the pretty little town of Yangshuo after our five-hour voyage down the Li, he just allowed us time to walk the few steps to a belvedere before hustling us into a waiting taxi and whisking us back to Guilin in time for dinner. *Embajador, vamos!* We got back in such good time – early afternoon – that he suggested visiting a cave whose artificial lighting effects would astound us. Much to his chagrin, we insisted on strolling through the city and exposing ourselves to contamination by political unrest.

Visit to an Imaginary Village

'Hung Xiuquan lived in this house and his brother Jenkan over there,' announced the headman of Hwa, a village two hours' drive from Canton.

It was a single-storeyed house in the village street itself, built of grey, sun-dried brick, and there was a wooden plaque over the door. Franz and I went inside, but it was a tight squeeze. The house consisted of one room furnished with a low bed, a straw mat, and a diminutive old table. A naked bulb hung from the ceiling. The room had no window, so the door provided the sole source of daylight – a minor inconvenience in an area where doors can be left open all year round. Hwa is almost on the Tropic of Cancer, fifteen degrees south of Peking.

The village headman showed us a larger building. This, he said, was the school where Hung had taught, and those were the foundations of his parental home. The imperial government had burned down every house in the village and wiped out the whole of Hung's family – forty people in Hwa alone.

I was puzzled. Until now, Hung had existed only in my mind's eye, and my description of him had accorded with that mental image. What puzzled me was that the surrounding landscape fitted the picture I had formed of it. I entered the museum in a rather apprehensive mood, hoping to be able to touch something once touched by Hung himself, as though physical contact might forge some magical bond between my mental image and reality.

The museum was quite impressive, certainly for a village of only three hundred inhabitants, and the headman had done his homework. He gave us a long lecture on the Taiping Rebellion, which had started at Hwa in

1852, on Hung's victorious march to Nanking, which he had christened 'the Heavenly Capital', and on his 'Heavenly Kingdom of Great Peace'. The headman pointed out that the rebellion had nearly toppled the dynasty, but made no mention of the many millions who died in consequence. He also neglected to mention that Hung had claimed to be Jesus' younger brother, and to have been appointed by their Heavenly Father to wage war on the demons of the Middle Kingdom and establish his Heavenly Kingdom in its stead.

The houses we were shown were modern, of course, and had never been occupied by Hung or any of his brothers. The school was just as modern.

'A hundred years ago,' I told the headman, 'when Hung Xiuquan had the evil spirit knocked into him by a box on the ear from John Wainwright Rogers, the missionary, the village looked quite different. It was a dirty place, and the village street was narrower. Hung's parents, brothers, and sisters all lived together in a small house which they had built of mud. The missionary's chapel stood at one end of the village. The mountains were much nearer in those days – just behind Hwa itself.'

The headman was a courteous soul. He said, 'What you say is entirely new to me. Did I hear you mention a missionary and a small church?'

Mr Qing, our old friend from the Canton Travel Bureau, had been briefed on my curriculum vitae. He gravely informed the headman that I had written a book about Hung and the Taiping movement.

A foreigner with a book about Hung to his credit? The headman looked impressed. Had I also mentioned Hwa?

'Of course,' I said. 'How could anyone write about Hung without mentioning Hwa as well?'

He knit his brow. 'And there used to be a church and a missionary here? Ah well, we're naturally ignorant of many things better known to people abroad.'

'You're too polite,' I told him quickly. 'My book is quite unscholarly – a mere novel. The missionary and the church are fictitious.'

'And the mountains?' he asked uneasily.

'The mountains were just as far from Hwa then as they are now.'

He looked relieved.

Home of a Rich Peasant

'You can see his house over there,' said our guide from Changsha. He was referring to the birthplace of another revolutionary.

It stood on a slight eminence above the village, surrounded by a few fields. We recognized it, of course. Anyone in China would have known the house at once. Representations of it could be found throughout the country – printed, painted, embroidered, woven into carpets, wrought in iron.

Shaoshan was colder than Hwa – not surprisingly, because it lay much further north in Hunan Province. Shielded from the rain by raincoats and umbrellas, we set off down the path that led from our rest-house to Mao's parental home. We passed the fish pond familiar to us from photographs that showed it covered with lotus leaves in summer. Here we threaded our way into the interminable stream of pilgrims bound for the house. Being foreigners, we were not made to wait outside with the crowds of rain-sodden devotees – our guide saw to that.

In the entrance hall, facing the door, I looked for the ancestral altar or small shrine mentioned in a book published in the early sixties. There was no altar to be seen, nor had our guide ever heard of one. Ancestor worship, he pointed out, was a reactionary custom peculiar to the feudalistic society of yore.

The house was spacious, even in comparison with a European farmhouse. The wash-house contained a large furnace and the kitchen a handsome brick-built stove. Shuffling slowly along with our fellow pilgrims, we passed a dining-room, three bedrooms, and a guest-room, then crossed the inner courtyard to the stables and outbuildings.

Mao had told Edgar Snow that his father started life as a 'Poor Peasant', worked his way up to 'Middle Peasant' status, and eventually, after entering the grain trade, became a 'Rich Peasant'. It was clear from the size and nature of the establishment that it could not have been run without hired help – in other words, without the 'exploitation' of agricultural labourers. Had he still been alive when the rural population was classified in 1950, Mao's father would undoubtedly have suffered on account of his Rich Peasant status. No one knows precisely how many landowners and Rich Peasants were killed in the course of the 'village class struggle', or land reform, but Western estimates vary between three and five million.

Although Shaoshan boasted a big, modern, multi-storeyed Mao Museum, opened in 1964, we were shown only four of its exhibition halls.

The rest were closed for alterations – a familiar excuse. 'Alterations' were still in progress when I revisited the place a year later.

None of the photographs, books, and press cuttings in the rooms on view dated from after 1927. The later exhibits in the other rooms presented an obvious dilemma. Many of Mao's fellow revolutionaries had fallen into disfavour or become traitors and non-persons. Should they be airbrushed out, or might some of them be rehabilitated? What was to be done with the photographs of He Zizhen, Mao's second wife, whom he had married in 1930 and ditched in 1937?

'That,' said our woman guide, pausing in front of a photograph, 'is Mao's brother Cemin, who died in 1943. He was executed by Kuomintang agents in Xinjiang.'

'And the boy beside him?'

'His son,' she said, turning to another photograph.

'Would that be Yuanxin,' I asked, 'the armed forces' political commissar in Shenyang?'

Yuanxin had been on good terms with his step-aunt, Jiang Qing, and was reputed to be a supporter of the Gang of Four, but that I had no need to point out.

The guide hesitated. Unable to take sole responsibility for supplying such information, she turned for help to the chairman of the local revolutionary committee, who was escorting us. He valiantly rose to the occasion.

'Yes,' he said, 'that is Mao Yuanxin.' We moved on. To judge by the chairman's expression, he was wondering whether some airbrushing would be in order, or whether it was still too early to decide. When I revisited Shaoshan a year later, the photograph had disappeared.

The Gang of Four

Shortly before Mao's death, so Geert Ahrens learned via the Albanian Embassy, the Politburo had agreed on the succession. Hua Guofeng would become Chairman of the Central Committee and, thus, of the Party. Wang Hungwen, the Shanghai 'helicopter', was earmarked as his deputy and Zhang Chunqiao, another member of the radical faction, for the premiership. The one great flaw in this arrangement was its failure to provide for Mao's widow. Jiang Qing and Yao Wenyuan, her chief propagandist, were to remain ordinary members of the Politburo.

The compromise broke down as soon as Mao died – if, indeed, it had ever been genuinely accepted by either camp – and the Gang of Four at once began to set the stage for a showdown. Acting in the name of the General Office of the Central Committee, they advised provincial and local authorities that, from now on, they were to take instructions from them in all matters of importance. Mao had been dead for only three days when Yao Wenyuan visited the capital's two big universities, Peking and Qinghua, and urged the students to send his widow affirmations of loyalty, together with 'memorandums summoning her to ascend the throne' – a traditional form of words. Wall-posters criticizing Hua Guofeng were displayed on the campus, though these were torn down by hostile hands. The widow herself did not remain idle. She twice visited the universities to drum up support. Red Guards suddenly reappeared in the streets of the capital, wearing arm-bands over their mourning bands and looking revolutionary.

At a meeting of the Politburo, Jiang Qing claimed the Party leadership for herself on the grounds that Hua Guofeng had demonstrated his incompetence. The Politburo failed to agree, so Hua proposed that the new situation should first be discussed in smaller groups.

Jiang Qing then, so it was said, forged two characters on an 'important document' and published it as Mao's exhortation to 'act in accordance with established principles', her object being to create the impression that Hua had suppressed a political testament left by her husband.

At Shanghai, their stronghold, the radicals issued arms to the militia, which was not subject to military authority. In Peking they contacted various senior officers and tried to win them over, but the officers informed Hua Guofeng. Mao Yuanxin, who was political commissar to the armed forces in Shenyang and had recently been playing an obscure role as middleman between the Politburo and his uncle, the late Chairman, was said to have launched some manoeuvres with the aim of marching on Peking when the time was ripe. We were told by a Chinese woman from Baoding, south-west of Peking, that the militia there had stormed the local arsenal, and that the city was in turmoil.

Again the four radicals demanded that Jiang Qing be appointed Party Chairman, and again the Politburo rejected their demand. They then began to mobilize their youthful supporters. A preliminary call to arms was sounded by the strident article prophesying that 'revisionist ring-leaders' would meet a bad end. A second and even more vehement article was due to be published on 8 October, but it never appeared.

On the evening of 6 October, a detachment of men from the Security Service or Guards Regiment 8341 entered Jiang Qing's house in Guan Yüan Park, in the western quarter of Peking, and arrested her. It is said that her servants spat on her as she was led away. Her three confederates were summoned to an evening session of the Politburo in Zhongnanhai Park, where the Central Committee Building stands. They arrived there separately and were arrested one by one.

Several of their closest associates were detained almost simultaneously, among them Mao's nephew, Mao Yuanxin. Senior Party officials from Shanghai were summoned to Peking for consultation. They tried to get in touch with the Gang of Four but could not locate them.

Their accomplices in Shanghai waited anxiously for the telephone call that would launch the coup. Three-quarters of a million rifles and three hundred pieces of artillery, together with ample supplies of ammunition, had been issued to the militia. Then came the phone-call from the conspirators' contact man in Peking, but it was not the call they expected. All he said was, 'My mother has had a heart attack.' Then he hung up.

Shanghai did not rise in revolt. News of the arrests spread fast, and the Shanghai conspirators had no desire to risk their necks for radical ideas, still less for a cause that was doomed to failure from the outset.

The radicals had numerous supporters, notably university students, industrial workers, and political commissars in the armed forces, but it would have taken a long time to mobilize, organize, and deploy them effectively. The radicals also controlled the media, which did more than mould public opinion: being the mouthpieces of authority, they transmitted the correct Party line to comrades throughout the country. For the most part, however, the radicals' supporters were inexperienced youngsters – opportunists or careerists insufficiently prepared for the latest turn of events. It was possible that the Gang of Four had modelled their plans on the Cultural Revolution and intended, like Mao, to call for the 'bombardment of headquarters'. They aimed to create a revolutionary situation by not only tolerating but actively promoting chaos in industry, communications, and government, this being the easiest way of overthrowing the moderates, who were still debilitated by the effects of the Cultural Revolution. Public disorder was the wave on whose crest they hoped to ride to power, just as Mao himself had regained his hold on the reins a decade earlier.

The plan was not entirely hopeless. Still cowed by the Cultural Revolution's reign of terror, the masses were open to intimidation. Many young people, in particular, had been disoriented by frequent changes of official policy and could readily be mobilized for radical campaigns. Undeterred by the fact that their strategy would cost many more lives, the Gang of Four never tired of citing Mao's dictum that revolution was 'no embroidery lesson'. When Hua Guofeng decreed help for the city of

Tangshan, they jeered at 'certain persons who use precautionary measures against earthquake damage and rescue operations as a pretext for suppressing the Revolution and neglecting to criticize Deng Xiaoping'.

But for all their cunning, Jiang Qing's clique set about things in an amateurish way. Mao's Cultural Revolution had culminated in a national tragedy; their attempt to repeat his strategy ended in farce. Mao had succeeded because he allied himself with Lin Biao and the armed forces, and because the latter obediently remained neutral until he himself employed them to suit his requirements.

Unlike Mao, the Gang of Four made no serious attempt to gain the good will of military leaders or any other power in the land; they made nothing but enemies. Under Mao's aegis, Jiang Qing had persecuted intellectuals and taken petty revenge on her personal opponents. The Four had lashed out ruthlessly, left and right, paralysing the country's political and economic life. Now they no longer had Mao to fall back on. Their sole weapon, as one of them aptly remarked, was the pen. They were fearless and resolute and unscrupulous in their choice of methods, but they overestimated their own strength and underestimated that of their adversaries.

When they were arrested, the Party leadership called them 'ultra-rightists' and, later on, 'ultra-leftists'. We referred to them as 'radicals', though their paramount concern may not have been the radical programme. They were primarily careerists – a community of political interests whose sole objective was the attainment of power by any and every means. Their ideological tenets varied, just as their campaigns were inconsistent and served merely to undermine their opponents' position. They advocated no idea that could have carried the people along with them.

The Chairman's Widow

Jiang Qing even got off on the wrong foot. In order to marry the young film actress in 1937, Mao had to repudiate his second wife, He Zizhen. The Yenan Politburo disapproved, and withheld its permission for a considerable time. It eventually sanctioned the match, but only if Jiang Qing undertook to abstain from all political activity. She more or less complied with this proviso until the mid-1960s, but not thereafter. Working closely with Mao, she fomented the Cultural Revolution and used it as her *entrée* to the Politburo itself. Jiang Qing had now become a force to be reckoned with, but she aimed still higher. She wanted absolute power.

The extent of her ambition could be gauged from her attempts to vindicate Wu Zetian (690–705), an Empress scathingly condemned by Chinese historians, all males, of course, or from her references to the allegedly exemplary reign of Empress Lü (188–180 BC). Her enthusiasm for prehistoric China's matriarchal society was unflagging. As she herself said, quite openly, 'Women can also be rulers. There will be empresses in communist society too.'

Since earliest times, Chinese bent on criticizing some prominent contemporary have habitually attacked some other figure who, however geographically or historically remote, has something in common with their real target of abuse. The discovery of such parallels calls for great ingenuity. In Jiang Qing's case, lampoons and wall-posters pilloried Indira Gandhi and Empress Cixi, when everyone knew these were merely proxies.

During the April riots in Tian An Men Square, demonstrators had chanted, 'We want no filthy empress!' Whether or not Jiang Qing really coveted the title and rank of empress, as popular rumour had it, is a debatable point, but she certainly aspired to be Chairman of the Party and Mao's successor – an ambition ridiculed by Mao himself.

Jiang Qing had been a moderately successful actress in Shanghai before she met him. She had also been married previously, but her marriage had been dissolved. Leaving Shanghai, she set off for Mao's headquarters in Yenan. Was it chance that brought her to his attention so soon, one wonders, or did she give destiny a helping hand?

Once she had gained power in the Cultural Revolution, she took revenge on all who had impeded her Shanghai film career or failed to recognize her talent. They were removed from office, ruined and humiliated, hounded because they knew too much about her past or were in possession of letters from her. Everyone will recall the press photos showing scenes of persecution in which her victims were paraded with placards round their necks and paper hats on their heads.

When the Gang of Four went on trial themselves, many of those who had survived persecution came forward and testified to Jiang Qing's petty acts of spite. While still in power, she had even had her former Shanghai landlady arrested and brought to Peking, where she was systematically browbeaten for fear of gossip about some compromising incident from the past.

Jiang Qing evinced a special hatred for Wang Guangmei, wife of President Liu Shaoqi, whose personal authority was second only to

Mao's before the Cultural Revolution. When Wang Guangmei, a comparatively young and good-looking woman, appeared in a long Chinese gown and a string of pearls during a state visit by her husband to Indonesia, Jiang Qing disapproved and took her to task. Wang Guangmei was unwise enough to ignore this reprimand, and Jiang Qing never forgave her.

During the Cultural Revolution, some of Jiang Qing's henchmen from Qinghua University telephoned Wang Guangmei and told her to come to the hospital at once because her daughter had been injured in an accident. In reality, they were holding her prisoner there. Wang Guangmei promptly informed her husband, who accompanied her to the hospital. The Red Guard reception committee were taken aback when their bogus summons conjured up the Head of State, plus bodyguard, as well as their captive's mother. Questioned as to the girl's whereabouts, they gave such vague and muddled replies that it soon became clear the story was a hoax. Dismayed, Liu Shaoqi drove off, leaving his wife to investigate the matter further. As soon as Wang Guangmei was alone and unprotected, the Red Guards seized her and hustled her into Qinghua University, where she was forced to don a long Chinese gown. Then, with a string of pingpong balls round her neck, she was hauled before a mass tribunal and abused. She defended herself staunchly, an eyewitness told me later, but her student captors kneed her in the back and pinned her arms behind her while activists in the mob yelled, '*Da dao!*' – 'Strike (her) down!' – or 'Down with cow-spirits and snake-demons!'

Wang Guangmei survived the Cultural Revolution, but her husband, who fell prey to Jiang Qing's machinations, did not.

Although Jiang Qing had reproached her rival for voguish extravagance, her own lifestyle bore no resemblance to that of the toiling masses. She was presumptuous enough to design a new female costume comprising a high-necked, loose-sleeved blouse and a full skirt – a synthesis of Western fashion design and that of the Tang dynasty a thousand years earlier. Replicas of this outfit were displayed in store windows and offered for sale on the instalment plan, free of clothing coupons, so that female comrades could demonstrate their loyalty by buying them. But nobody did. What self-respecting woman would have courted her workmates' ridicule by dressing in such a style? Window-shoppers gazed at the new creations and walked on quickly with covert smiles.

Jiang Qing loved luxury. Her American biographer, Roxane Witke, describes the choice fare served at her dinner parties, when fragrant little wreaths of orchids would be presented to each guest.

Chinese newspapers, which continue to tear her to shreds, claim that her Cantonese servants were obliged to wash the leaves on the shrubs at the entrance to her orchid garden before she gave a party. They further allege that a neighbouring dockyard had to stop work during her visits to Canton, on account of the noise, and that river traffic, too, was temporarily halted.

These stories may or may not be exaggerated. What is true is that she made the workers living opposite her board up their windows so that they could not see into the grounds. I drove past several months after her arrest, but the boards were still in place. Quite inured to living by artificial light, the residents had been too scared to ask for their removal.

Jiang Qing's lengthy interviews with Roxane Witke, the young American feminist and sinologist, took place in 1972. She used them to recount her life-story and propound her views on politics, art, and literature, evidently in the hope that the resulting book would become a companion piece to Edgar Snow's *Red Star over China*, which had gained Mao an international reputation at the end of the 1930s. However, Witke left China with only one of the tapes she had made of these interviews. They had apparently caused a rumpus in the higher reaches of the Party and provoked a marital altercation.

Bowled over by the preferential treatment she had received at Jiang Qing's hands, Witke paid tribute to her 'regal bearing' – 'a regality expressed by perfect posture, facial animation and exquisite timing'. The biography appeared when Jiang Qing was already behind bars. Its heroine, faithfully recorded by Witke, gives a highly cinematic account of her poverty-stricken childhood and her promising film career in Shanghai, which she self-sacrificingly renounced in order to devote herself, heart and soul, to the revolutionary struggle. This version of Jiang Qing's early life was soon dismissed as fictional by witnesses who preserved quite a different recollection of her years in Shanghai. The book is amusing because of the naïve way in which Jiang Qing's carefully calculated remarks are accepted at face value by her biographer, and the passages in which the two staunch feminists swap ideas on male society are particularly entertaining.

According to Jiang Qing, Mao fell in love with her at first sight. She says nothing of her own emotions, her love, affection, or even liking for the Great Chairman. 'Sex is engaging in the first rounds,' she observes at one point, 'but what sustains interest in the long run is power.' And in China as elsewhere, it should be added, power does not come easily. 'Throughout Chinese history,' Witke wrily, if somewhat clumsily, remarks, 'becoming the imperial consort was the fastest feminine means for upward social mobility.'

Jiang Qing was quick to learn this historical lesson, but the Chinese people were spared much tribulation when Hua Guofeng and his Politburo allies prevented the Chairman's widow from assuming power like an Empress Dowager in days gone by.

Shanghai

Early December

The approaches to Shanghai looked lovely from the air. We had still been flying very high when we crossed the Yangtze near Nanking, and the Changjiang – the Long River – was lost in haze like a dark ribbon on a monochrome background. Now we were low enough to pick out individual junks and sampans on canals and waterways.

We had left a brown world behind us when we took off from Peking. Even the villages were mud-brown and barely distinguishable from their surrounding fields. There was ice on the canals, but even the ice bore a yellowish-brown film deposited by the first dust-storms. Winter had come, and the earth would be brown for another five months. I buried my nose in a newspaper.

I had stopped reading by the time we neared Shanghai, distracted by nostalgia and uncertain whether my reunion with the place would be a pleasurable one. I looked out of the window. The broad plain stretched away beneath us, verdant even in winter, its surface crisscrossed by canals and ditches. Most of these waterways, which occur on average every hundred and fifty paces, run parallel to each other and intersect at right angles with transverse ditches – and so on for a hundred square miles or more. This cannot be the result of chance, but is evidence of a strong central government with a wide territorial sphere of authority. Far from indulging in bureaucratic caprice or love of order for its own sake, the administrators who made farmers dig their canals and ditches in a predetermined pattern were presumably concerned to regulate the influx and efflux of flood water.

No network of canals on this scale could have been excavated in short order, certainly not with the spades, mattocks, and wicker baskets that were the only implements available in former times. Seen from above, the waterways look neither chaotic nor rigidly and forbiddingly gridlike, but more like the ramifications of an ancient walnut tree in winter: an organism that has developed, not in a matter of years or decades, but in one or even two millennia.

We could now distinguish the junks' brown sails. Motor boats were towing strings of sampans hither and thither. Where were the junks going? What were the sampans carrying? Were all these toings and froings part of some grand economic design worked out by the Peking authorities?

Gulag prisoners sentenced to corrective labour had been assured that the canal they were toiling to construct would become a major arterial waterway. Many years later, Solzhenitsyn sat on the bank and waited. Nothing happened for a long time. Then a barge came past, heading south with a mountainous cargo of logs. Peace and solitude returned. After another long wait, a second barge appeared. This one was heading north. It, too, was piled high – with logs.

As in Russia, so in China?

Political Unrest

Three men were standing in front of a miniature wall-poster no bigger than a postcard. One of them was reading aloud with the aid of a flashlight.

The poster was affixed to the wall of a building – more precisely, to a wing of the former Hong Kong & Shanghai Bank, once one of China's most prestigious financial centres. Even if the trio had known this, which they almost certainly didn't, it wouldn't have interested them. They wanted to know what the tiny poster said. A couple of minutes' walk would have brought them to the Bund, Shanghai's waterfront boulevard. Displayed there was another wall-poster, if so it could be described. Measuring at least fifteen feet by twenty, it was brightly illuminated and alive with spirited caricatures. The principle feature was an outsize pan sizzling over an open fire, flames from which were licking over the rim. Inside the pan, some two dozen men and women with heads the size of pumpkins were hopping desperately from one matchstick leg to the other. They were the Gang of Four, whom we recognized, and their Shanghai henchmen in the Party and municipal government, whom we did not.

Before dinner we had viewed the harbour from the top floor of the Cathay Hotel, an old and once luxurious establishment now known as the Peace Hotel. The poster was in the street below. We asked Shanghai's Head of Protocol the names of the people in the frying pan. One of them, who was flinging his arms around with wild abandon – presumably because the soles of his feet were being scorched – was a man called Bai.

We casually inquired if the dinner on our programme for tomorrow would be hosted, as scheduled, by the head of the Foreign Trade Organization. Our mentor couldn't say. It wasn't. The director of the Foreign Trade Organization was dancing in the pan. His name was Bai.

The three men walked off, arguing, and the reader pocketed his flashlight. We went and peered at the postcard-sized sheet, but it was too dark to decipher anything. When I returned next morning it was gone – torn down.

But in Nanking Road, the main commercial thoroughfare, as in the Bund and other big streets, every available space was plastered with wall-posters. They all carried ferocious and sarcastic attacks on the Gang of Four, whose home town this was.

The Four were often portrayed as grotesques, many of them executed with talent and verve. The Chinese masses have always been good at kicking a man when he's down – or a woman. Jiang Qing came in for some particularly rough treatment. She was depicted living in the lap of luxury, wearing glasses from Japan, false teeth from Hong Kong, a wig from the United States, and – almost invariably – an imperial crown on her head. She and her three confederates were shown being trampled by booted feet, transfixed with spears, spitted on fountain pens, beaten to death with shovels.

Some exceptionally striking caricatures had been posted up outside Department Store No. 1 in Nanking Road. I stopped the car and went to take a few pictures of them. At once I was surrounded by fifty or a hundred people who hemmed me in so tightly I could scarcely move. They were neither friendly nor hostile, just curious; but for how much longer?

Polite, helpful, and inoffensive individuals can be unpredictable in the mass. What were foreigners doing in Shanghai? Why should they be interested in wall-posters? Could they be spies? My Chinese escorts from the municipal government hustled me back into the car, looking apprehensive. Dozens of faces pressed against the windows. A few youngsters thumped the roof and wings – playfully, so it seemed. When we started to drive on the crowd was slow to move aside. As the authorities in Peking had warned us, Shanghai was still in the throes of political unrest.

Our next port of call was Machine Tool Factory No. 1. After touring it, we emerged into the forecourt. Some men had propped ladders against the administration block and were hanging wall-posters. Attacking whom? The factory manager couldn't say – he hadn't read them yet. 'Perhaps the Gang of Four,' he replied, 'or their supporters here on the premises.' He laughed, but it was the Chinese laugh of sudden embarrassment which foreigners so readily misinterpret. Then he escorted us back to the car, looking grave. I refrained from inquiring if he had any personal cause for concern. The question was superfluous – I could see he had.

Our host at dinner was Mr Bai's deputy. I told him that people in Hong Kong claimed the wall-posters were officially controlled. Mr Bai's deputy gave a laugh, but not of embarrassment. 'Controlling them would be fine,' he said, '—if we could. We watch their drift, of course, but we don't intervene. There's no need. People must be given a chance to let off steam. Many things come to light in the process. The Gang of Four's supporters must be identified and brought to book. That could take a long time.'

'How long, more or less?'

'We've only just started. Another year, perhaps.'

It took far longer.

Puppets and Politics

The theatre was packed with adults and children in roughly equal numbers. Puppets representing the Chinese people entered from both sides of the stage. Members of the national minorities – Tibetans, Mongols, Zhuang, Uighurs, Miao in colourful costumes, soldiers, peasants, workers – ranged themselves in a semicircle beside the Sons of Han, or Chinese proper.

The puppets were a little over two feet tall. One rod supported their bodies while another two controlled their arms. They moved in a very lifelike way, operated by puppeteers stationed below the bottomless stage. One by one they stepped forward, condemned the Gang of Four, and extolled Wise Chairman Hua Guofeng. Their attacks on the Gang of Four grew steadily louder and more vehement.

All at once, four men entered the auditorium from the left – real men, not marionettes – and halted in front of the stage. They were supporting puppets representing the four accused – grotesque but excellent likenesses. The Chinese 'masses' on stage inveighed against each of them in turn. The puppets' operators bowed their heads on their chests in the traditional pose of a Chinese on trial. Under a rain of accusations from the stage, they started to tremble violently, and their heads sank still lower when the puppet tribunal screamed *'Da dao! Da dao!'* Only Yao Wenyuan, the Shanghai journalist, made no move to bow his head. He continued to stare insolently and impassively at the crowd on stage until he, too, was subdued by their redoubled cries.

The puppeteers took their puppets by the neck and legs and made a rapid exit to the right, so that it looked as if the Four were being thrown out bodily.

The audience applauded with gusto. Then we watched a performance of the lion dance.

Our escort from Shanghai's Protocol Section was a quiet man. He made no reference to the Gang of Four while accompanying us back to our hotel, only to the lion dance, which had shown a lion and its two cubs being schooled for the circus ring. The trainer and his animals were puppets, of course. Our escort asked if we had enjoyed it. The way the beasts kept falling off their spheres until they learned how to stand and propel them along – the way the old lion turned stubborn – the way the lion-tamer vaulted over his charges and back again in a flash . . .

'No politics at all!' said our escort. 'To think such things are possible again! Will they all come back?' He hoped but dared not believe so. The lion dance was a traditional piece. 'For many of the young people in the audience,' he went on, 'that was their first performance without a political moral. They won't know what to think – they'll be wondering what the lion dance really means, politically speaking.'

The Children's Palace

Grown-ups and children had to follow different routes from the gate in the street to the door of the Children's Palace. We could head straight for the entrance, whereas they had to scale a climbing frame, crawl through pipes, teeter across a horizontal bar, negotiate ditches and other obstacles. They could gain admittance to the Children's Palace only by completing this junior version of the Long March, which prefaced every day they spent there.

As far as we could tell, the children ranged in age from six to fourteen. Only the best-behaved and most progressive youngsters – primarily the offspring of government and Party officials – were privileged to spend a day or two a week in such surroundings. There were ten Children's Palaces in Shanghai, one to each urban district.

The youngest children, who had paraded in a room of their own, clapped when we entered and raised a concerted cry of *'Huanying!'* or 'Welcome!' Then one little shrimp stepped forward, raised a conductor's baton, and led his six- and seven-year-old peers in song. First came a hymn to Wise Chairman Hua, originally addressed to Chairman Mao but modified by the simple expedient of substituting one name for another.

There followed a choral tirade against the Gang of Four, whose dastardly characters and abominable crimes the youthful songsters sternly condemned. They wound up with a loudly chanted, thrice repeated chorus of '*Da dao!*' – 'Strike (them) down!' This they accompanied by scowling fiercely and smighting an imaginary Gang of Four to the ground with their clenched little fists.

The children in the other rooms also greeted us by clapping, dancing, or singing. They performed a shadow play entitled *The Cock and the Fox* with home-made puppets of transparent goatskin, made model aeroplanes and ships, or conducted simple chemical experiments. The members of one art class were seated in front of a plaster bust, pencilling it into their drawing books with earnest concentration.

In the last room we visited, some boys were busy throwing balls and firing darts from toy pistols. The targets in each case, which tipped over backwards when hit, were cardboard figures of Jiang Qing, Zhang Chunqiao, Wang Hungwen, and Yao Wenyuan. The Gang of Four were under attack even here.

Franz looked pensive when we left. What effect would all this have on the youthful psyche? If children were inoculated with hatred and aggression at such a tender age, she said, they would grow up to repeat the horrors of the Cultural Revolution. I expressed scepticism. Psychologists' claptrap was never more misleading than when it seemed self-evident, I told her. For all its pseudo-scientific jargon, it really belonged to the same category as palmistry, oneirology, dowsing, and astrology. If ever those youngsters repeated the horrors of the Cultural Revolution, it would not be because they had hymned their hatred of the Gang of Four at a Children's Palace. Their singing was merely a theatrical form of fun, just as the cardboard figures of Jiang Qing and her confederates were to them what Redskins had been to us.

The week before, a young English guest of ours had been strolling beside the lake in the grounds of the Summer Palace when two little girls approached her, giggling shyly. They eventually plucked up courage and asked her in broken English whether she would write something down for them. She tore a sheet out of her notebook and wrote: 'I like Peking. China is a beautiful country.'

The girls thanked her delightedly and were on the point of going when our friend asked them to return the compliment. They whispered together, still giggling, and inscribed a few Chinese characters in her notebook. Then they thanked her again and ran off. That evening she showed us what they had written. It was: '*Marxism-Leninism da dao! Mao Zedong da dao!*'

Those two little girls must have been shown the Great Chairman's picture before they could walk, told about the Great Helmsman in Peking before they could speak, encouraged to wave Mao's Little Red Book and sing hymns to him before they could read. Even now, they began each school day with a song composed in his honour.

We were dumbfounded when we saw their inscription. It was the first time we had encountered such a thoroughly negative attitude towards Mao – and in children, too!

Shanghai Memories

On the way to the puppet theatre that evening, we'd caught sight of our old home. Franz and I gave a simultaneous exclamation and the driver slowed.

It was dark, and the place looked just as it had done thirty-six years ago. The tall fence of woven bamboo was still there, and so was the little roof above the entrance. The house had been far too big for us, but accommodation was scarce and this was the only one on the market. A red brick building with two storeys and an attic, it was situated at the intersection of the Route Henri Rivière and the Avenue Pétain, in the French Concession. It would have looked equally at home in a French provincial town.

If I close my eyes I can still walk from room to room. Three steps led up to the kitchen and another twelve to the first floor. The room on the right at the head of the stairs was where our eldest son spent the early months of his life. He was born on the Dragon-Boat Festival – an auspicious date. The event was celebrated by the cook, the houseboy, the coolie, and the amah, all of whom were slightly fuddled by nightfall and all of whom clamoured to carry the baby when Franz arrived home from the hospital to find our front door garlanded with flowers.

Why, when one looks back on days gone by, is the sun always shining?

A sunny morning at the end of September 1940. It was not quite as hot and muggy as it had been, and I welcomed the change. I drove to the office by way of Avenue Joffre and Avenue Foch. When I left the French Concession and entered the International Settlement, the street changed its name to Avenue Edward VII.

Plane trees lined the avenue, and beyond them stood two-storeyed buildings, shops below, living quarters above. At this hour of the morning, straw mats could often be seen spread out on pavements at the mouth of side streets. Knowing what lay beneath them, I looked away, then looked again despite myself. Sometimes, if a mat was on the small side, a pair of feet peeped out. Pedestrians unable to skirt these obstacles stepped over them in passing. The mats concealed corpses.

There were tens of thousands of homeless people in Shanghai. Many had left the land for the city, others were townsfolk who had fallen on hard times and been evicted from their homes. They slept in alleyways, but now that the nights had turned colder the weakest of them were dying off. The householder who found a cadaver outside his door at daybreak would drag it swiftly to the nearest intersection and leave it there, covered with an old mat. He wanted no complications, no formal statements to the police. A stranger's corpse was no concern of his.

A truck made the rounds at nine o'clock. Two municipal employees toured the streets, jumping out whenever they spotted a mat. They took the corpse by its wrists and ankles and heaved it into the back, then drove on. Mats were stacked on the left, bodies on the right. Mats were converted into cash, bodies transported to a field on the outskirts of the city. There they were cremated.

How could we endure the sight of such misery? Not just foreigners like me, but the Chinese themselves – everyone who lived in Shanghai? How could we walk past beggars without even seeing them?

They were starving, crippled, and blind, male and female, young and old. The children were usually hired out and their scabs and sores paraded for inspection. Emerging from a restaurant, you would find a handful of urchins hopping around in front of the car like sparrows and chirping the words they'd been taught: 'No Papa, no Mama, no whisky!' The first time you heard it, you laughed and tossed them a coin or two.

They couldn't keep them, of course. All their takings had to be surrendered to 'bosses', of whom Shanghai had two; one in charge of the International Settlement and the other of the French Concession. The 'bosses' lived like kings, allowing their minions only just enough money to keep body and soul together and enable them to pursue their profession. It was they who rented out children and stationed beggars in the most likely places.

The 'boss' of the French Concession had a celebrated and highly remunerative showpiece. Just as people were streaming out of the cinema or the Chinese opera, a barrel would come rolling up. The boy inside had no legs and only one arm. With his torso wedged inside the barrel, he used his remaining arm to propel himself through the streets at quite a respectable speed. The money was collected by another boy trotting alongside.

As for us, we inhabited the world of the wealthy. So did our servants: Zhang the cook, Yüe the houseboy, Shu the coolie, and the children's nurse, who had no name and referred to herself simply as 'Amah'. Although their wages were minuscule by European standards, their only bonus being a sack of rice every Chinese New Year, they were rich in their own and others' estimation. To them, beggars in the street were invisible – creatures to be feared and shunned like lepers. Poverty could stick to you like pitch, infect you like an incurable disease. It was easy to lapse from wealth into poverty, but easier for a camel to penetrate the eye of a needle than for the poor to ascend – by dint of honest toil, of course – into the world of the wealthy.

We made donations to relief agencies and churches, but the recipients of their help were few. The mat-enshrouded corpses on the pavements were only a glimpse of China's poverty. No one lifted even a corner of the Great Mat.

Notwithstanding this, certain Chinese had made it their aim to abolish Great Poverty and Great Wealth into the bargain. The people of Shanghai spoke of them only in whispers, aware that they were already in the city. They were everywhere, in fact, but their plans were derided by the 'old China hands' whose experience of the country went back so many years. Secure in their wealth, they had grown accustomed to speaking with smug condescension of the Chinese and all that happened in China, none of which they took seriously. 'Pipe dreams' was their verdict on the plan to do away with Great Poverty. They were the pipe dreams of Mao Zedong and the Communist Party.

I drove up Avenue Edward VII and turned left into the Bund. The Bund was the city's most photogenic feature and the first to be seen by those who arrived, as most people did, by sea. On my right flowed the Huangpu, which always had several ocean-going vessels riding at anchor on its sluggish yellow surface. Presiding over the Bund stood the strongholds of the masters of Shanghai, the great British and American banks through whose colonnaded portals the visitor passed as though entering a temple. Over there stood the Customs House, the council chamber of the International Settlement, the luxurious Cathay Hotel, the British Consulate General, and beyond it Garden Bridge. The bridge was guarded by a Japanese sentry, and all who passed him had to doff their hats or caps in salute.

The German Consulate General occupied the top two floors of an office building at No. 2 Peking Road. Here, too, were the offices of the German Embassy, but only those concerned with the press, radio, and industry. The embassy itself was in Peking, still known in those days as

Peiping, or 'Northern Peace'. Peking had only one small English-language newspaper, one Chinese radio station, and no industry worthy of the name.

Even in the midst of World War II and after its occupation by the Japanese, however, Shanghai remained China's most important commercial centre. In addition to numerous Chinese dailies and periodicals, it had four big English-language newspapers and one German, the *Ostasiatischer Lloyd*. There were twenty-six radio stations, of which several broadcast in English and one each in French and German. At twenty-five, I was the youngest member of the German Embassy's Shanghai staff and responsible for broadcasting. I saw to it that our small German transmitter broadcast in English because many Shanghai Chinese and all the city's foreign residents, Germans included, were conversant with the language. I subscribed to Reuters, Associated Press, and United Press, whose reports I included in our news broadcasts so as to acquaint our listeners with the other side's views as well as our own. We also broadcast jazz rather than Wagner and military marches. Quite clearly, I had an underdeveloped sense of what was politically acceptable and unacceptable, and my efforts were bound to end in disaster. Before being recalled, I christened our German station 'The Voice of Europe' – somewhat prematurely, I fear.

The Grateful Chicken

Our acquaintanceship with Dr Huang went back to his days as an assistant physician at Shanghai's German hospital, the Paulun. His address took some finding, and we neglected to tell our Chinese guides that we were going out. Their insistence on accompanying us would hardly have suited Dr Huang in a country where consorting with foreigners attracted such suspicion. For the same reason, we visited him on foot instead of taking a taxi.

We asked after the Huangs' grown-up children, who were the same age as ours.

'Are they doing well?' I asked. 'Are they happy?'

'They're workers,' the Huangs said simultaneously, and laughed. They laughed, not because they found it amusing, but because it saddened them that their children hadn't gone to university.

'Children from professional families are refused permission to study on principle, unless their father happens to be an official in the university administration or some other recognized body. Then, anything goes – through the back door, as we say.'

To Chinese parents, nothing has ever mattered more than their children's upbringing and education. Passing exams, or at least the preliminary provincial examination, then progressing to higher examinations and finally to the supreme test of knowledge in the capital – such was the goal for two thousand years. Examinations were the ladder that led to senior posts, to success, prestige, and often to wealth. By climbing that ladder, men of peasant and artisan stock – even men from the merchant class – could become one of the scholar-civil servants who constituted the highest class of all. Only soldiers' offspring were debarred from taking this route.

But social advancement was not the main concern. Education alone could help one to become the 'superior person' of whom Confucius spoke and set one on the road to refinement and correct behaviour, loyalty and integrity. A knowledge of facts – expert knowledge – was often no more than a secondary aim.

Nothing ever grieved Chinese parents more than a work-shy son. Chinese literature teems with such object lessons. Dr Huang's children did not fall into this category; they *wanted* a higher education. In the old days they would have enjoyed better opportunities than most because they came from a professional family. Now, children from professional families were said to have a 'black family background'.

One of the Huangs' sons belonged to an oil-field drilling team. Another son was a lathe operator in a Shanghai engineering works. Their daughter, a would-be doctor, had been obliged to spend five years in an agricultural commune. At least she was back in Shanghai now, but working behind the counter in a department store. One of Dr Huang's colleagues was trying to get her a traineeship as a children's nurse.

'Through the back door?' I asked.

Mrs Huang spread her hands. 'What choice do we have?'

I described how well Romanian doctors lived because their patients had to deposit an offering on the surgery desk – cigarettes, vegetables, plum brandy, hens, geese – before they were even shown into a chair and asked what ailed them. An envelope containing a few banknotes would do just as well.

'But that's outrageous,' protested Dr Huang. 'It doesn't happen here.'

Mrs Huang smiled. 'We had an unexpected visitor yesterday,' she said. 'A chicken flew over the fence and into our garden.'

'With a slip of paper in its beak,' I asked, 'giving its name and address?'

Dr Huang smiled too. 'No, but it must have been footsore after walking all the way from a people's commune in Hungqiao. I could even tell you the name of the family who've been rearing it on their private plot. It made its way here out of sheer gratitude.'

The Poplar and the Willow

Early December

I have lost my proud poplar and you your willow.
Poplar and willow soar upward to the Ninth Heaven.

Thus begins a poem by Mao Zedong. Its meaning is not immediately obvious. Although this is a respect in which it fulfils one of the basic requirements of modern poetry, Mao was no revolutionary when it came to versifying. On the contrary, he adhered to classical Chinese conventions.

For the benefit of those who had failed to interpret the poem, the *People's Daily* explained its significance. By 'poplar' – in Chinese, *yang* – he meant his first wife *Yang* Kaihui, who was shot by the enemy. Similarly, 'willow' – in Chinese *liu* – was a reference to his comrade-in-arms *Liu* Zhixun, killed in 1932. The poem was addressed to Liu's widow.

It was originally intended that the English translation of this poem should be accompanied by an explanatory footnote, but Jiang Qing had balked at this. She did not wish English-speaking readers to get the absurd idea that Mao was still grieving for his first wife. The *People's Daily* went on to censure the editor but did not mention him by name.

We knew who he was, of course, and we knew he was in disgrace. Xinhua, the official news agency, had reported a few days earlier that Qiao Guanhua was to be succeeded at the Foreign Ministry by Huang Hua, Chinese Ambassador to the United Nations.

We heard from a Chinese source that Qiao Guanhua had approached Gromyko or some other senior Soviet official at the end of September, when the UN General Assembly was in session, and covertly solicited Soviet good will and support if a take-over by Jiang Qing and the radicals provoked disturbances verging on civil war. He was allegedly told that fraternal Soviet assistance would take a little time to arrange, and that the radicals would have to manage on their own for a week at least.

Had we been deliberately fed this information, or was it just one among many rumours circulating at the time? Two weeks later, Hua Guofeng's speech to an agricultural conference included some cryptic remarks to the effect that the Gang of Four, in planning their coup, had 'relied on aggressors' bayonets to support their puppet throne'. Thereafter, nothing more in this vein was ever said, and the accusation was quietly dropped.

Qiao Guanhua vanished from the stage on which he had played a major role for several years. How had this gifted man enmeshed himself in such a web of political intrigue?

On his return to China from Germany in the mid-1930s, Qiao became personal adviser to Zhou Enlai, then stationed in Chungking as liaison officer to the Chiang Kai-shek Government, and married his interpreter, Gong Peng. This did not, however, gain him an entrée to the revolutionaries' inner circle. He had not been a soldier or taken part in the Long March. Although everyone acknowledged his great intellectual ability, veteran revolutionaries tended to hold this against him. It aroused suspicion. Intellectuals had scruples, were ambitious, backed their own judgement against the Party's, thought and spoke at a rate that sometimes defied comprehension. Intellectuals were not to be trusted.

Qiao's career progressed slowly. He remained bogged down in the second echelon, where the Party made use of his intellect much as an employer exploits a craftsman's special aptitudes. Early in the 1960s, for example, he was appointed to help draft and edit a series of open letters to the Soviet Central Committee. Although their brilliantly reasoned arguments made a great impression, Qiao was overtaken on the Party ladder by old-timers who could not hold a candle to him intellectually. This rankled with him.

When Gong Peng died in 1964, he married again. His second wife was a friend of Mao's niece, Wang Hairong, with whom she had studied at Peking's Institute of Foreign Languages. Through her, Qiao Guanhua gained access to the inner circle of the leadership and the antechamber, as it were, of the Great Chairman's court. He also came into contact with Jiang Qing.

The Gang of Four disregarded the fact that Qiao did not belong to the old guard. Ever on the lookout for careerists, they noted his ambitious streak. Anyone who pledged himself to them could bank on promotion, and in 1974 Qiao Guanhua was appointed Foreign Minister. He owed his advancement more to Jiang Qing than to his old boss, Zhou Enlai. From now on, his allegiance belonged to her and the radicals. It was his sense of obligation to them that prompted him to join the April protest march against the riots in Tian An Men Square. Many people took this amiss. Hadn't the demonstrators in the square paid tribute to the memory of Zhou Enlai, whose close associate the Foreign Minister had been? Had he, the intellectual, defected to the radicals?

In a ministerial list allegedly drawn up by the Gang of Four and circulated in Peking after their detention, Qiao had been assigned a Deputy Premier's post. For all his intelligence, he had apparently failed to recognize the naïve and slipshod way in which the radicals were putting their plans into effect. 'He isn't intelligent,' one of his former aides told me, 'but too clever by half – and too ambitious. All the same, he isn't a bad man.'

Qiao Guanhua and his wife were now living under house arrest in their Peking home. He was writing his memoirs – not for public consumption, of course, but for the Party archives – in due detail and with due self-criticism. The house-arrest order was later relaxed. He and his wife were at liberty to leave the premises, but they didn't for many years, on account of the disgrace.

The Old Year and the New

At the turn of the year I sent Bonn a retrospective account of events in China since Mao's death and outlined the road that lay ahead. The Chinese, I wrote, were expecting wage increases. For more than a decade now, workers had been denied promotion from one wage group to the next. Without wage increases and bonuses, no increase in production could be achieved. China's communications network would have to be improved and the mechanization of agriculture extended.

The masses were expecting material improvements of all kinds and, more particularly, a liberal regime. The intellectuals were hoping for a return to the conditions that had prevailed in China during the mid-1950s.

It seemed to me that the Government aimed to fulfil these expectations and revert to the comparatively moderate policy pursued by Mao at that period. I was strengthened in this belief by the republication of his 1956 article entitled 'On the Ten Major Relationships'.

I felt a few qualms when the telex went off, wondering if I hadn't carried my predictions too far – if I hadn't been rendered over-optimistic by our few Chinese acquaintances and their burgeoning belief that fundamental improvements lay in store.

Our guests at lunch that day were Ted Youde, Britain's Ambassador in Peking, and his wife. Like Pierce Cradock, who succeeded him, Youde knew more about Chinese affairs than anyone else in the diplomatic corps. His own end-of-year dispatch to the Foreign Office had reported that everything pointed to a fundamental change of course in

China. Now that he had sent it, however, he owned to feeling uneasy too, and wondered if he hadn't been precipitate.

By the time lunch ended, we were in agreement: China *had* changed course, and fundamentally.

1977

1977

Anticipation

Jiang Qing and Zhang Chunqiao were hanging from a tree, side by side, their legs swaying in the wind. Both glared sullenly through their glasses. Above them hung Yao and Wang. They looked just as disgruntled, and no wonder. All four figures wore placards round their necks, but their names were defaced with the two bold red brush-strokes that identified them as criminals. The Gang of Four had been modelled in papier mâché, two feet tall, and children were amusing themselves by shaking the tree and watching them dance.

The tree stood beside Chang An Avenue, not far from the Peking Hotel, and the children sat perched on a wall behind it. The wall itself was obscured by a wall of humanity. Everyone was straining to read a poster visible only to those in the first few rows. One of the lucky ones was reading aloud in a piping voice. Passers-by lingered in the hope of catching a word or two. All I distinguished from the back of the crowd was Deng Xiaoping's name.

Next day some young people scaled lamp-posts in Tian An Men Square and adorned them with garlands and baskets of flowers. They were colourful paper confections. The weather was far too cold for real flowers – fifteen degrees of frost despite the brilliant sunshine.

Zhou Enlai, that universally respected figure, had died exactly a year ago. Small groups of people, mostly delegates from factories or neighbourhood committees, carried wreaths to the square and deposited them on a dais.

The huge open space was thronged with people. They posed for photographs in front of a big portrait of Zhou Enlai erected by a labour unit and read the wall-posters already on display or being hung. These handwritten sheets – several hundred yards of them – were affixed to walls, columns, and lamp-posts. Most of them were signed by works committees, neighbourhood committees, or groups with fanciful names, but one or two individuals had supplied the address of their labour unit. Particularly well-turned phrases or poems were transmitted by those in front to those at the back, many of whom were armed with pencils or ballpoints and jotted them down for subsequent discussion. Occasionally, someone would deliver a short speech.

The wall-posters covered many topics, but their commonest theme was a demand for the recall of Deng Xiaoping. They also attacked the people who had quelled the April disturbances, notably Mayor Wu De, the local Party boss, and Chen Xilian, commanding Peking's military district. Curses were heaped on the Gang of Four, but the authors' subject matter varied as widely as their arguments, demands, and personal attacks.

Our colleagues in Hong Kong, who felt convinced that these posters were officially inspired and controlled, reported as much to Bonn. Given the distance between Hong Kong and Peking, it was a pardonable misconception. Co-ordinated campaigns take on quite a different appearance because the central propaganda authority cannot assume responsibility for spontaneous demands of a divergent or conflicting nature. They are subject to guidelines and follow a strictly predetermined pattern.

The people around us realized that their leaders could not prevent them from paying tribute to the memory of Premier Zhou Enlai, as they had the previous April. Many approving remarks were scrawled at the foot of the wall-posters. The crowds were excited and happy – too much so to take offence at the presence of foreigners. Exaltation had banished fear. They were conscious of their collective strength and masters of their fate, at least for today. They comported themselves like free, proud individuals, betraying none of their usual diffidence and circumspection. That might return tomorrow, but now, in the mass, they felt supremely self-assured.

What had happened to them? Did anyone seeking a display of popular sovereignty have to visit Peking's Tian An Men Square to find it? Were these the New Men? Not at all. The New Man possessed a high degree of revolutionary consciousness, regarded the class struggle as 'the main link', staunchly upheld the campaign against right- and left-deviationists, and obediently followed the Party line, which perfectly accorded with his own desires. He would attend a mass meeting only if it had been convened and organized by the Party.

The crowds in Tian An Men Square were not ablaze with revolutionary fervour, not thirsting to storm some Chinese Bastille, but filled with anticipation. It surprised me to hear what they hoped for in the way of civil liberties – surprised me and revealed the inherent strength of a nation undaunted by decades of disappointment.

The square was not cleared at nightfall, as it had been last April. To show that they harboured no evil intentions and did not plan to remove the garlands and wreaths under cover of darkness, the authorities obligingly illuminated the square by turning on the street lamps.

People stood there reading throughout the night. It was only when the crowds thinned between 4 and 5 a.m. that our interpreter, Frau Gareis, managed to copy down substantial portions of the more important wall-posters. By the time she set off home on her bicycle, chilled to the marrow, the next crop of readers were arriving on their way to start the morning shift.

By noon the Gang of Four had disappeared from their tree. Some little bottles were hanging there instead, a few of them filled with red ink. I asked the bystanders what they meant. They laughed and said, 'Little bottles.'

'So I see,' I said, 'but why?'

They almost split their sides when the truth sank in. The Chinese for 'little bottle' is *xiao ping*. Though written differently, it is pronounced exactly like Deng's given name, Xiaoping. As for the red ink, it signified that he was a true revolutionary, not the 'black' counter-revolutionary the Gang of Four had made him out to be.

The Waiting Game

24 January

'I had several long talks with Deng Xiaoping eighteen months ago. I hear he's on the way back.'

'Yes,' I said, 'but slowly. I suspect it'll take a while yet.'

'Why?' Chancellor Helmut Schmidt took a pinch of snuff, staring out of his office window at the leafless trees in the grounds of the Palais Schaumburg.

'Because he's Hua Guofeng's toughest problem. Hua took over Deng's job last April. Now he's expected to recall him to the leadership, but he naturally doesn't want to prejudice his own position. Deng's position is strong enough already, out of office or not. The people know that Premier Zhou Enlai had earmarked him as his successor. Deng can afford to wait, Hua can't.'

'Why not? Who's forcing his hand?'

'Public opinion.'

'Public opinion?' Every syllable conveyed the deepest scepticism.

I reported on the mood of the crowd in Tian An Men Square a few weeks before and showed the Chancellor some photographs I'd taken. He kept the best ones but remained unconvinced.

'All right,' he said, 'so the people of Peking can state their wishes in writing and paste them up on walls. They're restive, and they pack a political punch as long as they're all together in the square. It was the same last April, but that didn't deter the Party leaders. They quelled the riots and proceeded to do what *they* wanted, not what the masses saw fit. Couldn't that happen again?'

'Not in this case. The April riots were aimed at the radicals – the Gang of Four. Hua arrested them three months ago. He can't revert to their policy and rescind the law a mere three months after taking over. No, he'll have to recall Deng and eat crow. So will the rest of the people who joined in the anti-Deng campaign and are still holding down seats in the Politburo. It'll be a real feast of crow all round, with Deng looking on and laughing. My Soviet opposite number thinks he'll let them fob him off with an advisory post. I don't agree. Deng must have some pretty definite ideas about his future policy and his status inside the Party and Government. He can afford to wait. Public opinion's on his side.'

The Chancellor said, 'I see. Quite a problem for Hua.'

'But Hua has another problem too. Those wall-posters that went up two weeks ago may be only a whiff of democracy, but how can anyone rule a nation over nine hundred million strong – indefinitely, I mean – if he's subjected to an imperative mandate from the crowds in the Square of Heavenly Peace? Mind you, the people's taste for issuing imperative mandates may diminish as time goes by.'

'Perhaps,' said the Chancellor. 'On the other hand, wouldn't it be better for the inhabitants of Peking to get their own way for once, instead of being constantly dictated to by a lone politician?'

Return of a Composer

Mid-March

I met Miss Li at a reception early in the week. She waited until we were alone, then asked if I could keep a secret.

'That depends,' I said.

'I'll tell you anyway. Beethoven's coming back.'

'What! That bourgeois – that princes' lackey and capitalist-roader?

Didn't you read what the *People's Daily* said about him and his music?'[1]

'Ah,' said Miss Li, 'that was years ago. Besides, it can't be true. Our great teacher Lenin was very fond of Beethoven.' She smiled.

'Is that the latest argument?'

'Yes. They're going to broadcast the Fifth Symphony on television.'

'When?'

'Soon. I'll let you know.'

On Wednesday she sent me a message to the effect that Beethoven might not, after all, be on the way back.

On Thursday it was rumoured – but only rumoured – that the Fifth would be broadcast on Saturday.

By Friday complete uncertainty reigned once more. On Saturday itself, the penultimate page of the *People's Daily* carried an announcement at the foot: there was to be a televised concert of Chinese compositions, among them a concerto for flute and *pipa*. A Chinese acquaintance expressed amazement. This was sensational news because the *pipa*, an ancient four-stringed lute, had been pronounced a feudalistic instrument by the radicals and banished from the concert hall. The paper made no mention of Beethoven.

Our language teacher, Mrs Xü, whose husband was a singer, excitedly assured us that Beethoven would be performed that very evening. That afternoon we received a call from a German press correspondent: Beethoven was still out, and he had filed a report to that effect.

The concert programme was finally announced at 7 p.m., after the television news. It featured the Chinese compositions listed in the press, plus another item referred to as 'Fifth Symphony'. The composer's name was omitted.

It was indeed Beethoven's Fifth – a distant relative of the original score, but Beethoven nonetheless.

A few months later we met the conductor, Li Delun, who became a good friend of ours. Forbidden to play European music for many years and too scared to practise it even at home, he and his orchestra had fought a hard battle with the rearguard of the left-wing radicals. There had been little time for rehearsals before the performance, but the ice was broken at last.

---

[1] Chao Hua in the Peking edition of the *People's Daily* on 14 January 1974: 'Absolute music, as composed in Europe during the eighteenth and nineteenth centuries, is a product of European capitalist society, which supports the interests of the bourgeoisie and serves the capitalist system. The content, ideas, and emotions permeating it are unmistakably bourgeois in class character. "Capitalism comes into the world, and from head to foot, from every pore, drip blood and filth." Thus wrote Karl Marx, and it is that blood and that filth which this music glorifies.'

Tolstikov's Tale

Mid-March

We were giving a dinner for a dozen-odd ambassadors and their wives. Vassili Tolstikov, the Soviet envoy, was a rotund, genial man with a wry sense of humour. Though wholly devoid of the ruthlessness and aggression I have sometimes met in other Soviet officials, he was held in the highest esteem by his fellow ambassadors from the Warsaw Pact countries. Tolstikov ruled the roost as no mere *primus inter pares* would have done, and none of them ventured to speak when he held the floor.

As First Party Secretary in Leningrad, Tolstikov had occupied an important rung on the Soviet Party ladder. He was now out in the cold, having been shunted off to Peking and given a post that offered scant political scope, but had resigned himself to this change in status and was soldiering on. I always enjoyed talking to him and his wife, a cultivated Leningrader with a wide knowledge of Chekhov and Tolstoy.

As soon as we were comfortably seated over our postprandial beers and whiskies, I asked Tolstikov if he had witnessed the attack on the Soviet Embassy in April of last year.

The Soviet Embassy stands in large, walled grounds originally set aside for captured Cossacks at the end of the seventeenth century and later allotted to the Orthodox Church. The embassy itself, with its big driveway and marble steps, its reception rooms, banqueting hall, and private cinema, is only one of many buildings on the site. It resembles a palace.

The approach roads are narrow. The one nearest the embassy was christened Anti-Revisionist Street a few years ago but reverted to its original name in 1980. The big wrought-iron gate at the end of this street is guarded day and night, like all embassy gates in Peking, by members of the People's Liberation Army. The embassy grounds contain a school attended mainly by the children of residents from socialist countries.

School finished at 2 p.m. on the day in question, and the pupils were on the point of going home. Tolstikov himself was not far from the entrance when he saw two Chinese trying to push past the sentries. At that moment an explosive device they were carrying went off, instantly killing both them and the three Chinese sentries. The blast was so severe that fragments of the victims' bodies rained down on the embassy lawn. The big windows of the first-floor reception room were shattered, and Tolstikov later showed me where plaster had been dislodged from the rear wall.

The sentries on the embassy gate were replaced within minutes.

Tolstikov said he called the Ministry of Public Security at once and reported what had happened. (I should have asked him for the number, which he must have had on file since the days of the Great Friendship. Peking had no telephone directory, and numbers were given to foreigners only on a need-to-know basis.) The Ministry took its time, however, and two hours elapsed before its investigators turned up.

Tolstikov allowed them to enter the embassy grounds and remove the bodies, but they didn't do a very thorough job. While hosing down the lawn, members of the Russian domestic staff found the top of a woman's skull and an identity card belonging to a mining engineer from Baoding, some hundred miles west of Peking.

Tolstikov endorsed the view that the bomb attack was not directed primarily at the Soviet Embassy. Of course, he said, its real purpose had been to embarrass the Chinese Government, but the underlying circumstances were still something of a mystery to him. The Chinese press had made no mention of the incident.

The same evening, the Chinese gave an official banquet at the Great Hall of the People, a long-standing function to which the diplomatic corps had been invited. Tolstikov attended it as a matter of course.

'We and our wives were standing in the great reception hall, drawn up as usual in order of seniority. Our host was Hua Guofeng, then Deputy Premier and Minister of Security. As soon as he came in, he walked straight up to me and shook my hand – in fact he held it for close on a minute without uttering a word. Needless to say, my fellow ambassadors interpreted this gesture as a sign of tacit agreement, and wondered what it meant.'

They must have wondered, though he didn't spell it out, whether Peking and Moscow had renewed the Great Friendship. I don't know if the East European ambassadors round the table had heard this story in such detail before, but it seemed that they hadn't.

Moral Sensitivity

Early April

The Hungarian Embassy had invited the diplomatic corps to a screening of a new Hungarian film at the International Club, a Chinese-run establishment.

Only hours before the performance, every embassy in Peking was circularized as follows:

URGENT!

The Embassy of the Hungarian People's Republic presents its compliments to the Diplomatic Missions in Peking. It regrets to have to inform them that the film show scheduled for today at the International Club cannot now take place and must be postponed until further notice. This unavoidable postponement has become necessary because the International Club, having regard to the moral sensitivity of its Chinese employees, declines to screen the film. The Embassy of the Hungarian People's Republic apologizes to those invited.

The Embassy of the Hungarian People's Republic takes this opportunity of assuring the Diplomatic Missions in Peking of its highest esteem.

The Hungarians later explained that the film had included a sequence of a young couple kissing.

A Hundred Days and After

Every government, in China as elsewhere, enjoys a hundred days' grace. Then questions begin to be asked – not in this case by the Chinese media, being organs of the Party leadership, but by the people. A hundred days pass quickly, at least for those in office.

Spirits in Peking had been buoyant at the beginning of January. The masses had made their views plain when celebrating the first anniversary of Zhou Enlai's death. They assumed that the Government would listen to them, and that Deng Xiaoping's return was a foregone conclusion. There were even a few hints in the press that the Government had got the message.

March came, however, and nothing happened. The hundred days were up. Incipient criticism could be detected among our closer Chinese acquaintances. What was the Government doing? Materially speaking, nothing had improved. We were even told that rations in one or two provinces had been cut. German technicians employed there reported that the Chinese were working without enthusiasm. They wanted more money.

Wages, which were divided into eight grades, had remained frozen for many years, just as individual workers had remained frozen in their wage groups. Their children had grown in size and number, but prospects of promotion were nil – they were imprisoned in a financial chrysalis. There was no hope of improving their standard of living, however hard they worked. Why didn't the Government do something? What *was* it doing? Where were all the promised improvements?

Conferences were held by the Party and Government. March brought a meeting of the 'extended' Politburo, which meant that the Politburo's twenty-five members sat in conclave with delegates from other central organs of the Party, the armed forces, the provincial authorities, and the Government.

The people of Peking took it for granted that the conference would recall Deng Xiaoping and inaugurate a grand new policy. They laid in stocks of fireworks, but they needn't have bothered. Extraordinary meetings of labour units and neighbourhood committees were convened, only to be regaled with interminable Party declarations. One victim of such a session told us that it had taken eight hours to read out these documents and interpret them. The leadership announced that it shared the public's esteem for Comrade Deng Xiaoping and intimated that its view of the April riots in Tian An Men Square differed from that of the Gang of Four. On the other hand, both Deng and the riots had been criticized by Chairman Mao. Mao's authority could not be undermined and his dictum revoked without more ado.

The order to clear Tian An Men Square had been given by Peking's First Mayor and Party boss, Wu De, who always looked like misery personified behind his thick-lensed glasses. Not only did the Pekingese hold him responsible for quelling the rioters, but he had been the last to criticize Deng Xiaoping in November, when everyone else had stopped. Wu De was one of yesterday's men. Although his unpopularity had been amply expressed by wall-posters, he remained in office – kept there, so it was said, by Hua Guofeng.

As though to prove that the worst was far from over, Chinese newspapers continued to insist that literature must serve the Party and the Revolution. Hundreds of thousands of intellectuals were still living in exile on the land, forbidden to write and teach or classified as 'right-wing elements' and compelled to do manual labour, their children debarred from higher education. Survivors of the Cultural Revolution kept their heads down because the colleagues who had then called the tune, the fanatical critics and inquisitors, were still ensconced at the desks beside them. What further blighted the intellectuals' hopes was the Party leaders' declaration that they wanted no wholesale settling of scores with those who had been 'misled' by the Cultural Revolution.

Things were progressing, if progressing they were, in a far from troublefree fashion. The big industrial conference in April was remarkable for the absence of southern China's two most influential political figures, the Party boss of Guangdong Province and the commander of the Canton military district. They did not attend because Deng Xiaoping, who was under their protection, had yet to be recalled.

Delegates to the conference were in broad agreement on major issues. Industry was to be stimulated, foreign trade promoted, and the people – within limits, of course – permitted greater freedom of speech. However welcome these aims, nothing definite was said about fulfilling them – nothing, for instance, about wage increases or China's acceptance of foreign credits. As for material incentives and workers' bonuses, structural reforms in agriculture and crash programmes for key projects in industry and communications, the delegates either shelved these issues or failed to agree on them.

All that emerged were two long programmatic leaders in the press calling for public order, discipline, and increased production, but appeals of this kind had lost their efficacy. The Chinese, who were tired of appeals, no longer listened to them.

Every realist in the country knew that the only person capable of taking major decisions and implementing them in the face of internal Party opposition was Deng Xiaoping, but Hua Guofeng still hesitated to recall him. Why? Because he might have threatened the position of veteran Maoists, not to mention that of Hua himself. Thus the Party's lengthy declarations counselled patience. Deng would be duly rehabilitated when the time was ripe, so any new demands, for instance on the occasion of the Festival of Souls in April, would be not only superfluous but out of place.

Some of our Chinese acquaintances believed these official pronouncements; others found it hard to disguise their scepticism. They had been duped and disappointed too often.

Hua Guofeng

Early April

Premier Filbinger of the German Federal State of Baden-Württemberg and his entourage of civil servants and journalists had been inspecting an infantry division based near Tientsin, sixty miles south-east of Peking. As we were climbing back into our cars, a Chinese official announced that the return trip to the capital would have to be speeded up a little. He had just been informed by telephone that the day's schedule now included an interview with a person of importance. His air of mystery only served to convince us that the person must be Hua Guofeng.

After greeting us in the small anteroom like long-lost friends, Hua led us off for the obligatory photographs. The protocol officials, who knew their business, shepherded us into position so deftly that no one could put a foot wrong. The photographer waited until we were all standing still, then took a picture. He took a second one for safety's sake. Tomorrow, as custom prescribed, the fruit of his labours would appear on the penultimate page of the *People's Daily*.

Hua was quite at ease. His movements were fluent, harmonious, and controlled without seeming studied. He was a tall man – roughly Filbinger's height but rather more heavily built. He did not gesticulate, sat quietly in his chair, spoke calmly. His manner conveyed that he had time to spare and no more appointments in view. He looked a patient man – a man whose mere presence would pour oil on troubled waters.

Hua, who comes from Shaanxi Province, grew up in a village and worked in the fields as a boy. His father was no Middle or Rich Peasant like Mao's, so he must have spent his childhood in very humble and impecunious circumstances. His formal schooling was rudimentary, and all he knew had been absorbed in the course of his Party career. He did not look ambitious. His comrades may have regarded him as comfortable and inoffensive. His expression was amiable. You got the feeling that he was at pains to endear himself to anyone he spoke to. His hands reposed serenely on the arms of his chair. They were strong but slender and well proportioned – not the hands of a typical peasant. Was it really Hua who had swept away the Gang of Four? Did those hands have claws of steel?

I couldn't see any.

Nothing he had said so far added much to yesterday's interview with Vice-Premier Li Xiannian, who was present again today and seated on Hua's side of the semicircle. Filbinger spoke of President Sadat, whom he had seen a short time before. He presented a shrewd and circumspect account of the German position. Hua abandoned his engaging smile and listened intently.

Did he have claws of steel and the ability to use them, or had he merely been thrust to the forefront by others? I found it hard to decide.

It was at Orşova, at the entrance to the Iron Gate. I'd been out hunting and was standing at the roadside, waiting for my Romanian gamekeeper-cum-guide, when a gypsy came past leading a bear. 'He looks friendly, that animal of yours,' I said. 'Why shouldn't he?' the gypsy retorted. 'He always looks friendly. He doesn't flatten his ears or bare his teeth like a dog – he doesn't always growl when he's angry, either, but when a man comes who is evil – the bear knows. You can stand beside him and he'll still look friendly, but then he'll lash out, and you've lost an ear or an eye or what-have-you.'

Was Hua Guofeng capable of lashing out like that? Maybe he was.

'We neutralized the Gang of Four in double-quick time,' he told Filbinger. 'Everything passed off without bloodshed, far better than we'd expected. We'd counted on serious resistance in Shanghai, but the people there erupted like a volcano and unmasked the Gang of Four's supporters.'

'Unmasked' was jargon for driven out of office and indicted.

Hua went on to speak of the damage done to Tangshan by last July's earthquake. 'Even here,' he said, 'nearly a hundred miles away, the shock was so severe I couldn't get out of my chair for what seemed a very long time. I was sitting at my desk, but the floor was swaying so much I couldn't get a foothold. I tried telephoning Tangshan when the tremors stopped but failed to get through. I managed to speak to Tientsin, which is closer to Tangshan. The damage there was considerable, so you can imagine what Tangshan looked like.'

That was Hua's sole reference to himself – his one and only resort to the first person singular. The earthquake had occurred at 3.25 a.m. He seemed to work very long hours.

A Chinese Mouse

Mr Huang looked like a mouse. Everyone was struck by the resemblance, though no one would have said so to his face. It was hard to speak to him anyway, because he was always on the phone. As our Chinese interpreter, Mr Huang bore responsibility for everything: obtaining air tickets, rail tickets, and travel permits, fixing important appointments, making reservations, dispelling misapprehensions. He spoke no German, but his English was quite fluent.

He continued to resemble a mouse when seated at his desk with the telephone clamped to his ear – an earnest, bespectacled mouse. When off the phone, he wore an amiable expression. He had also been known to laugh, but only rarely. Our other Chinese employees, even Lao Liu, kept out of his way and treated him with great respect. Did they see him as a lion rather than a mouse? Was it his job to report on them?

On Labour Day, when even the Chinese are excused work, Franz and I decided to watch 'the masses' at play – more precisely, to visit the Working People's Park of Culture and the Summer Palace grounds outside the city. Mr Huang accepted my invitation to accompany us with furrowed brow, much as if I'd presented him with the Gordian knot and asked him to undo it.

He came to collect us on the dot and showed us, with an air of quiet satisfaction, that he had procured three complimentary tickets of admission to the parks. We later discovered that these were quite redundant, but Mr Huang evidently felt that complimentary tickets were an ambassadorial *sine qua non*.

A festive, fairground atmosphere reigned throughout the parks. Parents were out walking with their neatly dressed children, hand in hand. If the children romped around, as they sometimes did, they romped with restraint and took care not to make a nuisance of themselves. We didn't see a single child crying. Boys and girls strolled in segregated groups, laughing and chattering. These were the same happy faces I recalled having seen at Chinese fairs forty years ago. There wasn't a New Man in sight. Firecrackers hissed and banged all over the place. There were booths where you could knock out Soviet tanks with miniature guns as they crawled across snowy wastes. There were carousels, obstacle courses, children's choirs, troupes of dancers, and a puppet theatre. People were rowing on moats and ponds. Shrubs and trees were bright with fruit and blossom, even at this early season of the year, but closer inspection revealed that they were made of paper or plastic. An enormous dragon brooded on the lake, waiting to make its entrance in tonight's display. Mounted on a small stage, a coloratura soprano sang an aria in honour of Wise Chairman Hua Guofeng. She was followed by a tenor and a bass who jointly assailed the Gang of Four and laid them low. The paths between the Summer Palace and the lake were so crowded that we could hardly get through, but the dominant mood was just as cheerful here as elsewhere. Many couples had perched on the lakeside railings with their children and were munching the steam-baked bread known as *mantou*.

Mr Huang held our blue complimentary tickets firmly and ostentatiously in front of him, as though presenting them for inspection. He wanted everyone to know that he was escorting us because he had been officially instructed to do so, not because he 'worshipped' foreigners and their alien ways.

I invited him to lunch at the Summer Palace's open-air restaurant. Mr Huang would only accept a cup of tea, on the grounds that he had over-indulged himself at breakfast. Although he didn't say so, of course, he was eager to avoid subsequent accusations of having lived-it-up in public with foreigners.

According to Mr Huang's colleagues, he had once studied Buddhism.

He himself was vague on the subject. Whatever the extent of his problems during the Cultural Revolution, they must certainly have caused him a lot of anxiety. Mice and lions are made of different stuff.

A member of the embassy staff passed our table. I gave him my camera and asked him to snap the three of us at lunch. Mr Huang made a self-effacing attempt to leave the table but was persuaded to stay. The picture came out well. The complimentary tickets showed up beautifully. Mr Huang was holding them in front of his chest like a blue breastplate to show that he was there on duty.

I asked him about his taste in English literature. He was in the middle of *Gone With The Wind*, and he explained why. 'I have to familiarize myself with reactionary literature,' he said. 'Unless I do, how can I pass judgement on it?'

I sympathized, having used an analogous argument during the war, and said I could lend him other books that would help to enhance his knowledge of bourgeois-capitalist life. Though disposed to accept my offer, he cautiously inquired what books I thought suitable for the purpose. I mentioned Orwell's *Animal Farm*. He asked if it had anything to do with agriculture.

'In a way,' I said. 'It's about pigs, mostly. One can learn a lot from it.'

'How interesting,' said Mr Huang. 'The biggest bestseller in China is a book called *How to Breed Pigs*. So far, it has sold nine million copies.' A flicker of alarm crossed his face. 'Of course,' he added swiftly, 'the works of Chairman Mao have sold many more copies than that.'

'Of course,' I said. 'That goes without saying.'

Orwell's book must have seemed admirably suited to the study of bourgeois-reactionary ideas. At all events, Mr Huang asked my permission to lend it to a friend whom he described as entirely trustworthy.

In the years that followed, I lent Mr Huang a number of books designed to deepen his insight into the capitalist world. He found Ed McBain's detective novels about events in the 87th Precinct exceptionally relevant, judging by the way he seized on every copy as soon as I'd read it myself. I bequeathed him my collection of McBains before leaving Peking. Caution reasserted itself, however. I discovered on the day of my departure that he'd presented them to the embassy library.

The Iron Rice Bowl

Mid-May

With a workforce of five thousand, the tractor factory at Nanchang was one of the biggest plants in Jiangxi Province. It had no manager when we visited it, but one of the half-dozen deputy managers, who appeared to be responsible for visitors, took us on a guided tour. We were the first foreigners he had shown round the premises.

The machinery was of pre-war standard, and many of the workers were standing around doing nothing. Even at a glance, we could see that productivity was low. The deputy manager conceded this. The factory's daily output was ten tractors. 'But we've only been back at work six months. Before that, the plant was idle for twenty-one months.'

'Nearly two years?' I said. 'Why was that?'

'Line struggles,' he replied simply.

It was a long story. Ever since the founding of the Chinese Communist Party, clashes had occurred between two 'lines' within it – eleven clashes, counting only the major ones. Power struggles as well as policy disputes, they were usually fought out at Party Headquarters. During the Cultural Revolution, however, everyone in the country had been forced to take sides.

Although the worst of the urban and rural conflicts were over, ill feeling persisted. How could people forget the brutality they had suffered at the hands of the other side? Decreeing peace was one thing, keeping it another.

'But the Chinese have always had a gift for compromise. Couldn't you negotiate and reach agreement?'

'No, out of the question. They wouldn't listen to reason. They were tools of the Gang of Four – right-deviationists, counter-revolutionaries.'

The deputy manager still got hot under the collar when he spoke of the other 'line'. Two years ago, he said, the majority of the workforce had been in favour of increasing output, but a member of the management with a minority of workers behind him declared that their first duty should be to implement the revolutionary line in Jiangxi Province; then they could think about production. Backed by some of Nanchang's Party leaders, the minority on the works committee accused the majority of obstructing the revolutionary masses – charged them with revisionism and an obsessive emphasis on production. Scuffles broke out in the factory grounds. The radicals were expelled and the premises occupied by the non-striking majority. They turned up daily, shift by shift, but were unable to maintain production because the minority cut off the power supply and held up consignments of spares and raw materials. Despite this, the majority continued to occupy the premises for fear of sabotage.

'But what about the provincial government – the revolutionary committee, I mean? Didn't they intervene?'

'They tried, but they were split too.'

'And the Army? The military authorities stepped in when strikes broke out at Hangzhou, didn't they?'

'In this province they'd already backed the wrong horse once. They kept out of it.'

'So production was at a standstill for twenty-one months. What did the workers and their families live on?'

'Wages continued to be paid, of course. We never abandoned the "Principle of the Iron Rice Bowl", even when things were at their worst. You can't smash anyone's rice bowl, not even your political opponent's, when you're engaged in a legitimate struggle between two lines. It was Mao's proletarian-revolutionary line versus the bourgeois-revisionist line of Liu Shaoqi.'

'So you and the majority supported Mao's line?'

'A hundred per cent, though the minority claimed that *they* were keeping Chairman Mao's banner flying and called us running-dogs of capitalism and Liu Shaoqi.'

'If your provincial revolutionary committee couldn't make up its mind which line was correct, couldn't you have consulted Peking – Zhou Enlai, perhaps?'

'Of course. Everyone consulted Zhou Enlai, but he wasn't all-powerful. There were others to be considered. The Gang of Four, for instance.'

'And Chairman Mao himself?'

He hesitated for a moment, then decided to ignore my remark. 'Party Headquarters had already sent one Politburo member to settle a provincial strike. That was at Hangzhou, but the person they sent was Wang Hungwen, one of the Gang of Four, and he only stirred things up. No, we had to deal with the situation ourselves. No one else could help us.'

'Not even Chairman Mao?'

'Chairman Mao had no wish to tread the Confucian path of the golden mean. He believed that, if there were no conflicts and no struggle to resolve those conflicts, the Party would become moribund. And that, in turn, would mean a cessation of progress.'

'I find that hard to understand.'

'Yes,' he said.

On Holy Ground

The house was of recent construction. Although we weren't asked to remove our shoes, the woman guide's voice became noticeably more subdued and reverential when we entered the modest, whitewashed farmhouse room. We were on holy ground.

'Chairman Mao,' said our guide, 'slept in that camp bed for many years.'

'Is that the original bed?' I asked.

'Of course,' she replied. 'He slept here between 1927 and 1929. His headquarters were in the Jinggang Mountains, and this is where he formed the first Chinese Soviet Government.'

'After which,' I said, 'the whole area was lost and not recaptured for another twenty years.'

'Correct.'

'And because all the houses had been destroyed, they were rebuilt, this one included. And because his original bed had disappeared, you got hold of any old bed and put it here instead.'

'Not any old bed,' the guide retorted with a faint smile. 'Chairman Mao never slept in *any* old bed. When the house was restored, we naturally installed a good, solid one.'

'Where did it come from?'

'I couldn't say. Perhaps from a depot maintained by the People's Liberation Army.'

'And that's the one?'

'Yes,' she replied, 'that's the bed in which Chairman Mao slept.'

In the course of our subsequent travels we saw a total of seven beds in which Mao had slept. The teacher-training college at Changsha boasted no less than two, because Mao had lodged there twice. Both beds were new. It would, after all, have been unseemly to exhibit a used article.

At Wuhu, a town on the Yangtze which we visited later on, we were shown a guest-house in which Mao had once stayed. The caretaker who had looked after him was produced to testify that all was as it had been on that momentous occasion. The bed was made up as he always liked, with one side left free for the books he habitually read so late into the night. A towel was draped over the bedside lamp to concentrate the light on whatever book he happened to be reading. Displayed on the bedside table were the cigarette butts he had left behind – a lot of them. They were encased in glass like sacred relics. A clothes stand supported his dressing-gown and several newspapers in wooden holders. All the newspapers dated from the time of his visit, but several characters had been inked over: they represented the names of persons who had since become non-persons. We were even shown, with due reverence, the bathroom and WC the Chairman had used.

But back to Jinggang. In company with some fellow ambassadors from Peking, we drove to the highland plateau. The gradient of the serpentine road, which had not long been built, was relatively gentle. Chinese advances in road construction were brought home to us when we were shown the steep track used by Chairman Mao on his way to inspect the sentries at the top.

'I have long aspired to reach for the clouds, and I again ascend Ching-kangshan . . .' Thus begins the authorized translation of the poem Mao wrote when revisiting this scene of his early revolutionary activities in 1965. We found ourselves looking down on a dense white carpet of cloud, pierced here and there by dark, wooded crests resembling islands in a sea of cotton wool. The air was clear, and mountain ranges could be seen in the far distance.

Behind the house stood a tree that had once been Mao's command post. Our guide was moved by his own stock phrases. 'This tree,' he said, 'lost its leaves and withered when Chairman Mao and his troops were compelled to withdraw from Mount Jinggang. It didn't turn green again till 1949, the year of liberation. Since then it has done so every year, and today – as you can see for yourselves – its foliage couldn't be finer.'

The guide conducted us to a boulder on which the Chairman had leaned, head in hands, while reading or lost in thought. From the awe in his voice, it might have been one of the stones which Jacob 'put for his pillows' at Bethel before dreaming of the ladder whose summit brushed the sky.

We were also shown two heavy wooden buckets which Chairman Mao had filled with spring water and borne up the mountain on a shoulder-pole to slake his soldiers' thirst. 'And behold,' I muttered in German, 'when he reached the top, the water had turned to wine.'

Claude Arnaud, the French Ambassador, gestured grandly at the peaks in their sea of cotton wool. 'And over there,' he said, 'he could often be seen at sunrise, walking on the clouds.'

The Great Harmony

Rice fields look their loveliest when the pale-green seedlings have just been planted. The size of a rice field is always proportionate to the size of man. Rice cannot be grown in fields that stretch in an unbroken expanse to the horizon because the water level cannot be evenly maintained and regulated over wide areas.

Every field is enclosed by a small, knee-high dam. This has two openings, one to admit water and the other, on the opposite side, to let it drain out. The seedlings stand with their roots and the base of their stems in water. Unless the water level remains constant, the ground dries out or the seedlings are swamped.

The dams trace a network of lines across the landscape. Rice-growing country is a subject for artists who prefer to capture space and perspective with pen or pencil. In hilly areas the dams form contour lines, but not with the cold precision of a survey map.

Fields ascend hills in a series of terraces with water flowing from one to another. Horizontals dominate the landscape, but the slender, bright green rice plants transform each field into a mass of verticals. The same shade of brilliant green clothes the entire landscape and is reflected in living water.

We had driven for hundreds of miles across broad plains and belts of hills, all of them devoted to the cultivation of rice. Even where thickets of bamboo sprouted from the sides of ravines, rice would be growing on the valley floor. Leaving Jiangxi behind us, we entered Hunan. Together, these two medium-sized Chinese provinces are almost as big as California. Inhabited by seventy million people, they lie in the Yangtze Basin, China's rice bowl.

Colo, I thought – I till or cultivate. *Colo, colere, colui, cultum*. The Latin verb has a variety of meanings. It can also connote worship, reverence, adornment – even cult. This was a cultivated, man-made landscape, but man, far from leaving a trail of devastation, had opened it up and made it accessible. Instead of subduing water by means of vast dams, he had gently tamed it with a network of ridges eighteen inches high.

Ariston men hydor – 'Water is best' – are the majestic opening words of Pindar's first Olympian Ode, but the great hydraulic civilizations first arose on the Indus and Nile, the Euphrates and Tigris, the Huang He and Yangtze, not in Europe, not in Greece. The connection between Asiatic social systems and a hydraulic economy was early recognized by

Adam Smith and John Stuart Mill. Karl Marx also explored these relationships in his later years, but the longer he debated them – according to Karl Wittfogel, himself a Marxist – the more confusion he sowed.

Karl Wittfogel's book *Oriental Despotism*, in which he endeavours to draw a picture of 'hydraulic societies', is a great and thought-provoking work in the manner of Spengler or Toynbee. Studies like these, which subordinate their coverage of vast areas and long periods of time to a single idea, present alluring vistas of their subject – alluring but misleading. National histories are tailored to fit the author's key idea, while anything that conflicts with his general picture is shrouded in a smoke-screen.

Wittfogel spent some time in China, but did he ever drive through rice-growing areas? Did he surrender to their impact, free from his preconceived theories? Did he have any eye or feeling for what there was to see, or did he, like Marx, derive his knowledge of the world of labour from books alone?

I incline to the latter view, for anyone who traverses the rice bowl of China will recognize that despotism and a strong central government were not the main determinants of social and economic activity. Many forms of despotism have also existed in anhydraulic cultures. Although a strong central authority was essential to the damming of rivers and the construction of large canals, what impresses one about rice fields is something quite else, namely a sense of orderly co-operation, not imposed from above but born of society itself.

We must have driven past myriads of rice fields, and still they swam into view. Each field got its water from the one above and gave it to the one below in a never-ending cycle of reception, utilization, and transmission. The landscape was a well-ordered, embellished, harmonious cosmos – cultivated in every sense of the word.

Being man-made, how could this landscape have failed to react on its maker? He who received water had to relinquish it. He who demanded consideration had to exercise it. He who drained off another's water not only injured his neighbour but disrupted the agricultural cosmos.

A landscape such as this was conducive to the idea of social harmony, of a civilized, orderly society in which each had his place and occupation and human beings were as well established as the five basic relationships between governors and governed, parents and children, man and wife, elder and younger brother, friend and friend.

The farmsteads of ancient Iceland lay many miles apart, separated by inlets, mountains, and trackless lava fields. They were far enough apart to be out of sight of each other, but distance was no deterrent. The Icelanders stopped at nothing, not even mounted forays at dead of night, to put a neighbour's home to the torch, carry off his cattle, or slaughter him in revenge for some similar atrocity of long ago. Even if they themselves perished in the process, they lived on in the sagas that glorified the deeds of the departed.

These feuds were also pursued before the Thing, or assembly, where Icelanders negotiated fines and indemnities with a great relish for ingenious legal arguments and casuistic quibbles. How much more scope for litigation they would have had if transported by some wave of a magic wand to Jiangxi or Hunan Province!

Though far from undisputatious, the Chinese are not litigious. They survived without lawyers for thousands of years, and the few that existed when Mao came to power were soon forbidden to practise. The ban on their profession has recently been lifted, but its current membership does not exceed one to every quarter of a million inhabitants.

The rice-bowl cosmos has to get by without law courts. There is no court before which one man can charge another with having drained off his water. In earlier times, such disputes were settled by the families or the village concerned; today the decision rests with 'the masses' – in practice, with the communes or, in serious cases, the regional authorities.

If the dispute is a minor one, the parties sit down together and speak their minds with a mediator present. In other words, they jointly seek a compromise. What matters is *jiangli* – talking rationally, showing common sense, acting humanely, avoiding friction. There is no insistence on absolute self-vindication. The essential thing is that neither party should lose face, be driven into a corner or humiliated.

The need for laws was long debated in China. The *fajia*, or 'legalists', were in favour of them, but the Confucian view prevailed. Laws might determine a person's outward behaviour, said Confucius, but they could not determine his nature or prompt him to become a 'superior man'. Instead of being regulated by laws, therefore, society should regulate itself by means of the individual's moral responsibility towards others.

Thus, Confucius' 'superior' person did not go to law over private disputes. Criminal acts were often left unprosecuted if the families succeeded in reaching agreement. Even the less noble-minded were well advised to avoid litigation, because civil suits caused nothing but trouble and exposed both parties to the risk of a flogging for their failure to come to terms in a spirit of harmony. The outcome was uncertain, too, because no civil code existed and judges based their decisions on custom, common sense, or bribery. To quote a rescript issued by Emperor Kangxi (1661–1722): 'I desire that all who have recourse to the courts [in civil suits] be dealt with mercilessly and in such wise that the laws disgust them, and that they tremble if ever they have to reappear before a judge.'

Settling disputes through a mediator was, and still is, common practice in town and country alike. If this fails, the parties consult their neighbourhood committee or labour unit. Even divorce suits have first to be submitted and substantiated to the satisfaction of the neighbourhood committee, which generally advises estranged couples to go home and try again.

The Chinese are not, as we are, subject to a remote authority that calls the individual to account in clearly-defined cases but otherwise leaves him in peace. They inhabit a society whose constraints on the individual's private life are quite automatic and have always been so. In the old days, villages or units of ten families were sometimes held collectively responsible and jointly liable for all that happened within their domain. Even during periods when this law was not in force, however, entire families had to pay for the crimes and misdemeanours of their individual members. If a senior dignitary fell into disfavour and was condemned to death, the same sentence often extended to all his kinsfolk, children and grandchildren included.

Even today, the pressures of the close-knit society in which every Chinese lives and works – his neighbours, his neighbourhood committee, his labour unit and its security adviser – weigh more heavily on the individual than any far-off court of law or civil authority.

Darkness was falling, and still we drove on through rice fields. The roads of Hunan Province, which we had just entered, were better than those of Jiangxi. Sometimes, when lights went on in houses near the highway, we caught sight of people sitting at supper. The glow from the naked bulbs overhead was mirrored in the flooded paddy-fields.

It was in this landscape and out of this society that *li* developed. The word has often been translated as 'rites' or 'ritual'. Both are correct, but *li* connotes more than that – more than the purely superficial. It means civilized, socially aware, responsible human behaviour. It means humanity and consideration for others. It means receiving water and, when one has used it, passing it on.

To Xunzi, one of the great thinkers of the third century BC, *li* was not only a social but a universal principle. 'Through *li*, heaven and earth unite in harmony, sun and moon shine, the four seasons come and go in succession, planets and constellations traverse the sky, rivers flow, all things flourish, men's desires and aversions are regulated and their joys and hatreds kept within bounds.'

Heaven had appointed the emperor to preserve the harmony between heaven and earth by means of moral behaviour, for political thought and action in China were directed towards a society that lived at one with itself, not towards freedom, democracy, or the greatest happiness of the greatest number. The requirements of society, not of the individual, were paramount. The individual mattered less and was not expected to take himself too seriously.

The Chinese were unconcerned with deliverance from evil or sin, nor did they aspire to a kingdom of heaven. Their dream was the golden age of *da tung*, the 'Great Harmony'. It was regarded as the beginning and origin of the Chinese social order and also as its end and objective. A celebrated passage in the *Liji*, or *Records of Rites*, describes it. Sun Yat-sen based one of his republic's two national anthems on the passage in question, which to the Chinese is full of moving, archaic weight. It reads as follows:

> When Tao, the Great Way, prevails, the state is common to all. The most virtuous are chosen and the most able appointed, truth is spoken and harmony maintained. That is why people do not love their own parents nor care for their own children alone. Instead, they see to it that the old can face death in peace, adults work in peace, and the young grow up in peace. Widowers and widows, orphans, childless, and sick are nourished by society. Men have their profession and women their home. Useful things are not discarded, but neither are they hoarded for oneself alone. People aspire to develop their energies, but they do not work solely for their own profit. Subterfuge and intrigue thrive no longer, and there are neither thieves nor robbers nor revolutionaries, so that the outer gate need no longer be locked. That is *da tung*, the state of Great Harmony.

Is that how the Chinese used to live? Is that how they live today? Are their relations really so harmonious? Far from it. What we have just heard is a self-imposed demand – a challenge. To meet it in full would exceed the power of man, but any civilization must be measured by the demands it makes on itself. What matters is not that people fail to fulfil them, but that they strive to do so. Not surprisingly, the Chinese have forsaken their aspirations very often, as often as Christians have failed to meet the standards set by Christ.

No Embroidery Lesson

I was shown round Ichun, a medium-sized provincial town in Jiangxi, by little Mr Wang. Little Mr Wang spoke English and came from Hong Kong. He repeatedly congratulated himself on being privileged to act as my guide. We had barely left the hotel and walked a few hundred yards when I discovered the reason for his self-congratulation. He wanted to join his brother, who owned a Chinese restaurant in Hamburg, and hoped I would help him get a visa.

His parents had sent him to the college for Overseas Chinese in Peking. From there he had gone on to Peking University itself.

'We had a hard time there when the Cultural Revolution began. They cut off my hair and my trouser-legs.'

'Why was that?' I asked.

'My hair was too long by Chinese standards, and my trousers were drainpipe trousers.' He pointed across the street. 'That building over there was our famous concentration camp.'

'Infamous,' I amended, because he'd asked me to correct his English, '—infamous would be more appropriate than famous.'

'Yes, of course. Thank you. Would notorious do too?'

'Certainly.'

'Well, it was very notorious.'

'Just a minute,' I said. 'Is this a guided tour or an English lesson? Anyway, it's a cinema, not a concentration camp.'

'It's a theatre,' said Mr Wang, 'but it was a concentration camp at the beginning of the Cultural Revolution because the jail was far too small. So was the theatre, for that matter. There was hardly room to sit, and only a few of the badly injured could lie down. One of them had a broken leg – it was so swollen they couldn't pull his trousers off. There was no lavatory, so the stench was appalling.'

'You were shut up in there yourself?'

'No, I only inspected the place.'

'You inspected it?'

'Visited it, if you prefer. I and my friends had been "subjected to struggle" in Peking, so we'd joined the Red Guards by then. There was a Maxim gun on a table in the middle of the stage, and behind it a youngster maybe sixteen years old. He kept the gun trained on the auditorium while other youngsters sat flanking him with sub-machine-guns on their laps. The people in the auditorium were forbidden to speak. If the boy with the machine-gun saw someone open his mouth, he'd yell, "Shut up, unless you want a bullet in your head!" I asked him what the people had done. He didn't know, but he said, "They're a bad lot, every last one of them. They'd be no loss to the world." One prisoner told me he'd been hauled out of bed at two in the morning – he still didn't know why. He begged me at least to let his family know where he was.'

'And did you?'

'No, I couldn't afford to get involved in a local matter. My Red Guard unit had sent me here to *gen huo* or *da chuan lian* – "light a fire" or "swap experiences". It was a very popular practice at the time. You could get to know the whole country that way. I've never travelled as much as I did in those days.' Little Mr Wang broke off, then added, 'There are other things I could tell you, but I don't know if I should.'

Of course he would – he couldn't stop himself. It was obvious that he hadn't grown up in the People's Republic. Chinese who had were more cautious and discreet.

'Go on,' I said.

'It was a few roads further south,' he began.

'A few blocks south of here would be more idiomatic.'

'Thanks. Anyway, I was walking down the street with three friends from Peking when we saw a crowd of people gathered round a truck. We went over to look. A man on the truck lifted a tarpaulin and showed us two dead bodies. They were the first ones I'd ever seen. They stank, and the heads were – well, it was sickening. The other side had hauled the men out of bed in the middle of the night and marched them off into a field. They were accused of spying on an ammunition dump and ordered to say who else was involved, but they both denied everything. The other side beat them and threatened to bury them alive unless they confessed. When they still refused to talk, they were forced to dig a pit and stand in it. The pit was filled in, first up to their chests, then up to their necks. When they still said nothing, it was filled in completely.

'The dead men's relations gathered round the truck, weeping and wailing. They were old people and children, mostly. According to them, the informer was a neighbour called Liu. Several of the crowd ran off to fetch him. He was hiding, but they found him and dragged him to the truck. He denied the whole thing, naturally, so they punched him and pushed him up against a wall. Some men took off their belts and flogged him. Then they tied him to a telegraph pole and went on flogging him. He swore he was innocent – he screamed and shouted – but nobody took any notice.

'Then a little boy brought a heavy bamboo shoulder-pole – the kind they use for carrying buckets of water. The men took it and beat the prisoner until he passed out and slid down the pole to the ground. Some-one untied him. Most of the crowd were for leaving him there, but a youngster with a Red Guard arm-band shouted, "Chairman Mao says revolution is no embroidery lesson!" Is that the correct translation?'

I nodded.

'So he took the shoulder-pole and beat the unconscious man to death.'

'Didn't you try to stop him?'

Mr Wang shook his head.

'Couldn't you at least have tried?'

'It was too dangerous.'

'But there were four of you.'

'And a hundred or two of the others. Even if they hadn't killed us, they'd certainly have beaten us up. Anyway, I'm not sure if my friends would have lent a hand – we Chinese don't like interfering. Besides, it might have got back to our unit in Peking.' Mr Wang paused. 'Chairman Mao really did say revolution wasn't an embroidery lesson. He said it back in 1927, in his essay on the peasant movement in Hunan.'

I made no comment. Why was he telling me all this? Just for the sake of a German visa?

The street was lined with wooden buildings, none of them more than two storeys high. The shutters were open, so we could see inside. We passed an establishment where sewing machines could be rented by the hour, then a little workshop in which three men were busy fitting wooden handles to mattocks and spades, then a bicycle repair shop. Sacks of chemical fertilizer were untidily stacked in the entrance of another building. There was much conversation but little actual work. Silence reigned only in the sewing-room, where time meant money.

Mr Wang said, 'It's impossible to understand what's going on today unless you know what it was like here during the Cultural Revolution.'

'Impossible for a foreigner, you mean?'

'Very difficult, certainly.'

He was getting it off his chest, I reflected, and only a foreign confidant would do. Perhaps he was right – perhaps you couldn't understand unless you'd actually been there. Unable to help him, I let him run on.

'The shooting had just broken out when our train reached Ichun – artillery as well as everything else – so we waited in the Red Guard office at the station. They brought in a woman who'd also been accused of denouncing someone. The local Red Guards were furious and punched her in the face. When her mouth started bleeding they wrapped her head in a red flag and went on punching her. That continued for half an hour or so. She kept shouting that she was innocent. "She's had enough," I told the Red Guards in the office, "—why not let her go?" They yelled at me. "You're from Peking," they said. "You've no idea what's been going on here. Shut up and mind your own business." So I shut up.

'It wasn't long before the woman shut up too. Once she'd stopped screaming and struggling, they took her by the legs and dragged her outside.'

I continued to look at the shops, but without registering their contents.

'There was nothing to be done,' said Mr Wang. 'Another time I was travelling by train from Peking to Nanking. It was full of Red Guards like me, all on their way to "swap experiences".

'There was an old woman in our compartment. She was being deported to Jiangsu with a placard round her neck stating her name and the crimes she'd committed. She wasn't allowed to take it off. Her husband had been a big landowner before the Liberation. As soon as the purges and the land reform began, they'd bolted to Peking, where her husband opened a little shop. That meant she was guilty twice over: her husband had been a landowner first and then a capitalist.

'They'd deported her for having exploited and oppressed the peasants. Now she was to pay for it by doing hard labour on the land herself. "City life is sweet," as the saying goes, and Peking was to be cleared of criminal elements.

'Whenever Red Guards passed the door they jeered at the old woman, and the rest of the compartment joined in. The most spiteful of all was a girl even smaller than me. The old woman had her hair done up in a – what do you call it?'

'A bun?' I suggested.

'That's right, a bun. Well, the girl grabbed her by the bun and banged her head against the partition – really hard. Then another girl and a couple of boys followed suit, and everyone started punching and slapping her. The first girl emptied the old woman's basket. Then she put it over her head and thumped it hard. Nobody wanted to see the old woman's face, I guess. The girl invited everyone who passed our compartment to give the basket a thump. She was laughing – she found it funny. I moved to the next carriage and stood in the crowded corridor. I didn't see the old woman when we reached Nanking. They'd thrown her out of the window.'

'How terrible. Why?'

'Because she was already dead,' said Mr Wang. Sensing that I found this answer less than satisfactory, he added, 'Perhaps they didn't want any questions asked at Nanking. They needn't have worried – nobody ever questioned Red Guards. Maybe they did it out of sheer high spirits.'

'High spirits?'

'I don't know if you can understand that.'

'Yes,' I said, 'I can. "Nothing is more terrible than man" – the Greeks knew that long ago.'

'But that girl! She couldn't have been more than sixteen by our reckoning – only fifteen by yours.'

'She was human too. But what did she actually have against the old woman? What did people have against the man you were telling me about – the one they beat to death?'

'Well, the old woman was a criminal – everyone knew that because of the placard round her neck – and the man was an informer.'

'But those were only allegations. Besides, there was no need to beat them to death.'

'I know, but people hated them.'

'Why, exactly? What was the source of their hatred?'

I reproduce Mr Wang's reply in condensed form, just as I noted it down at the time:

'It all really started on 25 May 1966, when Nie Yuanzi[1] put up her wall-poster at Peking University. In it she attacked the Party boss and rector of the university for conducting the new criticism campaign too academically and without sufficient drive. Acting on instructions from Kang Sheng, who was one of the worst of the Party leaders, she called on the masses to mobilize.

'When Chairman Mao had the text of Nie Yuanzi's wall-poster published all over the country, we realized that it represented the new official line – that we were expected to attack revisionist elements and counter-revolutionaries. We weren't quite sure who they were, not at first, so we picked on all the teachers we disliked most.'

'You'd joined in yourself by that time?'

'Yes, of course. Little by little, almost all our teachers came under fire. We hauled them in front of mass tribunals and called them to account. They had to stand there with their heads bowed. Sometimes we made them wear paper hats and placards.

'A few of them put up a fight. They were given a hard time and subjected to special treatment. Others came over to our side and denounced their colleagues. There was also a conservative faction that accused us of radicalism. It was utter chaos, but everyone was forced to take sides.

'The same thing happened at Nanchang University, here in Jiangxi

[1] As Party secretary of the Department of Philosophy, Nie Yuanzi was responsible for political guidance, ideological training, and compliance with political guidelines. She had no academic functions or qualifications, but was simply a Party official.

Province. It wasn't the students who launched the campaign – it was the Party, which wanted to mobilize them. Then the movement spread from the students to the workers. Here at Ichun, smallish groups of people met to accuse the local Party leaders of revisionism. The Party leaders fought back and condemned them as rebels. Everyone had to make up his mind. The only way of proving yourself a revolutionary was to join in the struggle between the two "lines" – that was the test of revolutionary sentiment. The conflict intensified when each side started to hold mass meetings. These were disrupted at first by individuals, then by hostile chanting from organized claques. When both sides held rallies on the same day, fighting broke out in the streets. A lot of people cut themselves lengths of the thick bamboo that grows in these parts, three or four feet long, and used them on their opponents. There were many casualties.

'By now, each of the two parties claimed to be revolutionary and described the other as revisionist. It was the same here as in Peking and the rest of the country. We called it "combating the self-styled red flag with the Red Flag". There were lots of wall-posters too, of course, all attacking prominent members of this or that faction. For a while, the two sides fought a running battle with powerful loudspeakers which broadcast their slogans all over town, night and day.

'A new phase opened when the Army came down on the side of the provincial authorities and put its stock of arms and ammunition at their disposal. Then came shootings, abductions, and murders – executions, they were called.

'The rebel faction, which was naturally at a disadvantage without arms, sent delegates to Peking to protest. They were successful. The "Cultural Revolution Supervisory Group", which had effectively replaced the Politburo, decided that the Army at Ichun was backing the wrong side and ordered it to stop. The order came from Jiang Qing and Kang Sheng, but the conservative faction refused to surrender its arms and occupied the Army's ammunition depot.

'At that, forty thousand men from the rebel faction surrounded the depot and presented the defenders with an ultimatum. The ultimatum had just run out when my train pulled into Ichun station. The rebels eventually stormed the depot after bombarding it with mortars obtained from Army stores. Many were killed.'

Having submitted his visa application to the embassy, complete with every conceivable form of testimonial and declaration, Mr Wang called on me in Peking four weeks later. We had tea together.

'You came to China at an inauspicious time,' I said.

'Still, there were times I look back on with pleasure.'

'For instance?'

His reply was unhesitating. 'The first year of the Cultural Revolution.'

'You mean when they docked your hair and your drainpipe trousers?'

'No, after that.'

'When you were sent to Jiangxi Province as a Red Guard liaison man?'

'Yes, but not only to Jiangxi! I got to know nineteen Chinese provinces in that time. You can't imagine what our mood was like. We could suddenly move around – we'd thrown off the shackles of university discipline. Bureaucratic rectors and principals quaked in our presence.

'We spent our evenings sitting in canteens or classrooms. We selected future targets and debated the wording of wall-posters: for instance, whether Professor Hong's misdemeanours should be described merely as "contradictions within the people", whether he was a straightforward royalist, opportunist, or reactionary, or whether the case was more serious and necessitated references to "a conflict between us and the enemy". Whether Professor Qiang should be numbered among the cow-spirits and snake-demons, or whether we should be lenient and attack her solely because she hadn't yet discarded the "Four Olds".[1] Many of our articles were witty, though some were pretty outrageous. On other days we'd hammer out charges to be brought against our teachers at mass meetings or draw caricatures and paste them up on the university walls. You know who I mean by Wang Hairong?'

'Mao's niece, the Vice-Foreign Minister? Yes, but I haven't seen her around for a while.'

'Wang Hairong was bound to vanish quickly, after a meteoric career like hers. She was still doing a special course at the Institute of Foreign Languages when the Cultural Revolution began. A conversation she had with the Chairman became compulsory reading throughout the country. Do you know it? No? I'll send you a copy.[2] The Chairman urged his

---

[1] The 'Four Olds' were: old ideas, old culture, old customs, and old habits.

[2] The following is an excerpt from the conversation:

Wang Hairong: 'We have an official's son who behaves badly. He pays no attention when the teacher speaks. He does no homework. He reads novels. Sometimes he stays in the dormitory and goes on sleeping, and sometimes, when our class or group has a lesson, he doesn't turn up at all. He makes a bad impression on all of us.'

Chairman Mao: 'Don't your teachers allow students to sleep during class or read novels? We should allow them to. Teachers should lecture less and get their students to read more. I believe that the student you mention will one day prove extremely able because he has had the courage to skip your course ... When you return to university you must be the first to rebel. Don't go back to the Institute on Sunday and don't take part in any meetings.'

Wang Hairong: 'I wouldn't dare. It would be an infringement of university discipline.'

niece and all of us to rebel against our universities and their teaching methods. We felt liberated. A lot of what Chairman Mao said about education was closer to the truth than our everyday experience of university life.

'You may find our mood a little hard to understand, but you wouldn't if you'd paid a visit to Tian An Men Square in February 1967. The side streets were plastered with placards and caricatures, poems and proclamations – attacking Liu Shaoqi, for example, or his wife Wang Guangmei, or Deng Xiaoping.

'Columns of students and workers marched through the streets with placards announcing that they'd deposed their superiors and replaced them with revolutionary committees. Fireworks were going off all over the place. It was thrilling, especially for youngsters from the provinces, who congregated at a special rendezvous bureau set up in the square.

'And as for the travelling I told you about! We all travelled free, of course – no tickets or travel permits needed in those days. The trains were so full, many passengers had to perch on the steps outside – some of them even dozed off and fell. The carriages were so crowded I once spent a whole day standing on one leg in the corridor. Another time I had to share the carriage toilet with three friends. The relationship between the sexes was quite different too. I won't go into details, but that was a form of liberation in itself. We won't forget that, any of us. It was a great adventure. There were new things happening all the time, and we were always in high spirits.'

'That's the phrase you used at Ichun, when you told me about the old woman in your compartment – the one who was branded a criminal because her husband had been a landowner and exploited the peasants.'

'Yes,' said Mr Wang, 'I remember. That was the other side of the coin. I can still see that young girl grabbing her by the hair – it was awful, but I already told you: you can't understand what's going on today unless you know what it was like here then.'

'You think it could happen again?'

Mr Wang thought for a moment. 'I don't think so,' he said, 'but I

Chairman Mao: 'Don't worry about that kind of discipline. Just don't go back to the Institute. Simply say you wanted to infringe university discipline.'

Wang Hairong: 'But I can't do that! I'd be criticized.'

Chairman Mao: 'I don't think you'll ever amount to anything. You're afraid of being rebuked for infringing university discipline, afraid of criticism and bad marks. You're scared of being expelled from the university and not admitted to the Party. Why are you frightened of so many things? The worst that can happen is that you get thrown out of the Institute. So what?'

wouldn't rule it out altogether. A lot of people are afraid it might. What do you think?'

'I don't see any pointers in that direction. Once bitten, twice shy – that's my personal forecast. Besides, history seldom repeats itself exactly. When something terrible happens to people, they keep looking over their shoulders. For decades now, foreign journalists have been delving around for signs of a Nazi revival in Germany. It does rear its head here and there within the lunatic fringe, of course, but any genuine threat to our country won't come from that quarter. New threats come from quite a different direction – one that people haven't been watching. I don't think there'll be a repeat performance if Deng Xiaoping is recalled and the leadership remains as united and flexible as it has been till now.'

'You may be right,' said Mr Wang, 'but you're basing your prediction on a whole lot of ifs.'

A Kiss from Jiang Qing

About a year after my conversations with Mr Wang, a young Chinese woman told me of her own experiences at Peking University.

'The disturbances began at the end of May 1966, after Nie Yuanzi had put up her wall-poster. Liu Shaoqi sent so-called working parties to the university to restore order, but on 18 June the situation got out of hand. Teachers who had been seized by their students were flogged, abused, or showered with ink in public. The working parties called a mass meeting and reprimanded the students for unworthy and un-revolutionary conduct.

'A few days later the university received a visit from Jiang Qing. She was accompanied by Chen Boda, who had once been Mao's private secretary and now acted as the Cultural Revolution's ideological interpreter. At another mass meeting, the exalted visitors were asked questions – prearranged questions, naturally. What the students who asked them wanted to know, most of all, was whether the manhandling of their teachers on 18 June had been a revolutionary act, a counter-revolutionary act, or simply a piece of politically neutral barbarism.

'Jiang Qing said nothing, but Chen Boda, after beating about the bush for a while, finally stated that the treatment to which university staff had been subjected did not constitute a counter-revolutionary act. As soon as we heard that, we knew that Mao and a section of the Party leadership not only approved of these outrages but actually wanted them to continue.

'A few weeks later, at the end of July, another big mass meeting was held at the university. Jiang Qing had again turned up and was sitting on the platform. Many students made speeches attacking the leader of Liu Shaoqi's working party. Peng Xiaoming, a seventeen-year-old girl who was still attending Peking University's secondary school, made her mark as a public speaker. She likened the working party to a fire brigade that had come to extinguish the cleansing fire of the Cultural Revolution. Meanwhile, the leader of the working party was compelled to stand beside the platform and listen to this tirade. When Peng Xiaoming had finished, she went over to him, removed her belt, and lashed him across the face with it. He didn't dare defend himself.

'When she had done with him, Jiang Qing summoned her to the platform, where she hugged and kissed her. It was a sign to us that all opponents of the radical line were to be treated as that man had been treated by Peng Xiaoming.'

I said, 'Rather unconventional, wasn't it, hugging and kissing someone in public?'

'Yes,' my Chinese acquaintance agreed, 'but Jiang Qing often acted in an extravagant way – after all, she was a mere actress. That the Chairman thought as she did became clear to us a week or two later, when Lin Biao gave a speech from the Tian An Men terrace. On that occasion, 18 August, a schoolgirl was presented to Chairman Mao. He asked what her name was. Song Binbin, she told him. Binbin is a pretty name meaning educated, refined, and courteous, but Mao said she ought to call herself Yao Wu instead – meaning roughly "Want-Fight". All the newspapers carried Mao's remark next day, which was another clue to what was expected of us.'

'And did the girl call herself Song Yao Wu from then on?'

'Yes, but it turned her head. She went off the rails and started beating people who made no attempt to defend themselves. They say she later did a spell in prison. Anyway, her christening proved her undoing.'

Jesuit Lies?

'No words can describe how ingeniously all things among the Chinese are so disposed, in a manner superior to the laws of other nations and directed towards public tranquillity and orderly human coexistence, that they cause themselves as few inconveniences as possible.' Leibniz based this statement, which he made in 1699, on reports from Jesuit missionaries in Peking. Were the Jesuits lying when they claimed, three hundred years ago, that the Chinese people lived in a state of prestabilized harmony? Were eminent sinologists like Richard Wilhelm, Arthur Waley, and Lin Yutang, that great idealizer and popularizer of the Chinese character, concocting a myth when they described how Chinese notions of harmony influenced the everyday life of Chinese society?

For two thousand years, every educated Chinese was expected to memorize *The Doctrine of the Mean*, a Confucian text. Thus, every schoolboy knew the words: 'Let the states of inner equilibrium and harmony exist in perfection. Then will a happy order prevail throughout heaven and earth, and all things be sustained and flourish.'

Were the Chinese deceiving themselves?

I had seen this 'happy order' for myself in China's rice bowl, though not as a form of prestabilized harmony. It is a system that for ever re-creates itself by adjusting imbalances, not by means of edicts and laws but by mutual consideration – by compromise and agreement on the reception, utilization, and transmission of water.

The cyberneticist would call this cosmos a control system that constantly stabilizes itself by means of negative feedback and cyclical adjustment. Elements disruptive of symbiosis within such a close-knit system are swiftly diverted by regulators and reduced to harmless proportions. This process fully corresponds to that employed by nature itself, which may be why the rice-field landscape resembles a cosmos in its own right. Individual freedom exists within this control system only insofar as it does not disrupt the whole.

We assume that there is something of the rebel – the Prometheus – in every human being. We carefully note the bounds set on freedom and are alive to the liberties the individual lacks. Why should members of the people's communes be happier and better balanced than those who enjoy the greater freedom of our own towns and cities? Perhaps because they concentrate less on the freedom they lack than on the freedom they possess and the opportunities open to them. Their system offers little scope to Promethean personalities, who are quickly cut down to size or removed. The Chinese have never philosophized about freedom. It is only now, after one or two earlier attempts, that freedom – and political freedom in particular – is becoming a burning issue, though only among students and intellectuals. If it spread to the countryside, that debate might have an explosive effect and destroy the control system mentioned above.

The system, it should be said, is far more vulnerable and less effective than it appears. It cannot control everything. Individual Chinese may adapt themselves more easily to society, but they, too, look for ways of cheating the system. They are not exempt from selfishness, passion, cupidity, and envy.

The system tends to produce superficial harmony by shelving awkward decisions. It glosses over problems or sweeps them under the carpet for the sake of an outward accord that will save the face of all parties. Grit gets into the works, causing the system to run hot. Alternatively, it is put out of gear by clumsy official intervention – the Great Plan, for example – and grinds to a halt altogether. These breakdowns have occurred quite often. China has seen many more rebellions in her time than the West, and there have been groups of Chinese in every period who preferred to quit the system – to 'drop out' and live in isolation like the bandits of the Liangshan moors in the novel *Water Margin*.

Sinologists of the French school have never attached much importance to these notions of harmony. Like Wittfogel's, theirs is a picture of a society groaning under laws and instruments of authority wielded by Chinese bureaucrats. They bemoan the lot of a people doomed to subjection by 'a hierarchic, authoritarian, paternalistic, and tyrannical state, a polypoid welfare state, a totalitarian Moloch of a state' – one alleged to have exercised 'complete control over all the activities of social life' and 'absolute authority at every level' (Balacz). This is an exaggeration. Did these eminent scholars spend all their time in China poring over dusty tomes? Did they never see how the Chinese actually live and come to terms with each other? Would they care to suggest how any country as big as China can be governed except by a centralized, bureaucratic administrative system? If scholars of the future were to judge our own way of life solely by laws, statutory provisions, and complaints of undue government intervention, they would form a lamentable picture of our everyday existence and wonder how we managed to breathe at all in such a stifling atmosphere.

Although Chinese bureaucrats have often been in the ascendant during the past two thousand years, or since the founding of the Han dynasty, the Chinese in general suffered more when administrative collapse brought anarchy, disorder, and the law of the jungle in its train. Realistic Chinese fiction teaches us that, even when it was corrupt and oppressive, the bureaucracy provided a minimum of security.

Government authority in China does indeed extend to every sphere of social life, and never in Chinese history has the bureaucracy been as powerful and overdeveloped as it is today. In earlier times, by contrast, civil servants were surprisingly thin on the ground. In the middle of the last century they numbered no more than thirty thousand, or one to every fifteen thousand inhabitants. In Germany we have one to twenty-seven. Urban and rural administration, together with the numerous functions which our Western governments needlessly usurp and regard as their prerogative, used in China to be undertaken by guild-like associations, local corporations, or groups of families. The Chinese have always been good at detecting areas of freedom and making themselves at home in them, especially in the towns, and at finding shelter in professional organizations, fraternities, and family units. Evidence of their bustling and cheerful urban existence can be found, not only in the accounts left by Marco Polo and Ibn Batuta, but in the Sung dynasty's urban monographs and attractive genre paintings.

The Jesuits described a country that was better administered during the seventeenth and eighteenth centuries than Europe. Modern critics charge them with ignoring the less admirable characteristics of the emperors they praised so highly. This may be true, but it is possible that their standards of comparison were based on certain contemporary European monarchs or ecclesiastical dignitaries. Beside them, Chinese emperors like Kangxi (Kang Hsi) or Qianlong (Chi'en Lung) must have seemed doubly impressive and regal figures.

The Jesuits gave an accurate description of China's prevailing scale of values, national and local institutions, and principles of government. They told the truth, just as Pericles told the truth about Athens in his oration for the dead in 430 BC, and as Polybius told the truth about Rome. They and other seventeenth- and eighteenth-century observers saw the world through eyes different from ours. They still believed in grand designs, still hoped for the establishment of a just world order and felt confident that this goal would be attained as man progressed. Our own eyes are focused mainly on the thwarting of grand designs by man's inadequacy.

It is true that the Jesuits omitted to describe how people in China failed to fulfil their country's commandments. Although they must have been aware that human weakness existed there, they saw no reason to labour and illustrate this obvious fact because it would only have undermined their position in the 'ritual dispute' with opponents in Rome.

The picture they transmitted to the West was incomplete, because it failed to reveal how often this system based on harmony had collapsed, burying millions of people in the process. It is nonetheless remarkable that, whenever major rebellions broke out and dynasties fell, the Chinese were often quick to construct a new system closely akin to the old, complete with new checks and balances.

Then Mao appeared on the scene. Progress was his Promethean goal, not stability. Mao aspired to permanent revolution, not harmony. He called on people to back the proletarian-revolutionary line and combat the bourgeois-revisionist. Only these two lines existed, and the conflict between them did not admit of neutrals or spectators. Those who blew neither hot nor cold were Laodiceans, to be spewed out of the nation's collective mouth. Anyone who invoked *The Doctrine of the Mean* was an enemy of progress, whose sole source of nourishment was revolutionary conflict. Strife between the two lines was the father of all things, but everyone had to decide for himself which was the correct or revolutionary line. Such was the touchstone of revolutionary consciousness. The only certainty was that the correct line could not be one that aspired to a life of harmonious concord like 'an embroidery lesson'. The correct line was the one prepared to undertake the most radical social changes in the most radical manner; the true revolutionaries were those who hated.

Mao's power had steadily declined since the failure of the Great Leap Forward. The Politburo no longer followed his lead, and derisive articles about him appeared in the press. From the early 1960s onward, policy had been increasingly determined by Liu Shaoqi and Deng Xiaoping.

Then he gave the signal for the Cultural Revolution. On 26 July 1966, he swam the Yangtze to show that he was still hale enough to do battle. He mobilized the young against the Peking authorities who were keeping the nation at work, quietly and steadily, and trying to thrust him, the prickly idealist, aside. He later preened himself on an idea new to the revolutionary textbook. 'Bombard the headquarters!' was the slogan of the wall-poster published at his behest. He impaled the nation on the horns of a dilemma – stirred up a spring tide that carried him back into power. Was the reacquisition of power his real motive for launching a cataclysm that claimed hundreds of thousands, maybe millions, of lives?

On 25 October 1966, during a closed session at Party Headquarters, he declared:

The Great Cultural Revolution has brought devastation in its wake. It is not surprising that many comrades have yet to recognize its significance. Although it has not long been in progress, it has tremendous momentum. The Peking University wall-poster had scarcely been published when the entire nation rose to its feet. Red Guards were on the move throughout the country even before the letter to them was published. You, too, are experiencing the full force of the spring tide. Being responsible for this havoc, I can hardly blame you for grumbling at it. I kindled the Cultural Revolution of the past five months . . . Previously, you concerned yourselves with industry, agriculture, and communications, but not with the Great Cultural Revolution. The same went for the Foreign Ministry and the Military Commission. What you never expected has now occurred. In my view, this spring tide is a good thing. Brains that have not thought for years will have to start thinking again under the impact of this tidal wave. At the worst, it was only a mistake.

The Soul of Shanghai

I revisited Shanghai a few days ago.

The city's outer shell was as it had been forty years ago, when I went there for the first time, but its soul – or whatever Shanghai may have possessed in the way of one – had fled. This is assumed to have happened when the communists occupied the city in 1949, or possibly one night a little earlier, when Chiang Kai-shek's National Government cordoned off the Bund with ultra-reliable troops and emptied the banks of their bullion. By the glare of headlights, the gold was carried across the Bund to ships berthed alongside and taking on cargo for Taiwan.

I doubt if Shanghai's soul went to heaven. The odds are that it headed in the opposite direction. That's where the action is, so rumour has it, and that – if presented with a choice – is where Shanghai's soul would have opted to go. It wasn't the utterly evil and vicious soul celebrated by sea shanties in the last century and popular songs in the early decades of our own. Its besetting sin was an excessive preoccupation with money. Safe in the knowledge that the city would wink at whatever they did – especially if there was a percentage in it – the rich of Shanghai exploited their wealth to the full.

Much that went on there was reprehensible, true, but a youngster of twenty-one doesn't immediately or invariably look for moral tone in the girl of his fancy – he tends to be swayed by other aspects of her person. Ensnared before he knows it, he accepts her as she is. Everything about her seems beautiful, even the flowers of evil whose scent intoxicates him most of all.

She is gone now, this seductive if less than immaculate oriental beauty – where to, we have already surmised – but why not describe her as she was in the heyday so few can remember?

Nanking Road, forty years ago . . . This, the city's main commercial thoroughfare, runs off the Bund at right angles and later becomes Bubbling Well Road. It is a relatively narrow street, with few buildings more than six or seven storeys high. Rickshaws by the hundred thread their way through a seething mass of humanity. The rickshaw coolies, who have bulb-operated horns on their shafts, toot incessantly. Nobody takes any notice, so they clear a path for themselves by shouting. The traffic policemen are white-uniformed, white-turbaned Sikhs with well-groomed black beards cocooned in hairnets. They do their best to keep things moving, but who cares? Certainly not the baker's boy. By some incredible feat of equilibrium, he cycles through the throng with one hand balancing a tray of oven-fresh cakes above his head and the other devoted to handlebars and bell. He is singing an operatic aria, and Chinese singers habitually shut their eyes when performing in the upper register. A Gurkha stands sentinel outside a jeweller's shop, his bushy beard as fearsome a sight as the kukri in his belt and the sub-machine-gun slung across his body. Discreetly escorted by her bodyguard, an elegant Chinese *femme du monde* emerges from the shop attired in a green cheong-sam slit far above the knee. She gladdens the eye as she boards her limousine. The bodyguard shuts the door and climbs in beside the chauffeur.

You can buy anything in Nanking Road, even without producing money. A foreigner from the West enjoys unlimited credit. You have to pay by cheque at the twenty-storey Wing On Department Store, but elsewhere you merely give your home or business address and sign the *chit*, or bill. At the end of the month or on pay-day, a date known to every shopkeeper, the *shroff* turns up, presents your *chit*, and collects his due. You are well advised to pay up. If you don't, the *shroff* will convey this fact to your boss or advertise it among your compatriots at the club. Shanghai withholds her favours from the insolvent. They must either borrow or clear out.

Only the *taipan*, the foreign business tycoon, counts in Shanghai. Politicians, generals, academics, artists, film actresses – none of these are revered in the same way. People speak with awe of the firm a *taipan* owns or manages, of his large house, his army of servants, his expensive wife and her jewellery, his Eurasian or White Russian mistress, his business deals and connections. Not of his collections. What should he collect in China – Chinese art? Certainly not. If anything, postage stamps. Postage stamps are not only valuable but portable.

Expatriate society is a superficial world dedicated to only one thing other than money: the dogged and unremitting pursuit of pleasure. It's amazing how much pleasure you can take without gagging on it.

At night you frequent bars, clubs, or cinemas showing the latest Hollywood movies. Or parties. Female party-goers discuss clothes, servants, and the curious ways of the Chinese. They also engage in coast gossip – the latest society tittle-tattle on the Dairen–Hong Kong circuit – and talk about money. Their menfolk talk about money too.

Weekends are a time to forgather at country clubs or the race track. Although greyhound racing is considered *infra dig.*, you can indulge in it once in a while. Visitors from home get taken to gambling dens patronized mainly by Chinese, or to opium dens where most of them feel sick after the first puff. There is a wide range of diversions for bachelors, from the comparatively respectable dance halls where Chinese, White Russian, or Eurasian girls dream of capturing a client, if not for life, at least for a nice long time, to the grosser delights of waterfront bars and brothels.

Shanghai is big-hearted and broad-minded except when it comes to casinos. In response to protests, these have been banished to Hungjao, beyond the boundaries of the International Settlement. Nobody minds where or how else you enjoy yourself as long as you don't harm your firm's reputation. Reputation matters in Shanghai. The merchandise you deal in may be suspect and your source of income shady, but contracts – even unwritten ones – are kept come what may. *Chop* is the term for your trademark and your firm's good name. No one who sullies his *chop* will ever do business again with a Chinese merchant. Your *chop* is sacrosanct.

The people of Shanghai are tolerant in other respects, even towards crime. Their city used to be a battlefield contested by two rival gangs, the Reds and the Greens. Now that the Greens have triumphed, crime in Shanghai is organized. Anyone requiring protection pays the Greens a retainer. The banks, which maintain small private armies of their own, turn into fortresses overnight when the Shanghai police go on strike. Artillery would be needed to take them, but the Greens harbour no such intention. Their joint 'bosses', Mr Du and Mr Huang, hold seats on the boards of three major banks. One of them, who used to head the CID in the French Concession, even has a street named after him. The *taipans* chuckle at this, satisfied that all is as it should be.

Shanghai is an extraterritorial treaty port wrested from China after the Opium War. The British and Americans call the tune in the International Settlement, the French Consul General in the French Concession. The British, French, Americans, Germans, and Russians represent only a tiny minority – a few tens of thousands in the midst of four million Chinese.

The white minority have no cultural needs that cannot be met by Hollywood movies. To the Chinese, however, Shanghai is an intellectual and cultural metropolis. Chinese literature, theatre, opera, cinema – all these flourish here. Shanghai means freedom, even to the communists who founded their party in the French Concession in 1921.

The white minority pay no heed to local developments. Doing good business with the Chinese doesn't even entail dealing with them personally; that can be delegated to the native office help known as *comprador*. The millions of Chinese in Shanghai can think, say, write, and do as they please. The foreigners in their midst consider it unimportant, and are doomed to persist in that attitude until overtaken by events.

Shanghai's soul has departed, leaving behind only a memory of those colourful days. It was an amiable soul, despite its preoccupation with money and pleasure. It enjoyed all that life had to offer and can surely have no regrets, even in its present abode. The shell it abandoned has been occupied by another soul.

'Should anyone succeed by dint of administrative measures in making the poor rich and the rich poor, then will the country be strong,' declared Shang Yang in the fourth century BC. In the new Shanghai of 1949, the communists began by expelling any of the rich who had not fled in time. The rich presented little difficulty, but the poor were another matter. Since poverty could not be eliminated, it was dealt out to all in roughly equal shares. Nanking Road is just as crowded as it used to be. Though not as colourful, the crowds are more so than in Peking. Shanghai's inhabitants are noisier and laugh more readily than their fellow countrymen in the north. The jewellers' shops and furriers have gone, but the department stores are better stocked than in other communist countries and the goods on display of generally better quality. They may be expensive, but people can live – if not in style, in tolerable comfort.

Karl Marx in Wuhan

November

It was a few years ago, at a hunting breakfast under canvas. I was seated on the left of Nicolae Ceausescu, President, Party leader, and incumbent of every other senior post in Romania apart from those entrusted to members of his family. After he had given me his views on Radio Free Europe's news broadcasts and I had given him mine on freedom of speech and information, he changed the subject. Rather than allow them to become completely impoverished, he was subsidizing industry in Maramuresh and other unfavourably situated districts on the Romanian–Soviet border. 'That's the way we do things under socialism,' he said. 'It wouldn't happen in a system like yours, where capital is invested solely with an eye to profit.'

I enlightened him on our own subsidization of regions bordering on East Germany, and told him he was much mistaken if he equated our free market economy with the sort of capitalism Marx had in mind.

'Granted,' said Ceausescu. 'Comrade Soviet Ambassador, Comrade Chinese Ambassador,' he called across the table, 'listen a minute! If Karl Marx came back to life today, I swear he'd completely rewrite *Das Kapital*.'

Ambassador Drozdyenko grimaced as if to say that nothing in Romania would surprise him. He raised his glass of *tsuika*, the local plum brandy, and sang out '*No rok!*' – a toast that absolved him from commenting on Ceausescu's hypothesis. Ambassador Lin of China made the interpreter translate it twice but said nothing, just sipped discreetly at his glass of mineral water.

Karl Marx never saw the inside of a factory – or only once, very briefly, on his way to take the waters at Marienbad – and was uninterested in getting to know the workers, whom he referred to as 'louts'. I wished, all the same, that he could have accompanied me to Wuhan to see the big continuous casting plant and cold-rolling mill being built there by a German consortium. More particularly, I wished he could have talked to the workers.

Wuhan stands beside the Yangtze, some four hundred and fifty miles inland but accessible to ocean-going ships of modest tonnage, and is a landmark in the history of the Chinese labour movement. It was the disturbances there in 1911 that led to the fall of the last imperial dynasty. In the 1920s Wuhan became the seat of the revolutionary government. During the Cultural Revolution and until very recently, 'political unrest' there had been such that, when I proposed to visit the place, the Foreign Ministry twice conveyed that my visit would be 'inconvenient' – to the Chinese authorities, of course.

Our sixty German technicians and fitters lived outside the city limits in Hotel No. IV. I did not see Hotels I to III, but No. IV was a modern multi-storeyed building with a spacious lobby, large, airy dining-rooms, numerous bedrooms, and a few small suites. Several floors were reserved for German personnel and several for the Japanese who were constructing a hot-rolling mill nearby. The Germans' tour of duty was six months or a year, though some of them had been there much longer. They earned good money and had little to spend it on, so a large proportion of their income could be salted away. Many of them had brought their wives and children. They lived out here in the plains, some distance from the city. The only way of getting to Wuhan was by bus, but they rarely visited it. Nothing worthwhile went on there. It was all Chinese.

But no matter. German firms being mindful of their employees' welfare and morale, a married couple named Kunde had been engaged to look after them. They themselves occupied four small but pleasantly furnished rooms, of which one served as an office. Frau Kunde did her own cooking because she and her husband, who were all for home comforts, preferred not to eat in the communal dining-room. Groceries could be purchased right next door at the well-stocked Friendship Store, which was reserved for the use of hotel residents.

The Germans had recently complained that only pork was on sale at the meat counter. The Chinese promised to ring the changes. They kept their word, but again the Germans complained: the meat tasted odd. The Chinese were puzzled. 'But dog meat's so good in winter,' they said. '—very warming. We had a hard job getting it. Dog meat's always scarce at this time of year.' So it was back to pork again.

We enjoyed an excellent Chinese meal in the dining-room, but studied the menu closely to be sure we got pork. Herr Kunde showed us round the spotless modern kitchen and the bar, where residents could dance as well as drink. In the grounds were a small practice football field and a huge inflated tent containing a tennis court. The big swimming pool nearby had been drained for the winter, but the ultra-modern bowling alley was in use every afternoon. Special slippers had to be worn to avoid scratching the parquet. We might have been in the home of some German *Hausfrau* in Swabia, not in central China.

Also in the grounds, between the hotel and the sports tent, was a modest basketball court. 'For the Japanese workers,' explained Herr Kunde. 'Their consortium installed it. Even the Japanese like a little recreation sometimes.'

'Is that all they've got?' I asked. 'Yes,' I was told, 'but they seem happy enough.'

The German consortium had even run to a school, complete with one teacher of each sex. The children were divided into two mixed classes, one six and the other seven strong. They could learn anything the teachers knew, including Latin, French, and chess. I inspected the school a trifle enviously, hoping that we would succeed in establishing one of our own at the embassy in Peking. We eventually did, though we never aspired to an inflatable tennis court or an electronic bowling alley. I yearned to take Karl Marx on a tour of Hotel No. IV. It would have been interesting to discuss his theory of impoverishment and the exploitation of labour under capitalism.

We travelled by bus to the site of the steel mill, which was visible from a long way off. Everything had been designed on a colossal scale. The 'sheds' were five or six hundred yards long and several hundred yards wide. The steel combine was managed by a revolutionary committee. Its chairman, who showed us round in person, strove to explain why work was nearly a year behindhand. He blamed it all on the Gang of Four. The German supervisors confirmed this but pointed out that the Gang of Four had been behind bars for more than a year. Productivity had risen, they said, but was still far from uniformly good.

I turned to the head of the revolutionary committee. 'Wages were supposed to be increased throughout the country on 1 October. Bonuses were to be paid for higher output. Wherever appropriate, you were going over to piecework. *Have* wages been increased here?'

'Not yet,' I was told, 'but they will be, backdated to 1 October. Anyway, political consciousness matters more than material incentives. Productivity won't increase until we get that right.'

This hoary argument, which dated from the time of the Gang of Four, had long since gone out of fashion in Peking. Hearing it reminded me that we were in the provinces.

A German technician who was installing a modern electronic control system expressed satisfaction with his Chinese assistants. He introduced them – three inconspicuous figures in blue dungarees. 'There's nothing they can't get the hang of,' he said. 'I've never worked with keener or more intelligent types.'

'What about all this complex wiring?'

'It's child's play to them. They keep the conduits absolutely dust-free, too. I'd like to take them home with me.'

In the next shed we found twenty or thirty men sitting around on crates, talking.

'They're improving their political consciousness,' the German supervisor told me. 'That's *kaihui* – political instruction.'

'They also play cards sometimes,' said a German technician in our party. '*Kaihui* usually happens three times a week.'

When questioned, the man from the revolutionary committee looked faintly embarrassed and told us that these classes would be less frequent in future.

The German supervisor elaborated. 'Under the Gang of Four, fifty per cent or more of the workforce used to sit around doing nothing – if they turned up at all. That's the only reason we're running late. The Chinese know it too. Workers undergoing *kaihui* in the old days used to be urged not to work so hard. Tell them the opposite now, and how successful are we likely to be? The "iron rice bowl" mustn't be broken, so they get paid whether they work or not. They *can* work, all the same. They did a better and far quicker job on the foundations of this plant than we're used to back home.'

'It's the same with the peasants in the communes,' I said. 'The majority are hard-working. They slave away from dawn to dusk, especially on their private plots.'

A Chinese worker was perched on a concrete pipe, eating rice and vegetables out of a bowl. I sat down beside him while the German supervisor and the chairman of the revolutionary committee discussed an administrative problem.

The worker, whose name was Zhang, described his daily routine to me. He rose at half past four while his wife made breakfast and prepared the cooked rice and vegetables he took to work in his dinner-pail. At half past five he set off for the bus that dropped him at the gates of the construction site. Meanwhile, his wife did the household chores, woke their two children, and took them to school before catching her own bus to the stocking factory where she worked. Zhang had been out of luck again today. The first bus was full and didn't stop. The second he failed to board because there were too many people ahead of him. The third offered standing room only. Zhang got to work well after seven o'clock. It had been raining, and because the Chinese had ignored their German technicians' advice to begin by constructing roads on the site, it took him twenty minutes to toil through the mud to his shed. Work should have started at seven, but only half the shift arrived on time. The German technicians were always punctual. They rolled up in a special bus at five to seven.

Zhang was allowed a one-hour lunch break in which to eat his rice and vegetables. After lunch he usually stretched out on a crate and grabbed some sleep. When work stopped at four o'clock he would have to trek back through the mud to the bus stop. There were buses in plenty, but the queue for them was invariably hundreds of yards long. Tempers often flared up despite the presence of supervisors, whose job it was to ensure that no one stole a march on his neighbours. By half past five Zhang would be on board a bus, standing as before and barely able to breathe because of the crush. The bus regularly got stuck in the traffic jam on the Yangtze and Han bridges. Although a few passengers left it there, he never seemed to get a seat.

I followed up my visit to the steel mill by paying a courtesy call on Li Fuxian, deputy chairman of the revolutionary committee of Hubei

Province, which has roughly forty-five million inhabitants. He, too, believed that intensified revolutionary consciousness was the key to eliminating arrears of work on the steel mill. He, too, argued that the Gang of Four had done a lot of mischief locally.

'Take the buses here in Wuhan,' he said. 'For a long time, there was no glass in the windows.'

I inquired the reason.

'Many people blamed it on young hooligans,' he told me, using the Anglo-Irish loan-word in currency throughout the communist world, 'but it wasn't quite like that. The culprits, I regret to say, were disorderly workers incited by supporters of the Gang of Four. When they couldn't board a bus at the end of the day, they simply smashed the windows and climbed in. Wuhan didn't have a single bus with its windows intact for months.

'The workers are less restive now. We replaced the windows and obtained fifty more buses, but even they aren't enough. We're awaiting another consignment. Meantime, we hope the supervisors will prevent a recurrence of trouble.'

'Some of them are armed with batons.'

'That I consider wrong,' said Li Fuxian. 'Our aim is to convince the workers by reasoned argument, but I'm afraid it's going to take time. The poison in their minds runs deep.'

It did indeed. Outside the steel mill, not far from the bus stop, stood a large, white-painted statue of Mao resembling a plaster cast. One morning as they were driving to work, our German technicians – and, of course, any Chinese workers who passed the spot – noticed that someone had hurled a bucket of red paint into the Chairman's face.

Zhang leaves his place of work at half past five but does not get home till half past seven or eight. After standing throughout the bus journey, he is tired. He is tired in the morning, tired at work. He works six days a week. Monday is Zhang's rest day, Wednesday his wife's. Whoever has the day off cleans the house, looks after the children, does the washing, and goes shopping. There are no vacations, but Zhang and his wife do get another seven days off a year: one each at New Year and on 1 May, three at the Spring Festival in February, and two to mark the country's National Day at the beginning of October. And so it goes on, year in, year out.

Zhang earns 55 yüan a month. His wife earns 35. They are saving up for a bicycle so that his wife can cycle to her factory and not be dependent on buses. A bicycle costs 160 yüan (£48), or almost twice their combined monthly income.

Zhang and his wife go to bed at about half past nine, each as exhausted as the other. A socialist fairy-tale would add that they are tired but proud and happy at not being exploited, like foreign technicians, by capitalist bosses. But this is not a socialist fairy-tale. I suspect that, if Karl Marx were to drop in on him one evening, Zhang might be tempted to ask some pertinent questions about proletarian poverty under capitalism and the happiness of workers in socialist countries. But then, he probably wouldn't dare to come out with them.

1978

1978

Oil Wells and Amazons

We had travelled all night by sleeper. At dawn the train pulled up beside an open platform. We were in the midst of a broad plain, flat and desolate for as far as the eye could see. This was the Shengli oilfield in Shandong Province, not far from Tsingtao. It had a population in excess of two hundred thousand people, but where were they? All we could see in the distance was an administration building.

Nothing grew here apart from sporadic clumps of coarse grass. The land, which had degenerated into steppe, was mottled with white patches of potash and salt.

Asphalt roads traversed this expanse, sometimes flanked by depots or rows of single-storeyed houses, sometimes unrelieved by anything for miles on end. Oil pumps dotted the landscape, all nodding as though permanently in agreement. There was no incentive to linger, even for a moment – nothing beautiful or even ugly. Here and there we sighted mounds of earth, some conical and others already flattened by the elements. The stones on top identified them as graves, but why there? Why not a hundred yards to the left or right? Who lay buried beneath these mounds? One might be close to a storage depot, another a few paces beyond it, another out in the middle of the plain, a long way from the road. It was as though someone had pointed to various spots at random and said, 'There!'

There were no mature villages here, not even a few successive rows of houses. This was nobody's home, but it produced a lot of oil. We were shown everything, not forgetting the Women's Brigade. All such units have since been disbanded, but in 1978 they still existed. Their purpose was to rear a female version of the New Man, a creature whose needs were minimal and whose sole aim in life was to serve the Party.

The eighty girls lived in huts built round a sandy quadrangle. Their average age was twenty, it seemed, and all were obeying Mao's injunction to the female sex to 'support half the sky'. Two of them came walking across the quadrangle, hand in hand. Like the rest, they wore a unisex outfit comprising slacks, jacket, and peaked cap. Our first port of call was a room where eighty rifles were kept in racks, one for every member of the brigade.

For defence against whom? My question evoked no smiles. The rifles were their military equipment, the girls informed us gravely. Presumably for use in the class struggle.

We toured the barrack rooms, each of which housed eight beds. On them, knitting or doing crochet work, sat girls who had just come off duty. Beneath each bed was an enamel basin, and beside it lay a straw suitcase, the sole repository for personal belongings. Against the wall stood a table with half a dozen books on it, all bound in red. I didn't bother to examine them – they had to be by the late Chairman. There were no lockers, no pictures apart from a photograph of Mao, no flowers, and no bedside lamps, just a couple of naked bulbs suspended from the ceiling. Once again, there was nothing that might have induced one to linger – nothing either beautiful or ugly. All the girls looked the same: identically serious.

The classroom, which doubled as a dining-room, was furnished with benches. The kitchen was deserted save for a girl seated at the table slicing radishes. *Mantou* was being steam-baked in the oven. Together with the radishes, this would constitute the brigade's next meal.

The girls were not employed as ordinary workers. They were called on only in cases of emergency – for example, to deal with a fractured valve or pipe.

We drove out to a derrick where three girls were busy replacing a length of buckled pipe. They moved more gracefully than men and looked quite attractive in their dungarees and grey-blue, rather oversized hard hats. As they raised the pipe and heaved it into position, they looked like US Marines raising the Stars and Stripes over Iwo Jima. Once the pipe was vertical, they gently and gingerly lowered it into the borehole.

Later they would be driven back to their quarters for a meal of *mantou* and radishes. And then? What did they do in their spare time? They could lovingly clean and oil their rifles and put them away again. And then? Go for a walk along the asphalt ribbon that stretched across the desolate plain? Count the number of paces between one telegraph pole and the next, or trudge across country, through salt-stained sand and clumps of sea holly, to the nearest grave? But what else? They knitted. They crocheted. They read aloud from the works of Chairman Mao. They attended political education classes and responded to questions with stereotyped answers learned by rote. To the outsider, they gave every appearance of being a sworn sorority of Amazons.

Yet no aspect of this picture, I feel sure, was authentic. It was just as spurious as the world-famous photograph of the heroes of Iwo Jima. True, the girls were entitled to feel proud. Out there in the wilds, they were supporting half the sky as Mao had ordained. They had shown the opposite sex a thing or two. But how long could pride sustain them? How long could they subsist on it, for instance on that one free, frightful day in the week when half the sky was being supported by others? How often did they quarrel with their room-mates? How strong was the communal pressure on an individual girl to steel herself for heroic endeavour?

The Chinese are born under such pressure, granted. They are made of sterner stuff and can endure more hardship than the average Westerner, but not indefinitely. How big was the turnover in the Women's Brigade? How often did a heroine crack under stress? Were these the New Man's female counterparts?

I don't believe it. Heroism is a scarce commodity. Subsequent investigation has shown that some of the most celebrated heroes of labour were guilty of overstating their production figures. Far be it from me to suspect these Amazons of such a thing, but the fact remains that they were deceiving themselves and us. They were playing a heroic role. That can be exhilarating for a while, but for ever? To the bitter end?

How long was it before they wearied of their heroic but husbandless, childless, homeless existence in the wilds? Or did they remain here for good, until buried in the grave that awaited them somewhere, sometime, in the surrounding steppe? Was this their new home? What did they think of while drifting off to sleep? What did they dream of at night? Revolution? Home? Derricks? Or lengths of pipe rearing into the sky and sliding gently into the ground?

The Revolution Betrayed?

Mid-August

I had just returned from leave. Peter Hauswedell, my adviser on the domestic political scene, brought me an article that had appeared during my absence in every major newspaper. He apologized for its length but urged me to read it.

The foreign experts who assisted the Chinese with their external propaganda were in turmoil, it seemed. Agitated meetings had taken place at the Friendship Hotel on the outskirts of Peking where they lived, and some of them had initially refused to help translate the piece on the grounds that it was riddled with revisionism.

The article, which had appeared on 24 June, was somewhat unappetizingly entitled 'A Basic Principle of Marxism. The Radical Reversal of Theory and Practice by Lin Biao and the Gang of Four.' The author had signed himself 'A Special Commentator', which meant that his message came from the Politburo itself.

The article's importance was beyond dispute, because it signalled a turning point in China's political aims and methods. Deng Xiaoping, whose hand was detectable throughout, had clearly sold his programme to the Politburo. My detailed report to Bonn was headed: 'Is China betraying the Revolution?'

The key sentences of the article sounded far from sensational to non-Chinese ears. They boiled down to an assertion that a political theory or 'line' could be correct only if borne out in practice:

'Practical results will show whether the line promotes the development of productive forces and is conducive to socialism and the interests of the masses. This is the sole criterion of the correctness or incorrectness of the said line.'

In other words, the development of productive forces took precedence over socialism. Marxist theory, the article went on, was 'a science but not a fetish.

'Theories are not immutable, eternal truths. They are amplified, revised, enriched, and developed by practice.' Some comrades could be heard to ask: 'If we put practice before all else and regard it as the sole criterion, where does that leave the ideas and pronouncements of Mao Zedong?' To this the article replied that Mao himself had called practice the sole criterion. Besides, it was wrong to fabricate a kind of religion out of Mao Zedong's ideas and worship Marxism-Leninism like a religious dogma. Revising obsolete principles in the light of current circumstances was not only necessary but normal and unavoidable. This was especially true at crucial junctures in history.

The article disclaimed any intention of renouncing Marxism-Leninism and 'Maozedongideas'. [1] On the other hand, all such ideas should naturally be tried out in practice. They had not passed the test once and for all.

The author was doubtless sincere in his oft-reiterated assertion that China would adhere to socialism as a matter of course. The only question

---

[1] Someone had persuaded the Chinese that, by amalgamating these words in foreign-language publications, they would metamorphose them into a system like Marxism. Maozedongideas, it should be added, are not just Mao's ideas but 'the crystallization of the collective wisdom of the Chinese Communist Party'.

was, what exactly *were* socialism, communism, and Maozedongideas? According to this article, the ideological system contained no fixed points from which to answer these questions. Neither Marx nor Lenin nor Mao could determine what was good and communistic; that was the function of practice alone, whose chief criterion was greater productivity.

The article mentioned that opposition to the principle of testing theories in practice did exist. This it simplistically ascribed to mental laziness and self-interest on the part of a few individuals.

Keeping our ears to the ground, we learned that the article was being debated nationwide, both at public meetings and in private. Some thought it pointed the way to a modern society, others feared that China would now embark on a revisionist course and betray the Revolution. Veteran Party officials were especially perturbed by this novel and different approach, for Marxism-Leninism and Mao's pronouncements had always been a rock on which to build. The words themselves were always quotable; only their interpretation called for care. Intellectuals, on the other hand, felt relieved. Already benefiting from the new course as it was, they hailed the article as a charter of liberation. The Age of Enlightenment must have seemed equally liberating to many eighteenth-century intellectuals and equally disconcerting to the devout. Yesterday the Party had smiled on those who merely waved Chairman Mao's Little Red Book; today, people who 'fabricated a kind of religion out of Maozedongideas' were branded as professional counter-revolutionaries. The mentally lazy would not be alone in finding it hard to reorient themselves.

Chinese friends and acquaintances in senior positions were candid about the difficulties they foresaw. Peasants and workers, who were used to adopting a practical approach, would be the easiest to convince. Not so the provincial officials who had built their careers on time-honoured slogans and thought that their faith in them was ideologically sufficient. Hardest of all to handle would be the lost generation – the young people who had grown up during the Cultural Revolution and learned nothing but political catchwords and Utopian ideas.

Middle-ranking officials in the provinces obstructed the transition to a new era like boulders on a mountain path. Many of them formed close-knit and deeply entrenched groups of local functionaries and powerful bosses who feared that a fresh wind would expose things far more damning than the mere fact of their entrenchment.

Hauswedell doubted if Chairman Hua Guofeng approved of the article. I disputed this, arguing that it would never have been printed at all without the Politburo's say-so. Hua himself had called for the modernization of China and re-established the Academy of Social Sciences, which was teeming with new ideas. All I doubted, given his predilection for consensus rather than controversy, was whether he approved of the article's trenchant language. I learned years later that Hauswedell was right, and that Hua Guofeng had opposed its publication.

Of one thing, however, there could be no doubt: Deng Xiaoping was the new development's driving force and prime mover. Hua shared the same fundamental aim – modernization – but balked at accepting the structural changes, economic and social, which any such process demanded. It was probable that he aspired to a highly industrialized China based on the sort of social system that had prevailed during the mid-1950s, when Mao was still 'good'. Reared on Mao's ideas, he could not conceive of any routes other than those mapped out by his predecessor in office. Whatever the Great Chairman had thought, said, and done was correct and must remain so. Such were Hua's limitations.

Cracks in the Wall of Silence

Is it possible to make any hard-and-fast statements about China? Must we call the country a vast enigma and leave it at that? Even if events there can be followed, are they open to interpretation?

The truth is that hard-and-fast verdicts on China are difficult to arrive at, but that the same applies to all countries of comparable size – the United States and the Soviet Union, for example. China is as big and regionally diverse as Europe.

Once dependent on a microscopic analysis of the press, we had now acquired many other authentic sources of information. We were no longer hemmed in by a wall of silence. Everything had changed within a very short space of time. Not only were officials more communicative, but the man in the street had lost his fear of us. Shop assistants ceased to dive for cover when we walked into a pharmacy and asked for a herbal cold cure. On the contrary, they volunteered advice and rocked with laughter at our solecisms.

Members of our embassy staff toured nearly every province in the country. Our travels took us to factories of every description, mines, communes, oilfields, canal construction sites, power stations, universities, agricultural and teacher-training colleges, schools, nursery schools, hospitals where operations were in progress (with and without acupuncture anaesthesia), laboratories and atomic research institutes, editorial offices, museums, theatres, department stores, temples, monasteries, churches, centres of regional and municipal government, factory and street committee rooms. I spoke to people from all walks of life and visited communes all over China, from Heilongjiang Province in the far north to subtropical Guangdong in the south and the Tibetan highlands in the west, from the oases of Turfan and Jiuquan in the Gobi Desert to central China and Shanghai.

In conversation with us, the Chinese now enlarged on their worries, their families, and their jobs. We often visited their homes, dropping in unannounced as well as by invitation. Our visits to people's communes and factories nearly always elicited frank admissions on setbacks, deficient planning, or unfavourable developments.

The information we obtained on our travels amplified what we were told by the Peking authorities, and our knowledge was further enhanced by conversations with scientists and artists, students, and journalists. Although they liked to show off well-kept and well-administered establishments, not run-down ones, this is a natural and world-wide tendency. We were very seldom confronted by a façade, but it did happen.

No one based in the capital of a country like China, with its vast extent and patchy communications, can hope to get to know the whole of it. Who, after all, even if he has lived there all his life, would claim to 'know' Europe or the United States? Taken together, however, our conversations in Peking and observations while on tour afforded us a picture of the country's prevailing state and salient problems. Any such picture is bound to be subjective, not only in presentation but in the selection and inclusion of the features that go to make it up. Describing a thing as it really is, or was, cannot be more than a goal to be approached but never attained.

Hong Kong used to be the principal observation post of the so-called China-watchers who kept an eagle eye on the People's Republic. It was particularly important to the United States, which maintained no diplomatic relations with China and had no representatives in Peking. Much could be gleaned there from refugees and Overseas Chinese who had been visiting relatives across the border. Most of these came from the south and many could paint a vivid picture of living conditions in that part of China, but few were capable of putting things in political perspective.

Evaluating these interviews was a laborious task, to be undertaken only by agencies employing a large number of multilingual personnel and working closely with the colonial authorities. They expended a great deal of money and manpower on constructing a mosaic picture of China, but they overrated their knowledge and kept it to themselves. Theirs was a remarkably static and rigid picture. While indicating political trends, it failed to reveal the nature and strength of the forces underlying them. The apparent accuracy of the information obtained – which was often negated by closer scrutiny – deluded people into believing that China's political leaders possessed the same information and drew the same inferences from it as the investigative agency – an intelligence service, let us say. This was seldom the case, however, because Western experts and Chinese politicians thought along quite different lines. However good they might be at compiling and collating facts, the former were rarely imaginative enough to put themselves in the place of the latter and forecast their decisions accordingly. The experts had no political experience of their own. They were political scientists with sinological training, not Chinese politicians, and the criteria that governed the Chinese leaders' decisions remained a mystery to them.

Whenever I read the findings of these agencies, I recalled the old rule that enjoins men in the field to use expert opinions as encyclopaedic knowledge rather than sacred texts and founts of revelation.

Only cautious use could be made of the Hong Kong press, because many suspect individuals and institutions offered their information and disinformation for sale on the local intelligence market. Far greater interest and value attached to the newspapers and periodicals that had special links with Peking. This applied less to *Ta Kung Pao*, Hong Kong's authorized communist newspaper, than to one or two smaller publications which occasionally received informative reports from Peking on trends and ideas within the Party leadership or one of its factions. These were papers used by certain individuals or groups at the top of the Party hierarchy – their identity was hard to determine and probably varied – to air news items or ideas which they were as yet unwilling or unable to publish in the Chinese press. All such articles were of interest to us in Peking.

Less informative were some of our talks with Hong Kong China-watchers who, although they perused the Chinese press with care and kept their card indexes in perfect order, asked the wrong questions, sought answers to questions long resolved by the Chinese leaders, or ignored questions to which answers were urgently required by Peking.

The Door Opens

Mid-August

We can depend on one thing alone, namely, that our scholars expound Confucian principles to the people. If, however, after being reared by the nation, these brilliant and gifted scholars abandon their traditional courses of study in order to follow the barbarians, correct attitudes will not develop and evil views will become rife . . . Scholars at work in the customary disciplines are now being instructed to study among foreigners. Your slave fears that they will not learn aright what they are supposed to learn there, and that they will be confused thereby, a thing entirely in keeping with the plans that are being forged by the foreigners.

Substitute 'Marxist' for 'Confucian', and this memorandum to the Emperor from Grand Secretary Wo Ren, drafted in 1867, could well have been published in the days when the Gang of Four and their left-wing radicals ruled the Chinese roost.

Early in August 1978, however, I heard quite another tune at the Ministry of Education. Summoned there by Vice-Minister Li Chi, I was informed that the Chinese leadership – in other words, the Politburo – had decided to send the cream of China's students abroad to study at universities there, live among foreign students, and take their examinations like all the rest. The Chinese Government would foot the bill.

Li Chi asked if we could accept a preliminary intake of five hundred students. I replied that our universities were open to all, foreigners included, as long as they possessed the requisite academic and linguistic qualifications, and undertook to consult my Government. When I asked how many students would be working abroad and where they would be sent, I was told that their precise number had yet to be determined but would certainly amount to several thousand – perhaps to as many as ten thousand. They were to study in the West, preferably, apart from a handful in Yugoslavia and Romania.

At the time, many foreign experts took a sceptical view of this plan. Our own Academic Exchange Service doubted whether the Chinese would be able to muster more than a hundred suitable candidates, if that. As for the US authorities and their sinological advisers, they doubted the ability of the reformist members of the Chinese leadership to carry out their programme at all, given the internal opposition it would arouse. One of my aides, who was equally surprised and almost as sceptical, asked an official at the Education Ministry whether the Chinese had fully considered the implications of such a step, pointing out that the students would import a lot of Western ideas when they returned. 'That's fine,' she was told. 'We couldn't wish for anything better – that's why we're sending them to you.'

According to Li Chi, it had naturally been pointed out to Deng Xiaoping that a few students might defect and remain in the West. His response to the memorandum was a marginal note stating that this contingency must be allowed for and accepted.

I discussed the Chinese proposal with some senior members of the Soviet Embassy staff at a Peking reception. Unable to disguise their apprehension and fully aware that their own Government would never have countenanced such a scheme, if only because of the many Soviet students likely to remain at large in the West, they sullenly poured cold water on it. In the first place, they said, it was far from certain that Deng Xiaoping would really manage to push it through, practical problems and bureaucratic obstruction apart. Secondly, the Chinese authorities would get a nasty shock when they discovered what sort of ideas their students brought home with them. Last but not least, Western countries would never be so foolish as to let thousands of Maoist agents loose on their own young people.

As it turned out, very few Chinese students elected to remain in the West when their time was up, and the vast majority exercised political restraint.

The sceptics were right inasmuch as the Chinese Education Ministry had some initial problems where preparation and selection were concerned. At the time of writing, however, some twelve hundred Chinese are studying in the German Federal Republic.

Intellectuals were now at liberty to resume contact with confrères in the outside world, read foreign books and periodicals, and in many cases travel abroad. Not only in Peking and Shanghai but elsewhere as well, they took an optimistic view of the future and hailed the change of course with enthusiasm. When talking to them in private, however, we detected a hint of uncertainty. Like many foreign experts on China, they wondered whether the new course would hold – whether the left-wing radicals might not stage a comeback and resurrect the motto 'All by our own efforts'. These reactionary forces had not, after all, been eliminated. They continued to lurk even now in government and Party offices, eagerly waiting for Deng Xiaoping's great new experiment to go adrift. The ideas propounded by Grand Secretary Wo Ren in his memorandum of 1867 to Emperor Tongji had still not been laid to rest.

Cain and Abel

Premier Maurer of Romania was regaling us with woodcock – eight of us in the dining-room of his mountain villa near Sinaia. He had shot the birds himself, and we listened to his exposition of the difference between woodcock and snipe with the respect due to a sportsman of note. At some stage in the meal, I can't recall in what connection, someone mentioned ideology.

'Ideology?' scoffed Maurer. 'That's a German invention – it doesn't explain a thing. You think our relations with the Soviet Union have anything to do with Karl Marx?' He turned to me. 'How many communist leaders have ever read him? Five per cent at most, believe me.' I must have looked incredulous. 'You doubt that?'

'Yes, I find it hard to believe.'

'Perhaps you're right,' he said. 'Maybe I was exaggerating – maybe only three or four per cent. I've rubbed shoulders with them all, and I should know. I'm one of the few who *have* read Marx – I've even lectured on him. The most the others know about him is what they've read in the *Short Course* – either that or they've dipped into *Principles of Marxism-Leninism*. All right, so Mao may have read the odd thing by Marx, but who else? Well, maybe the experts in the Academy or the Secretariat of the Central Committee.'

Five years later, I and a visiting German parliamentarian were in the Great Hall of the People with Vice-Premier Li Xiannian, then the most important member of the Chinese leadership apart from Hua Guofeng and Deng Xiaoping.

'Our relations with the Soviet Union,' said Li, 'did not deteriorate because of our conflicting views on Marxism-Leninism, but because the Russians tried to impose their policy on us.'

My German visitor, a social democrat and well-known professor of jurisprudence, would have welcomed at least a mild profession of faith in ideology and its bearing on practice, but like Napoleon – '*Tous ces idéologues . . .*' – the more practical communist leaders tend to play its importance down. Their prime concern is to do what is politically or economically expedient. After that, they appoint experts in the Central Committee Secretariat to find ideological explanations for the benefit of rank-and-file comrades. Western experts, whose knowledge of developments inside communist countries comes mainly from the communist press, are inclined to overrate the influence of ideology on concrete political decisions.

While still in motion, the communist movement has often, though not invariably, been propelled by ideology. Whenever Communist Parties gain power, however, ideology limps along in the wake of events. Its logic never enforces new decisions, creates new facts, or introduces new lines of approach. Those are the responsibility of the Party leadership. Ideology offers no serious resistance to the normative force of actual developments, which stem from decisions taken by the Politburo or its leading members, provided the latter are united in their resolve and not divided among themselves. Conversely, if ideologists receive instructions from Party Headquarters to adopt a new position on this issue or that, they turn like a weathercock – a rusty one, sometimes, but rust can be dissolved by applications of oil from on high.

Ideological changes are a sure sign that the Politburo has already embarked on a new course. This course must be ideologically interpreted and justified to obviate intrigue and rebellion on the part of internal critics and reorient Party officials in conformity with the new, cast-iron truth.

Ideology does, nevertheless, possess certain important and politically concrete functions in a communist-ruled country. It is the instrument with which the Politburo keeps the 'base' orderly and disciplined. Communist leaders can mould ideology like clay and represent the result as an eternal truth for acceptance by the masses. To Communist Party functionaries, however, it is a conceptual life-raft to be clung to in the interests of security and stability. No matter if the life-raft is encrusted with barnacles; those are the Party leaders' problem.

Journey to the West, an old Chinese picaresque novel, tells of Sun Wukung, the Monkey-King, who has a club he can make small enough to fit behind his ear or as long as a tower is tall. Such is ideology in the hands of the Party leaders: an instrument designed to keep both masses and officials in order. They can make ideology small – so small as to be barely visible – or wield it against internal opposition like a mighty, death-dealing club.

It was thus employed by Mao, Jiang Qing, and their henchmen in the Party leadership. Anyone who imagines that the Cultural Revolution sprang from ideological differences inside the Party is badly mistaken, and few Chinese would subscribe to that view. Ideology, it can be demonstrated, was not the origin of the Cultural Revolution but the bludgeon used by Mao to strike his antagonists down – his equivalent of Sun Wukung's club.

In combat with fraternal parties and the class enemy abroad, ideology has become merely sounding brass, potentially irksome but lethal no longer. The Chinese sometimes use it, like the 'three-worlds theory',[1] to explain and justify a foreign policy that enables their socialist country to maintain good and amicable relations with governments of widely varying hue – even with conservative or undemocratic governments like the military régime in Chile – as long as they lend themselves to incorporation in a united front against the Soviet Union. Quite clearly, a factitious construction of this kind cannot be exported and is incapable of inspiring the oppressed peoples of the world to engage in revolutionary wars of liberation. It is designed for China's use alone and valid only for a certain period and international situation.

But if ideological differences of opinion must be ruled out, what constituted the real reason for the estrangement and ultimate break between Peking and Moscow?

It was Peking's growing realization since the mid-1950s that the Soviet Union did not regard China as an equal partner, that the Kremlin assigned absolute priority to national interests, that China must be harnessed to the Soviet Union's national objectives, like the countries of Eastern Europe, and that she ran a risk of losing the sovereignty she had not long regained from the Western powers, this time to a 'fraternal' state.

As early as 1955, Khrushchev told Adenauer of his alarm at China's growing potential and openly proposed a *rapprochement* to counter the Yellow Peril. Did the Chinese first learn of this from Adenauer's memoirs, or did Khrushchev – who liked the sound of his own voice – talk in the same vein to other, less discreet politicians, possibly even from his own camp?

The Chinese were offended when Khrushchev used his celebrated secret speech to the Twentieth Congress of the Soviet Communist Party to demolish Stalin's image without consulting, or even informing, any of his allies in advance. His attack on Stalin's personality cult was an indirect slur on Mao as well. Did Khrushchev's abandonment of Stalin's course imply abandonment of the foundations of his foreign policy? Although Stalin, too, had often given the Chinese cause for complaint, they trusted him to persevere with his anti-American plans and protect his eastern flank by employing China as an ally and agent, as he had in the Korean War.

The Russians had signed an agreement with the Chinese guaranteeing

---

[1] The First World originally comprised the two superpowers, though qualifications have occasionally been attached to the United States' membership since 1978. The function of the Second World, which consists of the industrialized nations, is to isolate the Soviet Union and resist its hegemonic aspirations in concert with the Third World and the United States. The Third World comprises the developing nations, including socialist countries like China, one or two members of the Warsaw Pact (Bulgaria, Romania), and the Mongolian People's Republic.

them information about the manufacture of the atomic bomb. Quite suddenly, they went back on their word. Why? To ingratiate themselves with Washington?

China's decision to detach herself from the Soviet Union and pursue an independent line was taken during Khrushchev's visit to Mao early in October 1959, after his meeting with Eisenhower at Camp David. The Chinese were afraid that the 'spirit of Camp David', which had been conjured up by Khrushchev and Eisenhower without reference to Peking, might lead to a US–Soviet accord. This fear was heightened by Khrushchev's advice to China to stop bombarding Quemoy and Matsu, the offshore islands under Nationalist occupation.

'We used to call the Soviet Union our "elder brother",' Hua Guofeng once declared. 'After embarking on their revisionist policy, however, the Russians tried to bring us under their control and restrict our sovereignty.'

The Chinese have always been peculiarly sensitive in matters affecting their sovereignty. Mao assured Edgar Snow in 1936 that he had no intention of fighting for an independent China, only to hand the country over to Moscow. Khrushchev's advice to cease bombarding the islands, coupled with Russian proposals to install Soviet radio transmitters on Chinese soil and form a joint Pacific fleet – which would naturally operate under Soviet command and have the run of China's ports – finally convinced the Chinese leaders that Khrushchev planned to incorporate their country in the Soviet empire.

Despite the obedience owed by a younger to an elder brother, the Chinese severed their ties with the socialist family. The decision, as we have already said, was taken in October 1959. In the middle of 1960 the Russians removed all their experts and technicians from China, together with the blueprints for all major industrial projects. At about the same time, in June 1960, Khrushchev took advantage of the Bucharest Conference to launch an attack on China. He not only strove to justify his policy towards China and substantiate it after the event but questioned China's ideological stance at the bar of fraternal communist opinion. The Chinese later justified their own policy, with great stylistic finesse, in their Open Letters from the Chinese Communist Party to its fraternal Party in Moscow.

This exchange of blows did not last long. Nowadays, the heavy clubs of yore are brought out only on high days and holidays. Chinese discussion of the Soviet Union's socialist status now assumes quite a mild form and has even ceased to embody charges of revisionism, though that term has been replaced by others like Soviet hegemonism and social imperialism, which are just as pejorative.

'This split,' I was asked by Klaus Mehnert, the Soviet expert and political commentator, '—how long do you think it'll last?'

Mehnert had come to Peking as part of a delegation, and the two of us were driving out to the Great Wall in a long convoy of official cars. He had been a friend of ours since our days in Shanghai.

'According to Mao,' I said, 'ten thousand years.'

To a lover of precision like Mehnert, that wasn't good enough. 'But what about the new Chinese leaders?' he said. 'Won't their greater pragmatism convince them that they've more in common with the Soviet Union than the Western world – that they're wasting a lot of energy on this squabble and getting nothing out of it? Isn't it conceivable that China and Russia will develop a more relaxed relationship, leading in the end – however gingerly they embark on it – to a concerted foreign policy?'

'There's another side to the coin,' I said. 'The Chinese engage in similar dark conjectures whenever they hear the word *détente* or learn of American attempts to agree on arms limitation with the Russians. They wonder if those policies may some day lead to co-operation – however gingerly at first – between Moscow and Washington. Co-operation against whom? – that's the question they ask themselves. Who'll be excluded from the club? *We* quail at the thought that Peking and Moscow may start co-operating again, but Peking's direst nightmare is a vision of the two superpowers agreeing to rule the world in partnership.'

'It would be mine, too,' said Mehnert, 'but I don't see it happening, not for a long time.'

'Like ten thousand years?'

'I wouldn't like to put a figure on it.'

Once so closely allied, China and the Soviet Union have progressively drifted apart. They maintain opposing, or at least divergent, attitudes to almost every international issue. The thirty-year treaty of friendship and alliance, signed in 1950, was abrogated in 1979 and is no longer in force. In the field of nuclear armaments the Chinese very soon attained by their own efforts what the Russians had denied them. China's relations with the West are better and more troublefree than those of the Soviet Union. Hostility between Moscow and Peking, on the other hand, has steadily hardened in the past two decades, a process accelerated by Soviet support for Vietnam's supremacist policy in Indo-China and the invasion of Afghanistan.

Peking is pursuing a pragmatic policy, and an improvement in Sino-Soviet relations, or at any rate a more relaxed attitude, is possible. The likelihood of an *entente cordiale* has not, however, increased. On the contrary, a soberly pragmatic and unideological approach is bound to convince the Chinese of the existence of a concrete and profound conflict of interests. They must realize that, while the gulf between the two big neighbours can be narrowed, it cannot, in the foreseeable future, be closed.

Frontiers do not, as some writers claim, constitute the real bone of contention between China and the Soviet Union. Under the 'Unequal Treaties' of the nineteenth century, the Chinese empire ceded over half a million square miles of territory to the Tsarist empire. Deng Xiaoping once said, during a conversation in which I took part, that this was not the point at issue, and that China was prepared to acknowledge certain historical decisions. The genuinely disputed territory was only a small fraction of the total, he went on, so a modicum of good will should make it possible to reach agreement.

No such agreement has been concluded. The disputed areas, as we also heard through the Soviet Embassy in Peking, amount to little more than eleven thousand square miles, most of them in the inhospitable and almost uninhabited Pamir highlands and the remainder in the Ili region and on the Manchurian border. Given their nature and extent, agreement on these desolate frontier areas should not prove an insurmountable problem. Whether the Russians alone are being obstructive it is hard to tell, but there is a possibility that the Chinese, too, would prefer to leave this matter temporarily unresolved.

Whereas ten divisions were stationed along the Sino–Siberian border in Khrushchev's day, Deng Xiaoping estimated that, under Brezhnev, there were fifty-four of them, totalling one million men. Western estimates put the figure somewhat lower. The Chinese take the view that the Russians have not reinforced their Siberian garrison for defensive purposes and call for it to be reduced to the level Khrushchev found acceptable. In view of the Russians' rejection of far more modest Western demands at the Mutually Balanced Force Reduction talks in Vienna, and of their rigid and inflexible approach to military planning and policy, China's demands would seem to have little prospect of success.

The Soviet leaders know full well that not even a million men could win a conventional war against China because Chinese forces, in keeping with their 'people's war' strategy, would withdraw to the Yellow River or even beyond, swamping the invaders in three hundred million or more Chinese. Limited operations against China would nonetheless be feasible. It is this fact that keeps so many Chinese troops tied up on the northern and north-west frontiers and the Sino–Mongolian border. China would, however, be extremely vulnerable to Soviet attacks by air and sea.

Fears that mounting population pressure may one day prompt the

Chinese to spill across the Soviet frontier have long been rife in the Soviet Union. The more dispassionate architects of Soviet strategy and policy must nonetheless be aware that China is quite incapable of expanding in this way, even if she wished to. Expansion would require military backing, and China will remain militarily inferior to the Soviet Union for a very long time to come.

The Chinese, for their part, feel threatened by Soviet expansionism. They point out that the Soviet Union has steadily extended its sphere of influence in recent decades, in their immediate vicinity as elsewhere. They feel endangered by the Soviet invasion of Afghanistan and Soviet support for the 'petty hegemonism' of Vietnam, both of them neighbouring countries. The substantial reinforcement of the Soviet Pacific fleet, which has access to a Vietnamese port, is regarded by them as a threat to their own seaboard.

China continues to call for the abandonment of this expansionist acquisition of strategic bases. There is little likelihood, however, that the Soviet Union's world-wide interests will permit it to comply or tacitly exclude the Far East from its established policy without receiving major Chinese concessions in return.

Soviet and East European diplomats in Peking believe that the old policy of friendship still has many adherents among the Chinese. A few optimists further believe in the possibility of reactivating those forces and restoring the Great Friendship without the need for any appreciable Soviet concessions.

No one would deny the existence of some Chinese who look back with pleasure on their visits to the Soviet Union and preserve agreeable memories of their social contacts and friendly relations with its inhabitants. They make no secret of this, but all belong to an older generation whose experiences antedate the 'Ice Age'. A few veteran Party officials undoubtedly consider China's *ouverture à l'ouest* a dangerous development and secretly deplore the frigidity of her relations with the Soviet Union. Public opinion being overwhelmingly opposed to that view, however, they take care not to advertise it.

All else apart, the behaviour of many Soviet experts in China – their blatant condescension and frequent lack of consideration for their Chinese hosts – kindled feelings of resentment that are still perceptible today. 'They thought they had a monopoly of intelligence,' I was told by one Politburo member, 'whereas we Chinese were "stupid swine". I had two advisers who poked their noses into everything and made a point of ordering us about. In the end I asked them who was the minister, they or I. They were to speak only when I asked them for advice; otherwise, they were to keep their mouths shut. That really upset them. Soviet military advisers insisted on taking account of Soviet military experience and ignoring ours. After all, they said, they'd won the Second World War. They were annoyed when we cited our own military experience. After all, we retorted, we'd beaten the Japanese and Chiang Kai-shek.'

The Soviet Union is disliked in China and has done little to court popularity there. Moods of this kind can fluctuate, of course, or even undergo a sudden transformation. Right now, most Chinese are fascinated by the prospects opened up by co-operation with the West and unimpressed by what the Russians have to offer, which compares badly. Only co-operation with the West can lead them out of isolation and into the world. Intellectuals and young people find the West attractive for another reason: freedom resides there, not in the Soviet Union.

Why, with their country in the throes of political and economic controversy, should the Chinese leaders initiate a new debate about something on which widespread public agreement reigns? Concrete considerations are what inhibit pragmatic Chinese policy-makers from seeking an *entente* with the Soviet Union.

There is, for all that, a long-term possibility that the two powers will resume businesslike relations, start talking to each other again, strengthen their trade links, or adopt the same position on individual issues. To quote the East German Ambassador, Helmut Liebermann, relations between them may then become 'like those between the GDR and the FRG'.

A new treaty of friendship? China, the Middle Kingdom, has never in her history concluded defensive alliances with the countries on her borders, the single exception being her still valid treaty with North Korea. The quasi-alliances of the two World Wars can be ignored. As for the 'Treaty of Friendship, Alliance, and Mutual Assistance' signed in Moscow on 14 February 1950, it can only have reinforced the Chinese aversion to contractual ties of this nature. The probability is that China will conclude no more treaties of mutual assistance for years to come, least of all with the Soviet Union.

The Emperor and the Chairman

He was the greatest – he not only knew it but said so. Greater than all the other great rulers of the past, he never tired of proclaiming his greatness and having it carved in stone. He united his country, unified every aspect of it, stripped the ruling class of power, and transformed Chinese society from the bottom up. Millions had to die for the sake of his plans, but people didn't matter to him. Only one person counted in China, and that was himself.

We are talking, not of Great Chairman Mao, but of King Zheng, who ascended the throne of Qin as a thirteen-year-old boy in 246 BC and died in 210 BC, at the age of forty-nine.

Qin lay on China's western border. The country's population already included a substantial number of the same Tartars who lived in the deserts beyond the border, outside the civilized or Chinese world. This was the time of the Warring States, when the ten or twelve Chinese kingdoms fought each other for nearly three centuries. Qin itself was remote and on the periphery of the contest. 'The people of Qin have the same customs as the barbarian tribes Rung and Di,' it was said at the centre of the civilized Chinese world. 'They have the heart of a tiger or a wolf. They have no conception of good form, of family relationships and decorous behaviour. Beating earthenware pots, banging cups, twanging the pipa, hammering on hip-bones, crying "Woo-woo!" and thereby rejoicing the eye and ear – such is the "music" of the country of Qin!'

But music of this kind did not corrupt the people, as the philosopher Xunzi approvingly noted. It did not seduce them with dulcet and decadent melodies and rhythms. The people were simple and unspoiled and stood in awe of their government officials. The officials themselves were strict but just and unconcerned with anything but the good of the state and the welfare of its inhabitants. In short, everything in Qin was just as the philosopher would have wished – with one regrettable and crucial exception: the people of Qin disdained Confucius and the Confucians, whom they refused to tolerate. This was bound to lead to disaster sooner or later, Xunzi felt sure; but disaster was a long time coming.

Qin was to the kingdoms of ancient China what Sparta was to Greece or Prussia to Germany. Outsiders may have sneered at this unrefined country where the simple life was exalted into a virtue, but they respected and feared it.

The masters of Qin cared nothing for the opinion of the outside world. They wanted no truck with the Confucians and the humanism of their founder, whose doctrines they regarded as an unworldly ideology. Qin put its faith in the amoral, power-political philosophy of Shang Yang, a former Chancellor whose doctrines and statecraft had made the country strong.

In 221 BC, when King Zheng had conquered the other Chinese monarchies and united *tian xia* – the civilized world, or 'everything beneath the sky' – under his dominion, a new era began. To bring this home to everyone, Zheng graciously coined and adopted a new title in place of the old designation 'King'. He now styled himself Shi Huangdi, First Exalted Emperor. From now on the emperors were to be numbered – an endless succession of them, for the Qin dynasty was to rule for ten thousand years. But a mere four years after the death of the First Exalted Emperor, the Second Exalted Emperor took poison and the Qin dynasty became extinct. It had been in power for fifteen years, which seems to prove that ten-thousand-year empires are little more durable than Hitler's Thousand-Year Reich.

The new, unified Chinese empire disintegrated, but the old days never returned. The name Shi Huangdi, or Qin Shihuang, First Emperor of the Qin dynasty, became synonymous with terror. The eminent German sinologist Richard Wilhelm called him 'one of the greatest scoundrels and scapegoats in Chinese history'. Nothing, he wrote, could be more typical than the sympathetic way in which European scholars defended him against the supposed prejudices of Chinese historians and strove to invest him with a renown that had always been denied him in China.

Always? If Wilhelm meant to imply that it always would be, he was wrong. Later in our own century, Qin Shihuang acquired a potent Chinese advocate who tried to rehabilitate him after two thousand years of obloquy by Confucian China, which had represented him as evil incarnate. The Emperor could not have gained a more influential champion, but more of that anon.

So this was Mount Li, with the First Emperor laid to rest in its depths. The 'mount' was more of a mound, and not a very impressive one at that, compared to the pyramids of Egypt. Mount Li resembled a gigantic molehill, a cone of earth roughly one hundred and fifty feet high but very much broader at the base. Though plain and featureless in outline, it contained buried treasure, very little of which had so far been brought to light. Very little? That depended on your point of view.

As soon as he came to the throne, the thirteen-year-old monarch decreed that work should begin at once on his tomb. It was not a task he chose to leave to his successor. The tomb was to surpass in size and splendour all that had gone before. Zheng, as he then was, had an early awareness of his own importance and the way he wished to be regarded by posterity. His tomb was still unfinished when he died at the age of forty-nine, even though seven hundred thousand men were at work on it.

Mount Li is about an hour's drive from Xian, the capital of Shaanxi Province. We had skirted fields and driven through villages to get to it. This was the seat of an ancient civilization, but the fields, villages, and roads were indistinguishable from those we had seen in other provinces. China boasts no pyramids, no castles or palaces like Mycene, Tiryns, or Persepolis – no lofty marble temples like the Parthenon. The Chinese have always built with timber and sun-dried bricks.

The asphalt road is lined with trees. Twenty-two hundred years ago, it must undoubtedly have been flanked for miles by the huts or tents of the seven hundred thousand prisoners employed on Mount Li – unless, of course, they sheltered from the wind and weather in pits. The authorities would not have troubled much about their creature comforts. They were identified as convicts by facial tattoos and forced to dress in red. Most of them were castrated as well, a favourite form of punishment because it hurt, humiliated, and left a permanent mark without impairing its victims' capacity for manual labour. The hundreds of thousands of men who toiled here for the First Exalted Emperor have vanished without trace.

Maize fields stretch away on either side of the avenue. Mount Li itself is the sole outward sign of the work that went on here, though some of the labourers' remains will doubtless come to light as excavation proceeds. All the artisans and architects familiar with the tomb's design were walled up between the middle and outer gates to prevent them from betraying its secrets. They too will be unearthed in due course.

For the Emperor's soldiers, however, resurrection day has already dawned. Since 210 BC, when Hannibal was still fighting in Italy, the eastern access to Mount Li has been guarded by a whole legion of them – seven thousand soldiers, mainly infantrymen but also numbering specialized units of archers, unarmed warriors in karate-like poses, and charioteers complete with chariots and horses.

Many of them are not quite as operational as they were because their baked clay limbs have disintegrated. *All the king's horses and all the king's men, couldn't put Humpty together again* . . . In this case it is the king's horses and men who need reassembling, not Humpty-Dumpty, and hundreds of archaeologists are labouring to restore them.

They work in a glass-roofed building that looks like an enormous station concourse and covers Excavation Site No. 1, which is bigger than a football field. Beneath the roof stands the main body of the army, some six thousand strong. Shafts or trenches have been sunk to a depth of fifteen feet. Some of the pits are full of shards. Since no one has touched the site for twenty-two hundred years, however, the fragments are complete and have only to be reconstructed. Patience is the sole requirement.

We climbed down into a pit where relatively little damage had been done by the collapse of an ancient wooden roof. The soldiers, most of them intact, were in various stages of excavation. Buried to the chest, waist, or knees, they seemed to sprout from the soil. Many were slightly askew and one had lost his head. The sight of them standing there, patiently awaiting deliverance, was reminiscent of a baroque Resurrection scene. Here, however, the dead confronted us in tangible, three-dimensional form. We could gaze into their eyes – even touch them. They tolerated us in silence just as they had tolerated the removal of their weapons, a few years after the First Emperor's death, by a rebel general who felt that these could be better employed in the land of the living.

Not a button or rivet was missing from their accoutrements. Realism had not been carried to the lengths of portraying a man with buttons torn off or armour awry. Sergeant-majors must have been detailed to inspect the statues and check their buttons before acceptance. I counted two hundred alone on one well-armed foot-soldier. Belts, straps, and neckerchiefs were all in place, head-bands well braced. The inspecting sergeant-majors must have viewed the parade with professional approval.

The statues were not boring or monotonous to look at, but – of course – archaic Greek *kouroi* they were not. These soldiers had been produced *en masse*. The sculptors were not required to portray a festive procession like that of the Panathenaea and bring out its beauty in relief. Their task was to muster a well-disciplined army whose members could guard the First Exalted Emperor's slumbers for all eternity.

When the prefect of the guards, who together with his staff officers was found only some hundred paces further on, had stepped from his black-and-red lacquered chariot, an officer must have shouted something like 'Attention!' and reported to the prefect that the legion was ready for inspection. And that is how they have stood for the last 2,200 years, frozen in posture and mien. Some of them may be slightly askew and others may have lost an arm or a head in the course of their long vigil, but not a button. The buttons are all there.

Some six hundred statues had been unearthed at the time of our visit. In view of their precise alignment, however, and the inconceivability of there being a gap in the ranks where some rebellious statue had failed to report for duty, it was possible to visualize the rest of the subterranean host and inspect it in our mind's eye.

The soldiers were in military uniform poses, though deviations from the norm were permitted when consistent with regulations. Only the faces varied, doubtless at the Emperor's command. They may have been likenesses of his imperial guard – a strong assumption in the case of the officers. There are some remarkable portraits among them, but the faces are dispassionate and expressionless – the faces of men under orders.

Although Qin had been credited with producing large sculptures in the round by one or two written sources, no one had taken these reports too seriously. As recently as the 1960s, experts were claiming that large-scale Chinese sculpture had begun with Buddhism, or almost five centuries later. Then, in 1972, commune peasants digging a well near Mount Li – thirteen hundred yards to the east of it – came across a member of the First Exalted Emperor's guard. Whoever felt the more startled, peasants or soldier, this discovery heralded China's biggest archaeological sensation.

So we stood in the pit, face to face with the resurgent warriors, and looked them in the eye. We would have known them again in the street or in our dreams. Theirs were not the hard-bitten, worldly-wise faces familiar to us from sculptures of the Roman Republic. They were the faces of soldiers expected to obey without question, not think or give orders themselves. They were young faces still unmarked by life and living. Many had been smoothed and retouched to deprive them of expression.

These were no volunteers, no fierce devotees of the Emperor, no ardent defenders of their native soil. Their task was to suppress freedom, not defend it. The Emperor's wars were not theirs.

The house of Qin owed its ascendancy to Yang of the Gung-sun family, better known as Shang Yang or the Lord of Shang, a contemporary of Philip II of Macedon, father to Alexander the Great. The Confucians, and intellectuals in general, he execrated as 'lice' and 'pests'. They had no place or say in a country like Qin. Shang Yang was a believer in *Realpolitik* and a harsh judge of human nature. 'The people in general hate war,' he declared in the book attributed to him, 'but he who can persuade them to delight in it will attain supremacy.'

No delight in war could be discerned on the faces of Qin Shihuang's soldiers. Retouching had obliterated their thoughts. People in Qin were not supposed to think. Confucius had had the dangerous idea of educating people. Like the great philosopher Lao-tse, Shang Yang preferred uneducated subjects. Thinking was the business of the government and obedience that of the governed.

An Emperor who commissioned so many other portraits would surely have ordered a likeness of himself. The interior of the mound may yet yield one or more such effigies. Qin Shihuang would undoubtedly have employed the greatest sculptor of his day, but would anyone have dared to portray the Emperor as he really was? We owe the following description of him to one of his advisers:

He has a waspish nose. His eyes resemble slits. He is pigeon-chested and has the voice of a jackal. He is merciless, with the heart of a tiger or a wolf. In adversity he humbles himself, but when successful he devours men without scruple.

I am a common citizen in a homespun robe, yet he treats me as if I were his superior. Should he succeed in conquering the empire, we shall all be his captives. There is no staying long with such a man.

He not only stayed, of course, but became the Emperor's commander-in-chief. In any case, Shang Yang's book had emphasized that no excessive moral demands should be made on any ruler. 'A ruler called virtuous has no loyal ministers; a lenient father has no dutiful sons.'

Shang Yang nursed an equally low opinion of ministers who pursued Boy Scout ideals and desired nothing but good. 'Government by do-gooders leads to lawlessness and dismemberment; government by rogues, on the other hand, brings order and strength.' Hitler would have warmed to this philosopher-statesman.

Shang Yang's political doctrine was formally adopted by Qin and brought it dominion over the Warring States. He considered the traditional virtues not only superfluous but positively injurious. He enumerates them more than once: 'If the following ten evils exist within a country: etiquette, music, songs, history, the pursuit of virtue, moral doctrines, filial obedience, brotherly love, integrity and philosophy, then the ruler cannot make his people fight and decline is inevitable.'

The First Exalted Emperor was innocent of these ten evils.

His burial chamber in Mount Li is still unopened at the time of writing, but Sima Qian, the 'Grand Historian and Grand Astrologer' who lived a century after him, has left us a documented description. Being a replica of the universe, the vault should not be pictured on too small a scale. Its ceiling represented the star-studded night sky, its floor the earth. Traversing the latter were the Yangtze, the Huang He, and the other rivers of China. They ran with mercury, not water, and an ingenious contrivance made it appear that they were flowing into a miniature ocean. Erected in the chamber were model palaces, pavilions, and government buildings. The Emperor could not dispense, even in death, with an abundance of precious vessels – bronze, one imagines – and precious stones. His last resting place was lit by lamps filled with sperm oil and intended to burn for ever. Crossbows were sited at strategic points, strung and cocked so that they would automatically transfix any would-be thief who broke in. It is still uncertain whether the rebel general who robbed the imperial guards of their weapons may also have penetrated the burial chamber and helped himself to its treasures.

In the middle of the chamber, in a bronze sarcophagus, lay the Emperor. He was not entirely alone. His son, the Second Exalted Emperor of Qin, had thought it unfitting that 'those of his father's ladies who had borne no sons' should be sent home to their families in the customary manner. Instead, they were invited to join the Emperor in his tomb and buried with him. Their numbers, too, should not be underestimated.

By pursuing the policy whose principles we have sampled above, Qin Shihuang had 'established the unity of the world'. The Chinese equated the civilized world with the Warring States, just as their contemporaries in ancient Rome, Athens, or Alexandria equated their own civilized world with the countries bordering the Mediterranean.

The First Emperor compelled the princes and 120,000 noble families to move to Xianyang, the capital of Qin and the empire, where he made them build palaces like those in their former places of residence. This effectively removed them from the soil in which their power had been rooted.

Qin Shihuang divided the country into thirty-six military districts, each administered by a military and a civil governor appointed by himself and charged with keeping an eye on each other. He thereby substituted a bureaucratic for a feudal system of government. This administrative structure, with its division of power in the provinces between a military and a civil governor, endured for over two thousand years.

When one of his advisers suggested giving his sons provinces to hold as fiefdoms, Qin Shihuang submitted the proposal for discussion. His other advisers must have known that the Emperor wanted no trouble with recalcitrant princes, however, for they persuaded him to reject it.

Qin Shihuang was the great unifier. A capacity for unifying, not dividing, has always been the mark of greatness in China. Pluralism almost invariably brings disintegration, the Chinese feel, and disintegration, as we have already seen, was Shang Yang's greatest dread.

In 1949, Mao Zedong unified the nation. That was a great feat performed in the days when he was still 'good'. During the Cultural Revolution, which began in 1966, he rent the nation asunder. That, as the Party has formally stated, was a mistake.

Qin Shihuang, on the other hand, unified and standardized everything within reach, from writing and coinage to weights, measures, and axle widths. He even tried to standardize ideas. It was he who built the Great Wall, which incorporated stretches previously built by kings of the Warring States as a defence against the nomads of the north. He had canals dug and highways built, the latter fifty paces wide and lined with trees. Sima Qian tells us that hills were demolished and valleys filled in to avoid bends in this road network, which the People's Republic would be glad of today. The Emperor also drove the Huns back into the Ordos Desert and conquered territory as far south of the Yangtze as modern Vietnam, where a garrison was stationed near the site of Hanoi.

Even cosmological magic was obliged to take note that a new age had dawned. In place of fire, which had previously been the dominant element, Qin Shihuang pronounced water the element that was to promote and protect his dynasty. Black, not red, became the dominant colour, and life was henceforth to be governed by the number six. Six inches was the prescribed length and breadth for officials' hats and the strips of bamboo on which documents were then inscribed. The Emperor never left his office until he had completed his daily quota of 'paperwork' – twice times sixty pounds of it. He made sure of this by having the documents submitted to him carefully weighed every morning.

By the Emperor's command, the following words were carved on rocks and monuments: 'He regulated all things, verified facts, and gave each its proper name.' According to Taoist doctrine, 'things approach the Emperor and he gives them their names'.

Today, this task devolves on the Central Committee of the Communist Party or its Politburo. It is they who decide whether a man is 'black' or 'white', whether and until when Mao was 'good' and when he began to 'make mistakes'. Ordinary people anxious to avoid giving offence must be told what to believe or, at any rate, how to conduct themselves.

He who can name things is their master. This is illustrated by an anecdote about the Second Exalted Emperor, Qin Shihuang's son. Sima Qian tells us that Chancellor Chao Gao, who planned to usurp the throne, submitted him to a trial of strength. He had a deer paraded for the Emperor's inspection and announced that he was making him a gift of 'this horse'.

The Emperor laughed. 'Are you not mistaken, Chancellor? That is a deer, not a horse.'

But when he turned for confirmation to his retinue of officials and courtiers, the smile died on his lips. They were all looking grave and thinking hard. One or two declared that, in certain respects and from certain angles, the animal did indeed bear some resemblance to a horse. Others could not make up their minds, but a few courtiers, either reckless or devoid of political instinct, could not see the deer as anything but a deer. These latter the Chancellor ordered to be severely punished after the audience – probably killed or castrated.

That was the end of the Second Emperor, too. No longer competent to name things, he had forfeited his power over them. Power had passed to the Chancellor, who compelled him to take poison.

The First Exalted Emperor would never have accepted a deer in lieu of a horse. He had a monument erected to himself on a mountain, with a plaque extolling his achievements:

> He defines the law, leaving nothing in doubt,
> Making known what is forbidden.
> The local officials all have their duties.
> All is done correctly, all according to plan.
> There are no robbers and thieves.
> Men delight in his rule.

The last assertion was probably something of an overstatement. Living in his empire cannot have been much fun. Seven hundred thousand men were condemned to forced labour and employed on his tomb. More than a million toiled to construct the Great Wall, and only three in every ten returned. Countless others were conscripted for military service or put to work on roads, canals, and enormous palaces. The fields were denuded of labour and the people grew hungry. Food supplies became precarious, even in the capital.

Intellectuals suffered too. They hated the Emperor and he hated them because their constant talk of the past reflected on the glorious present and 'confused' the people. Mao, who had a similar problem with intellectuals, restricted their study of history to areas where they could demonstrate that the past was of service to the present.

The First Emperor had all history books and chronicles burned on the grounds that they were useless, one exception being the annals of Qin itself, which have survived. Works by great philosophers and collections of songs were also consigned to the flames. Only works of reference containing vital information and instructions – oracle books and treatises on medicine and agriculture – were spared. One copy of every existing book was kept locked up in the imperial library, but this itself was later destroyed by fire.

Neither the Confucians nor the entire Chinese people ever forgave the First Emperor for burning the books. The written and printed word has always enjoyed respect in China. It is now thought, however, that the Confucians exaggerated a little when they spoke of wholesale destruction, and that it would scarcely have been possible to confiscate and burn every book in the brief interval between the issuing of the decree and the Emperor's death.

No exaggeration attaches to their accounts of Qin Shihuang's ferocious anti-intellectual campaign. Confucian scholars, whose everlasting talk of the good old days under mythical monarchs had 'confused' the people, were hauled into court, where they traded accusations and denounced each other. Four hundred and sixty of them were found guilty and buried alive outside the capital, within sight of Mount Li. Others were sentenced to hard labour and sent to work on the Great Wall.

The Emperor's wrath could be terrible indeed. Once, while sailing down the Yangtze, he found his progress impeded by a contrary wind that sprang up on Mount Xiang. He promptly commanded that every tree on its flanks be felled. To visit even direr punishment on the mountain whose wind had denied him passage, make it lose face, and render it ridiculous in the eyes of the world, he had it painted red – the colour worn by criminals. The mountain must have suffered terribly.

On another occasion, while looking down from a hill in the palace grounds, he was displeased to note the size of his Chancellor's retinue. One of the palace eunuchs conveyed this to the Chancellor, who hurriedly dismissed a few of his escorts. 'One of you talked,' the Emperor said accusingly to his eunuchs and courtiers, and we can picture him glaring at them with slit-eyed fury. When none of them confessed to having warned the Chancellor, he made sure of punishing the culprit by executing every last member of his entourage.

'In the thirty-sixth year,' wrote the Grand Historian, 'Mars approached the Scorpion's Heart. A shooting star changed into a stone when it fell to earth at Dongzhun, and somebody inscribed on the stone: "After the First Emperor's death, the land will be divided."' When the Emperor learned of this, he dispatched his Prime Minister to investigate the matter. Nobody admitted having written the words, so he followed established practice and had everyone in the district killed. As for the meteor, which could not be allowed to go unpunished either, the Emperor had it melted down.

All to no avail, of course. Qin Shihuang died in the following year, as predicted, and his empire fell apart.

He was the greatest – everyone confirmed this, and he himself recorded the fact on stone throughout his empire – but happy he was not. He was a frightened and profoundly superstitious man. Three unsuccessful attempts on his life had left him with an abiding fear of death. He dispatched men in quest of the elixir of life and magic mushrooms with the power to ensure longevity, but most of them seized their chance and never returned.

His three hundred court astrologers told him only what he wanted to hear. More pernicious still were the Taoists under whose influence he fell. They taught that he who renounced the world could experience all-embracing unity – the *unio mystica* – and become a True Man. The True

Man does not get wet in water or burn to death in fire; he rides on the clouds and soars through the air, surviving for as long as heaven and earth continue to exist. Qin Shihuang decided to become one of these fortunate beings. He dropped the royal 'We' and styled himself 'The True Man'.

One of the Emperor's Taoist magicians advised him to guard against evil spirits by hiding himself away and concealing his whereabouts at night from all and sundry. He duly had banks, walls, or curtains erected to screen the routes between the 270 imperial palaces and pavilions situated in and around his capital. All were to be kept in readiness for him, lavishly equipped with bells, drums, and beautiful women, and no one was to divulge, on pain of death, in which of them he proposed to spend the night.

But peace of mind and happiness still eluded him, writes Sima Qian. Accordingly, he commanded his court poets to write poems and songs about the immortals and the True Men. Although these were sung everywhere by imperial decree, their practical effect was nil.

The Emperor's fears became still more intense during the last year of his life. We can picture him – a sharp-nosed, pigeon-chested, slit-eyed figure – hurrying night after night from one palace and pavilion to the next, fleeing ever further afield in his mortal dread of spirits and assassins, and then, when his fears were dispelled by the advent of day, striding boldly back to his imperial residence, there to bark out orders and sentences of death, left and right, in a voice like a jackal's.

One day, some magicians whom he had sent in search of the herb of eternal life returned with the news that it could definitely be obtained in Penglai, a sort of Chinese Elysium, but that some huge whales had prevented them from getting there.

The Emperor promptly put to sea in person. Stationing himself in the bow of his ship with a crossbow, he symbolically punished the whales that had barred the way to Penglai by skewering a large fish.

Back on shore again after a fruitless voyage, he fell sick and died while still a long way from his capital. Qin Shihuang's death was concealed by his retinue, which included his youngest son. Every day, meals and government dispatches were delivered to the imperial litter. The litter responded by issuing edicts duly authenticated with the imperial seal, among them one addressed to the Crown Prince, who had been banished for impertinence. It commanded him to kill himself forthwith – an order which, being a dutiful son, he reluctantly obeyed.

It was high summer, and the journey home took weeks. When the stench of decay from the litter threatened to give the game away, the

Chancellor had it closely escorted by a wagonload of salt fish. And so the First Exalted Emperor of Qin returned to his capital, a rather less regal and awe-inspiring figure than when he left it.

But that no longer mattered. What counted, historically speaking, was that this haunted, unhappy man with the raucous voice and narrow chest had conquered the Warring States and welded the civilized world into a single country. He had trampled on its inhabitants and coerced them into a Great Leap Forward – successfully, unlike his modern counterpart. Although they nearly perished in the process, they never forgot what it was to be united. Qin Shihuang had made them one nation.

What also counted, of course, were the millions who had died, the scholars buried alive, the books consumed by fire, but none of these could nullify the fact that, during his eleven years on the imperial throne, Qin Shihuang had laid the foundations of a political structure, the Middle Kingdom, that was to endure for thousands of years.

Qin Shihuang's youngest son, who had accompanied the litter and was well acquainted with the contents of the edict addressed to his elder brother, inherited the throne. He just had time to bury his father in Mount Li, seal the tomb, and plant the mound with shrubs and trees. Then, chafing under the burdens of imperial grandeur, his subjects rose in revolt. When matters came to such a pass that the Second Emperor could no longer distinguish a deer from a horse, his Chancellor ordered him to take poison. The Qin dynasty was extinct. Rebels occupied the capital, the library and palaces went up in flames and burned for many days, and the terracotta soldiers guarding the First Emperor's tomb were disarmed.

But the old days never returned. The new Han dynasty reunited the nation and retained a centralized, bureaucratic system of government. For over a century, scholars and rulers fiercely debated the cause of the Qin empire's swift collapse. Those in power ascribed it to the First Emperor's failure to apply Shang Yang's precepts with sufficient vigour and determination, whereas the Confucians put it down to the diabolical system itself.

The Confucian theory gradually gained acceptance, and the memory of Shang Yang, whose doctrine had carried Qin to imperial supremacy, was anathematized. No matter what the virtuous Confucians preached, however, they could not deprive the names of Shang Yang and the First Emperor of the evil lustre that continued to fascinate those who peered back into the dark recesses of history.

Mao Zedong, for example, made Qin Shihuang one of his schoolboy heroes, probably inspired by an early sense of kinship with the great author of change and revaluer of all values. Party literature subsequently called his burning of the books 'a progressive measure'. The Emperor had set greater store by the present than the past, whereas the Confucians, who had sung the praises of the good old days, were reactionaries by definition. Instead of accepting the new order, they had wanted to restore the old.

'Burning the books was intended to standardize thought,' declared the Party's ideological journal, *Hongqi* (*Red Flag*), in 1974, and standardizing thought was a good thing. That, after all, was precisely *Hongqi*'s own special function.

When Chairman Mao extolled Qin Shihuang at the second session of the Eighth Party Congress on 8 May 1958, Marshal Lin Biao objected that the Emperor had burned books and buried scholars alive. Mao laughed.

'What does that matter!' he exclaimed, according to the minutes. 'He buried four hundred and sixty scholars; we buried forty-six thousand. Didn't we behead a few counter-revolutionary intellectuals during the "suppression of the reaction"? I discussed this with certain democratic figures and told them: You're wrong if you revile us and say we're like Qin Shihuang. We've outdone the First Exalted Emperor of Qin a hundred times over. If you call us Qin Shihuangs and dictators, we fully accept that. But you still haven't made it clear enough, I'm afraid. We shall have to emphasize it a good deal more strongly. (Loud laughter.)'

What Are They Really Like?

Otto was back in Peking. He called me from the Peking Hotel and said he was sure I wouldn't mind if he brought Hildegard to supper.

'Of course not,' I said. 'Who's Hildegard?'

'A new addition to my Hong Kong office. It's her first time in China. She's a good-looker – a real sight for sore eyes.'

I told him to bring her right over.

'There's only one thing. She's got some wrong ideas about the Chinese.'

That, I told him, was secondary. We would join forces and dispel her misconceptions.

We sat on the terrace after supper. It was dark but still very warm. We'd lit some joss-sticks and put them on the floor to discourage the midges.

'The Chinese remind her of blue ants – that's what Hildegard said at lunch today.'

'But you straightened her out?'

'Right,' said Otto. 'I told her to watch the waiter. He'd been standing at the entrance to the dining-room for five whole minutes, staring into space. We wanted to pay – so did the people at three other tables, who kept timidly raising one finger – but he didn't notice a thing.'

Hildegard remarked, 'But I've watched Chinese labourers at work on a dam, shovelling earth and toting it away in baskets. They trotted the whole time.'

I told them the story I'd heard from our Ambassador in Tokyo, who'd been travelling by train from Peking to Ulan Bator, the capital of the Mongolian People's Republic.

'The train reached the border around midnight. It stopped there for two hours because the wheels had to be adjusted to fit the Soviet gauge. It was bitterly cold – forty or fifty degrees of frost. In the waiting-room he was accosted in English by a youngish Chinese woman who asked him a mass of questions about Europe and the outside world. When he countered by asking who employed her, the railroad or the customs service, the answer was no on both counts. She was just a married woman who worked in an office in the local town. She'd been studying English at the Institute of Foreign Languages, here in Peking, but the radicals had packed her off to the frontier – literally into the wilds. Her ambition was to become an interpreter in Peking. She naturally knew how hard it would be to obtain a permit to move back to the capital, but she proposed to try anyway. So, to improve her English, she met every trans-Siberian express that stopped there in the middle of the night, once or twice a week, and spent the two-hour stop-over talking English to foreign passengers.'

'I'm glad Otto's wrong about the Chinese,' said Hildegard. 'I'm glad they aren't all as lazy as he says.'

Otto was unrepentant. The would-be interpreter might be a hard worker, he objected, but she could hardly be described as a blue ant.

'She and the waiter are opposite extremes, surely,' Hildegard said. 'It's only natural for newcomers to China to summarize and generalize their first impressions. We're bound to get the wrong idea sometimes. You two have met a lot of Chinese over the years – you know their potentialities. For instance, aren't they a cruel race? Otto's told me one or two stories about the Cultural Revolution.'

'I could tell you many more,' Otto said.

'Well, how do you account for such atrocities?'

'Can you account for Auschwitz?'

'No,' said Hildegard.

'Neither can we,' I said. 'We can't explain what happened there any more than the Chinese I've spoken to can explain the atrocities of the Cultural Revolution. Society condemns them in Europe and China alike. The excesses that took place here assumed a different form, of course, but they were only possible because the authorities did nothing to stop them. They not only endorsed but encouraged them – for instance, when Jiang Qing publicly kissed a girl for lashing a defenceless political opponent across the face with her belt in front of a mass tribunal. Mao and the radicals had done away with *li*. What mattered to them was revolutionary consciousness, not moral standards.'

'But you can't pin all the blame on Mao and the radicals,' said Otto. 'History's full of similar examples. What about the Taiping Rebellion, or the Boxer Rebellion, or the state of civil war that existed here during the twenties and thirties? People were tortured and butchered just as cruelly then. Personally, I've always found the Chinese sinister in the mass. Why? Perhaps because the average Chinese renounces his individuality more quickly in a crowd than his individualistically-reared counterpart in Europe, and mobs don't have any moral standards. They're ruled by emotion and don't know what they're doing. The individual stops being himself and becomes part of a mass organism – an arm, a hand, a foot.'

'I wouldn't quarrel with that,' I said, 'but it's never very long in China before the unwritten laws of society reassert themselves and inhibit brutality.'

'What then?' asked Hildegard. 'Is it exorcised completely?'

'No, of course not, but it's suppressed again. Think of the male and female sadists who ran our concentration camps. We've all heard of some who went to ground after the war and led perfectly respectable lives. Did their brutality become dormant, or what?'

'Perhaps it found other outlets,' said Otto, '—perhaps it does in all of us. For instance, nothing disgusts me more than the smug hypocrisy of people who run around brandishing a moral yardstick without sparing a thought for their own murky depths. I know a radio commentator who's relentless in his insistence on moral integrity. He's a born grand inquisitor, hounding public figures and crying shame whenever they put a foot wrong.

'And the man himself? I was present once when he cruelly humiliated his girl-friend – the woman he was cheating on his wife with. One barbed remark did the trick. His daughter spent over a year in hospital, but he didn't visit her once. If you accused him of brutality, he'd just look uncomprehending. Yet there he is, still churning out commentaries like a stern moralist devoted to fighting for the right and exposing evil in high places. Everyone thinks he's the soul of honesty and integrity.'

Hildegard, who felt he'd have made a good subject for Shaw or Ibsen, wondered why modern writers didn't tackle themes like that.

But Otto refused to be sidetracked by Shaw and Ibsen. 'I look at it this way. They live encased in a strait-jacket made up of the five basic, traditional human relationships between governor and governed, father and son, man and wife, elder and younger brother, friend and friend. In every case but the last, one party is subordinate to the other. The Chinese have always lived under a strict set of obligations – a code that encouraged tyranny in superiors but muzzled and suppressed their inferiors. That accounts for all the rebellions in Chinese history, when people cast their social obligations and standards to the winds. The Greeks spoke of *ekstasis*, or standing outside oneself – being beside oneself, in other words. The atrocities committed during these bouts of "ecstasy" seem inexplicable to the Chinese once they're safely back inside their pattern of social norms and obligations – back in a state of *enstasis*, so to speak. To my mind, the ecstatic state occurs more often in Chinese history because the thoughts and aspirations of the Chinese are less centred on the individual than they are with us, and because they're more readily absorbed into a mass. But I can see you're dying to produce some arguments to the contrary.'

'Indeed I am,' I said. 'Remember Heine's description of mob violence during the Paris cholera epidemic? How two inoffensive passers-by were suspected of trying to poison people with some white powder they happened to be carrying – how a bunch of old women removed their clogs and finished them off, and how terribly the bodies were mutilated? And what about pogroms in Russia and lynchings in the States? No, cruelty's universal. It ran riot among our own people too, but not in the form of mob violence. Once it had disguised itself as the master-race ideology, it coldly and systematically exterminated millions of people.

'That's why your explanation's only a hypothesis. It may serve to interpret mob violence in China, but it doesn't account for similar phenomena elsewhere. Cruelty isn't a peculiarly or typically Chinese characteristic. It's inherent in all races, and the most we can do is gauge its degree of latency and discover what holds it in check. If that's what you're implying, I agree with you. As Hildegard just said, we ought to know the Chinese better than she does, having been here longer.'

Otto gave a wry smile. 'If I don't know all there is to know about myself, which I don't, how am I supposed to explain the Chinese? I only know they aren't blue ants or colourless, faceless people. Their personalities are just as unique and distinctive as ours.'

'Exactly,' I said, 'and they can't be reduced to a common denominator. Leibniz based his picture of the Chinese on reports from Jesuit missionaries. He described Chinese peasants and servants as treating each other with the civility typical of European aristocrats. They never displayed anger or hatred, always remained courteous and aloof. That's still true, but only superficially. At home, in the street, at market, on the waterfront – anywhere among the uneducated masses who haven't learned refined manners – the Chinese can be thoroughly rude and offensive to each other. They can also draw on an enviable stock of swearwords. Physical violence isn't uncommon either, even in the family circle.'

Otto laughed. 'We're confusing the poor girl. Perhaps the most one can say about the Chinese is what they *aren't*.'

'Like what?' asked Hildegard.

'Well,' said Otto, 'I'll confine my remarks to the Chinese of China. They differ in lots of ways from the Overseas Chinese, who can often be noisy, rude, inconsiderate, and hard to please. The Chinese of China are reared in a tougher social environment – one that eliminates or greatly reduces the characteristics that make it hard for people to rub along with their neighbours.'

'But what makes them different from people in other countries?'

'Many things. For instance, you don't find religious fanatics here, the way you do in Arab countries. The Chinese have always been tolerant in matters of religion. There wasn't any orthodoxy, so there weren't any heretics to persecute. Orthodoxy didn't exist here till Mao came along.'

'Here's another example,' I said. 'I've never seen a sign here of the Latin craze for ostentatious masculinity – the sexual display and machismo. There's something else as well. The Chinese don't cherish too high an opinion of themselves. Vain, ambitious, prestige-conscious people do exist in this country, but the average person doesn't take himself too seriously. He doesn't cling to life, either. If he can't escape humiliation, he'll die with remarkable facility. The Chinese consider self-pity undignified.'

'They aren't dogmatic,' Otto went on. 'They prefer to compromise. On the other hand, they can also be vindictive, malicious, garrulous, nosy, crafty, and morally censorious. They aren't above informing on each other, which is probably a legacy from the days when denunciation was a public duty. They're diligent, but only when diligence pays. It's never occurred to them to work for work's sake or attach any intrinsic value to such activity. The family, a square meal, congenial company, a few hours of leisure – those things have always been worth a little effort to them. They're as acquisitive as anyone, and more so today than in the lean years, but they can accept material deprivation more easily than most. When it comes down to it, they're content with very little.'

'Forty years ago,' I said, 'when I travelled through country districts and saw the peasants living in squalor, it surprised me how happy they seemed. I even heard them singing in the fields – and that was a novel experience to someone who'd just crossed the States as an amateur hobo, sharing freight cars with bankrupt farmers and unemployed labourers. They were just bitter, but these people were happy in spite of their poverty and the misery they had to endure.'

'They're happy by nature,' said Otto. 'That came over this afternoon, while Hildegard and I were walking in the Summer Palace grounds. The Chinese enjoy a good laugh – they take a naïve delight in little things. There are exceptions, of course – that goes without saying.'

'But they all love children,' I said, 'and vice versa. It's touching to see the care Chinese youngsters bestow on their parents and grandparents. How many times have you seen a European teenager carry his mother or father or grandmother to the station on his back because he doesn't own a bicycle?'

Otto nodded. 'Treating your parents with respect is considered a mark of refinement and good breeding. The same goes for older people in general. The last time I was in Shanghai I went looking for a shop in the old Chinese quarter. I couldn't find it, worse luck, but it used to have a sign up outside: "Old people and children not cheated here." Compare the scene I witnessed in Hong Kong a few days ago. I was having lunch with one of our compatriots, and the son of the house cracked a joke at his father's expense. The Chinese guests laughed, but you could tell they were shocked. People here don't poke fun at their parents, let alone criticize them to their faces. When the Chinese of old wanted to characterize barbarians, they said, "They treat their parents disrespectfully – they don't know the meaning of basic human relationships." To them, filial and parental love were two sides of the same coin.'

'What about the Cultural Revolution?' asked Hildegard. 'Were parents treated as respectfully then?'

'No,' said Otto, 'but then, the Cultural Revolution was a relapse into barbarism.'

I said, 'Leibniz made much of the courtesy found here three centuries ago, even among humble folk. It's still very noticeable, even today. I've often been amazed by the dignity and delicacy of veteran revolutionaries who received their only schooling in a barrack-room. But Leibniz said something else which still holds good today: he said the Chinese keep their distance in conversation and are generally more perceptive of other people's feelings. They cultivate friendships and make loyal, unselfish friends, but they don't have any time for the hail-fellow-well-met approach.'

'That's because they're proud,' said Otto. 'I think we tend to underrate the pride factor in our dealings with the Chinese. They'll turn down any kind of proposition, however advantageous, if it comes from someone they don't like and don't trust, or if it hurts their pride.'

'You meet that all the time in politics,' I said. 'They don't regard politics as an abstract problem to be solved like a mathematical equation. Politics and ethics have always been closely related in their ideas and dealings. To them, politics is something people engage in with people, and with some people they just can't communicate. They don't either like or trust them.'

'It's the same in business,' Otto went on, for his new recruit's benefit. 'You can't do business with them unless they trust you. The human element is central every time. Chinese entrepreneurs have built up vast businesses in Hong Kong and overseas, but they've always kept them in the family. If a firm grows too big, the various branches are delegated to brothers, sons, nephews, grandchildren, and so on. Huge, anonymous industrial empires aren't their cup of tea. They like dealing with *people*.'

I asked Hildegard if our duologue had left her any clearer on the subject of the Chinese.

She laughed. 'A lot of it was news to me, but from what you've just said the Chinese have a mixture of good qualities and bad. They aren't blue ants – in fact they differ so much it's almost impossible to generalize about them. They're a mass of contradictions. Like us, in other words.'

A Surprise Suggestion

End-November

I was buttonholed by Ambassador Tolstikov at an official Chinese banquet for Le Duan, the Vietnamese Party boss, and asked if I would see him sometime. It sounded rather urgent, so I invited him to call next morning.

We briefly discussed Le Duan's after-dinner speech, which had echoed an earlier speech by Deng Xiaoping and warned China against 'changing colour'. No one who recalled the context of Deng's remarks could fail to grasp the ominous nature of this allusion. Tolstikov, who also felt that relations between Vietnam and China were becoming increasingly strained, ascribed their deterioration to incidents provoked on the Cambodian–Vietnamese border by Peking's friend Pol Pot, possibly with Peking's encouragement. I replied that the Chinese seemed to want peace in that area and asked if he hadn't heard reports that the Vietnamese themselves had made incursions into Chinese territory. He said he hadn't.

Then he came to the real purpose of his visit. Our personal relations were good, he said. Couldn't we meet regularly – every two weeks, say – to exchange views on the situation in China?

As I saw it, this unwonted proposal implied that the Soviet Embassy lacked reliable information about China and was, or might be, unsure how to interpret such reports as it did receive. Or was there something more behind it? Tolstikov, who was most persistent, advanced a number of arguments designed to render his suggestion palatable. I could bring along two or three aides, for instance, and he would do the same.

I felt pretty certain that this proposal did not emanate from him but had been engineered by another branch of the Soviet establishment. However, we had no intention of enlightening the Russians on what we thought of the Chinese scene or what the Chinese had told us in confidence.

My response to Tolstikov was that our commercial, scientific, and cultural links with China were steadily multiplying, as he must know from the reports he had read, and that our political discussions with the Chinese were gaining in scope and interest as well as frequency. The workload of an ambassador at pains to cultivate these relations was so heavy that, grateful as I was for his proposal, I could not take it up.

Vassili Tolstikov quite understood my position, and our personal relations remained cordial and unstrained until his government recalled him.

The Chinese Card

Hua Guofeng, China's Party leader and head of government, had returned from his state visits to Romania and Yugoslavia – his first-ever trip abroad. The fact that he had visited Tito, the arch-revisionist, exemplified the change that was taking place in China. The Chinese Communist Party had already begun to study the Yugoslav self-administration model, that cross between the planned and the free market economy. Everyone was preoccupied with modernization and greater access to the West.

While Western correspondents took a surprised and often sceptical view of this development, the Soviet press betrayed concern. Realizing that China has always held a fascination for the West, the Russians had launched a campaign designed to demonize the country. China wanted a third world war, they claimed. She was pursuing a provocative policy and would be tempted to expand by population pressure. The West, and Federal Germany in particular, was sternly warned against 'playing the Chinese card'.

Although smoking-room strategists often toyed with the idea that the Chinese card might be brought into play in a conflict with the Soviet Union, no realistic politician took the idea seriously. 'Distant water cannot extinguish your burning home . . .' Zhou Enlai had used this Chinese proverb to the Romanians as long ago as 1971, and it had often been quoted since. When questioned about China's military potential by some US congressmen early in 1978, Deng Xiaoping told them he had little more to offer than 'empty talk'. His response in October of the same year, when asked by German journalists how China would support her friends if their security were threatened, was 'With our mouths'.

The Soviet press asserted that we were faced with a choice between Peking or Moscow, and must make up our minds at once. Close involvement in China's economic and modernization plans was in itself construed as a half-option in favour of China – one that might strain our relations with Moscow and render *détente* more difficult.

Nevertheless, the West had a legitimate interest in developing its links with China at a period when the country was becoming more receptive to us and more economically and politically attractive. China was not trying to export her revolution. It would not be in our interest for the Russians to have a political vacuum on their eastern flank – a weak country which they could ignore when framing their policy towards the West. From our point of view, an economically and politically powerful China would be an asset. It would make for stability in Asia, whereas a country as weak as China was during the first half of this century would exert a largely destabilizing effect.

Recognizing this and developing our relations with China accordingly does not, however, mean playing the Chinese card – a card we don't hold in any case. Only the Chinese themselves can do that.

Collective Guilt

They were reluctant to speak out.

For the benefit of my visitors, a party of ten German publishers, editors, and journalists, I had asked the Mayor of Shanghai to introduce some intellectuals who could describe their experiences during the Cultural Revolution. So there we were, ensconced in a drawing-room at the Jinjiang Hotel, but nobody cared to take the plunge.

The seven Shanghai intellectuals told us what we already knew. They stuck to generalities. Professor Ji Jin of Tongji University recalled that Tongji had been founded by a German, Paulun, and announced that it was to be reopened. The author Wang Shiyen described attacks by the Gang of Four on Shanghai's writers and artists. Xü Yülan, an actress and singer, told us that her colleague Su Qingtu had spent nearly a year in jail for writing eight letters to the Central Committee in Peking complaining of the cultural policy and mentioning Jiang Qing and Zhang Chunqiao by name. He had been led away in handcuffs.

'Now tell us about yourselves.'

Xü Yülan was the first to pluck up courage. She had a beautifully modulated voice, and even those of us who knew no Chinese took pleasure in its sonorous cadences. She had been compelled to work in a commune for ten years, hoeing fields, cleaning out stables, and so on, but wasn't allowed to sing a single note. Her opera company was broken up and its stock of props and costumes scattered to the winds.

Jin Jingchang, an architect and town planner trained in Germany, had not pursued his profession for more than a decade.

'So what did you do instead?'

'I worked on a technical dictionary.'

'Were you molested?'

'Yes,' someone said at last. 'We were all subjected to struggle.'

I explained the term. 'Subjected to struggle' meant interrogated, browbeaten, pilloried in front of mass tribunals, forced to undergo house searches, led through the streets wearing a placard and a paper hat.

'Were you physically assaulted as well,' asked one of the journalists, '—punched or beaten, I mean?'

The answer, when it came, was subdued. 'Yes, but the Gang of Four are a thing of the past. That time is over and done with.'

They were reluctant to talk about it, and least of all about their own experiences, save possibly in private.

But Theo Sommer, an associate editor of *Die Zeit*, dug his heels in.

Deng Xiaoping had told the visitors only a few days ago that China's experiences during the Cultural Revolution had been both good and bad. Good as well as bad? Theo Sommer confessed himself puzzled. Throughout his tour of China, he had heard nothing but the bad sides of the Cultural Revolution. Which were its good sides, and to what extent had it been influenced by Mao? Hadn't he initiated it?

Everyone was evasive except the writer Wang Shiyen, an elderly man with impressive features. 'We understand your questions,' he said, 'but we cannot answer them today. We prefer to leave them to the judgement of history.'

That was plain enough, but not for Theo Sommer, who remained politely insistent. Everywhere he went, he said, he heard tales of the misdeeds of the Gang of Four. He realized that this was a case of *pars pro toto*, and that the phrase embraced their ultra-leftist supporters, not just the Four themselves. On the other hand, what of the newsreels and press photos showing hundreds of thousands of people cheering Mao Zedong, Lin Biao, and the Gang of Four? What of those forests of hands ecstatically waving Little Red Books? Didn't they prove that everyone had joined in? If the nation had balked, the Cultural Revolution would never have wrought such havoc, so wasn't everyone equally to blame for what had happened? Wasn't everyone guilty in some degree?

Theo Sommer's notions of collective guilt were lost on the Chinese. 'What could we have done?' they asked.

That night, perched on our hotel beds and drinking some of the Scotch we'd brought with us, Sommer and I debated the question.

I levelled an imaginary pointer at an imaginary Great Wall separating China from the Christian West – one wall among many. Evil inherent in the human heart? That, as Xunzi taught so long ago, can be mitigated by upbringing and education. The evils of this world? Original sin, inherited from Adam and Eve? Try those concepts on the Chinese, and they look mystified. They have no intention of shouldering another's guilt. The Lamb of God, which taketh away the sin of the world? What sin? ask the Chinese.

Nineteenth-century missionaries who came to China to save four hundred million souls had many a tale to tell of these obdurate heathens who, heedless of the moral depravity rife in their country, flatly denied the existence of guilt and sin.

Even the educated made things easy for themselves. He who committed a crime got punished and received his just deserts; he who committed a crime but slipped through the net of justice by means of bribery, perjury, or cunning had simply been lucky. Although uneducated people thought he risked being brought to book by Yan Wang, the King of Hell, predictions of that kind could not be proved and were probably no more than idle talk. Besides, there was plenty of time before the day of judgement, so why not enjoy it? Going around in sackcloth and ashes, doing penance, self-abasement and self-chastisement – none of these achieved anything. The Confucians set no store by them. Superstitious folk might sometimes reflect on their misdeeds – in a shipwreck or earthquake, say – but the notion of collective guilt did not exist.

Nor does it in Japan. Ruth Benedict pointed this out, shortly after World War II, in *The Chrysanthemum and the Sword*. The soul of General Tojo, whom the Americans executed as a war criminal, now resides with those of other national heroes in the Yasukuni Shrine in Tokyo. Members of the Japanese cabinet still go there and make obeisance to them – all of them, including that of Tojo, who was responsible for the attack on Pearl Harbor, the war, millions of dead, and Japan's defeat. What he did was essentially wrong, but he paid the price. No responsibility attaches to the Japanese people.

Although recent sinological research indicates that an awareness of sin did exist in China at the end of the Ming dynasty in the sixteenth century among adherents of a certain school of philosophy, it was short-lived and restricted to a small circle.

Confucianism, the prevailing doctrine, rejected such ideas. Self-examination and self-criticism it had always demanded, but never remorse or penitence. The Party, too, requires self-criticism in certain circumstances, but a comrade merely confesses his mistakes and errors; the Party has never yet infused its members with a sense of sin – fear, certainly, but not sin. The intellectuals we'd met earlier that day had been humiliated during the Cultural Revolution. Not having committed suicide like thousands of their colleagues, they smarted at the humiliations inflicted on them. Their silence was a mark of shame. They felt disgraced.

Such was the gist of my rather didactic and far too long-winded lecture to Theo Sommer, who listened with admirable patience.

Some months later, on 6 February 1979, a group of Chinese girls wrote to the periodical *China Youth*, the Party's official organ for young people, asking the selfsame question Theo Sommer had put to the Shanghai intellectuals.

'How was it possible,' they demanded, 'for the Gang of Four to run so amok in recent years? Why did the Chinese people allow it? They were, quite clearly, the worst criminals in Chinese history ... Although the Gang of Four and their supporters managed to gain a surprising amount of power, they were a mere handful. Why couldn't hundreds of millions of Chinese unmask and overthrow them in time to prevent this disaster? . . . Referring to Louis Bonaparte's counter-revolutionary *coup d'état*, Karl Marx said, "If the French assert that their nation succumbed to an insidious attack, one remains unconvinced. How was it possible for three upper-class confidence tricksters to take a nation of thirty-six million people by surprise and capture them without resistance?" '

The editorial answer was that no blame could be attached to the French people themselves, as even Marx had conceded. 'In other words,' the periodical went on, 'the view that individuals can be held responsible for historical advances and setbacks cannot be upheld . . . The Gang of Four's emergence in China had profound social and political roots and was a consequence of history. The Gang of Four took advantage of the fact that our laws were inadequate, and that we possessed no legal system and institutions on which to rely.'

So the people weren't at fault, nor was the nation. The blame lay with economic, social, and political conditions. History itself spawned the Gang of Four – history or possibly, even, Hegel's *Weltgeist*. What could the nation or the individual have done to combat such a development?

Happiness and Mrs Yü

Mrs Yü apologized for the fact that her home was so much smaller than our ambassadorial residence. We reassured her by telling her that our own home in Germany was far less grand than our quarters here.

Mrs Yü, a fifty-eight-year-old librarian, had retained her maiden name in keeping with the modern custom. Her husband, Professor Sung, worked at a physics institute. The family occupied a 'four-corners-yard' in a small side street. The single-storeyed house was built around a rectangular courtyard. All its windows and doors looked out on this yard, whose only access to the street was a narrow passage. There was just enough room in the yard for a walnut tree, and a few flowers and pot-herbs were growing in one corner. The house was picturesque but uncomfortable, Mrs Yü told us. Coal-fired stoves provided the sole source of heat, and two rooms only were kept heated in winter. To reach the kitchen or the lavatory, you had to cross the yard in all weathers. Mrs Yü had no refrigerator or vacuum cleaner, freezer or washing machine. Water for washing had to be heated on the gas stove, and the Chinese use a lot of water.

The household numbered seven: two parents, three sons, a daughter, and a daughter-in-law. As they all worked, they had no money worries. We asked Mrs Yü to describe her day for us.

She got up at five o'clock, washed, cleaned her teeth, got dressed, and made breakfast. The first meal of the day consisted of a sort of rice soup accompanied by vegetables and *mantou*. The daughter and daughter-in-law, who were also up and about by this time, lent a hand with breakfast before helping to wash and prepare the vegetables for lunch. The family did not eat meat every day.

Mrs Yü took fifteen minutes to cycle to the library where she worked from eight till noon. She went home for lunch like her daughter, who worked at a hospital and brought back *mantou* or boiled rice from the canteen. Her husband also lunched at home. Two of her sons took dinner-pails to work and the third ate in the cab of his truck.

Mrs Yü returned to the library at two and worked till six. She did her shopping on the way home – not such a problem now that queues were a rarity in shops and markets. Mr Sung, who worked at home in the afternoons, had the saucepans on the stove by the time his wife came home. Everyone, including their sons, helped to get supper ready. After that came washing-up and the rest of the housework. All three sons spent two hours a night in front of the television set, taking an adult education course. Their studies had been cut short because of their father's political difficulties during the Cultural Revolution, and they were now trying to catch up – according to Mrs Yü, with little prospect of success. By half past nine or ten the lights were out. This was the family's unvarying routine, six days a week.

Mrs Yü was allowed ten days' vacation a year, but not all at once. She had to take them one at a time, perhaps to coincide with a visit from friends or a special shopping expedition.

Were women better off now than they had been?

Yes and no. In the old days, before she married, she'd done nothing but housework. Living 'like a frog in a well', she'd seen nothing of life or the city. Peasant women, too, had worked in the home and were seldom seen in the fields. Today, women had equal rights. They were permitted to work in the fields and factories like men, and could also do heavy manual labour – not that they were always paid the full rate. Equal rights hadn't gone as far as that – not everywhere, at least – but things were progressing. To a woman, equal rights meant that she had to do most of the housework as well as holding down a job.

If happiness could be measured at all, I said, were Chinese women happier today than they used to be?

'Yes and no,' Mrs Yü repeated. 'Women in modern China have more rights, but that isn't happiness in itself. In the old days, a woman with a reasonably amiable husband, a reasonable standard of living, and a brood of well-brought-up children – sons, I should have said – could be perfectly happy without any rights at all. On the other hand, there were many women who had no rights and were unhappily married as well. They were treated like slaves and subject to the whims of their mothers-in-law, especially if they hadn't borne a son – so much so that suicide often seemed the only way out. A lot of women chose that escape.'

'Today they can get divorced.'

'They can,' said Mrs Yü, 'but just you try it sometime! Europeans consult a lawyer and go to court, but with us the neighbourhood committee comes first. Our society has always been opposed to divorce. Still, at least it's a possibility.'

'So the women of today *are* happier?'

Again Mrs Yü hesitated. In the old days a woman's happiness had consisted in bearing as many sons as possible. She lived for the family, not herself. It was sons who perpetuated the family and ensured that its ancestors received punctual and reverent sacrifice, whereas a daughter left her family and joined that of her husband. The happiness conferred by numerous offspring no longer existed today, when a woman was expected to be content with two children at most. What if both were daughters who married into another family? How could one's own line survive? Didn't the family count at all these days? If not, what did? What did one live for? Not the Revolution, surely!

Mrs Yü could not imagine how people filled the void created by the knowledge that their family would become extinct when they themselves were no more. The new had replaced the old too rapidly. The novel conception of a one-child family would alter people's relations with children and other people – with society in general. The conception of happiness itself would change.

But things hadn't changed for Mrs Yü. Her family numbered seven, all of whom earned money and paid it into the family exchequer administered officially by her husband but effectively by herself. She made Mr Sung a monthly allowance of 15 yüan (£4.50) for pocket money. They were saving for the marriage of their second son, who was engaged. His fiancée would not be granted permission to marry until she had completed her nurse's training, by which time the couple would be twenty-eight. They had known each other for two years, and sometimes the girl came visiting.

Mrs Yü spoke kindly of her future daughter-in-law. It went without saying that she would embark on marriage as a virgin. Premarital relations are rare in educated circles. The eight thousand students at Peking University live on the campus in segregated hostels resembling barracks. Students do fall in love, of course, but they forbear to parade their feelings. They 'go together', but not even hand-in-hand when others are looking, nor do they go to bed together. Such exceptions as do occur are very rare indeed. Many may doubt this assertion – mistakenly. That is the way things are in China, though not, perhaps, for very much longer.

Mrs Yü and the rest of the family were happy with the second son's choice. She would fit in well. 'She's an unassuming person,' said Mrs Yü, 'and that can't be said of all young women today. Many are in the market for money and accept the man who earns most. They're also keen to know whether their intended partner has a good education and job prospects, or whether he comes from a politically compromised family.'

'In other words,' I said, 'their choice is determined by precisely the factors that used to guide parents in choosing a husband for their daughter.'

'In many cases,' said Mrs Yü, 'but not always.'

Grandchildren? Her daughter-in-law, the wife of her eldest, truck-driving son, was hoping to obtain permission from her labour unit to have her first child next year. Whether she would later be allowed to have another was doubtful. Whatever happened, Mrs Yü intended to retire in two years' time. Then she could devote some time to her grandchild. She hoped it would be a boy.

1979

1979

Punitive Action

18 February

The Chinese called their invasion of Vietnam, which had just been announced, a punitive action. To me it seemed more like a military adventure. As recently as November, a senior Chinese Foreign Ministry official had told me that his country would refrain from military action, even if the Vietnamese continued their provocations on the border, unless Chinese territory were deeply penetrated. This was entirely in keeping with China's current policy, which sought to project the image of a new, peaceful China whose efforts were exclusively centred on economic development.

That image had now been destroyed, and fears of the Chinese giant were bound to revive among the countries of East and South-East Asia. Hanoi having recently signed a treaty of friendship and alliance with Moscow, I did not discount the possibility of serious Soviet counter-measures.

The previous afternoon our Chinese staff had been summoned to attend a political meeting. Newspaper articles described the situation on the Sino-Vietnamese frontier as grave, and the Chinese press had reported that the inhabitants of the border areas were requesting military protection from continual Vietnamese incursions. To one who recalled the 1930s, this sounded ominous. Similar appeals for help had usually been published on the eve of an invasion.

According to a member of our staff who had phoned me the night before, more and more reports suggested that China was invading Vietnam. In the morning, Xinhua had announced that Chinese troops had already crossed the border in response to persistent Vietnamese frontier violations. Peking simultaneously proposed that all outstanding disputes between the two countries be settled by negotiation.

The real reason for China's 'punitive action' was that Vietnam had extended her sphere of control to the whole of Indo-China by conquering Cambodia as well as Laos. There were fears in Peking that the Vietnamese would consolidate their position in the occupied territories and then push further afield. It was also feared that they would allow the Russians to develop air bases in their country as well as the naval base at Camh Ran.

The State Department and one or two senior officials in Bonn feared that firm and resolute opposition to Vietnamese policy would drive the Vietnamese ever deeper into the Russian embrace, and felt that we should try to strengthen their links with the West by means of economic co-operation. To judge by the arguments they put forward, advocates of this view at the State Department were motivated by a strong sense of guilt. In their desire for reconciliation and atonement, they dismissed the fact that their policy would only encourage Vietnam in her aggressive and expansionist aims. They were labouring under a delusion if they thought the Vietnamese leaders would renounce the Soviet option in return for generous material assistance.

The Chinese, who were less naïve, denied that Vietnam's growing dependence on the Soviet Union represented a threat. On the contrary, they said, it would teach the Vietnamese a salutary lesson about the treatment to which dependent countries were subjected by the Russians.

'Vietnam may become an Asian Cuba,' I was told by a senior Chinese Foreign Ministry official, 'but only within limits. The Vietnamese are no Cubans. They didn't fight for independence from the Americans only to become dependent on the Soviet Union. They'll discover for themselves that dependence on Moscow is intolerable in the long run.'

Next day I called on Vice-Foreign Minister Zhang Wenjin and discussed the 'punitive action' for an hour-and-a-half. He told me that China had no set objectives, geographically speaking. The intention was to teach the Vietnamese a lesson and, having done so, to withdraw. I objected that it would be hard to tell when the lesson had sunk in. Zhang conceded this but pointed out that the Indians had learned their lesson very quickly in 1962. The current campaign was unlikely to last any longer than its Indian counterpart. He hoped that the Vietnamese, whose megalomania had inhibited them from negotiating on issues such as the expulsion of Vietnamese of Chinese descent, would soon see reason.

I asked if the danger of intervention by a third power would not increase the longer the operation lasted. Zhang replied that this danger had been taken into account, but that the conflict would remain localized and limited. He discounted Western fears of escalation. The Soviet Union would not have time to launch wide-ranging operations against a country of China's size. The most he could imagine was a series of minor frontier incidents or similar provocations. The Chinese Government had conducted a careful and objective analysis of all contingencies. China would withdraw her troops exactly according to plan.

We went on to discuss at length whether and how the conflict might be dealt with by the United Nations.

On 22 February I received a visit from Ambassador Shcherbakov of the Soviet Union, Tolstikov's successor, who had been in Peking for many months without evincing any eagerness to pay the usual courtesy calls on his foreign colleagues. Some opined that, as the Ambassador of a superpower, he felt no obligation to do so. He had recently been making up for lost time.

Ilya Shcherbakov had started life as a schoolteacher and worked his way up the Party ladder. He had been responsible in the Central Committee Secretariat for relations with ruling Communist Parties, served as Minister Plenipotentiary in Peking many years earlier, and completed a ten-year tour as Ambassador in Hanoi.

With his ruddy complexion and small moustache, Shcherbakov looked less like a Party functionary than a character in a Chekhov play. His movements were precise and deliberate. One could picture him sitting down at his desk, straightening his pencils and rulers, pen and pounce box, removing his pince-nez from a waistcoat pocket, polishing them, putting them on his nose, and ringing for his clerk.

We took tea together in the library. He wielded his cup with white, well-manicured hands. His expression was dispassionate and not unfriendly, but there was a hint of steel in his gaze. We discussed Vietnam as a matter of course, and I found him surprisingly frank on the subject.

I said, 'Your Government recently concluded a treaty of friendship and alliance with Hanoi.'

'Quite so, and we shall abide by all its provisions.'

'What does the treaty provide for, now that the Chinese have invaded?'

'Consultations,' he replied. He looked at me keenly to see if his meaning had sunk in.

'Ah,' I said, 'consultations.'

'Yes, and they'll take place in Moscow very soon. You can depend on that.'

'You think the Vietnamese will be able to handle the situation by themselves?'

Shcherbakov not only thought so but reiterated his belief at a later stage. The Soviet Union, he said, would welcome negotiations between the two sides, but Chinese troops would have to pull out of Vietnam before they could get together. 'We have no wish to be drawn into this conflict. Committing Soviet forces would be an extremely grave step – one that would fundamentally alter its character. Moscow is quite alive to the consequences of such a step.'

'I gather from what you tell me,' I said, 'that the Soviet Union intends to act responsibly, not widen the conflict.'

'*Da, da!*' he replied, smacking the table top in confirmation. 'Responsibly!'

No abuse was levelled at the Chinese. Shcherbakov referred only once, and without any particular emphasis, to Chinese 'aggression'. My impression was that he took a detached view of his country's new allies. He had told Ambassador Sato during his introductory visit the day before that the Vietnamese were disappointed that Tass had reported the Chinese invasion in such moderate language.

His comments on the military situation were as sober as might have been expected from someone so closely resembling a Chekhovian civil servant. Chinese forces had penetrated Vietnamese territory to a depth of nine or ten miles in places. Elsewhere, they were still pinned down on the frontier. The terrain, which he knew well, did not favour an invader. The Chinese offensive would be restricted to existing lines of communication because jungle and mountains on either flank prohibited the deployment of large formations. The Chinese were amply equipped with weapons manufactured in, or under licence from, the Soviet Union. So were the Vietnamese, but theirs were more modern by twenty years. They also possessed stocks of captured American equipment, which was very up-to-date. Every word Shcherbakov said on the subject underlined his stated belief that the Vietnamese were not reliant on Soviet aid and would be capable of containing the situation on their own. Just as he never vilified the Chinese, so he said nothing good about the Vietnamese.

Peter Hauswedell, our internal affairs counsellor, had discovered that although the Chinese deployment had started weeks ago – a fact already known to us – the decision to invade was only a few days old. Very senior officials were apprised of it by Party Document No. 11, only two days before fighting commenced. Other officials first heard the news on Saturday morning, when forward elements had already crossed the border, and the general public on Saturday afternoon.

Our domestic staff were preoccupied with other matters. Taking advantage of a recent snowfall, Old Liu and Little Wang had built a big snow panda outside the kitchen door and stuck a bunch of flowers in its paw. Whether coincidentally or not, it was facing the switchboard room presided over by pretty Miss Wen.

On 28 February I gave a dinner for Vice-Foreign Minister Zhang Wenjin and Assistant Foreign Minister Song Zhiguang. South-East Asia was our main topic of conversation, and they both presented a very frank account of the political and military situation. I was equally candid when they asked me for a summary of German press opinion, which was unfavourable.

Turning to Cambodia, I said that the country would be in a far better position if Pol Pot had not forfeited international sympathy by imposing such a barbarous régime. When Zhang Wenjin agreed, I asked why China had failed to remonstrate with him.

'Our views were no secret to Pol Pot,' Zhang said, 'but it's true that we were restrained in our criticism. We felt that our own recent past disqualified us from lecturing others.'

This was an honest reply, and one that merited acceptance. Chairman Mao had shown less restraint in June 1975, when he congratulated Pol Pot on his 'tremendous victory' and 'the abolition of all classes at a stroke'.

On 5 March, Zhang Wenjin received the ambassadors of Western Europe and America. He informed us that Chinese troops had just been ordered to withdraw from Vietnam, having attained their objectives, and pointed out that the punitive campaign against Vietnam had taken rather less time than the one against India in 1962.

Few campaigns in European history were undertaken purely in order to teach someone a lesson. Their more usual aim was to force another country to its knees, render it docile, or seize part or all of its territory. In China, by contrast, punitive campaigns have been known since very early times. Most of them were directed against the nomadic tribes of the north and west, who repeatedly invaded the more prosperous Middle Kingdom. China's military expeditions seldom aimed at territorial aggrandizement. Their purpose was to inflict damage on an enemy and deter him from further encroachments.

This particular campaign was over. The Chinese had probably counted on scoring a swifter military success, but Vietnamese resistance proved stiffer than they expected. Weaknesses had shown up in the Chinese command structure. The senior officers, who were elderly and hidebound, led their men in the style of thirty years earlier. Supplies and reinforcements failed to turn up on time, and the difficulties of the terrain had been underestimated.

Until now, the impression created by Hua Guofeng's Government was that China's efforts were wholly centred on modernization – that she would pursue a low-key foreign policy and lay no claim to regional policing powers. Her invasion of Vietnamese territory had demonstrated the falsity of this impression. The effect of the campaign, therefore, was twofold.

On the one hand, it lent the Chinese 'face' in the eyes of many Asians.

Vietnam having few friends in the area, they relished China's partial humiliation of a people who arrogantly claimed that their 'defeat' of the United States had made them the world's strongest military power after the Soviet Union. It came as a welcome surprise that the Chinese had correctly gauged the Soviet reaction, even though the ink was scarcely dry on the Soviet–Vietnamese friendship treaty. The Kremlin's limitations had been exposed for all to see.

Against this, there were revived or intensified fears in a number of ASEAN countries that China regarded South and South-East Asia as her stamping ground and meant to wield a political, military, or subversive influence there.

The Russians had demonstrated yet again that their response to critical situations is not as rash or irrational as is feared by many Western politicians, who warn against provoking them into ill-considered moves by taking too firm a stand. There are times when they like to create the impression that their patience is exhausted, and that those who continue to try it must be prepared for the worst.

In this case, cool deliberation must have convinced them that their scope for military intervention was limited. Their aloofness towards their Vietnamese allies showed that they were unwilling to give Hanoi a free hand – in fact they may not have been too displeased that this latest development had increased Hanoi's dependence on them.

Federal Chancellor Helmut Schmidt called Russia's response to the Chinese invasion 'wise'. If he meant that the Russians had carried out a sober appraisal of their interests and possible courses of action, the epithet was apt. If he meant that they had acted wisely because they wanted to keep and promote world peace, this would be harder to prove. Nine months later they invaded Afghanistan, not for the preservation of world peace but in furtherance of what they took to be their own national interests.

The Chinese and the Sense of Shame

Chinese women were absurdly prudish, Herr M. complained bitterly – far more so than their sisters in any other socialist country. Herr M., who was making a television documentary about the women of China, cited an example.

While on location in Kaifeng, he had auditioned a delightful young engine driver and outlined the questions he proposed to ask her in front of the camera. She was quite prepared to answer all his questions save one, namely, whether she'd ever been in love. That would embarrass her, she said. She'd be bound to blush, and everyone would see because the film was being shot in colour. So saying, she turned crimson.

'And we hadn't started shooting!' sighed Herr M. 'What a shame – what a picture she'd have made! Back home you can ask folks anything you like and they don't turn a hair. Nobody blushes these days except in romantic novels.'

Yes indeed, what a shame!

Many people call *Jinpingmei* or *Kin Ping Meh* an erotic novel. Lin Yutang himself puts it in that category, like all Chinese, although it is one of the greatest novels in Chinese or any other language and defies such narrow classification.

Written four hundred years ago, *Kin Ping Meh* depicts every facet of contemporary life in a provincial Chinese city: wealth and poverty, corruption and integrity, crime and lubricity. The amatory exploits of its hero, Ximen Qing, though far from being its only theme, figure prominently. The erotic scenes are described with such gusto and love of detail that the English translator of the four-volume, unabridged edition (*The Golden Lotus*, London, 1959), was sometimes reduced to the same condition as the pretty young engine driver in Kaifeng. To spare his blushes, he reproduced the more daring passages in dry and pedantic Latin.

The book has been widely read in China. Emperor Kangxi, whose own brother had translated it into Manchurian, banned it as pornography in the seventeenth century. His edict seems to have been ineffective, for at least fourteen different editions appeared in that century alone. Emperor Qianlong, who reimposed the ban in the eighteenth century, was just as unsuccessful.

Once, when I was sitting in the embassy library with Günter Grass and half a dozen well-known Chinese authors, male and female, Grass inquired if our guests had read the novel. Not only had they read it, but they admitted as much without turning pink. Xie Bingxin, who was eighty, actually laughed.

Could it be obtained at any bookstore? asked Grass. This time the laughter was general. Of course not! Even if it were published in an edition of half a million copies, it would be sold out at once. Any new book sold out within hours, as we were well aware, but *Kin Ping Meh* . . . No, most of them had borrowed it from libraries.

Libraries open to all and sundry?

Oh, no, only members of the Writers' Association.

Now that the Gang of Four were no longer at the helm and far greater freedom was in prospect, said Grass, might the novel not be republished?

Here the going got harder and the replies more hesitant. No one cared to pronounce on the theme of greater intellectual freedom. Although Bai Hua, the young soldier-writer, had delivered a courageous address on the subject at the Writers' Congress only a few days earlier, he now said nothing.

Opinions were divided on whether or not it might be feasible to produce a new edition of the novel. Someone – I think it was the poetess Ke Yan – mooted the possibility of an expurgated version. There was general agreement that the book should only be made available to adults. Didn't such restrictions exist in Germany too?

Yes, I replied. 'Morally injurious' literature could not be sold to minors in Germany either.

Someone else suggested that the novel might be published *neibu*, meaning 'for internal use only'. Even in imperial China, it had to a certain extent been sold *neibu*, or under the counter, and no one had ever discovered the author's identity. In the old days, educated people who wished to be taken seriously thought it better to disclaim having read such a notorious piece of fiction. They would have been ashamed to admit it.

Really? I said. Well, their prejudices seemed to have lived on. Whenever I passed some favourable comment on *Kin Ping Meh*, my Chinese friends would sigh and draw attention to the far more sophisticated *Dream of the Red Chamber*. *Kin Ping Meh* was cruder, admittedly, and I thoroughly appreciated the subtle characterization of *The Dream of the Red Chamber*, a novel of which I was also fond. On the other hand, I often became bored with the effeminate ways of its principal character, Bao Yü; with the ivory-tower effusions of the poetry club; with Bao Yü's problems in regard to maidservants and their delicate sensibilities; with the burial of flower petals in gardens; with people's habit of bursting into tears at the drop of a hat or going into a decline and lapsing into weeks of melancholia – in short, with the affectations and artificial problems of a great feudal household remote from real life. It had always puzzled me that, even in a communist country, literary critics found it possible to accept the parasitical existence of the Chia clan with only mild reprobation. It was Chinese prudery, then as now, that seemed to me to have denied *Kin Ping Meh* due recognition for its robust but often humorous social criticism, its all-embracing social compass.

Günter Grass wanted to know if our guests would dare to write a realistic description, either now or in the near future, of what two people did in bed together.

'For me the question doesn't arise,' said Wang Meng. 'I've no desire to, with so many other burning issues on my mind.'

Wang Meng and all the other writers present had suffered persecution for many years. Most of them had been rusticated and compelled to work in people's communes. Wang Meng himself had spent seventeen years living in Uighur territory on the Sino-Soviet border. I still recall what he said when he visited me in Germany some time ago:

'Many things in the West escape my comprehension. Literature, films, the visual arts, life in general – they all impress me as over-sexualized and boring. I'm disappointed, not because I'm a prude, but because I ask myself: Are *these* your concerns in a world on the brink of an abyss?'

Yet Wang Meng must have been aware that in China, and Chinese universities in particular, underground literature of a purely pornographic and wholly unpolitical kind now flourishes alongside the political variety. They are copied by hand, but a change is already under way. The growth of tourism and of China's contacts with the West is bringing about a rapid increase in the smuggling of pornographic books and pictures. Western magazines of the *Playboy* genre fetch high prices on the black market. Shanghai already maintains a thriving trade in 'dirty pictures', which are surreptitiously offered for sale on Nanking Road as they used to be in times gone by. Although some of this merchandise is said to be indigenous, imports from Hong Kong, Japan, Germany, and America are in greater demand, reputedly because they 'offer' more.

We are sometimes told that prudishness and sexual inhibitions, which provide psychologists with such welcome scope for their many conflicting theories, are simply a product of Christian moral concepts. Although it is probably true that Christian moral inhibitions have done a great deal of mischief on this side of the world, non-Christian China is far more prudish and her sexual modesty far more effective, even today, than in our Western, Christian world. Thomas Meadows, a pioneer sinologist of the last century, found much to criticize in the classical philosophers of China because they had still to see the Gospel light. On the other hand, he commended them highly for the fact that none of their sacred books or annotations contained a single sentence 'that may not be read aloud in any family circle in England'. One suspects that the Holy Writ presented him with greater problems in this respect.

No dictatorship, that of the proletariat included, can tolerate permissiveness, hence the brief duration of the Soviet Union's 'free love' phase. The strict tabooing of love in China cannot, however, be ascribed to socialism alone, still less to the sole influence of Chinese tradition.

Western opinion-makers often urge the public to cast off taboos because they are restrictive of freedom. As a corollary, they proclaim it heroic to destroy taboos and play with fire. Neither course of action is truly meaningful or truly heroic because closer scrutiny reveals that the taboos have long been dismantled and the fire has cooled.

It cannot be denied that freedom is restricted by the taboo of sexual shame, but is a 'shameless' society worth striving for? Do its assets exceed its liabilities?

'And they were both naked, the man and his wife, and were not ashamed.' That, according to the only report we possess, is how it was in the beginning. The picture did not change until the two inhabitants of Paradise had sampled the fateful apple. 'And the eyes of them both were opened, and they knew that they were naked; and they sewed fig leaves together, and made themselves aprons.'

Since then, shame has been one of mankind's fundamental characteristics, a potent force in all societies that attach a high value to mores and morality, responsibility and good order. Shame sets bounds on what is permitted in social life. A force productive of tension, it can destroy human beings as well as limit their behaviour. History is littered with the names of those who preferred death to disgrace. Western examples are relatively few, Chinese innumerable.

Although it is undoubtedly true that freedom reigns in a 'shameless' society, every passing day confirms that passion is being replaced by tedium, superficiality, aimlessness, loneliness, emptiness, and despair.

Early Chinese literature contains some ardent poems addressed by young girls to their lovers. Their outspoken invitations and thinly-veiled allusions to the pleasures of love are far from shameless, but neither are they coy.

Confucian commentators of later date were gravely perplexed by this. Like the interpreters of the Song of Solomon, they eventually decided to place an allegorical construction on such verses, though many of their exegeses were so factitious and far-fetched as to be almost unintelligible.

Although the Confucian interpreters are no more, some of these lyrics would cause problems in China's modern, communistically puritanical society. It would, for instance, be hard to imagine the following words, which were composed long before Confucius' day, being sung by a choir of women soldiers arrayed on stage or in front of a television camera. They occur in the *Shijing*, an anthology of popular songs:

> I implore you, young Zhung,
> leap not into our yard,
> burst not through our sandalwood!
> Not that I should be sorry if you did,

> but I fear people's wagging tongues.
> How I love you, young Zhung!
> But I so much fear
> what people say.

The author of this veiled invitation to Zhung, her lover, was not ashamed of herself for making it. Her action was not a sin in the eyes of Heaven, nor was her song a denial of erotic passion. It merely camouflaged what would, if openly displayed, have been an infringement of custom. Even in earliest times, love was *neibu*.

The girl's only fear was of wagging tongues – of what the neighbours would say if they saw young Zhung making his way to her through the hedge. She was afraid of being disgraced.

Just as 'shame' possesses a dual significance in English, so the Chinese word *chi* can mean both disgrace and the sense of shame – and *chi* is an important concept in Confucian ethics:

'The Master said: "If the people be guided by laws, and if it be endeavoured to keep order through punishment, they will seek to avoid punishment but will have no sense of shame. If they be guided by virtue, and if it be endeavoured to keep order through the rules of propriety, they will have a sense of shame and will, moreover, become good."'

Laws can govern people's outward behaviour only, whereas the reasons for their behaviour repose within them. The refined and educated or 'superior' person does not eschew crime for fear of punishment. He does so because he is deterred by shame, or fear of disgrace.

The missionary Richard Wilhelm translates *chi* as 'conscience', but the Chinese have never associated it with obedience to divine commandments, nor can it be equated with Socrates' *daimonion*, the inner voice that admonished him whenever he threatened to offend against what was mentally discernible as good.

Chi, or shame, was what a person felt when he had offended against *li*, meaning decency, convention, good form, and much else besides. But the person who did so – who was guilty of unseemly and irresponsible conduct – was committing no sin and violating no divine commandment. Although he had transgressed the cosmic order of things, that and the earthly social system were congruent.

It is strange that the Chinese should have devoted so little discussion to the concept of shame, almost as if they considered it such a natural disciplinary power that no words need be wasted on it.

Education, says Confucius, renders a person capable of perceiving and adopting the norms of ethical conduct. The basis of ethical conduct is the categorical imperative embodied in this negative version of our own popular dictum: 'Do not unto others that which you do not wish done unto yourself.' Sense of shame, it is further stated, will deter a person from transgressing this rule.

Thus the courts of ancient times did not so much punish a crime definable in terms of evidence as penalize the state of mind that led to its perpetration. Judicial verdicts and sentences are still coloured by this attitude. In the penal code of the Qing dynasty, which remained valid until the beginning of the twentieth century, forty lashes were prescribed as the punishment for 'shameless conduct'. Shameless conduct itself remained undefined because everyone knew what it was. We, on the other hand, live in a shameless society, where it would be difficult to reach a consensus about what is shameless and what is not.

In China, whenever an offence against the rules of society became common knowledge, social retribution was swift and severe. The 'shameless' person lost face and reputation, but only if his disgrace became known, if the story leaked out – if people started talking. So it was, at least, among the common folk or Old Hundred Families. This may be one reason for what strikes non-Chinese as an inordinate love of secrecy: the fear that, whether in the family, the village, or the government, matters may come to light which outsiders would regard as disgraceful, an occasion for gossip or even ridicule.

Those guilty of grave offences – gross shamelessness, so to speak – were naturally brought to trial. Penalties for the *xiao ren*, or Little People, tended to be harsher than those meted out to educated persons, who were (or were held to be) far more sensitive to punishment and keenly aware of their disgrace even before it had been advertised. They suffered not only from gossip but from a personal awareness that they had violated the code in which they had been reared. They internalized their shame, which could in certain circumstances affect them like the sense of guilt and sin from which it differed so greatly. Shame could not be mitigated by atonement. There was no authority, earthly or celestial, that could acquit them of shame by way of the confessional or by the direct exercise of divine clemency. All that could blur the memory of disgrace was future good behaviour and active remorse.

Because shame and disgrace can wound so deeply, the 'superior' person takes care not to make his neighbour lose face or give him grounds for shame. He refrains from casting suspicion on him and rebuking him in another's presence. The least gesture, the mildest reproach, can be profoundly hurtful.

I recall an occasion when Jiang Nanxiang, China's Minister of Education, was a guest at the Press Club in Bonn. The walls were lined with humorous caricatures of German politicians in animal guise. The Chinese visitor made no comment, but his surprise and bewilderment were all too plain. How could anyone degrade a person, especially a politician in office, by depicting him as a fox or a squirrel? In the case of someone expelled from decent society, someone with a 'black' past – a non-person or member of the Gang of Four, for example – anything goes. Where such people are concerned, the Chinese have no qualms about calumny and character assassination.

The sanctions applied by society to those who have transgressed its code are harsh and cruel, as Chinese children learn at a very tender age. They are reared, not in abhorrence of guilt and sin, but in fear of disgrace.

Although the legal penalties imposed on an educated person may once have been milder than those meted out to common folk, he was often harder hit by the moral condemnation of his peers. 'It isn't done' was a punishment in itself, a rebuke that might lead to the ostracism of him who had violated the code of honour of the educated class – and that, in a society where no one could seek refuge in anonymity, constituted a severe penalty.

Censure as a form of punishment is not unique to the Chinese world. Among the patricians of ancient Rome, the censor's enunciation of a *nota censoria* sufficed to bring a person *infamia* and destroy his good name. This rebuke was administered not only when a law had been broken but in the case of acts within the law but considered unjust.

Shame is stronger than any law. In one of the earliest Chinese novellas, the tale of Prince Tan of Yan, a knight at the Crown Prince's table sings a satirical song about a guest whom he considers to have been unduly privileged. The guest, however, declares himself willing to risk death to avenge an old insult inflicted on the Crown Prince by killing its author, Qin Shihuang, China's First Emperor. At this, the author of the lampoon is overcome with shame. When the guest passes him, bound for an attempt on the Emperor's life, he cuts his throat 'in token of farewell'.

We meet similar incidents in Japanese literature and history. The *samurai*'s honour carried more weight with him than laws with the mass of the people. It compelled him, if disgraced, to commit *seppuku*, [1] or disembowel himself. In the old days, European officers who had violated their code of honour were under a similar compulsion. In extreme cases of dishonourable conduct, which far from always constituted a penal offence and might simply mean that they had incurred excessive gambling debts, they either resigned or shot themselves.

[1] The word *harakiri* ('belly-slitting') is not commonly used in Japanese because of its crudity. *Seppuku*, the sinicized rendering of the same character, is considered less extreme.

Just as the Chinese ruling class was expected to display a superior sense of responsibility, so it based its claim to rulership on a superior moral sense and an adherence to a stricter code of behaviour.

Where statutory penalties are concerned, said Confucius, a man will try to evade them by subterfuge, lies, and legal quibbles. This he will do without the least embarrassment, whereas the person answerable to a code of honour will achieve nothing by splitting hairs.

Confucianism aspired to extend the strict code of the educated élite, insofar as this was possible, to the people as a whole. It wanted to render laws redundant by raising moral standards, and to use upbringing and education to transform Little People into Superior Persons who had no need of laws because a sense of shame would deter them from unseemly conduct.

The Gang of Four and their supporters, too, believed that people's awareness of a code was more effective than laws and edicts, and that education would remould the human being, transforming him into the different and superior creature known as the New Man. Daily political indoctrination was designed to enhance comrades' revolutionary consciousness, however, not their moral sense. The ultra-leftists held that, once the entire nation was imbued with revolutionary consciousness, production would rise to a level adequate for subsistence, and universal justice would prevail.

But they failed to create the New Man. The demands made on people's revolutionary consciousness changed so often that the one remaining constant was absolute obedience.

The Chinese Communist Party of today is less at pains to cultivate revolutionary consciousness. Instead, it falls back on old-established injunctions of the kind that also occur in the Confucian moral code – as, for instance, when it urges people to learn and heed 'the Five Virtues' (decorum, courtesy, cleanliness, discipline, and morality) and 'the Four Decencies' (decency of mental outlook, language, behaviour, and environment). Modern Chinese films ask: What is true love? What is nobility of mind? What does sacrifice entail? What constitutes true happiness? And, just as the Confucians drew their examples from anthologies of edifying tales full of dutiful sons, virtuous daughters, and righteous officials and judges, so the people – and young people in particular – are once more enjoined to follow the example of Lei Feng (1939–62), a model soldier and hero of labour who spent his short life doing good deeds.

But, just as the Confucians failed to educate the masses into paragons of virtue, so the Communist Party's efforts in the same direction are bound to miscarry. Life in a society of sanctimonious and superior people would bore the Chinese to distraction, especially as one of their favourite pastimes is to note and comment on their neighbours' moral conduct. Tongue-wagging – malicious gossip of the sort dreaded by young Zhung's admirer three thousand years ago – is still a constant and ubiquitous threat.

The following story was told to me by a Chinese acquaintance who had been sent to work in a factory during the Cultural Revolution. It appears that one of his fellow workers, a young woman, had an affair with a married colleague whose family lived far away in the country, and who saw his wife for a few days a year at most. Accused by their workmates of sleeping together, the couple denied it. Nobody believed them, and a mood of hysteria developed, particularly among their female workmates. They were watched and spied on. Eventually, after keeping them under surveillance, members of the People's Militia succeeded in catching them in bed together. They were promptly arrested and marched off to the factory, whose Security Bureau personnel interrogated them with relish and broadcast the results of their inquisition to the rest of the workforce. Neither of them was permitted to go home throughout this time. They were held in isolation at the factory and compelled to sleep there until the board of inquiry ended by reprimanding them both.

But that was not the end of the affair. The young man had lost face and incurred ridicule. To be an object of derision and a target for detractors whom one cannot escape is hurtful beyond endurance. Icelandic sagas record that strong men could be so humiliated by satirical poems that their sole recourse was to flee the country. The Chinese worker had no such alternative.

The girl fared still worse. Her father beat her when she came home – she was in her mid-twenties – and then turned her out. Her family wanted nothing more to do with someone whose reputation bore a stain that could never be expunged, so she had to live with her disgrace. She was assigned to a labour unit which refused to release her for employment in another part of the country, where no one knew her story. Now that her family had disowned her, she too was deprived of human society and a means of escape.

I never heard how the story ended, but suicide is the usual outcome in such cases. Where shame is a living force, social sanctions against those who commit some disgraceful act are harsher than in societies ruled by laws alone.

Many Chinese emperors subjected their ministers and court officials to ungentle treatment, as we already know. They castrated, bisected, quartered, or simply beheaded them. Emperors of a milder disposition abstained from such unrefined methods. If need arose, the Son of Heaven sent an unwanted official the *bailing*, or white silken cord (actually a ribbon), which the unfortunate man proceeded to use in keeping with custom and propriety.

Although he had served the empire well and was loyal to the Emperor, General Nian Gengyao fell prey to slanderous intrigue. Emperor Yongzheng (1723–35), who resolved to get rid of him, sent the General a long, polished letter of farewell enclosing the silken cord. The Son of Heaven concluded his missive as follows:

> As I peruse this State Paper, I shed bitter tears. As Lord of the Universe, however, I am bound to exhibit unswerving justice in the matter of rewards and punishments. I remit the penalty of decapitation and grant you the privilege of suicide. With lavish generosity and merciful forbearance I have spared the lives of your entire family, with one exception. You would have to be stock or stone, if, even in the face of death, you failed to shed tears of joy and gratitude for the benefits bestowed on you by the Imperial Master whom you have so foully betrayed.

Although physical violence was often employed against officials during the Cultural Revolution, Red Guards and people with a high degree of revolutionary consciousness preferred to humiliate their opponents and make them look ridiculous. The widow of Marshal He Long, whom the Gang of Four abducted and murdered, records that his jailer, instead of giving him rice in a bowl, tipped it on to the floor of his cell so that he had to lap it up on all fours, like a dog.

Educated persons – dignitaries and public servants – were seldom chained or tortured in the old days. If convicted of some grave misdemeanour, they were sentenced to wear a white hat that would advertise their crime and keep its memory alive. The same disgrace was visited on many politicians, scholars, and public servants, both senior and junior, during the Cultural Revolution. To this day, refractory prisoners in penal establishments are made to wear 'the cap of a bad element', so that disgrace will dog them even in the company of convicts like themselves.

Thousands of people jumped to their deaths during the Cultural Revolution, merely to avoid humiliation, sometimes after Red Guards had thrust them into an upper room with the window obligingly opened in advance. These victims of persecution, most of whom were intellectuals, acted as etiquette and education prescribed. 'The spirit can be killed but not humiliated . . .' They, too, preferred death to dishonour.

Some days before leaving Peking we received a visit from Mrs Yü, who had brought us a farewell gift. It turned out to be a magnificent old court robe, richly embroidered from collar to hem. We were in two minds about accepting it.

Mrs Yü told us that the robe had belonged to her husband's grandfather, a mandarin of senior rank, who had worn it on ceremonial occasions. Red Guards had burst into her home during the Cultural Revolution, bent on subjecting her husband to 'struggle'. They searched the whole house and purloined several articles of value, notably a watch and a camera. When they came across the ceremonial robe, they forced her husband to put it on. Then they gummed a piece of wrapping paper to the back, scrawled the characters for 'royalist' on it, stuck a dunce's hat on his head, and paraded him through the streets. Mrs Yü begged us to accept the robe as a gift. She and her husband no longer wished to keep it in their home, she said, but we ourselves might appreciate its handsome embroidery.

So the Red Guards had dressed her husband in this ludicrous costume and led him through the streets to roars of laughter from their comrades. Although they had humiliated him, not us, we experienced a vicarious pang of shame. In China, where shame and *li* count for more than they do with us, this treatment must have been almost too much for him to bear. Arrest and imprisonment or exile to the provinces he might have forgotten, but not the disgrace of that day.

Our reluctance evaporated. When Mrs Yü had gone, we took a closer look at her gift. A scrap of brown paper still adhered to the back. We have never removed it.

The Prince

Prince Sihanouk tended to screech when excited, his voice rising to a falsetto capable of shattering glass. 'Pol Pot,' he cried, 'is the Cambodian people's Public Enemy Number One. He has murdered millions of my fellow countrymen, and the ones who are left will starve to death without help from the rest of the world – and I'm here in Peking, unable to do a thing. I resigned as Head of State in 1976, not because Pol Pot amended the constitution and abolished the monarchy, but because he'd started to butcher my people. Hundreds of thousands died after the capture of Phnom Penh in 1975, when he drove them out of the towns and into the countryside.'

A sudden silence fell. He laughed abruptly and handed round some nuts. We sipped our China tea.

Twice in the past year I had given the Cambodian Ambassador letters for Prince Sihanouk from a friend of his in Germany. We hadn't known if he was a prisoner – indeed, we hadn't even been sure of his survival. The Cambodian Ambassador, whose table I always shared at official banquets in the Great Hall of the People, had promised to pass the letters on. Now I inquired about them.

'Nothing!' the Prince exclaimed. 'I received nothing! They locked us up in the palace and put iron bars over the doors to prevent anyone from entering or leaving. When Ceausescu and Deng Yingchao, Zhou Enlai's widow, paid state visits to Phnom Penh and asked to see me, Pol Pot told them I wouldn't receive them. *Imaginez-vous!*

'Once every three months, one of his aides would come and collect me in a big Mercedes and drive me out into the country, just so everyone would think I was backing that criminal. My people are a cheerful people – always happy – but when they saw me they wept!'

The high-pitched voice broke into a giggle. It was an antidote to distress and embarrassment.

'Just imagine, they wept when they saw me!' He giggled even louder. 'Ten members of my family have disappeared – daughters, sons-in-law, grandchildren. Do help yourself to a pastry – they're all we could get at the Friendship Store here. The Chinese made inquiries about them, but they still haven't received an answer. They never will, either. So now, as you can see for yourself, there are only the three of us left. We three and Aunt.'

The small white Pomeranian was begging for a titbit from Princess Monique. She picked the dog up and handed it to her son, the Little Prince, who took it outside.

'*Et voilà, le chien!* He escaped too, but our people we abandoned.'

'It all happened so quickly,' said Princess Monique, 'but we couldn't leave the dog behind.'

Sihanouk nodded in confirmation. 'Out of the blue, when Vietnamese troops under General Giap were already in the suburbs, the Chinese turned up and invited us to Peking. If we wanted to catch the last plane out of Phnom Penh, they said, we must drive straight to the airport. So we did. We didn't even bring coats with us. It's always so warm at home, we never stopped to think how cold Peking can be in January.'

Sihanouk hadn't shown his face or received any visitors in the ten weeks since then. The Chinese had told us that he was engaged in Buddhist spiritual exercises and didn't wish to be disturbed. Knowing what he thought of Pol Pot and being aware that discretion wasn't his forte, they may also have urged him to keep himself to himself.

At the end of March, however, he invited a handful of Western journalists to an off-the-record press conference on the understanding that he wouldn't give an interview or pose for pictures. Needless to say, the lure of the camera proved too much for him.

He had been told by Peter Scholl-Latour, a TV reporter, that I was anxious to visit him for a talk about Cambodia. I received an invitation next day. It was headed 'Telegram' but had not come through the usual channels. Chinese thrift and common sense had prompted the messenger to act on his own initiative. Why take Sihanouk's invitation to the post office, where it would have to be copied out and forwarded to me? Instead, he brought the telegram form straight to the German Embassy by bicycle. It wasn't much further than the post office.

Sihanouk was living in the old Legation Quarter, in what had once been the French Ambassador's residence. This, complete with a private cinema and a forty-metre indoor swimming pool, had been placed at his disposal by Zhou Enlai when he was staying in Peking prior to Pol Pot's takeover.

The new residence, which post-dated the earthquake, was a box-like building containing a large number of lofty, oversized, uncomfortable rooms. We were seated in one of these now, in the customary semi-circular formation. The Prince had left it up to us whether we came accompanied by one aide or two, so we had brought along Thomas Fischer-Dieskau, our economic counsellor, and his decorative wife Ingeborg. The invitation had spoken of '*Un dîner en toute intimité*'.

We were greeted in the driveway by Sihanouk's son, whose age I put at seventeen, but only after negotiating a reception committee of Chinese protocol officials and security men. The Chinese were clearly concerned for the Prince's safety. When he came to dinner with us a few weeks later, policemen were stationed all along the five-mile route from his residence to the embassy, and the embassy itself was completely cordoned off throughout his visit.

Sihanouk and his wife, who were standing in the middle of the big drawing-room, came forward to greet us. The Prince ran a hand over his shaven, almost cubic skull and explained that his Buddhist devotions would soon be completed. His eyes, which were always on the move, missed nothing. Piercing at times, they moistened at every mention of the Cambodian people. His voice was almost invariably animated, shrill, and emotional, though he sometimes turned tearful or giggled and took refuge in the Asiatic laugh of embarrassment. When speaking of matters close to his heart – the loss of his daughters, the sufferings of his people, Pol Pot's brutality – he tended to theatricalize in a humorous way designed to mask his feelings.

Sihanouk was fifty-eight. His half-Italian wife, a tall, slender woman, looked ageless – possibly in her forties. Her gestures were graceful, her voice was soft and friendly, her manner immutably serene. Looking at her, one was reminded of a Raphael Madonna and wondered how any such creature could exist on our planet. After dinner, while we were watching a film in which many of her friends appeared, now dead or missing, I saw her surreptitiously wipe away a tear.

'When we were detained,' said Sihanouk, 'the Princess did all the housework herself – scrubbing, dusting, washing, ironing.'

'Cooking too?'

'Cooking?' fluted the Prince. '*I* did the cooking, naturally. If there are two things I'm good at, they're cooking and ruling a country. But the days were long, and all I could do was cook, so I started learning languages. There were some language courses in the palace record library. On Monday I studied English, Tuesday Italian, Wednesday Russian, Thursday German. *Guten Tag*,' he went on, '*wie geht es Ihnen? Haben Sie schon gegessen?*'

'No,' I replied, 'we haven't eaten yet.'

His Royal Highness had not only cooked the dinner but written out the menu cards himself. They bore the Cambodian royal arms in gold. Could he really have found the time, before dashing to his car on 6 January, to pick up a stack of blank menus and stuff them in his pocket?

The meal began with some clear soup with a few peas floating in it. This the menu defined as *Consommé Royal Printemps*. The prawns that followed, which were known at our own table simply as *da xia*, or big prawns, became *Coquilles de fruits de mer Nantua*. The high-ceilinged dining-room was so vast and uncongenial that the table in the centre looked small and forlorn. The Little Prince joined us for dinner but said nothing. Aunt, we learned, was supervising operations in the kitchen. Franz asked the Little Prince if he intended to study in France like his father. Their Royal Highnesses greeted this question with a silence that seemed to fill every corner of the spacious room.

At length, Sihanouk informed us that he and his wife were not unnaturally anxious, in view of their daughters' disappearance and presumed death, to keep their son with them. Their other son, the brother of the Little Prince, had been denied admission to the house because of his avowed support for the Pol Pot régime. He was now living somewhere in Peking – quite where, the family neither knew nor cared.

The Prince's voice had risen an octave, and his wife was gazing angelically at her plate. We made appropriate noises of sympathy and regret, but Sihanouk had the bit between his teeth.

Unfortunately, he said, the Little Prince was also giving cause for concern. I tried to generalize the conversation by ruefully referring – *hélas!* – to the many and various worries common to all parents of children in this modern age, but His Royal Highness refused to be diverted from the case in point. The Little Prince thoroughly enjoyed the company of girls, he declared. He respected them like sisters but left it at that. *He couldn't make up his mind!*

The last words were delivered at full blast.

'*Honi soit qui mal y pense . . .*' Did my ears deceive me, or had someone – possibly Ingeborg Fischer-Dieskau – breathed rather than whispered it in my direction?

I made the transition from the particular to the literary by alluding to the principal character in *The Dream of the Red Chamber*, Bao Yü, who had given his father like cause for concern, but my words were drowned. The Little Prince's attitude, we learned, was in sharp contrast to that displayed at the same age by his male parent – a circumstance widely reported and discussed at the time.

But of course, we said – all the world was aware of that. Nevertheless, the Little Prince's attitude might change. He was still very young, and once he fell prey to a grand passion . . .

He might look young, retorted his father, but he was already twenty-six and would soon have to reach a decision. '*Comprenez mon émotion!*'

We sympathized with his feelings. It may have been that the Little Prince had his eye on someone other than his parents' choice, but his personal preferences counted for nothing. What mattered was the dynasty, which had ruled – as Sihanouk casually but rather vaguely remarked – for 'some two thousand years'. What mattered was Cambodia.

The Little Prince was visibly relieved, and Princess Monique rewarded me with a look of angelic gratitude, when I loudly expressed surprise and delight at finding that the next item on the menu, neatly inscribed in His Royal Highness's own hand, was *Kalbsleberwurst au Porto* accompanied by *Pommes de terre frites*.

Now it was my turn to solicit understanding for *my* emotion. Sihanouk, clearly gratified that his efforts had not gone unappreciated, announced that this dish was a new *création* concocted especially for the occasion. The can of calf's-liver sausage, identified as such in German on the label, had been found among his household stores. After blending and enriching its contents with certain herbs and a quantity of chopped, steamed onion, he had topped off the dish with cheese and browned it in the oven. The composition of the port wine sauce he owed to a recipe confided to him by a chef in a small Provençal town. We toasted each other in a fine, dry Bernkasteler Doctor. I was touched. Peter Scholl-Latour's TV team had recently photographed Sihanouk holding this, his very last bottle of German wine. Now he had opened it in our honour.

He would like nothing better, he said, than to retire to his modest villa on the Côte d'Azur. He could not foresee any political role for himself while Pol Pot still had a say in the affairs of Cambodia. He intended to remain in Peking for the time being, but he had made it clear to Deng that, if he came to power again, Cambodia would be a neutral country enjoying friendly relations with China and the Soviet Union alike.

'And with its immediate neighbours?' I asked.

'Of course!' exclaimed the Prince. He saw no problem there, thanks to his good relations with Vietnam's political leaders. I made no comment on this frail line of argument. A policy of neutrality had already failed him once, yet he seemed eager to resurrect it.

'Cambodia,' he went on, and his voice became shriller, 'will be the Switzerland, the Austria, of Asia. The problem is Pol Pot. The Chinese are pressing me to co-operate with him, but the policy I pursue is Cambodian, not Chinese. Pol Pot is a madman, pure and simple. Would a sane man abolish money as a medium of payment? Isn't anyone who destroys all a country's hospitals and exterminates its doctors and intellectuals deranged? Isn't anyone who revels in murder crazy? There were seven million Cambodians when he came to power; now there are only four million. By next year, if he persists in his present policy, there will be only half as many. The Chinese claim they want to liberate Cambodia. Whom do they propose to liberate if there's no one left alive?'

'How do you account for the fact that people still follow him?'

'Well,' he said, fixing me with a keen and far from friendly eye, 'these things happen, n'est-ce pas? Don't you remember? Surely you can't have forgotten how effective fanaticization and intimidation can be? Pol Pot now relies on mountain tribes and jungle hunters to do his dirty work. Worst of all are the children, many of them only twelve years old. He issues them with automatic weapons, and they delight in shooting anything that moves – people included. The Chinese keep telling me that Pol Pot has changed. They ought to know better. They've often tried to persuade him to adopt a more humane policy, but it's done no good. There'll be a protracted struggle between Pol Pot and the Vietnamese *Wehrmacht*' – he used the German word – 'and my people will be wiped out in the process. Either that, or they'll starve to death.'

He went on to criticize China's policy towards Vietnam. 'I've told Deng Xiaoping that the only way he'll ever teach the Vietnamese a lesson is to conquer the entire country, down to its southernmost tip. Otherwise they'll never learn.'

The Soviet Union came in for some bitter reproaches. The Russians were clumsy opportunists who exploited others for their own ends and then, when it came to the pinch, backed down. Cowardice, declared the Prince, was the most they could muster. But they would get away with such a policy only once, he predicted.

The German Democratic Republic, too, earned Sihanouk's contempt. He had annoyed Bonn by helping the East Germans to secure formal recognition in Phnom Penh. Several years later they had badgered Pol Pot, too, for permission to establish an embassy there in the hope of countering Chinese influence on the Russians' behalf. Only when their scheme had failed, and not before, did they discover that Pol Pot was committing crimes against humanity.

As we passed through the hallway, heading for Sihanouk's private cinema on the other side of the courtyard, we presented him with our ritual gift, which had been cleared by the security men and was standing on a table. It was a case of Ockfener Bockstein, a wine quite similar in character to Bernkasteler Doctor.

The colour film had been shot in Cambodia a dozen or so years before. It presented a blithe and cheerful picture of the country and its inhabitants. Nothing but beauty met the eye at every turn, and of problems there seemed to be none. How could it have been otherwise in a land ruled by a benevolently paternal prince who had even written the music for the film himself? The first song was entitled *Monique*. When the lights went up and we rose to leave, the composer sang us a reprise of the melody. Princess Monique had long since dried her tears and was smiling, a Raphael Madonna once more.

That was only the first of many enjoyable meetings. Prince Norodom Sihanouk had no country, ruled no nation, wielded no power. He had no money, either, but he had not been abandoned entirely. He lived in a sumptuous house with a big swimming pool and a cinema where he could screen his sixteen films. He entertained guests, cooked for them in person, and wrote out the menu cards himself.

Even in this uprooted state, he contrived to be a political force. He remained magically suspended in political space, a feat of levitation baffling to all who witnessed it. He was independent and remained so, though his political stance continually varied and could change in the course of a single evening.

The Chinese regarded him with scepticism because of his erratic, impulsive, and contradictory opinions, which he either voiced in interviews or aired by the simple expedient of calling up Agence France Presse. Though dubious at times of his reliability, they cultivated him, one assumes, because they had heard that different standards prevailed in Cambodia, and because this man of a thousand wiles might yet rule again in Phnom Penh.

Many of Sihanouk's plans had very shaky foundations, but their sole purpose was to tide him over till the next plan took shape, and the next, in a process that would culminate in his resumption of power. That this was only a question of time, he managed to convey to all who met him.

Sihanouk was a great play-actor – a conjurer with an inexhaustible colony of rabbits in his hat – but he never lost his dignity. His self-command was absolute and his eye for political openings and opponents' mistakes never deserted him. He directed fierce and often unfair criticism at friend and foe alike, concealing the most outrageous gibes beneath a veneer of polished courtesy. It delighted him to demonstrate his independence of great powers by informing them that his opinion differed from theirs. He combined Buddhist meditation with an epicurean lifestyle. He played the saxophone and 'composed' – that is to say, he devised melody lines and employed professionals to write orchestrations and arrangements. He also wrote film scripts. We later saw more of his sixteen films, all of which glamorized their Cambodian setting.

To call Sihanouk a patriot would be an understatement. He lives for the people who in turn supply him with the breath of life. He is the father of his people, just as his ancestors used to be in days gone by. That, perhaps, was the magical energy source that kept him hovering in midair, a political force devoid of any real power base. He suffered just as his people did, using histrionic gestures to conceal his despair.

Bartered Brides

Bride purchase is forbidden. The marriage law, one of the first to be enacted by the communist government, prohibited the giving of betrothal gifts to a bride's father because it effectively transformed an engagement into a commercial transaction. It further prohibited the arrangement of marriages by third parties – parents and go-betweens. The wishes of the bride and bridegroom were to be the sole determining factor.

In rural areas, however, the situation remains as it has been for thousands of years. Marriage continues to be a transaction between two families and is generally arranged by a go-between, who earns a handsome fee for his or her services. After marriage the bride moves in with her husband, who usually lives with his parents. This deprives the bride's family of 'manpower' and transfers it to the bridegroom's. The bride's family must therefore be compensated, sometimes on a generous scale.

The cottage, which had been carefully swept and tidied for the occasion, formed part of a village near Lake Taihu, in the Suzhou district. My visit had been arranged by the commune directorate, and I was seated at table with a middle-aged couple and their twenty-four-year-old son.

We drank tea, but only because I was there. The family usually avoided such an expense by drinking hot water, which is reputed to ward off colds. Everything the Chinese eat or drink is beneficial to some organ or a prophylactic against some ailment. Tea, of course, helps to combat numerous ailments, depending on its type and origin. I praised the peasants' tea. They regretted that it was only quite ordinary tea, though their son found it passable.

The son had been granted permission to marry. This was the biggest thing to have happened in years. The couple described their laborious negotiations with the bride's father, who seemed to have annoyed them more than somewhat. He had begun by drawing up a sort of balance sheet. 'I have raised, fed, and clothed my daughter for twenty-three years,' his argument ran. 'Even if I underestimate my expenditure on her – even if I put it at only one mao a day – it adds up, over twenty-three years, to 839 yüan [roughly £250].

'We beat him down considerably, of course,' said the bridegroom's father. 'He used to be a Middle Peasant, so we told him he ought to be glad that his daughter was improving her revolutionary status by marrying into a Lower Middle Peasant family. He replied that his son was serving in the Army, and the Army had taken no exception to *his* political status, but that was a feeble argument. Then,' the bridegroom's father went on, 'we discussed betrothal goods. The bride's father wanted the Three Turning Things for himself and the Thirty-Six Legs for his daughter. That we agreed to.'

It emerged that the Three Turning Things were a bicycle, a sewing machine, and a clock, while the Thirty-Six Legs were those of two beds, a cupboard, two tables, and four chairs. 'In addition, he wanted three complete sets of clothing for his daughter. We agreed to that too – after all, they didn't have to be of the finest quality.'

'Still,' interjected the peasant's wife, 'we're having to dress her three times over from head to foot, from cap to shoes. Underclothes, too!'

I asked the son if he had known his future bride long.

'No,' his father replied. 'She comes from a neighbouring commune, but the go-between naturally brought us her date of birth and horoscope.

Someone who understands these things compared them with our son's and found they matched. He only saw the girl last week.'

'Did you take to her?' I asked the young man. He blushed and said nothing. Obviously, the girl had appealed to him.

'Yes,' said his father, 'there's the modern age for you. In the old days we began by inquiring whether a girl was fit for work, whether she had learned how to sew, whether she was obedient or had an evil tongue. Nowadays, young men only want to know what a girl looks like.'

'What was so much better about the old days?' the rebellious youngster demanded, joining uninvited in his elders' conversation. 'In the old days, all you knew about a girl was what the go-between told you, and go-betweens are terrible liars.'

But the father hadn't finished enumerating his expenses. There was the wedding itself to be considered, and skimping on that was a false economy: you only lost face if you did. The wedding would be the greatest event in his son's life – something to be talked of for a generation.

The wedding feast would be held outside in the farmyard, or, if it rained, in the labour brigade's assembly room. Even if the guest list were restricted to relatives, workmates, and a few representatives from the labour brigade directorate, it would soon reach the hundred mark.

The villagers ate meat only on major public holidays and at weddings. 'We've already fattened the two pigs,' said the bridegroom's father. 'We also have some ducks and chickens, but many things will naturally have to be bought in town. Although one isn't supposed to spend too much on weddings these days, the meal is bound to cost about 150 yüan.'

In Germany, I said, trousseaux and dowries used to be – and sometimes still were – the responsibility of the bride's parents, not the bridegroom's. I had to repeat this because the trio thought they'd misunderstood me. They continued to find the idea incomprehensible. What! The *woman* had to provide her own clothes? A pity they didn't introduce our system in China!

'But perhaps,' the son put in helpfully, 'the bride has to do that only when she suffers from a *mao bing*.' Translatable as 'small defect' or 'minor infirmity' – a squint, for example – *mao bing* could also have meant, in the present context, a bad character or a politically unfortunate family background.

'No,' I replied, 'even when she doesn't have a *mao bing*.'

This set the seal on their incomprehension. Clearly, Westerners were different and had different customs.

'So how much will you have to spend in all?' I asked.

They hesitated. Heavy expenditure on such things was undesirable,

246

as the Party, the press, and the commune directorate kept emphasizing. The betrothal gift itself, or the financial compensation paid to the bride's father, was strictly illegal and had to be kept secret, though I felt certain that the precise sum had long been known to, and debated by, everyone in the village.

After joint consultation, they arrived at a figure of 1900 yüan, or roughly £570. The whole family had been saving up for four or five years, paying their wages into the communal exchequer administered in theory by the paterfamilias but in reality by his wife.

This they would continue to do after the wedding, except that by then they would have acquired another productive member whose additional 'work-points' would in time repay their outlay on her.

The Grand Design

Peter Dreyer of the *New York Journal of Commerce*, who had already discussed China's economic plans with other EEC envoys, asked me what I thought of them.

I told him that the modernization programme announced a year ago had aimed too high. Now that its sights had been lowered, a longish period of consolidation would follow.

Dreyer asked if I thought the Chinese capable of achieving their reduced targets.

Provided their political leaders maintained a united front and won public confidence, I told him, my answer was yes. Modernization would take longer than they thought, however. The Chinese themselves spoke of a new Long March – and rightly so, in view of the regional, economic, social, and political tensions that were bound to arise. Energy was scarce despite the country's big reserves of primary sources, notably coal and hydroelectric power. The communications network, too, was inadequate, and no new economic policy aimed at greater productive specialization could succeed unless goods were transported more quickly. There were plenty of other problems as well, but if Dreyer really wanted a long-term forecast:

'Yes, I'd still call the outlook good. The Chinese are intelligent and hard-working when hard work pays off. Everything now depends on their political commitment to modernization and capacity for organization. Political commitment exists at the top, but the Chinese leaders must persuade their provincial officials to adopt the policy and assume responsibility for it at the local level. This will be hard and take time. China's central administrative bodies are obsolete and inadequate. It won't be easy to overcome the planners' bureaucratic inertia, but even that should be possible as long as the Chinese leaders persevere in their quest for practical solutions – solutions measurable in terms of success – and don't knuckle under to outdated Marxist-Leninist dogma. What matters is that they should remain united and not abandon their objective half-way. If those conditions are fulfilled, the experiment can succeed.'

Dreyer referred to his previous interviews with other EEC ambassadors. 'They all take a far more pessimistic view. Some of them dismiss these modernization plans as utterly Utopian.'

'I think they're wrong,' I said. 'China's objectives are less Utopian than those of the European Community.'

Confucius Revisited

In the large monastery at the foot of the Taishan, the sacred mountain in the East Chinese province of Shandong, is a stone column dating from the fifth century. It bears an inscription of which rubbings can be obtained on request. The four massive characters, each of them well over a foot high, read: 'The works of the classics – great and erect.'

Do they still stand great and erect in the China of today? After being forced to quit the stage for a while, they now stand once more, albeit half in the wings. Even when Confucius, whom the Chinese call Kung Fudse or 'Master Kung', does make an appearance, he sometimes does so wearing a luxuriant beard and a leonine wig and spouting a jargon that might almost mislead the audience into thinking him a German – Karl Marx, for instance.

Whether on stage or in the wings, however, Confucius still wields an influence. He has become so deeply ingrained in the Chinese during the past two millennia that they register surprise and pleasure – today, at least – when told that they have just echoed an idea propounded by Master Kung. If they are surprised, this is because the young and middle-aged have no knowledge of him. In China as in Europe, schoolchildren no longer read the classics.

Politburo members of the older generation are still familiar with them. Fang Yi once told me that his first task, on going to school, was to memorize the Chinese classics without understanding a single word of them. They were not explained to him until he knew them by heart. I asked him if he thought this method of teaching a good one. Very good, he replied.

My permit and itinerary mystified a woman clerk in the Shanghai Travel Bureau. 'You visit the strangest places,' she said. 'What takes you to Qüfu?' I replied that it was the home of one of China's greatest men. I refrained from calling him *the* greatest. That would have puzzled her still more, because he, as everyone knew, had been a native of Shaoshan in Hunan Province.

Embarrassed, she asked a colleague whom I was referring to. She laughed and looked slightly shamefaced when told. I inquired if she had ever read any Confucius. No, she said, but she knew all about him because of the anti-Confucius campaign which the Gang of Four had launched against Premier Zhou Enlai a few years ago.

Now, however, people were starting to read him again. His works could even be bought in bookstores, though they were always sold out within days. 'The Reassessment of Confucius', an article by the fifty-year-old philosopher Li Zehou, stated simply: 'Whether you like it or not, Confucius is back and here to stay.'

So the darkness that enshrouded the classics is starting to lift. Although it is impossible to tell whether the ordinary Chinese is genuinely alert to them and expects them to supply practical aids to existence, the Cultural Revolution's attempt to hurl them into the abyss of oblivion has proved a derisory failure.

Not that the Red Guards failed to do a thorough job at Qüfu. Gangs of youthful revolutionaries not only demolished Confucius' memorial stele but vented their fury on it with sledge hammers. The shattered remains now lie strewn with wild abandon beneath the ancient thujas. All that still stands, perhaps because it defied demolition, is the plinth on its stone foundation. Beyond it can be seen a bare, muddy mound, evidently of recent date. This is another relic of the Cultural Revolution.

It marks the spot where Red Guards went digging for the Sage's remains, which had lain buried there for nearly two-and-a-half thousand years, doubtless with the intention of scattering them to the winds or playing football with the skull as their fellow revolutionaries had done at Babaoshan, the Heroes' Cemetery, with the skulls of deceased Party dignitaries. Having excavated the site to a depth of twenty feet without finding any traces of a coffin or human remains, they announced that Kung had never been buried at Qüfu at all; it was just another of the Confucians' innumerable lies.

'So what's the truth of the matter?' I asked our guide, who headed Qüfu's office for the preservation of ancient monuments. His name, like that of half the town's inhabitants, was Kung, which identified him as a member of the Master's family.

He smiled. 'The Red Guards were only amateur archaeologists, fortunately. Where *they* were digging, they'd never have found a thing.'

'But how can anyone be sure he's buried here? The stele they smashed was comparatively modern, wasn't it?'

'Yes, roughly five hundred years old – it dated from the Ming dynasty. However, we found an older stele on the same site. That one dated from the Han dynasty, or about two thousand years ago. It could be argued that even that stele was erected five centuries after Confucius' death. True, but what matters is that this is his family's burial ground. His son's grave is over there, his grandson's over there, his pupil Zigong's over there, and thousands of his descendants lie buried in the forest – down to and including members of the seventy-sixth generation.'

'What about the seventy-seventh?' I inquired. 'Where is his latest direct descendant now?'

Mr Kung looked impassive. 'Living in Taiwan,' he replied.

'And his wife's grave?'

'Only men are buried here.'

I had first visited Qüfu as a student in October 1936, travelling fourth-class on the Peking–Nanking railroad. Leaving the train at Yanzhou, a town too small to merit a hotel, I found lodgings for the night at the Steyler Mission.

Qüfu and Confucius' tomb were twelve or thirteen miles away. There was no bus service, and I could not have afforded to rent a car, even if one had been available. The fathers were unable to give me the name of a hotel in Qüfu either, so I was forced to do the round-trip in a day. The procurator of the mission station entrusted me to a rickshaw coolie named Han, a youth little older than myself. To Han, who resembled a horse and could trot like one, twenty-five miles in a day was a gentle stroll.

We set off down the narrow street at first light, passing beneath two multi-storeyed gatehouses whose delicate contours stood silhouetted against the paling sky. Outside the door of every house, small portable stoves were being tended by children operating bellows of unfamiliar design – twin-chambered contrivances which maintained a steady draught. Housewives sat on doorsteps grinding corn for their families' breakfast gruel between two horizontal, hand-held millstones. I felt like a traveller in time transported to the Middle Ages.

The feeling persisted when we reached open country. Peasants were already at work in the fields. Men hauled ploughs through hard, dry, clayey soil, bent almost double in their harness, while women guided the ploughshares. Outside each village was a threshing floor of tamped mud on which peasants crushed sorghum straw beneath massive log rollers. Wind sent the chaff flying as their womenfolk tossed it into the air with wooden paddles.

We passed no vehicles other than a few handcarts fitted with sails, which seemed to cruise across the plain in a curiously nautical manner. The peasants travelled on foot, their loads suspended from either end of a shoulder-pole.

The sky was high and blue, the autumn air so clear that the horizon seemed infinitely distant. It was here, two-and-a-half thousand years ago, that the princes of Lu had ruled their small domain. These were the roads which Confucius and his disciples had tramped or travelled in crudely constructed wagons. The plain was a dry yellow expanse devoid of rising ground. The villages consisted of small houses thatched with straw and built of unbaked mud bricks, yellow and dusty as the plain itself. There was not a tree to be seen. The peasants ploughed, harrowed, threshed, and served as their own beasts of burden. They wrested a meagre living from poor soil. When, if ever, had anything changed here? The further we went, the more I felt that time had stood still.

The sensation became even stronger that evening, on the return journey. At dusk, when it was almost too dark to see, the peasants wearily gathered up their belongings and went home. They neither spoke nor sang as they had during the day.

It was then, quite suddenly, that I felt I was in another age – not in ancient China, which might have been understandable, but traversing biblical country in biblical times. I couldn't identify the source of the picture conjured up by dim figures passing in the dusk as we made our way along these country roads. The feeling lasted only a minute or two, then faded, but it left me strangely uneasy. It was as though I had crossed some forbidden frontier – as though, if only for a few fleeting moments, I had genuinely emerged from the confines of time itself.

But to revert to our outward journey. To the peasants, the sight of me riding in Han's rickshaw or walking beside him was a novelty. I was a sensation – a man with yellow hair! They stopped working as we passed and inquired who I was, where I came from, where I was going. Han came in for some good-natured banter because he was hauling a *da bizi* – a long-nose – all the way to Qüfu, but he gave as good as he got. Whether or not his repartee was made at my expense, the peasants laughed.

Han insisted on my remaining seated when we reached the gates of Qüfu, arguing that he was a rickshaw coolie, not a tourist guide. He clamped the shafts beneath his arms and began to trot. With my weight offsetting his own, he positively soared along like a giant in seven-league boots.

Our first stop was the big Confucian temple, with dragons and other monsters carved on the columns of its broad façade. Greece and Rome having taught me how columns ought to look, I wrinkled my nose a little. Next, Han took me to Kung Lin, or Confucius Forest, a long way out of town. This site, which was twice the size of Qüfu itself, had been bestowed by the Emperor on Confucius' family so that all the Master's descendants – male descendants only, of course – could be buried near their illustrious ancestor.

The area is dotted with tall deciduous trees and thujas, many of them centuries old. Grass grows beneath the trees and flowers adorn the clearings – a rarity in eastern China, where municipal parks are bare of grass and every square yard of the plains is devoted to the cultivation of grain or vegetables, never to pasture. The winding paths in Confucius Forest diverge and converge like waterways, haphazard and unplanned. Everywhere beneath the trees, not close together but isolated and in no discernible order, stand funerary steles erected during the past two thousand years, tutelary stone lions, horses, and fabulous beasts. A pavilion and a small temple flank the path.

Han stopped and grounded his shafts so abruptly that I fell rather than climbed out of the rickshaw. Pointing to a medium-sized stele, he announced that it marked the burial place of Master Kung.

I was very dubious. Could this be all? Many of the tombs we had passed were far more impressive. This one had no tutelary figures, no carving or ornamentation, but it was *his*. The stele, a massive slab of grey stone some ten feet high, stood on a plinth with a flat stone base. The seal-script inscription did not include the character for Kung but merely referred to the Master by his posthumous honorific, 'King of Literature'.

Confucius was a lover of music and ancient poetry. Music must have wielded a powerful influence over him, for we are told that while studying Zhou music 'he forgot the taste of meat for three months on end'. Where philosophy was concerned, he devoted no thought to any of the questions that were exercising the pre-Socratics at about the same time. Like every Chinese philosopher since his day, Confucius had but one concern: the life of man in society.

'May I venture to inquire the nature of death?' asked a pupil. The Master's reply: 'If one has yet to know life, how can one know aught of death?'

Confucius died at the age of seventy-two in 479 BC, ten years before the birth of Socrates. His pupils bore him to his grave and mourned there for three whole years, but Zigong, the one whose company he liked best, built himself a hut nearby and mourned him for as long again. He was mourned as a great teacher and a great man whose life had been a failure – who had failed to attain his goal. He died unrecognized and unappreciated by the world at large; only his pupils knew him for the person he was.

'The Master said, "To hear in the morning that the world is in order, and then, in the evening, to die – that would be no bad thing." '

But the world was far from in order when he died. Eager to fulfil his political ideas and test them in practice, he had desperately sought office in Qüfu, at the Prince of Lu's court. He eventually secured a post but resigned it after only three months, when its full insignificance dawned on him. Already in his late fifties, Confucius became an itinerant scholar. He offered his services to various neighbouring princes, but none had need of a man who claimed to have a mission and spread novel, dangerous ideas. This pathetic and wholly fruitless quest was not without its humorous side.

'Kung?' said a frontier guard. 'Isn't that the man who knows that what he has in mind won't work but perseveres regardless?'

After more than ten years, when he was almost seventy, Confucius returned empty-handed to Qüfu, where he studied and taught. He lived on tuition fees but did not turn away pupils who could not afford to pay. The Chinese have always been mindful of his example when financing the education of poor but talented youngsters.

Confucius does not appear to have been a great orator. He spoke slowly and had an aversion to expert wordsmiths with a brilliant turn of phrase.

'To learn and employ one's knowledge at the appropriate season; is that not happiness?'

Those are the opening words of Confucius' *Analects*. He himself died without having put his knowledge to use, aware beyond doubt that he had failed, yet no other man has left so deep and millennial an imprint on any nation's culture, life, and ethics.

Yang Bo was one of the Vice-Governors of Shandong Province, a province with a population of seventy million. Having met during an official Chinese tour of Germany, we renewed our acquaintance at a dinner in Peking. When I casually regretted my inability to revisit Qüfu, where I had once been forty-three years earlier, he invited Franz and me to become the first foreigners to visit the town as soon as the worst traces of the Cultural Revolution had been removed.

Our sleeper – no fourth-class travel for me this time – pulled into Yanzhou at dawn. Yang Bo had sent a car to meet us, so there was no need to make the round-trip by rickshaw. We drove out of town along a sizeable arterial road. I had wanted to see something of the old quarter, but it was only on the return journey that our guide showed us a few narrow old streets which, to his surprise, I found more attractive than Yanzhou's modern housing developments. The two elegant arches had gone. So had the women grinding corn with querns and the children tending stoves in the street. The road to Qüfu was indistinguishable from any European highway and quite unreminiscent of Han, the rickshaw coolie. I wondered if he, too, had survived the passage of time.

The plain was not as broad and the sky not as high as of old. Every farm track and field was lined with trees – young trees of which the oldest were probably coeval with the People's Republic. The countryside was crisscrossed by power and telephone lines. We passed trucks laden with big earthenware jars, horse-drawn carts, cyclists, and peasants wheeling pigs to the nearest commune for sale or slaughter. The irrigation ditches were equipped with electric pumps, and small tractors could sometimes be seen in the fields. The wheat looked in good condition. No peasant would be harnessing himself to a plough when autumn came.

Our guide informed us *en route* that we were to be accommodated in the guest wing of the Kung family's palace. Yang Bo and his wife were there to greet us when our car drove into the courtyard, having preceded us by a day from Jinan, the provincial capital. They were delighted that their secret had been kept and insisted on showing us round in person.

When we came to the shattered remains of Confucius' stele, I asked Yang Bo why the government of Shandong Province had been unable to prevent such vandalism.

'The government itself was split,' he replied. 'Anyone who mounted a campaign against the terrorist gang might have been persecuted himself. After all, we didn't know which members of the Politburo backed the Peking students and student teachers who were terrorizing the town, or who was at the bottom of it all. Or rather,' he added after a momentary pause, 'I suppose we did, really.'

He fell silent, then started to describe what had happened. A small 'action group' of Red Guards – students from the Beida, Peking University proper, and Qinghua University, together with others from the College of Education and a technical college – had invaded Qüfu in September 1966, eager to efface Confucius' memory once and for all. For three whole months, they terrorized the town and destroyed irreplaceable antiquities.

And the local inhabitants?

'They were frightened. Nobody knew where the real power lay.'

We drove back into town. The temple and palace precincts, which cover fifty acres, are second only in size to the Forbidden City. They contain the Hall of Memorials to the Sage, the Bell Tower, the Drum Tower, some triumphal gates, a thousand-odd stone memorial pillars, thujas reputed to be two thousand years old, and the Great Pavilion of the Constellation of Literature, a poetic circumlocution for what might prosaically be termed the library. The Temple of Confucius is the largest and most sumptuous of all.

Yes, there were the same old dragon-encircled columns. Although my reaction to their un-Greek appearance was more indulgent than it had been, I still found them unappealing. This was not, of course, the original little temple built soon after the Sage's death, nor the Tang dynasty temple of the eighth century, nor yet the Ming dynasty temple of the fifteenth, but an eighteenth-century product of the Qing dynasty, which had revelled in excessive ornamentation.

Looking through the central door in the hall's broad façade, one sees a large portrait of Confucius displayed on the rear wall. This is new, and deputizes for the ancient statue that has served as a model for every effigy of Confucius in China. The original statue and those of the Sage's principal successors and disciples were destroyed by the Red Guards, who bore their fragments away and dumped them in some undiscovered spot. The temple's greatest treasure comprised some unique old musical instruments. These, too, were destroyed, but a row of angular 'music stones' can still be seen suspended from a beam. Two thousand years old or even older, they emit a note that is clear and pure but not particularly resonant.

We are told that, during his long peregrinations, the Master played some music stones in the town of Wei. 'Then a hermit passed by, and said, "He who strikes the music stones within is truly afflicted by the sorrows of this world."'

Although the main buildings had already been restored, many others were still encased in scaffolding. Work was proceeding apace because the Master's birthday would once more be celebrated on 23 August next. 'What is more,' said our guide from the house of Kung, 'it will be celebrated in keeping with ancient ritual, complete with the songs and dances of old.'

This was sensational news. A mere four years after the anti-Confucius campaign, there was to be a revival of the ancient ceremonies that had lapsed with the fall of the Qing dynasty in 1911. Surviving eyewitnesses described these as exceedingly impressive. Summoned by the nocturnal booming of drums in the drum towers, brocade-clad celebrants emerged from the temple by torchlight and performed traditional dances to an accompaniment of gongs, music stones, or ancient wind, string, and percussion instruments.

We were shown the temple dedicated to Confucius' father and mother. His wife had also been accorded one, though not for several centuries after his death, because some emperor's spouse – one with feminist leanings, perhaps – had taken pity on her memory. The Sage's wife can hardly have had an easy life at his side, obliged as she was to feed and house pupils of whom some were gentlemen of mature or advanced years. Additionally obliged to fend for herself during the Master's ten-year absence abroad, she fully deserved a temple of her own.

The Master, it should be said, makes no mention of her – she was only a woman, after all. He does, however, mention his son, whose lamentable reluctance to study has disqualified him from the privilege of a temple.

Confucius did not proclaim his wisdom from on high, but used simple and straightforward language. He not only taught that solicitude, beneficence, and love of one's neighbour should be the basis of all political dealings but exemplified this principle in his personal relations.

'The pupil Fanqi asked the Master, "What is benevolence [*jen*]?" The Master answered, "Loving all men."'

Confucius was frugal: 'The Master said, "With coarse rice to eat, with water to drink, and my bended arm for a pillow – I still have joy in the midst of these things. Riches and honours acquired by unrighteousness are to me as a floating cloud."'

He was also humane: 'On returning from Court to find the stables burned down, he said, "Was anybody hurt?" He did not inquire after the horses.'

A little pavilion stands in the temple precinct at the spot where once grew the peach tree beneath which the Master used to converse with his pupils. It may have been there that he asked them what they would do if a prince appointed them to govern.

The first claimed that, within three years, he would persuade people to regain their courage and recognize their obligations. The Master was sceptical. The second proposed to improve people's material circumstances within three years to such an extent that they would have enough to live on. The third, eager to impress the Master with his modesty, merely aspired to become an acolyte in the temple devoted to imperial ancestor worship.

'Diän, what say you?' The fourth pupil played more slowly on his lute, allowed the notes to die away, and laid the instrument aside. 'Ah,' he said, 'my desires differ from those of our three friends.' The Master said, 'No matter. Let each of you state his heart's desire.' Then said Diän, 'My dearest wish would be, in late spring, when one is already wearing light attire, to bathe in the river with a few grown friends and boys, or to repose in the cool woods, singing songs the while, and then return home at dusk.' The Master sighed and said, 'I favour this man here.'

In other words, Confucius was anything but the prig his devotees made of him as time went by.

Adjoining the temple precinct, on either side of a longitudinal thoroughfare three hundred yards long, stands the extensive palace complex in which we, too, were accommodated. We had an atrium house to ourselves, and leading off our courtyard, with its single tree, shrubs, and flowers, were other 'guest-houses' of similar design. One of these was occupied by Yang Bo and his wife, while another contained the dining-room in which our hosts entertained us to an evening meal.

The palace precinct is almost as large as that of the temple. We toured the Academy Building, the Examination Hall, and the Office of Seals and Decrees, an extensive archive which, though it goes back only nine hundred years, contains a complete record of the period. We also inspected the Office of Rites, the Hall of Justice, and the Office of Music and Ceremonies. One whole office was reserved for correspondence with the imperial court.

The private quarters of the Master's seventy-seventh descendant proved disappointing. Evidently at pains to keep up with the times, he had discarded some of the old Chinese furniture and replaced it with store-bought pieces dating from the 1920s. The veneer was already peeling off. In one corner we saw a grandfather clock. This was also of 1920s vintage and had probably come from a Shanghai department store.

We were shown the bedroom, which contained a bed so low and obscured by ornate carving that sleeping in it must have seemed a foretaste of death. Adjoining the bedroom were the rooms of the seventy-seventh descendant's principal wife and senior concubine. That of the junior concubine was smaller and situated at the far end of the building. Being too inferior, she was not permitted to share meals with the family.

Confucius' descendants were invested with princely rank two thousand years ago or more. The succession was occasionally disputed and had to be determined by the emperor, perhaps because some son of an inferior concubine laid claim to rights he did not possess.

In addition to Confucius Forest, the house of Kung owned most of the town and a sizeable proportion of the surrounding land. They also received grants from the imperial exchequer, and the emperors knew why.

For many hundreds of years, the palace at Qüfu was the focus of a process whereby Confucius the man was transformed into the founder of a doctrine and, ultimately, into a saint – the place where that doctrine was tailored to the requirements of Confucian scholars and imperial policy alike. That which Confucius himself had been denied – power and influence over the political, ethical, and cultural life of China – accrued to the Confucians and remained in their keeping for two thousand years.

For all of those two thousand years, Confucian officials administered the country. Dynasty succeeded dynasty, rebellions and civil wars brought havoc in their train, but the social conventions and attitudes espoused by these scholars endured until the beginning of our own century.

Although they dogmatized and simplified the Master's precepts, they not infrequently laid down their lives for them. Equally, although they produced exemplary and morally superior figures at every stage in history, they often hampered progress with their moral pedantry and rigid, humourless dogmatism. Anything prescribed by the Master and hallowed by antiquity was great and good. Always ready with a quotation from the classics, Confucians habitually invoked them, much as Mao and the Marxist classics are invoked today. Apt quotations deputized for reasoned argument.

This constant invocation of antiquity, of the Master and the classics, was one of the chief reasons why China's social structure remained so stable. Generation-gap conflicts were precluded by veneration of antiquity and one's parents. Even when they did arise, they never attained the intensity typical of our own age, in which they have become a prime cause of instability and are largely responsible for rapid changes in fashions, opinions, and political attitudes, the more so because youth and novelty are credited on principle with the bonus of truth.

In China that bonus belonged to the old, and anyone who produced a new idea was at a disadvantage. Though conducive to stability, the prevailing outlook fostered sterility, narrow-mindedness, and the entrenchment of abuses. While it also formed an undoubted cause of the many rebellions in Chinese history, society soon resumed its wonted course and bowed to the guidance of antiquity and the classics.

Mao's slogan – 'Destroy the old, construct the new!' – was the first attack for two thousand years on the principle that salvation reposes in tradition. Young Chinese of today have not forgotten this slogan, but the

Party is striving to restore stability. Indeed, it surpasses the Confucians in hidebound severity when it puts shackles on intellectuals and artists and tries to steer them along Party-sanctified lines.

The Confucians found it as hard to cope with Confucius the man as St Paul with the mortal persona of Jesus. Master Kung often embarrassed his latter-day adherents, who either explained away the many awkward passages in his recorded sayings or simply pronounced them spurious. In every other respect their approach to his utterances was deadly serious, even when he was joking and said so. Confucius differed from what they were or aspired to be. He was human in his very contradictions, as the *Analects* plainly show. Although he made heavy demands on other people and himself, he did not carry them to extremes. His cast of mind was Chinese in its sheer common sense. He offered his services to a usurper and discussed politics with a noblewoman of unsavoury repute. Even his pupil Zilu was perturbed by this, and later Confucians wanted to delete the passage on the grounds that it was defamatory. Their moral position was as lofty as that adopted by so many of our own youthful moralists when passing judgement on their parents' generation. Confucius said, 'To decline office is to neglect one's duty. He who wishes to preserve his personal purity countenances confusion in social relations. A superior man takes office and does as best he can. That the right principles will not prevail, he knows full well beforehand.'

The last sentence is a surprising and moving admission on the part of one who constantly enjoined his fellow men to strive for moral perfection.

Confucius could be impatient and acrimonious. He once struck a pupil on the shin with his stick when angered by his behaviour. Though capable of tolerating contradiction and bowing to persuasion, he could tongue-lash pupils in a spiteful and sarcastic manner. He was a past master at detecting ulterior motives and unmasking hypocrisy with a single sentence. When asked if one of his pupils was making progress, he replied, 'From the way he seats himself in grown-up people's places and fails to stand aside for his elders, I should call him less intent on making progress than on getting ahead in a hurry.'

Anything but self-righteous, Confucius acknowledged his mistakes and shortcomings. Humility and modesty prompted him to underrate his own importance. He died in ignorance that he had attained his goal after all. His aim, in an age when the times were out of joint, was to promote the development of firm opinions and the recognition of true values, not false. In this he succeeded.

It was only the teachings of Confucians in later centuries that metamorphosed him into an unctuous proponent of sage banalities, of devotion to duty, obedience, punctilio ('If the mat were not straight, he would not sit down'), and absolute submission to family and state.

Just as Jesus has been obfuscated by the Church and Marx by Marxism, so Confucius' personal qualities have been obscured and his teachings simplified, distorted by Confucianism, and reduced to a dogma composed of handy formulas.

Is this inevitable? Should it be taken into account, if they wish their influence to outlive them, by all great teachers and innovators?

Deng Xiaoping

He is a little man – the smallest of the world's leading politicians, perhaps, but not the least significant. If all of them were paraded in order of importance, he would surely merit a place near the front.

He never talks about himself, any more than do the other Chinese leaders, though his would be a longer and more interesting story than most. He never, for instance, mentions what he and his family suffered in the days of his ostracism and humiliation. So fierce were the personal attacks on him that his life itself was thought to be in jeopardy. One of his closest friends in the Politburo assured me that, had anything happened to Deng, he would have shot the Gang of Four with the revolver he always carried. I accepted this statement at face value.

Deng Xiaoping has been unseated three times in the course of his career. His first fall from grace came in 1933, at the age of twenty-nine, when he backed Mao's policy against that of his rival Wang Ming. The second and more serious instance occurred in 1966, during the Cultural Revolution. He did not resurface until seven years later, in 1973. Stripped of all his posts for the third time in April 1976, the year of Mao's death, he was not reinstated until August of the following year.

He never speaks of his days in the political wilderness, nor of his three rehabilitations, though journalists have often pressed him on the point. It would make quite a story – 'The Greatest Comeback Since Lazarus!' – but his lips remain sealed.

He is ready enough to talk about his age and what he proposes to do in the years that are left him. He was once asked, while visiting South-East Asia in 1978, whether China would still be communist in the year 2000. His response, as reported in the press, was: 'I don't know. Speaking for myself, however, I shall remain a Marxist-Leninist till the day I die.'

I called on him in September 1977, one month after he had been restored to Party and government office, accompanied by a German parliamentarian. The latter questioned him on the possibility of a future *rapprochement* between China and the Soviet Union. Deng's reply contained another allusion to his age:

'Being seventy-three years old, I myself will not live to see any such *rapprochement*. Comrade Hua Guofeng is fifty-six. He will live to see the turn of the century, but not a *rapprochement* with the Soviet Union. None can be expected, either, in the following generation. What will happen after that, I don't know. No one can see that far ahead.'

I met Deng many times, usually when visitors arrived from Germany. Almost buried in his armchair, he listened with keen attention and often opened the proceedings with a reference to his advanced age. It would not be long, he said, before things became too much for him. 'How old are you?' he asked me. I told him. 'What!' he exclaimed in horror. 'I'm eleven years older!'

'At your age,' I told him, 'Adenauer became Chancellor and remained in office for fifteen years.'

Deng said he wouldn't last that long. Watching him light one cigarette after another, I successfully resisted the temptation to tell him that, if he continued to smoke as heavily, he could well be right.

He went on to speak of Adenauer with great respect, quoting extensively from his memoirs. Khrushchev, he recalled, had tried to persuade the Chancellor to join the Soviet Union in countering the Chinese 'menace'. 'That was in 1955,' he said, 'when we still thought the Russians were our best friends.'

Deng was witty, sarcastic, and acute, but never volatile or garrulous – never anything but circumspect and in full command of himself. He would listen long and earnestly before replying in measured tones, framing his ideas in elegant, vivid, cogent language. He was invariably courteous, even when his opinion differed from one's own, though I once saw him laughingly restrain himself from flying off the handle at a country in the Middle East.

He could grow impatient when bored by people with nothing of interest to say. Repeated and ostentatious glances at his watch having failed to silence another visiting parliamentarian from Germany, he twice spat noisily into the big spittoon between them. Eventually, when the visitor persisted in elaborating his ideas, he tapped the face of his watch. I could understand his feelings too well to construe this as an act of discourtesy.

Our visitors during 1978 included a party of German journalists. I had told them that the Americans hoped to normalize their relations with

Peking in the coming year. They asked Deng if he considered this possible. He laughed and expressed the hope that it would happen before the year was out. They laughed too, because it was already mid-October, but the laugh was on them. Only two months later, in December 1978, Peking and Washington resolved to establish diplomatic relations.

Deng is fond of stating unpalatable truths. During 1978, a few new Japanese films were shown in China – the first modern films to be imported since the Cultural Revolution. One of them told the story of a Japanese country girl who was sold to a white slaver before the First World War and resold by him to a brothel in Borneo. The brothel sequences and scenes of violence were depicted with a realism that shocked Peking audiences. Outraged letters appeared in the press, and the authorities withdrew the film. When told of this on his return from a tour of South-East Asia, Deng gave orders that it should be re-released and shown on television as well. 'Our people,' he is reported to have said, 'must see what can happen to women in a capitalist society, nor must they turn a blind eye to the real state of things in our own country, where secret prostitution exists even today.'

But Deng Xiaoping should not be thought of as a liberal. The posters on Democracy Wall received his initial blessing and encouragement. Once these outbursts of criticism had fulfilled their purpose and started to question the Party's authority, however, he had them suppressed.

'The newspapers are to be left in peace,' ordained Frederick the Great, who once, while riding through the streets of Berlin or Potsdam, suggested that an unflattering caricature of himself – a kind of wall-poster – should be hung in a lower and more prominent position. But a joke could go too far, even for Frederick's taste, and he himself decided when that point had been reached. Deng resembles him in many ways. He is courageous, sharp-tongued, humorous, quick-witted, sceptical, autocratic, and sometimes unjust.

In 1961, when he had made a number of decisions affecting the development of the people's communes without consulting Mao, the Great Helmsman's furious reaction was, 'What emperor decreed this?'

In his great *Self-Criticism*, to which reference will be made below, Deng stated: 'Late in 1964, Chairman Mao criticized me for being a kingdom unto myself. At first, somewhat shaken by this, I nonetheless consoled myself with the thought that I was neither an avaricious person nor a seeker after power.'

This is true. He covets neither money nor power, has never been accused of plotting with others to acquire them, and is not the type to engage in petty intrigue. One of his aides assured me that any conjectures to the effect that Deng laid claim to the post of premier, or had done so after Mao's death, were utterly false. He had always taken the view that this post should be held by a younger man.

Deng is, first and foremost, a realist. When questioned about China's revolutionary objectives in South-East Asia, he replied, 'We don't propose to export our revolution. We have no wish, after all, to export our poverty.'

He is fully aware how backward his country is. 'Foreign friends,' he once remarked at a conference, 'have told us that China is twenty years behind the rest of the world in development. That was a very polite verdict. The true disparity amounts in many fields to thirty years, in others to fifty. We shall find it very difficult to attain the world level by the end of this century, let alone surpass it, even approximately or at least in some areas . . . We are as backward as we are because we cut ourselves off from the world for so long. We felt like the tiny principality of Yeh Lang, which considered itself the navel of the world and believed that it could ignore the kingdoms around it until the latter had had enough and swallowed it up. That's why we now want as many Chinese as possible to travel abroad, and many foreigners to visit us. I don't know, but there may be some people in Germany who suspect us of wanting to influence you politically in one direction or another. They need have no fear. We won't do that.'

Deng can be caustic in the extreme. He has no patience, least of all with stupidity and nebulous Utopias. In his view, those who produce no results or are past achieving them should quit, not cling to office. To use his own crude but graphic imagery: 'Anyone who sits on the privy and strains, and nothing happens, should go and make room for the next in line.'

I never heard him speak of ideological objectives, of transforming society, of the antithesis between town and country, of permanent revolution or the inevitable conflict between two lines. My own impression is that, like Napoleon, he takes a less than serious view of what is proclaimed by *tous ces idéologues*. He prefers to be guided by facts. Marxism, Marxism-Leninism, and Maozedongideas are valuable, but only if they prove their worth in practice. (The latter proviso is often omitted today, but that is another story.)

What earned him most opprobrium during the Cultural Revolution was his assertion that private agriculture was producing better results than the communes, and that the proper inferences should be drawn. Why? Because, in the words of a popular proverb, 'Black or white, the cat that catches rats is a good cat.'

Jiang Qing once charged Deng, at a mass rally of Peking students, with having decried the expression 'communist spirit'. This was probably because he found it too woolly and easy to manipulate. 'No matter who has introduced a thing,' he once declared with reference to Mao's precipitate establishment of the communes, 'if that thing is impractical and doesn't work, it must be changed. We can't afford to worry whether we shall lose face in consequence.'

He is not a master of tact, as we can see, and his store of respect for the luminaries of his day – even for the founders of Marxism – is limited. They paid him back for this during the Cultural Revolution. Even when he repudiates them, however, his public pronouncements treat them with dignity and propriety. This extends even to Mao, at whose hands he suffered so much, and contrasts with the treatment meted out to Stalin by Khrushchev.

In 1958, Mao relinquished the presidency to his old comrade-in-arms Liu Shaoqi, ostensibly because he wished to devote himself to basic questions of theory and the exalted tasks of supreme leadership. From then on, Mao's authority waned in proportion as Liu Shaoqi's influence on policy increased. Liu's closest associate was Deng Xiaoping. Though widely known to be a realistic, vigorous, and courageous man, Deng was still overshadowed by the other prominent leaders, political and military, of the revolutionary period.

The Cultural Revolution, Mao's device for regaining power, was primarily directed against Liu Shaoqi. Having marched at Mao's side for forty-six years – since 1920 – Liu was now to be isolated and destroyed. Deng Xiaoping was given a chance to redeem himself. It was intimated that he might get off lightly, yet again, if he engaged in public self-criticism.

This he did on 23 October 1966, at a working session of the Central Committee. The following extracts, some of them idiomatically and syntactically bizarre, are taken from the standard English translation of his speech:

The big-character poster that Chairman Mao put up at the Eleventh Plenum bombarded the headquarters of comrade Shao-chi [Shaoqi] and myself. In his poster Chairman Mao incisively pointed out the nature of our mistakes. He declared, 'By adopting the reactionary stand of the bourgeoisie, carrying out a bourgeois dictatorship, they (meaning Liu and Teng [Deng]) have repressed the surging tide of the Cultural Revolution. They have manipulated the facts, belied right and wrong, encircled and suppressed revolutionaries, stifled opinions differing from their own by imposing a white terror, and generally revelling in their power, what they have done is to increase the arrogance of the bourgeoisie and deflate the morale of the proletariat. Is this not indeed foul!' This criticism of the Chairman's is absolutely correct and has struck on the very heart of the matter . . .

Now that the mistakes have been corrected by Chairman Mao and the Central Committee, a broad mass movement is unfolding . . . Tremendous results have been achieved and our young people have been given a rare chance to learn and test themselves in struggle. The Chinese people are being revolutionized and the socialist future of the country is assured. This not only marks a new age for China but also marks a new age for the world . . .

My recent errors are by no means accidental or disconnected; they have their origins in a certain way of thinking and a certain style of work which has developed over a considerable period of time . . . In retrospect, my last few years have been marked by a steady regression, and due to my laxity in the study and use of Mao Tsetung Thought, I have made a number of mistakes . . . My distancing myself from the masses and lack of contact with reality is directly connected with my failure to follow Chairman Mao and my lack of proper study. As a result, I have become accustomed to lording it over others and acting like someone special . . . Till recently I have not been aware of my attitude and still felt myself superior and infallible . . .

Recent events have revealed me as an unreformed *petit-bourgeois* intellectual who has failed to pass the tests posed by socialism . . .

What I need to do is reflect on my past actions. I need to earnestly study Chairman Mao's works, reform myself and correct my mistakes. By so doing, I hope to be of some use to the Party and the people in the latter years of my life and make up, in some way, for my past misdeeds . . .

The above is only a preliminary self-criticism. I hope all comrades present will give their criticisms and suggestions.

Long live the Great Proletarian Cultural Revolution!

Long live invincible Mao Tsetung Thought!

Long live the great teacher, the great helmsman and the great leader Chairman Mao!

This document is hard to fathom and evaluate. Was Deng being sincere in his professions of regret? Hardly, save perhaps when passing one or two strictures on his 'style of work'. He had earlier expressed himself quite differently on the subject of Mao's personality cult. When reinstated after Mao's death, he not only set about dismantling it but also succeeded in banishing portraits of Hua Guofeng from public places. If he now regards the Cultural Revolution as a disaster, he must surely have done so then. How could so self-assured a man have abased himself so deeply? Did he fear for his personal safety? Is even he a prey to occasional fears? One cannot tell, but he gives no such impression. Fear would never prompt him to self-abasement, in any case. His more likely response to a threatening situation, like that of many small men, would be intensified belligerence.

I think his self-criticism was a deliberate political ploy – the only one that offered a chance of political survival. He must have realized, when faced with the task of drafting this admission of guilt, that no other course would save him from political, and possibly physical, extinction.

Far from interpreting Deng's self-criticism as an act of defection or a betrayal of his principles, the general public saw it as an affliction which he, like many others, had been compelled to take upon himself. Quite how distasteful he found it to make such an admission of guilt, however, it is hard to judge.

Sima Qian, Grand Historian and Grand Astrologer to the imperial court, once pleaded with the Emperor on behalf of a defeated general. Angered by his intercession, the Emperor had him thrown into jail and castrated. He was later reinstated and allowed to complete his great historical work, an invaluable source of information to posterity. During this second term of office, Sima Qian wrote a letter to a friend who was in prison under threat of execution. In it he explained why he had accepted all the humiliations heaped upon him:

> We all love life and fear death . . . Perhaps I was cowardly and wished to remain alive, even if I forfeited my honour. But I know, nonetheless, what is seemly. Even an inferior slave woman is capable of taking her life . . . No, it was not cowardice. If I concealed my feelings, clung to life, and uncomplainingly suffered myself to be covered with filth, it was only because I did not wish my innermost thoughts to remain unspoken, and because I could not bring myself to quit the world without having completed my great work . . . Had I decided on death, it would have had no more effect than the loss of a single hair by nine oxen. No one would have credited me with having laid down my life for a principle. On the contrary, they would all have believed that I had departed this life because I was at my wit's end, and because my crime allowed of no alternative . . . Only concern for my unfinished work made me accept the worst of all punishments without showing the fierce anger I felt. When I have at last completed my book I shall place it in the archives, there to await the advent of one who understands it. When it becomes known to the world, I shall have washed off the stain of my disgrace. Ten thousand humiliations of the kind I had to undergo would not be too much to suffer to attain that end.

But all this I can confide only to a superior person. To speak of it to the many would be pointless. For anyone in as questionable a position as mine, self-justification is no easy matter. The world has ever been fond of suspecting people's motives.

Like Sima Qian, Deng Xiaoping shouldered the burden of humiliation in order to complete his work. Although Deng Xiaoping was humiliated in another way, he too must have debated whether death might be preferable. Many others chose to die. Deng did not, and the Chinese nation owes him a debt of gratitude on that account. His death would have had 'no more effect than the loss of a single hair by nine oxen'. No one would have credited him with having laid down his life for a principle. On the contrary, they would have thought he had departed this life because he was at his wit's end, and because his crime allowed of no alternative . . .

Deng's admission of guilt did not preserve him from further criticism, harassment, and humiliation. He was paraded in front of a mass rally wearing a paper hat on his head and a denunciatory placard round his neck. His son Deng Pufang was arrested, interrogated, and urged to denounce his father. This he staunchly refused to do despite the maltreatment that has left him permanently crippled.

Deng himself was sent for re-education to a cadre school, where the authorities compelled him to wait at table on his fellow 'students' and companions in misfortune. He then spent some years working in a factory. After Lin Biao's flight and posthumous condemnation, he re-offered his services to the Government. He was recalled two years later, in 1973, becoming Deputy Premier and a close associate of Zhou Enlai, who earmarked him as his successor. It was not long, however, before he ran into difficulties.

In 1975, he clashed publicly with Jiang Qing at the agricultural conference in Dazhai. When he painted a gloomy picture of China's economic position and cited examples from Sichuan Province, Jiang Qing broke in with the assertion that people were far better off than before. Deng flatly contradicted her.

Refusing to be intimidated by the attacks made on him, his policy and supporters, Deng crossed swords with the radicals. Many Chinese believe that his popularity has never been greater than at this period, when he was conducting government business on behalf of Premier Zhou Enlai, already a very sick man.

Zhou enjoyed the people's love and respect. He was kind and humane, honest and upright, but all he did was carry out Mao's policies. Although he mitigated injustice wherever and whenever possible, he never seriously opposed the Chairman or failed to let him have his way. Reared in the Confucian tradition, he remained steadfastly loyal to Mao, both before his illness and in its latter stages. His image is idealized today, perhaps to contrast it with Mao's. There is a general avoidance of pointed questions. How, for instance, could a man whose political acumen was admired by all his foreign visitors, notably Henry Kissinger, have failed to foresee the disastrous effects of Mao's return to power through the Cultural Revolution? Why did he not support Liu Shaoqi? Why did he not range himself on the side of Peng Dehuai, who was the first to state openly that the emperor was naked – that Mao bore responsibility for the disastrous Great Leap Forward – and who ceased to be the Army's senior Marshal and Defence Minister and became an enemy of the Party overnight?

When Zhou died early in 1976, Deng became the focus of the people's hopes. It was the people who demanded his return to the leadership when the left-wing radicals were arrested. Hua Guofeng hesitated, perhaps because he felt no match for Deng's intellect and experience. When he did at last recall him, however, respect for Hua himself grew steadily because he was seen as a moderating influence on Deng's precipitate reformism. Fearful that the boat might be capsized by an over-hasty change of course, many Chinese found Hua's approach more prudent and circumspect.

There were times when Deng and his supporters had to draw in their horns. In summer 1979, for example, his stock sank so low that many people, including our colleagues in Hong Kong, thought he was finished. But of that there could be no question. Deng and his supporters were systematically consolidating their position. Representatives of the old-style 'two-whatever' policy, meaning those who had always endorsed whatever Mao said or did, were gradually ousted from the Politburo.

What differentiates the Chinese Communist Party from other ruling Communist Parties is that it once, when the People's Republic was founded, enjoyed a large measure of public confidence. This it has lost. Deng Xiaoping, who acknowledged this, realized that his first aim must be to regain that confidence. He has not yet managed to do so.

Many of Deng's political and economic moves were audacious and went to the limits of what he could accomplish in the face of opposition from the 'whateverists'. Even he, however, conducted his debate with them in the style of a traditional 'two-line struggle' in which decisions are taken by a select few.

Factory managers are now elected by their workers just as delegates to regional assemblies are elected by local voters, but political posts, both central and provincial, are filled as they always were. The people are not consulted. Neither is the Party itself, discounting a few senior members of the Politburo and the Central Committee. Chinese communists speak of a dictatorship of the proletariat, but where or when is 'the proletariat' ever consulted? What *is* the Chinese proletariat, anyway? Is it identical with the Party? Whatever the truth, it has no say.

The manner in which senior posts are filled remains as arbitrary as ever, with the result that the leadership suffers from structural instability. Deng Xiaoping is aware of this problem. He has so far failed to solve it, just as he has so far failed to impose a retirement age on public servants. Resistance inside the Party leadership and among provincial functionaries may be proving too strong for him.

Deng has not yet dared to bypass the Party and appeal to the people direct, fair though his chances of success would be. In his place, only one man would have taken the bull by the horns and regarded the move as dialectically progressive, but he is dead.

To Tibet by Turboprop

Tibet is inaccessible, even today. Our ancient turboprop began by flying west for five hundred miles, not south, to avoid an eighteen-thousand-foot range whose name I cannot even recall. The mountains on our route did not exceed twelve thousand feet. Rugged and jagged though they were, cultivated fields could be seen on their highland plateaux, just short of the snow line. Cultivated by whom? we wondered. Who lived up there and what did they live on?

Visible from afar, plumes of smoke rose from a cluster of tall chimneys. They could only herald the approach of Xining, where a heavy vehicle plant had been built in the wilds. I had always imagined Xining to be a small desert outpost, possibly still enclosed by walls, but I was mistaken. It turned out to be a sizeable industrial city with an impressive level of air pollution. Xining and its factories soon receded into their own miasma, to be replaced by the sight of Koko Nor glittering in an expanse of yellow desert. It was as blue as its name implied. Far to the north rose the white giants of the Xilian range, once listed in Western atlases as the Richthofen Mountains, after the great German geographer.

The Qaidam (Tsaidam) Basin was arid and desolate – featureless except where punctuated by salt lakes that dazzled us like mirrors lying upturned in the sand. Only once did we sight a caravan route. It emerged from a mountain range and traversed a broad sandy basin, running straight as an arrow for thirty or forty miles, then crossed a pass in the next mountain range and debouched into yet another basin. Situated beside it in the midst of this basin, which stretched from horizon to horizon, was a farmstead with three narrow fields – the whole no bigger than a postage stamp. Water there must have been, but what sort of people lived there? Who would have spent a lifetime alone in the desert, a week away from the nearest living soul? Who could have endured an existence of such utter solitude?

The Chinese for Golmud is *Go-erh-mu*. It used to be merely a name on the map – a trail marker. Not even a hut had occupied the site, though there may have been a well. We caught sight of Golmud as our plane banked steeply to the left and headed south for a gap in the mountains. Now the railhead of the line from Lanzhou, which was to be opened in the next few months, it proved to be a medium-sized industrial town. Golmud's factory chimneys did not belch as impressively as Xining's, so industrialization still had some way to go there. The sight of Xining had made us a little blasé.

The town stood on the edge of the desert, at the foot of a bare mountain range. A long conduit, presumably fed by snow water, ran down to it from the rocky heights above. Golmud marked the beginning of the oil pipeline and road to Lhasa. Our plane followed this road for many miles. Peering down at it, we could count the trucks that would take as much as a week to reach the Tibetan capital.

Later, when our route diverged from the road, we flew over barren wastes and mountains which, though bare of snow, had massive glaciers brooding in their ravines. Lakes glinted here and there, emerald green on the mountain saddles and turquoise on the highland plateaux. Every ten minutes or so, we flew over wide, gravel-strewn riverbeds, dry save for relatively narrow channels filled with water. After mistakenly identifying three of these watercourses as the upper reaches of the Yellow River, we gave up and consoled ourselves with the thought that all the great rivers of East and South-East Asia rise in Tibet: the Huang He, Yangtze, Mekong, Salween, Brahmaputra, Ganges, and Indus. We were bound to have flown over one or another of them.

Our plane touched down smoothly at an altitude of twelve thousand feet, and we stepped straight into a minibus waiting at the foot of the steps.

Lhasa Light

The road was unpaved but could have been worse. After two hours of it, our Chinese companion pointed to a pair of small hills in the distance. One of them, he announced, eyeing me expectantly, was the Potala. I feigned the keenest amazement and interest, but I was disappointed. The hills looked tiny – dwarfed by the mountains flanking the valley in which they lay. My own mental image of the Potala had been far more impressive.

Once we reached Lhasa and stood at its foot, however, I took everything back. The Potala is an architectural complex too vast to absorb at a single glance. Using the hill as a foundation for the massive walls of the monastery and temple, it transforms the hill itself into architecture, clothes its ascending flanks in masonry, and crowns its summit with gilded roofs.

We drove into the courtyard of a small guesthouse – Lhasa still had no hotel – and got out of the bus. We were not allowed to carry a bag, nor even a handbag, being still unused to an altitude of twelve thousand feet, and were pursued upstairs to our room by solicitous cries of '*Manmande!*' (Slowly!)

The altitude we got used to in a day or two, but not the light. This is Tibet's most astonishing feature, and one that never loses its impact. Everything looks new, fresh, and different in this white light and dust-free atmosphere. You feel you could reach out and touch everything in sight – not only the nearby Potala, which dominates the Chinese quarter, but the distant mountains as well. Every contour and fissure stands out with clarity and precision, as if viewed through powerful binoculars. But that is not all. The green of the highland pastures, the grey of boulders, the vivid red of geological strata in walls of rock – all these colours register their true intensity. No haze dulls their brilliance. There are no blue distances like those depicted by our old masters. Distant prospects here are as vivid as the foreground.

The sky is deep blue, the clouds are purest white, and the world looks freshly washed – the world, that is, with the exception of the Tibetans themselves, who never wash. That, too, can be clearly seen by Lhasa light. It is a white light, but pure and pellucid, not harsh and cold. The red frequencies in its spectrum are probably weaker. It is silvery, almost white, even at sunrise, when it falls on the grey walls of rock beyond the Potala.

One sunset during our stay was as dramatic as the sky in Altdorfer's *Battle of Arbela*; another conjured up a soft silver aura beyond the gilded roofs of the Da Zhao Si, the old quarter's principal temple, while the sky overhead was already growing dark. At night the sky is black and the stars barely flicker. They are clearly visible even near the moon, like punch-holes in a black lampshade.

Ancient and Modern

Lhasa has a modern quarter and an old quarter inhabited respectively by Chinese and Tibetans. Few Chinese can be seen in the old quarter and few Tibetans in the new. Even the children who swarmed around us in the former lagged behind, one after another, when we entered the street lined with modern buildings.

The new quarter was laid out in 1951, after the Chinese occupation. Its boring architectural features include a single-storeyed department store patronized mainly by Chinese and seldom by Tibetans, schools, administrative buildings, the offices of the Lhasa *People's Daily*, our own small guesthouse, and barracks and offices enclosed by long walls too high to see over.

The focal point of the old quarter is the Tsug-lag Khang. Around this temple runs the Barkhor, or Street of Eight Corners, which pilgrims must tread in a clockwise direction if they hope for any benefit in the world to come. To avoid being jostled by curious crowds, we rashly sacrificed such preferential treatment as we might have received in the hereafter by proceeding anticlockwise.

The houses were two-storeyed, and the gaps in their massive, rough-hewn boulder walls were filled with smaller natural stones. The prison, one of the finest ancient buildings in the Street of Eight Corners, was constructed of masonry more massive still. Small shops sold haber-dashery, aprons, cooking utensils, pots, and spices. Wherever the street widened, but also from the flat roofs overhead, children were flying kites at a remarkable height – five or six hundred feet, we estimated.

Ragged, grimy pilgrims clustered round the temple's wrought-iron gate, praying and prostrating themselves in the dust. Others were making their way round the Street of Eight Corners in similar fashion – clockwise, of course, or their exertions would have gone unrewarded.

We were admitted to the temple without having to wait in line, a privilege to which the expense of our Tibetan tour entitled us. It is open only three days a week, like the Mao Memorial Hall in Peking, and Lhasa's daily quota of visitors is limited to fifteen hundred – not that anyone counts them too carefully. The abbot told us that visitors had to be limited in number because there were so few monks to deal with them.

Why were there so few?

Many had emigrated, he said – to India, for example. Others had rejoined the laity. What about recruitment? Young men, said the abbot, were attracted to different vocations nowadays. Many were eager to serve in the Tibetan Army, for instance.

The abbot had a good, strong face. I wondered what he thought while trotting out such stock untruths. His expression gave nothing away. Could anyone become a monk? But of course, he said. I inquired the age of the youngest. He pointed to a robed figure sweeping the courtyard. Fifty-one, he said, impassive as ever.

The chapel doors were heavily chained and padlocked. The abbot had them opened for us. Presiding within were Buddhas and horse- or ox-headed gods, most of them attended by deities of junior rank. Of the latter, many were engaged with evident relish in the gruesome task of dissecting people with a wide range of implements and in a wide variety of ways. Not that we regretted it, details were hard to discern by the dim light of wicks floating in big bowls of rancid butter. These did little more than give off the acrid stench that never deserted our nostrils in Tibet, whether in temples or private houses. The only electric bulb, which dangled from two wires, dazzled rather than illuminated.

The most sacred object in the temple and the whole of Tibet is the statue of Buddha Sakyamuni, which a Chinese princess of the Tang period brought as a dowry from Chang An, then the Chinese capital, a thousand years ago. Sakyamuni sits in a side chapel measuring roughly ten feet by twelve. He has been so often and so heavily restored over the centuries that no stylistic features of the Tang period can be detected. He is hung with strings of turquoise and coral and lavishly adorned with silver and uncut precious stones, but the silver doesn't gleam and the jewels don't sparkle. The whole statue bears a thick coating of greasy dust, and the walls and ceiling are black with soot from guttering butterfat lamps. One is tempted to import a buxom German *Hausfrau*, issue her with a vacuum cleaner and a bucket of silver polish, and leave her to it for a day – better still, two or three days. After that, a few rented spot-lights from Cartier would work wonders.

The Potala

At the foot of the Potala stands the so-called Revolutionary Museum. It shows nothing of the Tibetan people's revolution – not surprisingly, since no revolution took place here. The most it could show would be the country's occupation by the Chinese or the anti-Chinese revolt of 1959.

The museum's actual function is to illustrate the horrors of lamaist rule, and in that respect it houses some impressive exhibits. There is, for example, a collection of mummified, severed human hands, one of which is conveniently mounted on a handsome ebony handle for use as a back-scratcher. Also on display are some iron skewers, needle-sharp and perfectly designed for their intended task of putting out eyes, a selection of thumbscrews, and sundry other instruments of torture. The true lama never killed an ant, far less a human being, but he was at liberty to flay people alive. The cured skins of adults and children bear witness to this practice, though what offence the children could have committed remains a mystery. They may have been the offspring of criminals – either that or twins, who were put to death on principle, usually with their mother. Photographs taken during the reign of the last Dalai Lama – he would have been a child at the time – show Tibetans with their noses lopped off and their eyes put out, and others with their heads cemented into walls. We can, I think, dispense with further examples.

Even if one bears in mind that this is a museum devoted to anti-lamaist propaganda, and that such atrocities may not have been the rule, it is clear that the lamas' hand lay heavy on the people. This we know from earlier, non-Chinese accounts, though the propaganda skilfully disseminated by exiled lamas in India makes no mention of such things. On the other hand, the Revolutionary Museum contains no photographs of atrocities committed by the Red Guards or of the numerous Tibetan monasteries and temples destroyed by the Chinese, mostly during the Cultural Revolution. Our Chinese guides said nothing when we inquired about them, hoping that we wouldn't press the point.

Towering above the propaganda museum at its foot, the Potala stands there like a cross between a fortress and an oriental Vatican bereft of its Pope. We made our way through a labyrinth of halls and devotional chambers or chapels. Many flights of stairs were as steep as ladders. The funerary statues of earlier Dalai Lamas occupied several floors. They sat cross-legged, with their hands in their laps. The feet and hands were dimly lit by a scattering of unshaded bulbs. The heads and shoulders were lost in gloom but could just be discerned when our guide shone his flashlight upwards. The Dalai Lamas had not, so we were assured by a Chinese who had lived in Lhasa for decades, been buried seated inside their statues. Instead, their cadavers were dissolved in acid. Some of this was heavily diluted and sold as an elixir, while the rest was stirred into the clay from which the funerary statues were made.

In the galleries and several of the halls, large expanses of wall were covered with paintings in miniature style whose iconographic interpretation would keep the world's centres of Buddhist study busy for decades – if ever they were published. They are still a jealously guarded secret, however, and the attendant who dogged our steps was careful to ensure that we took no illicit photographs. I became bored with the paintings' stereotyped succession of figures – as, for instance, when they depicted whole armies of gods and angels, saints and common mortals – and was tempted to dismiss them out of hand. But then, suppressing my facile preconceptions with an effort, I looked more closely and was rewarded with the sight of some lifelike and superbly painted scenes complete with remarkable, psychologically perceptive portraits no bigger than a thumbnail. Lost in admiration, I found it hard to tear myself away from one postcard-sized patch of wall, which showed a Dalai Lama on his way to China, and developed a sudden hatred for the attendant whose vigilance prevented me from coming away with one little snapshot, one tiny memento of our visit.

But the tour had to proceed. We passed a large number of Bodhisattvas adorned with dusty jewels and turquoise necklaces, as well as dozens of creatures from the lamaist pantheon, teeth bared and faces contorted with fury, whose function was to awe and terrify the faithful. These effigies do not convey the *tremendum* one experiences in the presence of God, but seem intended rather to instil fear of the priesthood and retribution in the world to come. The remarkable thing, however, is that this religion, too, appears to have possessed a sublime theology of which little is known. Although something can be sensed of its solemnity and pervasive power, its effect in these gloomy, labyrinthine passages is chest-constrictingly oppressive.

It was a relief to regain the light of day, the silvery light of Tibet. Standing on the Dalai Lama's terrace, we gazed across Lhasa at the mountains on the other side of the valley – so close, it seemed yet again, that we could almost reach out and touch them.

Buddhas and Barley

We were at fifteen thousand feet, having driven across country in our Toyota minibus, and had already paid a prearranged visit to a commune. Now we caught sight of a village some distance from the road and expressed a wish to visit that too. The driver pulled up.

A boy was standing beside the road. He stiffened when he saw us get out and hurried on ahead. We followed him along a narrow path and crossed a stream by way of some stepping stones.

We seemed to have the village to ourselves. The street was flanked by mud walls six or seven feet high. It was impossible to see into the yards beyond, and the gates were secured with heavy iron locks of strange design. Presumably, the locals didn't trust each other.

The boy reappeared with two old men in tow. Through our Tibetan interpreter, who had now caught up with us, we learned that the boy had been attending school for nine years and acted as the commune's accountant. There were fifty children in the village, of whom thirty-seven went to school.

Hanging from one gate was a red plaque inscribed 'House of a Renowned Family' in Chinese characters. The Tibetan characters below meant the same, no doubt, so one of the family's sons was a soldier. We asked if we might see inside some houses. Yes, we were told, except that all the gates were locked. Everyone else was at work in the fields. 'The houses are all much alike,' said the old men. 'The only ones you can see are ours or the boy's.'

'And the house where the little children are,' the boy put in.

Explaining that we had no wish to inspect every house in the village, we accepted their offer. Every gate had to be unlocked with a huge iron key before we could enter. All the houses were enclosed by a small yard containing a tree or two, a few shrubs, and some herbs. Sunflowers supplied the only touch of colour.

The first house we visited had mud walls reposing on a foundation wall of massive boulders. The door was surmounted by a small projecting roof improvised out of sheet metal, whereas other houses had canvas awnings. Ulrich, our son, filmed everything in sight for a television documentary.

Outside, a cauldron of water stood propped on some stones. Two big hanks of yak wool straggled across the yard, which was spanned by several lengths of yellow plastic string. For drying clothes on, suggested Ulrich. This drew a laugh from me and his brother Wolfram. 'Drying clothes?

Unglue your eye from that camera for a moment and take a look at those two old men. Their clothes have never seen the inside of a washtub – they're stiff with dirt. You can bet they've never washed their faces either.'

'So what's the string for?' Ulrich demanded.

We inquired. For drying herbs or fruit, we were told.

Though rather on the untidy side, the yard could not have been called chaotic. In a word, it looked homely. Its population of hens and cats thought so – you could tell.

This particular house had two rooms. The kitchen, which doubled as a store-room, was windowless and almost dark inside, with a hole in the roof to let the smoke escape. It was hard to imagine cooking in there.

All the living-room windows were properly glazed. In the centre stood a wooden post, and perched on top was a big china insulator of the type found on telegraph poles. Sure enough, some flex led up to a bulb suspended from the ceiling. Low beds stood against the wall, and the small table in front of them supported a mountain of woollen blankets. The bench against the opposite wall was covered with tattered old rugs.

The mud walls were unplastered, the ceiling and exposed beams black with soot. One of the beams had a meander pattern painted on it in white-wash. This was believed to bring good luck and repainted at the beginning of every year. Pictures of Mao hung everywhere, though one wall carried a portrait of Hua Guofeng as well. There were no devotional objects to be seen: not a prayer-wheel, not a Buddha, not a Tantra – nothing, even though we had turned up unannounced. We forbore to ask about this. Later, we learned that all such things are officially banned. Up in the remote highlands, where people live in tents and are less strictly regimented, things may be different.

At one of the houses we visited, a young woman was standing in the kitchen doorway parching peas in an enormous pan while a dozen or so children played outside in the yard. As soon as they saw us, they stopped playing and gathered round, wide-eyed with curiosity. Apart from doing her housework, the young woman acted as nursery-school teacher to the children whose parents were working in the fields.

We asked one of the old peasants if he was better off today than before. 'We have more to eat,' he replied.

When we pressed him for details, he gave them without hesitation. Though independent in the old days, he had been obliged to surrender the bulk of his barley crop to the feudal lord who owned the village – fifty or sixty sacks as opposed to the nine or ten he was permitted to keep himself. That had been too little to provide for his family's needs and next year's sowing.

And how were things today?

Today everyone worked for the commune, which sold its crop in town and reinvested or distributed the proceeds. Food was more plentiful now. What sort of food? Barley, of course, but peas and turnips as well. Butter and milk, too.

He certainly seemed contented, but we were only sixty miles from the capital. Other people, even including our Chinese guides, had told us that conditions in more remote parts of the country were worse to the point of famine, though this itself might have been an understatement. Being nothing more nor less than tourists skimming the surface of Tibet, we were wholly dependent on Chinese interpreters when conversing with the local inhabitants.

I asked the old peasant if he ever saw meat.

Yes, but only rarely. Now, being harvest time, was the best season for meat. What sort of meat? Yak, mutton, beef.

Ulrich had been filming the peasant's face throughout this conversation. His skin was like leather, wrinkled and almost immobile, and his eyes peered out at us through narrow slits devoid of lids and eyebrows. He might have been of one stuff with the boulders in his native fields. This was no man to be thrust aside; destroyed, perhaps, but never moved against his will.

Ulrich sensed this too. He did a thing he seldom does when the light's good unless there's something important on his mind: he lowered his camera.

'I'd be surprised,' he said, 'if that man's ever suffered from depression, frustration, stress, or a mid-life crisis.'

Knowledge Means Power

'When I came to Tibet twenty years ago, I helped to set up schools here. That was our first priority. One village informed us that it wanted an elementary school. Until the Dalai Lama and the nobles fled, its five hundred inhabitants had been serfs. Only three could read and write, and they were the feudal lord's overseers. Schools,' said Ah Wang, 'are the prime requirement. They'll change the face of Tibet.'

Ah Wang was a Tibetan, but he belonged to the Tibetan minority in the neighbouring province of Sichuan and had attended a Chinese school there. Being bilingual, he could act as a channel of communication between the Han, or true Chinese, and his fellow Tibetans. He was now deputy head of the Xinhua news agency's office in Lhasa.

But he was still talking about schools. Parents, he said, wanted to send their children to school to turn them into intellectuals. 'An intellectual is almost like a lama. Before 1950, when the Chinese occupied this country, only three schools existed here.'

'And today?'

'Today there are over six thousand elementary schools with two hundred and thirty thousand pupils, over fifty secondary schools with twenty thousand pupils, twenty-two intermediate technical schools, and four colleges of higher education.'

The communist authorities are using education as a means of combating lamaism and religious beliefs, but they would be unwise to pin too many hopes on it. Lamaism remains strong, and education provided by Han Chinese is regarded as suspect.

Although I have been unable to verify Ah Wang's assertion that there were only three schools in the whole of Tibet before the Chinese marched in, there can be no doubt that the lamas took a jaundiced view of education for the masses.

This attitude was not unknown in Chinese history: 'In ancient times, those who knew the way did not enlighten the people but strove to keep them in ignorance. The more knowledge the people possess, the harder they are to govern,' wrote Lao-tse. His opinion was shared by Shang Yang, the Han Chinese whom we met while visiting the tomb of the First Emperor. He wrote:

> If study becomes popular, people will abandon their fields and busy themselves with debates, high-flown phrases, and discussions based on false assumptions.
>
> If the people are artless, they will seldom be inclined to treason; but they will be useless if they see that glib-tongued itinerant scholars succeed in gaining honour in the service of their prince.

Where have we heard such ideas before? From Hitler, among others. 'On no account,' he declared during one of his meal-time monologues, 'must the population [of Eastern Europe] be permitted a higher education. If we fell into that error, we should be breeding future opponents of our régime.'

So the peoples of Eastern Europe were to become slaves, or, as the Chinese used to put it in their early feudal days, 'talking animals'. Confucius, by contrast, held that rulers should have two aims: to make the people prosperous, and to educate them. His view prevailed. The Chinese communists, too, assumed responsibility for public education as a matter of course. Even when fighting for their very survival in

Jiangxi Province during the late 1920s and early 1930s, they set up hundreds of schools and reduced the illiteracy rate – or so they claimed – from ninety to twenty per cent. The pupils, most of them adults, were naturally taught to read and write with the aid of primers that preached hatred of Kuomintang landowners and love of the Red Army. In this the communists were only following the example of mission schools, where literacy was imparted as an aid to reading the Gospels.

In Mao's China, politically oriented education was skilfully blended with propaganda and a set of moral demands on the individual. The results it achieved were not only remarkable but almost uncanny. During the 1950s, almost all the Germans who arrived in free Hong Kong after years in communist custody declared that they had been justly imprisoned. Mystified Western observers spoke of brainwashing and credited the Chinese with demonic powers of persuasion.

But there was nothing demonic about it. The autobiography of Pu Yi, the last Chinese Emperor, clearly demonstrates how a gentle and un-remitting appeal to man's social conscience and better nature – how a blend of patience and magnanimity, justice and severity, overt and veiled threats, subtle and incessant propaganda – ended by converting the ex-Emperor into a devotee of the new régime, whose darker aspects he either failed to perceive or, won over by his long re-education, dismissed as fortuitous and temporary.

Let there be no misunderstanding, though. Not everyone was treated with such consideration and psychological delicacy. Many other stories are on record of prisoners who were subjected to brutal and inhuman treat-ment, but not to education in any genuine sense.

It is nonetheless true that, in its own sphere of control during the war and throughout the People's Republic thereafter, the communist move-ment brought about a moral uplift and renascence. What contributed to this was the still austere lifestyle of most communist leaders themselves, coupled with military discipline, an uncorrupted administration, and the existence of moral standards to which rulers and ruled adhered in like measure.

What of the millions who were killed 'after the Liberation'? What of the landowners, rent collectors, shopkeepers, Kuomintang supporters? What of the capitalists?

Chinese society came to terms with their liquidation in a remarkably short space of time. They were regarded simply as casualties of the Revolution, members of a class that had no place in a new society with new and different moral standards. Even from Chinese who openly in-veighed against the atrocities of the Cultural Revolution, I heard peculiarly mild and sympathetic verdicts on the 'purges' of the early years, as though their victims were merely the price to be paid for the building of a new China. The fact that these victims included many Chinese who had fought to liberate their country from Japanese occupation was taken for granted. 'Regrettable, but what do you expect? It was a revolution.' My inability to endorse this convenient view was met with incomprehension.

Widespread loss of human life did nothing to quench the hopes of the Chinese, and especially of the younger generation, in the early post-revolutionary years. They were setting out to construct a great new country, and the mood was one of eager anticipation.

The Communist Party under Mao did not for long harness this passion to the development of something new, ready and willing though the people were. It soon became apparent to the Party leaders that educated, cultivated individuals took a more critical view of everything, not excluding the Party leadership itself. This was unwelcome to Mao and still more so to the Gang of Four. Teaching ceased at schools and universities soon after the Cultural Revolution got under way. An entire generation lapsed into semi-educated ignorance – a condition from which it can never wholly recover.

The Winking Owl

Although the dances of the Han Chinese, or Chinese proper, can be graceful and a pleasure to watch, they are dances devised for the stage. The Uighurs, a Turkic people, have dancing in their blood, and perform with fire and zest. Only yesterday, at the Turfan oasis, we had seen an Uighur emerge from behind a sand dune carrying a species of lute. He told our Chinese interpreter that he had been working in the fields, but that he had accompanied some impromptu dancing during the midday break.

Tonight's performance at the theatre in Urumqi opened with a hymn to Chairman Mao sung by a mixed choir. It was a long time since we had heard such a thing at Peking, but Urumqi, the capital of Xinjiang Province, is over three hours' flying time from Peking, half-way between the Yellow Sea and Europe.

A ballet followed. At the rear of the stage, bordered with black crêpe, hung a portrait of Chairman Mao. The *corps de ballet*, representing the Chinese people, mimed sorrow and veneration before it. Then a lone dancer bounded from the wings – a bearer of glad tidings, to judge by his radiant expression and athletic leaps. From one moment to the next, unbridled joy overcame the grieving throng. Some sprang hither and thither while others quickly but devoutly removed the late Chairman's portrait. One of the nimblest and most exuberant dancers vaulted on to a companion's shoulders and hammered a nail into the wall, some distance to the left of the original one. He only went through the motions, of course, because the second nail was already there. Mao's portrait was then hung – off centre – in its new position.

Nothing being so painful to the Chinese eye as asymmetry, it was easy to foresee that visual balance would swiftly be restored in some pleasing manner. Sure enough, the small orchestra in front of the stage emitted a noisy flourish. Flutes and *erhus* shrilled, trumpets blared, drums rolled and cymbals crashed. Then, with sprightly tread, some ten young comrades of both sexes entered from the left bearing a large picture above their heads. They did not exhibit it to the audience until they reached the centre of the stage. It was, needless to say, a portrait of Wise Chairman Hua Guofeng.

The crowd on stage had respectfully cleared a path for the procession and its precious burden. Children wearing Young Pioneer neckerchiefs turned cartwheels and bounded for joy. Their seniors and elders saluted the picture by bowing low in something very akin to the traditional kowtow. Arms were extended in supplication as the Wise Chairman's portrait was borne past. Another dancer vaulted gracefully on to a companion's shoulders, pretended to hammer a nail into the wall on the late Chairman's right, and helped to suspend his successor's portrait from it. Once the latter had been garlanded with colourful paper flowers by other dancers, male and female, symmetry was restored.

Such was the resemblance between the two portraits that it took a keen eye to distinguish the new Chairman from the old. Hua had even adopted his predecessor's hairstyle, so the absence of a mole on his chin was a convenient aid to differentiation.

The Chinese people bowed low, almost to the ground, before the pair of portraits. They raised their arms as though entreating benediction, then danced off left with heads still bowed. Meanwhile, pink spotlights played on the faces of the two Chairmen, the old and the new, and the orchestra accompanied their apotheosis with the biggest din their instruments could produce.

'A Herr Küng called,' my new secretary announced. 'He'd like to see you.' I raised my eyebrows. 'Not Professor Küng of Tübingen – the one who had all that trouble with the Pope and lost his licence to teach?'

It was the man himself. Hans Küng visited the embassy at my invitation and we closeted ourselves in the library.

'Well,' I said, 'has Peking University offered you a chair?'

He laughed and called my suggestion a trifle premature. He was still teaching at Tübingen University, but Peking's Academy of Social Sciences had invited him to lecture on 'Science and Religion'. Part of his lecture, which he had already delivered, dealt with the personality cult and the element of pseudo-religious belief in communism. To his surprise, his remarks had been greeted with approbation, not hostility.

Two Chinese journalists came to dinner with us not long after Küng's visit. One of them, I knew, had a landscape by the painter Huang Yungyü in his office. I'd admired it because, instead of adhering to the usual dry, academic style, it was unconventionally dramatic and employed a novel range of colours. I recalled having heard that Huang had incurred disfavour during the Cultural Revolution for depicting an owl with one eye open and the other shut.

One of our guests confirmed this story. The radicals had found the picture provocative and asked Huang what he intended it to convey, pointing out that no other Chinese artist had ever depicted an owl with one eye shut. Anyone who produced such a bizarre picture must have some ulterior motive, they insisted, and Huang's assertion that it held no deeper meaning was sheer effrontery. They felt satisfied that his owl was 'black' painting, because the idiomatic significance of 'closing one eye' was that a thing would soon pass and should not be taken too seriously. Did he mean that the Cultural Revolution would soon pass, and that communism should be regarded lightly?

Huang Yungyü had had a hard time, said our other guest. He had been 'subjected to struggle' and banished to the forests of Manchuria.

We went on to discuss the role of the owl in Chinese folklore, and ascertained that the Chinese, too, believed its cry to be a portent of death.

As for Hans Küng, said our guests, he had been absolutely right to stress the existence in China of political superstition. One example of this was the anthem *The East Is Red*, which likened Mao to a star.

'It was far worse during the Cultural Revolution,' they assured me, '—far worse than it is today. Before peasants picked up their hoes to weed a field, they had to turn to the east and salute Chairman Mao. Workers kept his picture beside their lathes and did the same. In schools, government offices, hospital wards – even in aircraft flying at thirty thousand feet – you could see people asking his picture for instructions in the morning and reporting to it in the evening, when they engaged in self-criticism. What you saw at Urumqi were scenes reminiscent of a temple or church. Never mind, though – picture-worship will soon be abolished.'

'Only where Mao is concerned,' I asked, 'or will the same apply to Chairman Hua Guofeng?'

They prevaricated slightly. 'That dance you saw at Urumqi – it wasn't typical. The clocks in Xinjiang are a little slow. The era of the personality cult is over, but they haven't caught up yet.'

'That's as may be,' I retorted, 'but I saw something similar at Shanghai in December 1976 – a truckload of people beating drums and cymbals with all their might. They were celebrating the publication of Chairman Hua's official portrait a month earlier. I wondered at the time if it was going to become a monthly ritual.'

'It hasn't, as you've seen for yourself. The personality cult is pseudo-religious – rather like your veneration of saints – but "Liberate thought!" and "Learn from the facts!" are slogans designed to wean people from a superstitious faith in the hoot of an owl or the sanctity of the Chairman of the Central Committee. We're appealing to them to think scientifically, not believe in dogma.'

'So I often hear it said,' I replied, 'but even some of your most emancipated and undogmatic articles begin with a pseudo-religious invocation.'

Our guests demanded chapter and verse.

'Well,' I said, 'a recent article stated that, where intellectual curiosity and respect for knowledge are concerned, socialism surpasses all other eras and social systems, and that it offers intellectuals the greatest chance of developing their talents to the full. I'm sure the three of us could easily cite a dozen or more instances to the contrary.'

'An article may *begin* that way,' I was told, 'but then it's qualified by an allusion to maldevelopments and shortcomings or defects. That's what matters most from our point of view. We only write our articles for the sake of what comes after the "buts".'

'Granted,' I said. 'That principle certainly applies to press comment in all socialist countries where "buts" aren't prohibited. With us, what matters most comes first. But even allowing for our difference of approach, the preambles to many of your articles – the ones that paint socialism as superlative in every last respect – well, they're hardly calculated to convert the non-socialist. He tends to equate them with the rattle of a prayer-wheel or whistling in the dark. To be frank, you may criticize individual maldevelopments and shortcomings – you often present them quite objectively, in fact – but you never question the system itself.'

'You're asking too much of us.'

'No,' I said, 'I merely mention that because I think it's what your readers want. We've all seen wall-posters demanding to know why Taiwan has developed more rapidly than the People's Republic. Your Chairman and other Chinese politicians have lately been exploring the reasons for the post-war "economic miracles" in Germany and Japan. If you presented a sober and objective comparison of economic development in Taiwan and the People's Republic, North and South Korea, East and West Germany, I think you'd be inundated with letters from readers eager to know the reasons for its disparity.'

They laughed. 'We get them already,' they said. 'Our system has many flaws – we realize that, and we're looking for ways of remedying them, but we haven't reached the stage where definitive answers can be given. That's why we don't favour any grand public debate on the comparative merits of your system and ours. Questions like that need careful formulation, not snap judgements. Once our society has consolidated itself – once it has overcome the effects of the Cultural Revolution and rule by the Gang of Four – we'll be able to debate them publicly. Till then, stability takes precedence.'

I forbore to comment on this fine revolutionary sentiment. 'I see,' I said. 'So you'll accept that the owl has its present uses and confine yourselves to telling your readers not to criticize it?'

Both our guests laughed. 'Exactly. But as time goes by we'll enlighten them on other forms of superstition – picture-worship, for instance. First things first, though.'

'Because stability takes precedence?'

'Exactly!' they chorused.

Two days later, *Guangming Ribao* published a reader's letter. 'Comrade Editor,' it began, 'the owl is a useful bird.' It went on to state that the owl caught as many as six hundred fieldmice a year, yet countryfolk considered it a bird of ill omen and a harbinger of death. The newspaper should urge people to protect it and dispel such superstitious beliefs.

The letter was signed: 'Two Soldiers of the People's Liberation Army.'

Democracy Wall

'What am I to do?' demanded the wall-poster in big characters. That was in November 1978. The poster adorned a wall in Wangfujing, Peking's main shopping street – not that it bears the remotest resemblance to Fifth Avenue, Bond Street, the Ginza, or their elegant counterparts in any

European capital. Wangfujing rivals them only in pedestrian density, which probably accounted for the poster's location. It had been affixed to a building near the offices of the *People's Daily*, only five minutes' walk from Tian An Men Square. Brush-inscribed on yellow paper, it was of medium size.

'What am I to do?' was no rhetorical question. The author of the poster, a woman, was soliciting advice. A substantial crowd had gathered round and were reading in silence. I reproduce the text from memory:

WHAT AM I TO DO?

Two years ago, early on the morning of 5 April, my husband went to the Square of Heavenly Peace to see if the police had really dared to remove the wreaths we had laid there on the Qing Ming Festival, in honour of Premier Zhou Enlai. That evening he failed to come home. Next day, I questioned his friends and the members of his labour unit, but no one had seen him. Then I went to the police station, where I was very unpleasantly treated and told nothing. I assumed that the police had arrested my husband. Although I returned every day, they still refused to tell me anything. They were anxious to get rid of me, but no man can simply vanish.

A month later, I was sent for by the Security Police. Someone came and told me that my husband had been killed in a brawl during the 'counter-revolutionary demonstration' in the Square of Heavenly Peace. My husband was no brawler. He always avoided fights. Then someone else came and gave me an urn containing his ashes. I was made to sign a receipt and sent home.

My husband and I were happily married. I could not have borne life without him if it had not been for our two children, but it was hard to care for them because we had no relatives in the city who could have looked after them while I was out at work. However, a member of my husband's labour unit helped me by taking them off my hands from time to time. A year ago we got married, and he moved in with me. I am now expecting his child.

A few days ago, just as I was washing the children and putting them to bed, and while my husband was chopping vegetables for supper, somebody knocked at the door. I opened it, and there stood my husband – my *first* husband, whose ashes were in the urn. I thought he was a ghost. They had arrested him during the disturbances in the Square of Heavenly Peace and taken him to a prison outside Peking. He was forbidden to write anything but a confession, not that he had committed any crime. Now he has been pardoned.

We went together to the Security Police and returned his ashes. Now I am married to two men.
WHAT AM I TO DO?

Like the first line, the last was brush-written in big characters. Passers-by read the poster in silence, then walked on looking pensive or dismayed. What answer could they have given her?

Though somewhat phlegmatic and not easily roused, the Pekingese have long memories. They not only recall what happened in Tian An Men Square at the beginning of April 1976 but continually refer to the subject.

For weeks, a wall-poster fiercely attacking Wu De, Peking's Mayor and Party boss, had hung in a side street in the western quarter of the city. It was Wu De who had called on the demonstrators to disperse on 6 April 1976. By November 1978, his position had become so weak that he dared not have the poster removed. He was replaced as head of the capital's Party and administrative machines but retained his membership of the Politburo. To a populace beginning to flex its muscles, this was not enough.

Almost overnight, the atmosphere in Peking became politically explosive. There was nothing fortuitous about this development. A so-called Central Working Conference had been in session since 10 November 1978. Attended by the country's political leaders, it was preparing the ground for a plenum of the Central Committee. The participants sat in secret, of course, and no details of their deliberations were officially released.

The Pekingese had nonetheless become aware that important decisions were in the offing. From the press, which had for some weeks been backing the victims of the Tian An Men riots, they gathered that a new wind was blowing. According to 'small-path news', or informed rumour, ex-Mayor Wu De and Chen Xilian, Peking's military commander, had engaged in self-criticism at the Central Working Conference. It also transpired that a new course was under discussion, one key issue being a reassessment of the Tian An Men disturbances. Only a year ago, Hua Guofeng had told a working conference that the demonstration was a counter-revolutionary act, and that this had been reason enough to suppress it.

The Pekingese not only disagreed but said so. Their memories were still green. From 17 November onwards, or about a week after the conference opened, there was a sudden increase in the number of wall-posters calling for a frank account of events during the Tian An Men riots. This was not engineered or inspired by any particular faction. Realizing that opinions on this issue were divided within the leadership itself, the capital's inhabitants had sensed their opportunity and seized it. They expressed support for Deng Xiaoping and his backers at the conference, who were demanding that the events of 1976 be aired in public.

What would they have done if the working conference, at which the whole of the leadership was represented, had solidly opposed such an airing? Doubtless kept quiet, at least temporarily, but their memories of those days in April 1976 would have remained undimmed.

A poster on the wall of the building next door to the *People's Daily* offices, which our interpreter, Frau Gareis, saw on 9 November, complained that the author was still suffering political discrimination because of his involvement in the April disturbances. Although the newspapers wrote a lot about rehabilitation and restitution, he had seen no concrete evidence of either. People should not believe a word they read in the press, declared the author of the poster. Everyone on the editorial staff of the paper next door was a liar. The editors of the *People's Daily* did not take these accusations lying down. While calling them unjust and exaggerated, however, they conceded that the man had a point and offered to raise his case with the authorities.

Most of the wall-posters in Wangfujing described personal experiences, protesting against illegal imprisonment and political persecution, but others complained of poor dental treatment, discourteous service in shops and stores, or official harassment. In the middle of November, those with grievances to air discovered that a long brick wall near the Telegraph Office was particularly well suited to the displaying of wall-posters. It was this ugly expanse of brickwork which Peking's foreign correspondents christened 'Democracy Wall'. Though situated some distance from the city centre, it was big enough to accommodate really long articles – and popular protests abounded, especially in regard to the Tian An Men riots. The posters that appeared on the wall near the Telegraph Office urged the authorities to come clean on the subject and demanded that all who had given orders to quell the demonstrators be punished. A few of them even attacked Mao, but Tian An Men continued to be their principal theme – for the moment. The following are verbatim extracts:

The people are indignant. They are disgusted by attempts to conceal the identity of those who contributed to, and are implicated in, the great tragedy of 5 April 1976. All such persons should publicly and truthfully render an account of their murders and arrests, and of their suppression of the revolutionary people's movement . . . We call for a committee of inquiry to tell the nation the true facts of the tragedy, namely:
Who were the ringleaders? Who pronounced the revolt a crime?
Who was in supreme authority when the revolt was put down?
Who ordered thousands of members of the militia and security services to mobilize for the purpose of suppressing the people in Tian An Men?
Who ordered these fascist hordes to assault the revolutionary masses

288

of the working people in Sun Yat-sen Park, the Imperial Palace, and the Palace of Culture?

How many lives were lost in all, not only in Peking but throughout the country?

Without a nod of assent from Chairman Mao, would the Tian An Men incident have been described as a 'counter-revolutionary act'? In our view, the time has come to reassess Chairman Mao . . . We are on the verge of a new historical epoch. China stands at a crossroads in her history. Which direction will she take?

This period saw the publication of an anthology of the poems that had been deposited in Tian An Men Square or read aloud there in April 1976, in memory of Zhou Enlai. Some of them were moving compositions imbued with the fervour typical of all hymns to freedom, and many attacked the radicals. After some hesitation, Hua Guofeng had inscribed the book's title – *Collection of Poems of Tian An Men Square* – in his own handwriting and sent it to the publishers' collective for reproduction on the cover. Alive to the direction of the prevailing wind, he realized that, as Minister of Security during the riots, he was personally vulnerable. He now strove to associate himself with the movement that was demanding an exposé. This increased his dependence on Deng Xiaoping, whose removal from office in 1976 was largely, though not entirely, a consequence of the events of the time.

Prompted by the rash of wall-posters, the Peking edition of the *People's Daily* published 'The Truth about the Tian An Men Occurrences'. Such, at least, was the title of a long, two-part article that appeared on 21 and 22 November. Readers were now informed that responsibility for the earlier, false account of events lay with the Gang of Four – whom else? – and especially with their propaganda chief, Yao Wenyuan, who had spoken and written of a planned and organized counter-revolutionary act. This was untrue, the paper said. On the contrary, the demonstrations had formed part of a spontaneous revolutionary campaign.

Formal assessments or reassessments of this kind carry weight in a country such as China. Anyone imprisoned for participating in a counter-revolutionary campaign could now demand his release and rehabilitation. Whether he would succeed was another matter, of course, for many of the officials who had decreed his imprisonment were still at their desks. Though important in all communist countries, the official classification of an event is particularly so among the Chinese. It had always been their rulers' task to *name things* 'so that the human spirit is not beset by misunderstanding'.

The naming of things has always been, and still remains, an aid to governing the Chinese people because, once names and terms have been laid down, they can no longer alter them at will.

The Chinese love to represent things in black and white. The 'black' person is better avoided, whereas consorting with a 'white' person can pay dividends. When the demonstrations in Tian An Men Square were counter-revolutionary, the subject had to be approached with discretion. When they became a revolutionary act, approval of them could be openly voiced and punishment demanded for those who had suppressed them.

A person could also be black if he had a black class background, a black political past, or black ideas. One could speak of black music, black painting, and black literature.[1] But the Chinese like to quantify, even about things that are a mixture of black and white. Until Mao's death, the Cultural Revolution was ninety-five per cent good and five per cent bad. Stalin was seventy per cent good and thirty per cent bad. One poster I saw on Democracy Wall bore the following marginal note in a reader's handwriting: 'Mao was thirty per cent good and seventy per cent bad.'

Two long pieces in the *People's Daily* gave an account of what had happened in Tian An Men Square. Though essentially correct and consistent with our own information, it omitted a number of important details. There was no mention of the demonstrators who had been clubbed to death in the Park of Culture, behind the walls of the Imperial Palace, nor of the person or persons on whose orders the riots had been quelled. Had a member of the Gang of Four been involved, the newspaper would have spoken out, so whose name had it suppressed?

Was it Wu De, the city's chief civil administrator, who had addressed the mob through loudspeakers and called on them to disperse? Or was it Hua Guofeng himself, then Minister of Security? One of the articles referred to a 'black element' in the municipal security services, but this could hardly be identified with Hua.

The decision had rested with one man alone. One man alone could have issued the crucial order and taken responsibility for it, and that was the advocate of permanent revolution.

One can picture him on the day when the spirit of revolution turned against him. There he sat in his home, only a few hundred yards from Tian An Men, huddled in an unpretentious armchair. He was very ill – unable to walk or even stand unsupported. His speech had degenerated

---

[1] 'Unhealthiness' is less reprehensible. Things that rate as unhealthy – *bu liang* – include boasting, overstating production figures, sartorial extravagance, and unduly long hair in young men. During the Cultural Revolution, any instances of physical violence, torture, and vandalism that had not been decreed or sanctioned were attributed to excessive zeal or described as 'unhealthy' practice.

into a series of grunts and croaks intelligible only to his secretary and a handful of intimates. Still entirely lucid, he often resorted to a scribbling pad when the spoken word failed him.

He must have read his minions' doctored reports on the latest developments in Tian An Men Square. Did he see through them? Did he credit them? Revolutionary spirit? That reposed with him alone. As he saw it, what had reared its fiendish head in Tian An Men Square was the spirit of disorder, not revolution.

Did he give names to the things that confronted him, as was a supreme ruler's right and duty? Or did he turn them over in his mind, with the dialectical leaps he mistook for philosophical thinking, and leave others to find the synthesis and name for what was afoot, to wit, counterrevolution? For that there was only one remedy: it had to be crushed. We do not know how he acted that day, but we can guess.

A Chinese friend told me that Mao liked to emulate an emperor in a Chinese opera, bidding someone a polite and gracious farewell but intimating to his courtiers by means of a covert glance, an almost imperceptible gesture, that their imperial master would rest easier if the man in question disappeared. The disappearance was discreetly arranged – so discreetly that it never came to the emperor's ears. Absolved of responsibility, he preserved an untroubled conscience. Chronicles of his reign would contain no record of any covert glance or almost imperceptible gesture.

The *People's Daily* articles were long. They said much about the incidents in Tian An Men Square but nothing about Mao Zedong's verdict on them. They told only half the truth. Public dissatisfaction persisted.

The Chinese for wall-poster is *dazibao*, meaning 'big-character communication'. Wall-posters are a long-established institution in China, and literary allusions to them can be found at an early stage. In a society devoid of popular assemblies, parliaments, and press, they provided a suitable means of airing personal grievances.

They now became a means whereby public opinion could express itself directly. Putting up wall-posters was one of the freedoms guaranteed by the constitution. Their incidence in normal times was sporadic. People wrote out notices announcing that they wished to swap apartments or places of employment and pinned or pasted them to lamp-posts, telegraph poles, or buildings. Just occasionally, someone would inquire why his daughters, who had been rusticated to northern Manchuria during the Cultural Revolution, were still forbidden to return. Journalists and diplomats tipped each other off whenever they spotted a wall-poster whose significance was political rather than personal.

But there were also times when passions ran so high – as, for instance, on the anniversary of Zhou Enlai's death or in Shanghai after the Gang of Four's arrest – that wall-posters blossomed everywhere. They then became symptoms of popular ferment. Even after the ferment subsided, they continued to hang there for weeks, tattered by wind and weather, until every vestige of them was removed during a clean-up campaign.

Ten days after they first appeared on Democracy Wall, there was no sign of any diminution in public unrest. More and more posters went up, and the wall seemed to be turning into an institution, a sort of Chinese Hyde Park Corner where anyone could find an audience for his complaints.

Although many posters were devoted to personal grievances or Utopian theories of the Hyde Park Corner type, most carried vigorous political protests. Initially levelled at the officials who had quelled the Tian An Men disturbances, this criticism gained in scope and intensity as November drew to a close. The system itself was called into question.

At the same time, people were calmer than they had been during the early days of the movement – calmer and more self-assured. Most of those who stood around in groups were between twenty and thirty-five. They belonged to the generation that had been smitten by the tornado of the Cultural Revolution – a battered, uprooted, restless generation whose political alertness and courage may have been a product of their ordeal by fire.

Some young people debated what they had just been reading while others sat on the ground and copied out passages taken down by one of their number. The more interesting posters attracted such crowds that it took a long time to get within eyeshot of them.

Below is a selection of extracts from the posters that appeared there:

We expressly request the Government to build a cemetery for the 90 martyrs murdered during the revolutionary unrest of 5 April.

[Signed] A Young Person of 5 April.

A reader had ringed the figure 90 in red pencil and written beside it: 'Only 90?'

Written in bold brush-strokes:

The Party has betrayed us. It promised us democracy, but what we have is the dictatorship of the proletariat!

A pro-Mao wall-poster had been damaged, apparently by people trying to tear it down. It was also covered with scrawled comments. For example:

We've heard enough of such slogans in the past few years!
Slogans like these are no substitute for the truth!
If you're trying to scare us, you'll have to do better than that!
Ludicrous!
Dog's fart!

The poster that caused the greatest stir was drafted by a twelve-strong 'Democratic Forum' based in the southern province of Guizhou. This called for a general settlement of accounts with the 'superstition and idolatry' of previous years:

> America is capitalistic. It is the most highly developed country in the world. It has a history of only two hundred years, but it has been able to develop so fast because it is free from idols and superstitions . . . Democracy is essential to scientific progress. China's First Emperor, Qin Shihuang, has been dead for two thousand years, yet the tyrant's shadow still looms over us and we hear his whip crack whenever there is talk of democracy and human rights.

The American columnist Robert Novak, who visited Peking at the end of November, inspected Democracy Wall as a matter of course. Bystanders crowded round as soon as he announced, through an interpreter, that he would be interviewing Deng Xiaoping next day. If they had any requests, he said, he would pass them on. The Chinese quickly jotted down their requests and queries on slips of paper and handed them over. 'But how,' they asked, 'shall we know what Deng replied?' Novak reassuringly promised to return at seven the following evening.

In conversation with a Japanese politician next morning, Deng Xiaoping described the wall-posters as an absolutely normal phenomenon. 'They prove that our country's situation is stable. Our constitution permits them. We cannot gainsay that, nor should we criticize the masses if they avail themselves of their democratic rights and put up wall-posters. If the masses are angry, they must be able to vent their anger. Not all the masses' opinions are carefully considered, but that we can't insist on. Anyway, it isn't such a bad thing . . .' It appears that he said as much to Novak the same afternoon. I never heard if Novak passed on all the questions and requests he had been given. In any event, he failed to keep his appointment at Democracy Wall.

John Fraser, correspondent of the Canadian daily *Toronto Globe and Mail*, volunteered to address 'the masses' in Novak's place – address them, that is, without being able to speak a word of Chinese. He had been his paper's ballet and theatre critic until only ten months before, and had no previous experience of China.

At half past eight that night, Peter Christian Hauswedell called me to say that people had turned up in droves – about three thousand of them, he estimated. (Fraser himself, never a devotee of understatement, later put the figure at ten thousand.) Hauswedell, who was calling from a public phone in the Telegraph Office, said that the crowd had applauded wildly when Fraser told them through interpreters that Deng had described the Wall as a good thing. They were now forming up with the intention of marching to Tian An Men Square, but seemed in a peaceful mood. Hauswedell proposed to follow at a safe distance and see what happened.

He was amazed how smoothly everything went, and how quietly the column formed up with no apparent help from stewards or organizers. The demonstrators asked foreigners to photograph them and keep a written record of the proceedings, saying that they wanted the rest of the world to know what view the Chinese took of freedom and democracy.

When they reached Tian An Men Square and assembled at the monument to the dead of the Revolution, Deng Xiaoping's statement was read out again. The crowd cheered Deng, Hua Guofeng, Zhou Enlai, freedom, and democracy. Then they turned to face the Great Hall of the People and sang the *Internationale* and the national anthem. It was, Hauswedell reported, a stirring scene.

I had some Chinese guests that evening and could not leave the house until just before ten. Driving to Tian An Men, I found the square almost deserted. It was cold – about twenty degrees of frost – and a biting wind blew dust into my eyes. The weather could hardly have been less suited to an open-air rally. At Democracy Wall, which was inadequately lit, people were reading wall-posters by flashlight.

Here I saw more figures than usual clustered beneath the leafless trees. They all looked bulky and shapeless in their thick quilted trousers and jackets, which are often worn over several layers of clothing. As far as I could tell in the gloom, most of those present were youngish people. One group was loudly debating Mao's merits to a barrage of interjections from the fringes of the crowd. I sometimes had to shut my eyes, the wind was so laden with dust, but the Chinese continued their debate regardless. Being less warmly clad than they were, I decided to go home.

As I drove past Tian An Men, the lamps in the square went out. The Great Hall of the People, too, was in total darkness.

Peter Hauswedell and Ute Gareis were back at the embassy by the time I got there. We retired to the library and drank a brandy against the cold. Still under the spell of what they had seen, my companions described the night's events.

I could well understand their emotions. They had been present on one of those rare occasions when individuals discover a common purpose, when human beings in the mass not only feel but *are* capable of great things – capable of anything, even ill-considered actions – because they cease to think while the sensation lasts.

People can be gripped by the passionate intensity of such moments, even as mere observers. I can understand this, though mass exaltation has always impressed me as sinister in its lack of lucidity, logic, and reason – sinister, too, because it so often ends in disaster.

Fraser and Novak had tried to mediate between the Chinese leaders and 'the masses' at Democracy Wall. Their attempt may have been motivated by hopes of a newsworthy sensation, but it was also naïve and imprudent. How could they, being ignorant of the Chinese language, have felt confident of holding the crowd in check? It was their good fortune that the situation did not get out of hand.

Fraser's wife, who writes under the name Elizabeth MacCallum, produced a long article describing how her husband's visit to Democracy Wall established a miraculously cordial relationship between the Frasers and the Chinese people. Their telephone rang at all hours of the day and night. Thanks to this flood of information, the correspondent of the *Toronto Globe and Mail* became acquainted with the true state of affairs in China while other correspondents less able to feel the collective Chinese pulse – not to mention uninformed diplomats – were groping around in the dark. If I read the article aright, it was a fateful moment, not only for the Frasers but for the Chinese people. Elizabeth MacCallum's piece was entitled 'How My Husband Brought Democracy to China'.

A year later, when the Chinese still hadn't democratized themselves despite Fraser's efforts, he left the country. Disgusted by their failure to see reason, and by the idle chatter of colleagues and diplomats who insisted that the time for democracy had yet to come, he went home and wrote a book. This he called simply *The Chinese – Portrait of a People*.

On each of the two succeeding nights, wall-poster readers again resolved to march from Democracy Wall to Tian An Men Square. Historic fervour tends to cool overnight, however, and no real sense of occasion declared itself.

Furthermore, many readers and authors of wall-posters were disappointed to read in the *People's Daily* that Deng Xiaoping, so recently cheered to the echo, had told his interviewers that a number of the views expressed on Democracy Wall were ill-considered and unconducive to national stability. 'We must explain these things to the masses and know how to lead them . . .' This remark was interpreted – rightly, no doubt – as a thinly veiled threat.

A few days later, base units of the Party in Peking and Shanghai received a confidential directive urging citizens not to attack Mao by name in speeches or wall-posters. The same directive, which was probably circulated elsewhere, stated that debates should not in future be held in the street. Labour units and neighbourhood organizations were described as the proper venues for such discussions.

A young Chinese with whom I discussed this move waxed bitter on the subject. 'Don't get the idea that Deng Xiaoping really thinks these wall-posters are a good thing,' he told me. 'It suited him nicely, of course, that they should demand the truth about the Tian An Men riots during the Central Working Conference, while he was trying to impose his plans on veteran Maoists like Wu De, Wang Dongxing, and the rest. It embarrassed Hua Guofeng into the bargain. That's why Deng temporarily favoured a little more freedom. The wall-posters were a genuinely "good thing" from his point of view, but only while the conference lasted. Now that he's obviously come out on top, discussion is to be transferred to the units, where a closer check can be kept on it.'

Although posters continued to go up, Democracy Wall no longer drew such crowds. Many people travelling to or from work used to stop and read the latest additions; now the majority walked or cycled straight past. The inhabitants of Peking had demanded that the Tian An Men riots be recognized as a revolutionary act. That recognition had been granted, and it was probable that politicians formerly persecuted by the leftists would be rehabilitated in growing numbers. Wall-poster demands for freedom, democracy, and guaranteed human rights had lost their novelty. In addition, official newspapers were contributing to the chorus of criticism – less passionately, perhaps, but in the main more cogently. The press was publishing readers' letters that might otherwise have appeared in the form of wall-posters. Hence, less attention was devoted to wall-posters themselves.

Students were conspicuously absent from the ranks of those who expressed their views on Democracy Wall. When questioned on the point, they pleaded pressure of work. Political agitation and indoctrination, together with conscription for agricultural labour, had robbed them of so much time in the past few years that they had to concentrate on their examinations. They were weary of politics. To those of them who had hoped that the Cultural Revolution would overthrow the old world a. d conjure up a new and better one, it was now apparent that their former course had been an aberration – a policy that had merely destroyed things and built nothing in their place.

Academics and intellectuals took a sceptical view of wall-posters.

Surfeited with political demands whose only effect was unrest, they had no wish to stick their necks out. They were still haunted by fears of the Cultural Revolution. In any case, they said, there was a general, albeit superficial, trend towards liberalization. Intellectuals were in demand once more. They had regained respect and ought to rest content with that. No one could foresee how long the new phase would last, but they meant to make the most of things while it did. At best, the protesters were sincere and enthusiastic youngsters with nothing to lose. Many of their complaints were justified, of course, but it was extremely doubtful whether they would achieve anything by voicing them. On the contrary, their demands might plunge them into a hazardous political adventure, blight the frail flower of liberalization, and prompt the authorities to take repressive measures. I heard equally sceptical comments, even from Chinese journalists who were boldly campaigning for greater freedom in their own professional sphere. Although foreign news agencies reported what wall-posters were saying only a stone's throw from their offices, they claimed never to have read them. Under present circumstances, they said, their demands could not amount to more than political Utopianism.

With the waning of public interest in Democracy Wall, the character of the posters changed. Most of their authors were young people who had been sent to work on the land during or after the Cultural Revolution, and who had now returned, legally or otherwise, to the capital. They were unemployed. Having quit school or university a decade earlier, they realized that they could not make up the ground they had lost. Some of them may have lacked the courage to resume their studies. They were a lost generation – politically exploited, disenchanted, embittered, and aggressive.

The authors of these posters formed groups of like-minded individuals. Once diverted from their original course, they had no desire to return, as the students had, to the same old rut – not that many of them were given an opportunity to resume their former routine. They wanted something new – new, at any rate, for China: democracy, human rights, freedom of speech, a free press, and legality. Some posters were moving and spirited appeals composed with the passionate intensity that only long-suppressed emotion can engender. Reading them, one sensed that their authors had the courage of their convictions. They were outspokenly critical of conditions in China, of ossified officialdom, of political tyranny exercised by administrators in many parts of the country, of the privileges enjoyed by arrogant functionaries at every level, of bureaucracy and mendacious propaganda. Their criticisms were not only acid but often well directed.

They called for democracy and human rights, though many of them had only the vaguest notion of what those concepts signified. With touching naïvety, they would sometimes ask foreign visitors to Democracy Wall how the democratic system worked and what limits were imposed on freedom within it.

Although the wall-posters sometimes referred in general terms to the 'Yugoslav model' or the greater efficiency of the so-called capitalist system, I was struck by their failure to mention the issues that pre-occupied the Chinese leaders. Inadequate communications, the energy gap, overcentralization, lack of industrial specialization, lack of incentives – these problems they never touched on, still less explored in depth. This, too, was understandable, for the authors of the posters were inexperienced in such matters. They lacked the comprehensive picture of the Chinese economy essential to any discussion of these subjects.

Peking was the centre of the protest movement. Shanghai's equivalent of Democracy Wall was considerably smaller and its posters milder in tone. The same applied to other provincial cities, so groups of protesters converged on Peking in the hope of evoking a bigger response and alerting foreign correspondents to their demands. The 'Enlightenment Society' of Guizhou Province, in south-west China, displayed posters of outstanding stylistic and graphic merit, and artists from the same province exhibited pictures whose total divergence from Chinese tradition carried echoes of early Expressionism. Günter Grass swapped one of his own etchings for a print by one of these artists.

Novel and unprecedented forms of protest occurred. Impoverished, half-starved peasants from agriculturally backward parts of China – backward and badly administered too, no doubt – turned up in Peking without travel permits and rail tickets and presented themselves at the red gate of Zhongnanhai Park, hoping to petition the Central Committee. Refused admittance, they staged a sit-in outside the gate, where they were filmed and photographed by foreign press representatives.

Stung by these protests, the Party leaders announced that they were sending a thousand commissioners to tour the provinces and investigate abuses there. However, even a thousand quasi-ombudsmen proved insufficient to deal with thirty years of unsupervised rule by local Party officials. There was no decrease in the influx of petitioners from rural areas.

The Chinese tend to be insensitive to the sufferings of those outside their family or immediate circle. Suffering, they feel, has always been the lot of man, and fortunate is he who has a family to fall back on in time of need. The ragged, hungry peasants continued to sit around, unaided by public authorities and neighbourhood organizations, who told themselves that any attempt to help would encourage countless other unfortunates to descend on the capital.

Although protesting peasants and plaintive wall-posters made little impression on the inhabitants of Peking, they were a constant preoccupation of the foreign correspondents based there. Some of these journalists were criticized by their Chinese colleagues for their daily visits to Democracy Wall. Accompanied by interpreters, they would note the contents of the latest posters and transmit them to their papers or agencies in the belief that they were presenting a true picture of China's internal situation. By evening, their reports would be beamed back to China by the Voice of America or some other broadcasting service and heard throughout the country. This often lent undue weight to demands which most Chinese regarded, if not as bizarre, at least as individualistic and unrepresentative – for instance, pleas in favour of free love or the legalization of brothels. These figured in foreign news broadcasts as if they were the universal and burning desire of the entire Chinese nation.

The more outlandish a demand, the greater its news value to editors back home – indeed, Peking-based correspondents received frequent requests for juicy items from Democracy Wall. Appeals for freedom and democracy had begun to pall. Stronger meat was required, and journalists unable to extract anything of interest from wall-posters would converse with bystanders through the medium of an interpreter. This was bound to turn up something spicy.

Although most correspondents were restrained and honest in their reporting, some foreign newsmen had fewer scruples. They kept in close touch with the authors of the wall-posters, who realized that a symbiosis of this kind might yield world-wide publicity. These correspondents seldom visited the provinces except on the annual group tours arranged for them by the Foreign Ministry's Information Section. They were surprised by the critical views which they now, for the first time, heard from Chinese lips. This, they felt, was the voice of the people. They overlooked the fact that it was only the voice of a small, politically militant minority, not that of the thousand million Chinese with whom they neither maintained nor sought any contact. Morning visits to Democracy Wall and evening assignations with angry young men satisfied them that they knew the truth about the state of the country and its manifold problems.

This somewhat naïve form of journalism, coupled with attempts to 'bring democracy to China' with the aid of youthful malcontents, harmed the protest movement and discredited it in the eyes of many Chinese, not only in the eyes of the Party leaders.

Some foreign correspondents hit on ingenious ways of getting in touch with protesters. John Fraser, for example, stuck a poster of his own on Democracy Wall. This announced that he had lost a gold ring and invited the finder to contact him. He gave his telephone number – Peking, as already mentioned, then had no directory – and was promptly bombarded with calls from young protesters eager to pour out their hearts.

Militant writers soon took to producing and selling small hectographed news sheets, mostly in very small editions. The publishers gave foreign correspondents advance notice of when they and their merchandise would appear at Democracy Wall. The news sheets cost next to nothing, but foreign correspondents were charged ten times the normal price by authors who frankly conceded that the premium was a form of subsidy. The journalists paid up readily, though some of them made it clear that they expected more of these underground publications than nebulous talk about freedom and democracy. Chinese acquaintances in the Foreign Ministry's Press Section claimed that public debates and protests had been fomented in this way. One underground paper soon adopted a more attractive layout and was immaculately printed, but the contents were tamer than of old, so a suspicion arose that it had been cornered by some official organ of the Party.

This was certainly not so of the most interesting mini-magazine, *Tansuo* (*Exploration*), whose editor, Wei Jingsheng, was a young man with a turbulent political past. A former Red Guard who had been rusticated and imprisoned by the left-wing radicals but later amnestied, Wei kept in active touch with over a dozen foreign correspondents. He also begged a duplicating machine from a member of the British Embassy, but without success. One issue of *Tansuo* featured a graphic and well-written account of his time in a political prison.

Veteran Maoists at Party Headquarters were indignant at the latitude granted these young protesters, but they were not alone in thinking it high time for the leadership to 'restore order'. Even moderates began to waver when the protesters kept up their foreign contacts during the punitive campaign against Vietnam, and when foreign newsmen filed reports on military matters of which they had presumably been informed by youthful activists at Democracy Wall. Criticism inside the Party was directed primarily at Deng Xiaoping, who had called the wall-posters a good thing as recently as November 1978. Now that the Vietnam campaign, for which he bore prime responsibility, had not gone entirely according to plan, Deng was forced on to the defensive. Addressing senior members of the Central Committee's bureaux and commissions on

16 March 1979, he criticized the wall-posters and the protest movement in general. Although his speech was not published, we learned its gist from several different sources.

A few days later, Wei Jingsheng took Deng to task in *Tansuo* on the grounds that he was trying to blame the democratic protest movement for delays in the Party leadership's political and economic programme. Wei wrote:

> Does Deng Xiaoping want democracy? No! He declines to understand the people, who are living in penury. He does not wish them to regain the power wrested from them by functionaries intent on their own careers. Speaking of our spontaneous popular movement for democratic rights, he claims that all we seek is an excuse to foment unrest.
>
> We ask: What do you understand by democracy? How can there be any talk of democracy if the people cannot even express their opinions freely?
>
> The people are banding together and demonstrating because they wish to complain of injustice, because they wish to prefer public charges, because they want democracy. They are demonstrating against hunger and dictatorship . . .
>
> The people must be careful that Deng Xiaoping does not develop into a dictator.

This, of course, was a 'good thing' no longer, and freedom of speech had gone too far. A Party directive banned all wall-posters, books, and periodicals hostile to the 'four basic principles': socialism, the dictatorship of the proletariat, the leadership of the Communist Party, and Marxism-Leninism-Maozedongideas.

That left few legitimate targets of criticism.

Only a few days after his special issue of *Tansuo* appeared, Wei Jingsheng was arrested. In October, while Hua Guofeng was in Europe and Deng Xiaoping was in charge of government business, Wei received a sentence of fifteen years' imprisonment 'for having supplied a foreigner with military intelligence, and for having publicly agitated in favour of overthrowing the Government, the dictatorship of the proletariat, and the socialist system in China.'

The newspapers devoted much space to letters endorsing the sentence – a sure sign that it was generally considered too harsh, by intellectuals in particular. A year earlier, Deng had said, 'If the masses are angry, they must be able to vent their anger. Not all the masses' opinions are carefully considered, but that we cannot insist on. Anyway, it isn't such a bad thing . . .' His present concern was to make a public example, nip an evil in the bud – stifle more serious criticism by inflicting draconian punishment on a minor offender.

'In imposing penalties,' Shang Yang had written two thousand three hundred years before, 'minor infractions of the law should be regarded as serious. If no minor offences are committed, there will be no danger of serious ones occurring. This is known as "ruling the people while in a state of law and order".'

The press found it peculiarly reprehensible that the dissidents, so they claimed, should have asked foreigners for money and political material 'for use in agitation against the socialist system'.

Wei Jingsheng admitted at his trial that he had passed on items of military intelligence. At the same time, he denied that they could have influenced the course of the Sino–Vietnamese conflict, or that he had received payment for them. He testified that Ian Mackenzie, Reuters' senior Peking correspondent, had offered him two or three hundred pounds sterling, but that he had neither seen him again nor received the money. Reuters counterclaimed that Wei had volunteered military information, but that Mackenzie had declined it.

According to some Chinese writers whom I saw and talked with not long afterwards, Deng Xiaoping considered Western criticism of Wei's sentence and the new restrictions on wall-posters to be unjustified. The foreign press wanted to impose a behaviour pattern on Chinese society for which it was not yet ready. When asked before his visit to America in January whether he would be discussing human rights with President Carter, he had replied that he thought it inappropriate: he would then be obliged to say a great deal about contempt for human rights in the United States, and that would scarcely be polite to his host.

Wei Jingsheng's harsh sentence cost Deng a lot of popularity, above all with those who had advocated his return to the leadership and demonstrated in favour of him and his policies in Tian An Men Square. They shared Wei's desire for greater democratization and accused Deng of indiscriminately lumping them together with the more Utopian members of the wall-poster set.

Deng Xiaoping is no liberal, as we have already said. Like 'idealistic', 'liberal' is, in communist parlance, a pejorative term. Liberal connotes unprincipled, vacillating, irresolute, aimless, indisciplined, and tolerant of what is bad. Liberalism leads to loss of authority and faith in socialism, to Western-style democracy, anarchy, immorality, drug addiction, corruption, and pornography. All these things went hand in hand, Party veterans believed, and unlimited freedom of speech would only have sown confusion, especially among young people who had yet to recover from the effects of the Cultural Revolution. Were they really expected to let the wave of protest spread to universities and tolerate the growth of a student movement like that which afflicted the West in the late 1960s?

Said Shang Yang: 'If, from a condition in which law and order prevail, the people become lawless, and if one seeks to master this lawlessness, it will only increase. Lawlessness should thus be suppressed while authority and good order prevail.'

Zhao Cangbi, the Chinese Minister of Security, told me that reported crimes had risen from four hundred thousand in 1978 to six hundred thousand-odd in 1979. The catalogue of offences was long and reminiscent of former times. The highest incidence of criminality and indiscipline occurred among young people who had returned from the land to the cities and were now unemployed. This group also produced most of the wall-posters or underground newspapers calling for freedom, democracy, and human rights. To the Party's *terribles simplificateurs*, the inference was clear: there was nothing to choose between any of them.

Freedom was likewise demanded by authors and journalists of the younger generation, whose articles and speeches exposed them to certain risks. Though just as impassioned in their pleas, they were more purposeful. However, even they had little time for the liberalism so often held up as an ideal by their Western colleagues. They felt themselves to be servants of the people. Bounds were set on freedom by morality and a desire to serve, rather than harm, the people and the state. One visitor to the embassy, a writer who had lectured an invited Chinese audience on life in Germany, left some of his listeners puzzled. Why, they asked, did he paint such an unfavourable picture of our country – why did he pour scorn on so many aspects of life there? The Chinese are unaccustomed to such an attitude. In the presence of outsiders, nothing but good must be said of one's family or country. Though necessary, self-criticism should be confined to one's own four walls; no whisper of disgrace must leak out. A Chinese autobiographer of the last century was rebuked by critics for admitting his mistakes. 'It isn't done' remains the rule. One 'does it' only when condemned to do so – when compelled to advertise one's own disgrace.

China's political leaders have enlarged the scope of press comment. Many published articles are critical of conditions inside the country. BBC TV foreign news items are relayed from London. Cinemas show foreign films, preferably those containing some useful moral, and foreign books are published in translation. But the Chinese leaders reserve the right to determine the speed of democratization and the latitude granted to the media. They have no wish to foment unrest or a revolutionary situation. They want neither permanent revolution, nor counter-revolution, nor – God forbid! – another Cultural Revolution. The erstwhile revolutionaries have become evolutionists. As men grow old, they view the world with different eyes.

China is to be modernized, but in a manner and at a speed to be determined by her leaders, in other words, the Politburo. Mistakes have been made. These will be rectified, say China's rulers, but they refuse to be coerced into detours or retreats by public opinion. They have quite enough opposition to contend with inside their own ranks.

Although freedom of speech has been restored to a small extent only, the Party has already come under fire from the masses – indeed, its candidates encounter overtly hostile propaganda during low-level democratic elections. In view of these warning signs, what are the Chinese authorities expected to do? Democratize the entire country at a stroke, introduce the secret ballot – make Party and government officials run for election? That, they tell themselves, would be sheer madness. The Chinese people aren't ready for complete democracy.– Deng Xiaoping himself has said as much.

So they stick to the old and well-tried system of government advocated by Confucius and Mencius. Government tends the governed, and the district administrator, like his precursors in every imperial dynasty, remains 'father and mother' to those who dwell within his jurisdiction. The Government is *ren zheng*, a solicitous and beneficent institution with the people's best interests at heart. And that is precisely how the Party leaders regard themselves.

'A government founded on the principle of benevolence towards the people, like that of a father towards his children; that is to say, a paternal government whose subjects, like infants unable to distinguish what is truly beneficial or harmful to them, are coerced into purely passive behaviour . . . is the greatest conceivable despotism . . .' In the course of their history, the Chinese have come to terms with this Kantian form of despotism. They acted on the principle 'government *for* the people' and sometimes approximated to a government *of* the people, but it is only today, for the first time ever, that one or two pleas have been made for government *by* the people – an institution for which, proclaims a paternal voice from on high, the Chinese are not yet old or mature enough. Once again, stability has taken precedence over any experiments likely to endanger it.

Much of the criticism expressed by wall-posters and underground newspapers was caustic and relevant. It only scratched the surface, however, because their authors tended to argue in terms of Marxism-

Leninism and the socialist classics. The roots of the evil remained untouched by critics whose sentiments were laudable, but whose arguments were weak in comparison with, say, Soviet dissidents' cogent attacks on their own socialist system.

Many foreigners in Peking overrated the importance of wall-posters. They brimmed with enthusiasm whenever they read new and vehement demands or blistering attacks on current conditions. It escaped their notice that the people of Peking had largely lost interest in them. At the end of 1979, Democracy Wall was closed. Its authorized substitute was a wall in a suburban park where few people ever went apart from a handful of foreign journalists. The chapter seemed closed.

Intellectuals had their careers to consider. They were faring better these days, in any case, and had no wish to jeopardize the new trend by pushing their demands too far. As for students, they were eager to pass their examinations and make up for lost time.

There remained the hard-luck cases, the victims of the Cultural Revolution, the rusticated townsfolk who had since returned but found it difficult to reintegrate themselves because the ranks had closed in their absence. There remained a small band of angry young men. Many of their arguments may have been superficial and many of their ideas muddled and Utopian, but they did not lack courage.

They will be followed, beyond all doubt, by people better equipped politically to hit harder and demand more. Discussion of freedom and democracy has not been terminated by the sentence passed on Wei Jingsheng and the closure of Democracy Wall. It has only just begun.

Prohibitions may check this development for a while, but not for ever. It remains to be seen whether China's leaders retain the initiative – whether they manage to control the pace and extent of democratization – or are forced to give way. In this respect, the democratic model adopted matters less than whether ordinary Chinese are given any chance at all to express their views and share in the policy-making process. Any attempt by their leaders to revert to despotism will render modernization impossible – that much is certain. Will it become apparent to senior functionaries reared on other ideas that their old style of leadership is inappropriate to the present day? They might do worse than consult the sages of long ago.

One of China's earliest written sources, *The Book of Documents*, has this to say on the subject:

The people should be cherished, not despised.
The people are the root of a country . . .
Even humble folk may surpass me in wisdom and virtue.

305

If the king errs often in governing,
discontent and danger will result.
Before it comes to that, some remedy must be undertaken.
In dealing with millions of people,
I should feel as if I were driving a team of six horses
with a rotten rein.

Mystery-Mongers

Franz Josef Strauss visited Peking before my time, early in 1975. Chinese officials collected him from his government guesthouse for an excursion to the Great Wall, leaving his party of aides and newsmen behind. My predecessor had arranged a dinner for the entire delegation and some high-ranking Chinese guests, but the Bavarian Premier failed to turn up until the meal was over. The fault was not his. He had been whisked off by air to see Mao Zedong, who happened to be in Central China at the time – at Hangzhou, I believe. The journalists had been hoodwinked, but why? There was no discernible reason other than the Chinese love of secrecy.

An aura of secrecy surrounds the most senior Party and government leaders. Like princes and ministers of the imperial era, they dwell in seclusion from the common herd. No details of their way of life are ever made public. They sweep through the streets in big, funereal Red Flag limousines whose rear windows are shrouded in black silk curtains.

No Chinese emperor kept an appointments diary. He sent for people, foreign guests as well as subjects, whenever the fancy took him – sometimes before dawn, for audiences usually began before sunrise. Anyone whose presence was requested by the emperor had to hurry. Once, when Henry Kissinger was unexpectedly summoned from his Peking guesthouse for an interview with Mao, even Premier Zhou Enlai became fretful when he failed to respond with sufficient alacrity. A summons from Mao was tantamount to an imperial command.

Strauss's escorting newsmen were not alone in being hoodwinked during his visit in mid-January 1975. Strauss himself was left in ignorance that an important political event was then in progress. Not that he or the journalists knew it, several thousand delegates to the National People's Congress spent half a week in conclave at the Great Hall of the People, right in the heart of Peking. Neither Mao nor any of the senior functionaries who received Strauss breathed a word about this parliamentary session. The German visitors learned of it only when they got back to Munich and read the newspapers.

I once accompanied Gu Mu, the Vice-Premier responsible for industrial construction, on a visit to Germany. The Chinese Ambassador in Bonn, Zhang Tong, showed him an article in *Die Welt* criticizing the lack of drive and interest shown by Chinese workers employed at the Wuhan steel plant.

'Well-meant criticism,' was Gu Mu's verdict. 'The real state of affairs is even worse. A good article – it ought to be published in China.'

I thought of the outcry it would provoke among German trade union officials if one of our own cabinet ministers well-meaningly advised his fellow countrymen to work harder – like the Japanese, for instance.

The article was reprinted, unabridged and without comment, in the Chinese newspaper with the biggest readership of all. Though produced in an edition of over nine million copies, it was never put on public sale and could not be subscribed to by foreign embassies such as ours.

Cankao Xiaoxi, usually translated *Reference News*, was the name of this confidential publication. It contained nothing but reports and articles culled from foreign newspapers and news agencies, some of them – like those disseminated by Tass – hostile to China. Readers were intended to feel that they were being presented with an objective picture of world events and international opinion. Only *ganbus*, meaning functionaries or cadres, received *Reference News*. The term *ganbu* extended to heads of production groups and managers of small state-owned stores and workshops.

Reference News was confidential, as we have said, and functionaries could often be seen hastily laying it aside when we entered their offices or places of work. Despite this, we frequently, though not regularly, came into possession of copies whose outspoken criticism sometimes surprised us. *Reference News* once carried two long and objective articles on China by Fritz Ullrich Fack, co-editor of the *Frankfurter Allgemeine Zeitung*, and Theo Sommer, associate editor of *Die Zeit*, who had recently visited the country. Though critical in many respects, they too were reprinted in full.

During China's military operations against Vietnam, *Reference News* reproduced an article from a Hong Kong newspaper. This stated that, although opinions might differ on the necessity for the campaign, it should now be persevered with and brought to a successful conclusion.

The Chinese functionary who read such a lukewarm tribute to the wisdom of the Vietnam enterprise felt that he had been taken into his leaders' confidence. He inferred – and may well have been meant to infer – that opinions differed inside the Party leadership itself. Being a *ganbu*, he knew more than the non-*ganbu*: he was a recipient of confidential information.

Still more confidential was *Da Cankao* or *Cankao Ziliao*, *Big Reference* or *Reference Study Material*, a publication that appeared twice daily until 1980 (only once a day thereafter) in an edition of over a million copies. This larger journal often reprinted long and even more critical articles on China from the foreign press. It was restricted to middle-ranking or senior functionaries who thus knew more, and were recipients of higher-grade information, than petty officials of junior status.

These intelligence digests owed their existence to a directive from Mao. First produced in relatively small editions, they were printed in larger numbers and distributed to a wider circle during the Cultural Revolution. The radicals often used them for their own ends – as, for instance, when a small Shanghai newspaper reprinted some pseudonymous articles written during the 1920s by Zhou Enlai. Because the confidential journals were restricted to material of foreign provenance, the radicals made arrangements for a Hong Kong newspaper to reproduce Zhou Enlai's articles and couple them with the charge that he had been a traitor responsible for the deaths of thousands of communists in 1927, when Chiang Kai-shek carried out his Shanghai bloodbath. *Cankao Ziliao* was then at liberty to carry this Hong Kong smear as a 'foreign press report'.

The above publications, whose contents naturally leak out, keep the Chinese people better informed about events abroad and international opinion than the inhabitants of other communist countries. They do not, however, contain any criticism of Marxist-Leninist principles.

The top echelon of the leadership has access to confidential bulletins and circulars of even more limited distribution. These, as we already know, were carefully manipulated by the Gang of Four during the Tian An Men riots of April 1976. I never saw one of these documents, but they doubtless contain items that any Western newspaper could print without detriment to national security. Whereas the vast mass of officials in other communist countries have to subsist largely on rumour, their directives from Party Headquarters being seldom explained or justified in detail, the Central Committee of the Chinese Communist Party often circulates documents with a variable distribution list finely attuned to the rank and security status of their recipients: some to senior officials only, others to regional Party secretaries or functionaries, and others to all Party members. These communications explain and justify the Party line with the aid of transcripts or documents such as Mao's letter to Jiang Qing.

At political meetings and indoctrination sessions, too, a careful distinction is drawn between the truth destined for the general public, the truth that may be imparted to the ordinary *ganbu*, and information of a highly confidential nature such as proposed amendments to the law, the rehabilitation of non-persons and banned literary works, or discussions relating to the person of Mao Zedong. Where these matters are concerned, the general public learns nothing until a decision has been reached. Many films, especially foreign films, are shown to selected audiences, just as a large proportion of the books printed in Hong Kong and the People's Republic are *neibu*, or for restricted consumption only. The criteria governing the selection of those granted access to such films or books are vague and fluctuating.

Keeping things secret, shutting oneself off, erecting walls around one's house and family – all these practices accord with ancient Chinese custom. The Chinese not only fear gossip but have good reason to do so. Shang Yang stated that every citizen had a duty to inform on his neighbour. If he did not, his complicity earned him punishment as severe as that visited on the person who had spoken slightingly of a magistrate, the government, or – not that this often happened – the emperor himself. The practice of shutting oneself off is correlative with the desire to inhabit a lively, close-knit community.

We have already illustrated the strength of Chinese society's pressure on the individual, a pressure exerted not only by the authorities but by neighbours and labour units as well. Areas of freedom do exist within the family, but even these are limited in number and scope by the demands of the family itself, more in rural districts than in towns, and less so today than formerly.

When the extended family or clan still constituted the building block of the social structure, it allowed the individual even less scope for personal development. Although it protected him, it insisted on absolute obedience, subordination, and integration. Where outsiders were concerned, it demanded reticence about family matters. The family was a unit that bore collective responsibility and collective liability. Its members stood or fell together. 'If a man be appointed an official, all his dogs and poultry likewise go to heaven.'

If a minister was stripped of office, every civil servant belonging to the same clan lost his job and, usually, his personal fortune as well. If the emperor had a minister beheaded, any members of his extended family who were spared a like fate could count themselves lucky. Examples of collective liability can also be found in recent times. The children of any man proclaimed a 'right-wing element' during the latter half of the 1950s had to abandon their university education and take up ordinary jobs.

Deng Xiaoping's entire family shared in his persecution, as we have seen. Although Mao is still called a great revolutionary, where are his children today? Where is his niece Wang Hairong?

In view of this talent for secrecy and long experience in collective self-containment, it might be supposed that confidential matters never become public knowledge in China. This is not so, however. The Chinese are inquisitive as well as secretive. Secretiveness automatically breeds curiosity, and the Chinese are great talkers. Jiang Qing complained that Mao himself was fond of 'little broadcast' gossip.

Knowledge of confidential matters is a functionary's privilege – the thing that sets even the most lowly *ganbu* above the common herd – but wherein lies the value of his superior status if he cannot parade it? The urge to show off often prompts him to communicate inside information to this person or that – in the strictest confidence, of course.

The spread of confidential information, or 'small path news', is substantially assisted by one particular group of whom the Constitution and Party statutes take no account. Western observers, too, have devoted surprisingly little attention to this group, even though it represents a distinct and recognizable component of the Chinese social edifice.

I refer to functionaries' children, who blithely transgress the barriers of secrecy at every level. They use the crumbs of superior knowledge that fall from their parental table as an aid to personal prestige. They always know when the wind has changed direction, or when prudence prescribes a low profile, or when a particular functionary or 'line' can be criticized without risk to oneself – indeed, with every prospect of winning high commendation. During the Cultural Revolution, they were the source of much information about new campaigns or changes of course or intimate goings-on in high places.

Some functionaries want no privileged treatment for their children. Hua Guofeng is often cited as a case in point, but most people regard him as an exception. Functionaries' children are different from those of the *lao bai xing*, or common folk. They rise in the world with their parents but can also fall with them, so friendships with the offspring of senior officials can be politically compromising. Parents discourage their daughters from becoming involved with officials' sons. 'Door must match door,' runs an old Chinese proverb, and door can also mean 'family'.

Functionaries' privileges are a serious and emotive topic. The son of a middle-ranking official got into Peking University 'by the back door', meaning that he was enrolled without passing an entrance examination. When his fellow students found out and 'unmasked' him, he was forced to leave. Next year he succeeded in passing the entrance examination and resumed his studies. He announced his return in a wall-poster and displayed it on the campus. It was true that he had entered the university last year by the back door, he said, but he was not the only one of his kind – just the only one to have been expelled because his father's position was insufficiently senior.

Functionaries' children attend the best nursery schools, are admitted to Children's Palaces and taught in 'fast classes' reserved for gifted youngsters. They pass their examinations and make rapid academic progress. Many are taken on foreign tours or granted scholarships to study overseas. They also have more money to spend. Their parents present them with cameras or cassette players acquired on trips abroad. They do not live in cramped apartments where each resident is limited to forty-three square feet of floor space, but in small houses, or even in the Olympian seclusion of Zhongnanhai Park.

On the other hand, we should not forget that even they live very modestly compared to Westerners of the same age, and that many of our working-class youngsters fare far better in the way of motorcycles, cars, cameras, stereos, foreign travel, educational facilities, and job prospects.

But egalitarianism has been exceptionally strong and radical in China since the Cultural Revolution. Confucius and Mencius taught that a man could find happiness in the social stratum into which he had been born. This did not entirely preclude advancement through personal efficiency, and children were encouraged to model themselves on imperial ministers, advisers, or governors who had come of humble stock. In general, however, people pursued a livelihood within their own class and accepted their superiors' privileges as a fact of life.

Nowadays, the Chinese watch jealously to ensure that no one enjoys more privileges than anyone else. This is why functionaries' children steer clear of children from ordinary families. They never invite them home for fear they may gossip about what they see there. They shield their private lives from the gaze of curious outsiders, and they ride, like their parents, in big official cars with black silk curtains.

The smoke screen that not only enshrouds the private lives of the ruling class but obscures the functions of government and the nature of the Party leaders' decision-making process has lifted a little in the years since Mao's death. Even so, many decisions affecting policy and personnel selection remain wrapped in official twilight. One cannot help feeling that the Chinese leaders might gain more public confidence if they drew back their black silk curtains and conducted affairs of state in a more open and universally visible manner.

Ghost Town

The old city wall must have been about thirty feet thick. Like everything else here, it was built of unbaked brick and had been disintegrating for centuries. We climbed it for a view of the ruined expanse that had once been a sizeable city. Not a house was standing, though we could still follow the layout of the streets. Some big blocks of masonry in the distance were all that remained of a palace and a temple.

Everything was yellow with dust. Not a speck of green met the eye: not a tree, not a shrub or blade of grass. It was two years since rain had last fallen here, we were told – all two millimetres of it. The desolate Turfan Depression stretched away beyond the city wall. Huoyan Shan, the Fiery Mountain, loomed on the hazy horizon like a mighty wall, its red flanks scarred with precipitous ravines by the torrents that had once coursed down them.

This was the mountain that had barred the path of the monk Tripitaka and his companions on their pilgrimage to India. They had all stood aghast at this obstacle, wondering what to do, until Sun Wukong, the Monkey King, exerted his magical powers and helped them across it. Somewhere here must lie the ruins of the temple in which Tripitaka had taught for a year. *Journey to the West*, that old Chinese picaresque novel, recounts the many miraculous and adventurous features of his pilgrimage. It was here, I seemed to recall, that a sorcerer had assumed the shape of the King, hidden him at the bottom of a well, and reigned for years, deceiving the Queen and the entire court, until Tripitaka turned up and Sun Wukong released the real monarch after a hard-fought battle with the cunning usurper.

A romantic soul would gladly have lingered here alone in the moonlight, gazing at the ruined and deserted streets and bringing them back to life in his imagination. Gao Chang, once the principal city of the Turfan oasis, in the midst of the Tarim Basin in desolate Xinjiang Province, would have inspired a late Victorian ballad writer or provided material for Burne-Jones and the other Pre-Raphaelites. They would have resurrected its erstwhile inhabitants. We would have seen the King of Gao Chang in a gorgeous brocaded robe – a tributary gift from the Emperor of China, whose annals made it appear that it was the Chinese court which received tribute from Gao Chang and not vice versa. We would have seen him strolling in his garden, surrounded by bodyguards and jesting with the ladies of his harem, who were also gifts from the Emperor of China, or riding out into the highlands of Bogda Shan to hunt with falcons and cheetahs. Or an ambassador would have arrived on camelback with a caravan from Samarkand. After riding for weeks through the desert, he would have glimpsed the city's lofty walls, the domed roofs of its royal palace, the white stupas of its Buddhist temples. He would doubtless have rejoiced at the prospect of spending some enjoyable weeks in Gao Chang while resting his camels and his consignment of Ferghana horses for the court of the Chinese Emperor. He himself, being really a merchant and only an *ad interim* ambassador, would not have lodged at a filthy, noisy, verminous caravanserai, but at the luxurious mansion of some fellow businessman, reclining on sumptuous Khotan carpets and served by beautiful Uighur or Kazakh slaves, male and female, who understood his native Turkic.

But alas, there was no romantic soul among us – or certainly no latter-day Pre-Raphaelite with easel and brushes at the ready. *This* ambassador hadn't ridden on camelback from Samarkand. He had driven from Urumqi in a 'Shanghai' car and was escorting his former boss, Gerhard Schröder. The Chinese authorities had invited our erstwhile Foreign Minister to visit them in his capacity as an 'old friend'. Having tried without success to forge formal links with China as long ago as 1964, Schröder had paved the way for the establishment of diplomatic relations between Bonn and Peking during talks with Zhou Enlai in 1972.

Now, as we looked down on the ruined city from its crumbling wall, we speculated on the probable number of Gao Chang's inhabitants. A hundred thousand, hazarded Mr Jung, secretary of the Foreign Affairs Committee. If not more, said the rest of us. At all events, its population must far have exceeded that of modern Turfan. Turfan is a wretched little village compared to Gao Chang, and smaller even than 'the Old City at the Confluence', another ruined site on a highland plateau.

But how had those hundred thousand people contrived to live in the Turfan Depression? Had its rocky terrain been swathed in vegetation? Used there to be a river here? Was the *kereding*, or network of subterranean watercourses that bring melted snow from the foot of the mountains, far more extensive than it is now?

Why were urban centres as big as Gao Chang and the City at the Confluence abandoned? Where did their inhabitants go? A romantic soul might have devised a romantic answer to this enigma, but one of our Chinese companions claimed to know the reason. Actually, he cited three possibilities in quick succession: either the water supply failed, or the people fled in terror from the Moslems, or the Mongols drove them out. But where did they go? He couldn't say. Either to Gansu in Chinese territory, or else in the opposite direction, to Kashgar. Modern Turfan was largely inhabited by Uighurs, he said. This was true – we had already encountered many of them – but it was also apparent to us that the local roost was ruled by Han Chinese.

Surrounded by desert and inhospitable mountains, Turfan is the lowest and hottest spot in China – five hundred feet below sea level and fifteen hundred miles or more from the Yellow Sea. During the first century BC it was China's most important garrison town in Central Asia and a bastion against the Huns. From there, Chinese armies thrust many hundreds of miles westward to Lake Balkhash and the Caspian. Turfan was also a major staging post on the Silk Road that linked China with the West two thousand years ago. The Chinese repeatedly lost control of it. For many centuries, it remained a small oasis kingdom, often overrun by Huns, Mongols, and Turkic tribes. Ever since the time of the Han Emperor Wu Di, however, or since the first century BC, every dynasty had regarded Turfan as part of the Chinese domain and sphere of influence.

Our route to Turfan had taken us through a valley flanked by massive, precipitous walls of rock. It was only later, when we emerged into the plain, that we saw, towering behind us, the eighteen thousand-foot summit of Bogda Shan.

The mountains were grey and bare – grey as the rocky bed of the mountain stream beside the road. As we descended further into the Turfan Depression, however, we noticed that the willows on the river bank were faintly tinged with red. Only eyes that had grown accustomed to monotone grey would have detected so subtle a shade. It was early April, and the catkins' reddish glow was a harbinger of spring.

The valley widened, and before us lay an infinity of desert: the rocky Gobi and the sandy Shamo. The asphalt road ran straight as an arrow across the broad grey expanse, with its shimmering, indistinct horizon. There was not a living creature, not a tree or bush, to be seen – nothing that might have prompted the eye to linger. The Gobi and the Shamo were as flat as a billiard table.

Insulated from the desert by the windows of our car, we could only guess at the sensation which so many travellers had sought to conjure up in print or paint, only to find that its true essence eluded them. I myself, who had experienced the indescribable in other deserts, could not have defined it.

A long way from the road, a man was riding a camel with another camel trotting riderless behind. He must have been heading for some destination, presumably along a track which only he could discern in the endless, stony waste, but to us in our motorized cage he seemed bound for

314

nowhere from nowhere. I envied the man. What, I wondered, would it be like to get out and accompany him on the second camel? Uncomfortable, certainly. The saddlecloth would be infested with fleas, and the most I would get for supper would be flat cakes of bread and cold mutton fat. But we would ride off into infinity, and at some stage, perhaps, if only for an instant while swaying along or resting when we halted for the night, I might experience the *unio mystica*, that great and all-embracing unity of which the Chinese Taoists also spoke. Such are the fleeting moments for which a person should live – the moments when he becomes a True Man . . .

I banished my romantic impulse. There would be no riding off into infinity, neither now nor ever again. Those adventurous days were long gone.

'So the Chinese have a long expansionist tradition,' Gerhard Schröder was saying.

'Yes and no,' I said.

'Meaning what?'

We were still some way from Turfan, so I took my time and delivered a brief lecture.

Chinese imperial policy during the past two millennia cannot be cited as proof positive either of an expansionist tradition, or of its opposite. China adopted an expansionist policy during the second and first centuries BC, under the Tang dynasty in the seventh century AD, and under the Mongol and Manchu emperors. Nevertheless, the 'policy of the long rein' was devised and pursued as long ago as two thousand years.

Any overview of Chinese history will disclose that the evidence against expansionism is vastly preponderant. At every juncture, in complete contrast to the West, we find a deep-rooted and often passionate aversion to all wars of conquest.

The most obvious and eloquent manifestation of China's non-expansionist policy is the Great Wall. Any nation that encloses its territory with a wall many hundreds of miles long, built at the cost of innumerable lives and huge sums of money, demonstrates that it means to preserve its possessions, not augment them by force of arms.

Any understanding of China's foreign policy in former times must be based on her ancient conception of the world. This comprised 'heaven', or *tian*, and 'that which is under heaven', or *tian xia*. At the centre of *tian xia* lay China, or *zhong guo*, the Middle Kingdom. This was not just one country among many, but human civilization in its entirety. The fringes of the Middle Kingdom, or 'outer world', were inhabited only by barbarians.

But the emperor presided over the whole of humankind. In springtime, when he ploughed eight sacred furrows beside the Temple of Agriculture and sowed them with rice and four varieties of millet, he not only guaranteed the growth of rice and millet in China but ensured that all things would thrive elsewhere in the world, even among barbarians who were ignorant both of cosmic harmony and basic human relationships. Those who failed to acknowledge him as the Son of Heaven contravened the world order, not the political claims of the Chinese Government. Although it might have seemed logical to coerce barbarians into a proper appreciation of the world order, the Chinese never came to any such conclusion.

'The King of Qi inquired of the philosopher Mencius whether he should annex the land of Yan. Mencius replied, "Would the people of Yan rejoice if you annexed their country? If so, you should occupy it. If the people would not rejoice, however, you should refrain."'

Confucius also advised against conquering distant lands, arguing that, attracted by China's moral and cultural superiority, their inhabitants would come there of their own accord. The Chinese would then civilize and pacify them.

Chinese history often records how scholar-civil servants warned against crossing swords with barbarians. 'Have you not heard,' wrote the poet Po Chuyi, a contemporary of Charlemagne, 'that the First Minister of Kaiyuan does not reward military operations on the frontier? It is not his wish that the troops should develop a spirit of aggression.'

In our millennium, wars of conquest were undertaken only by non-Chinese rulers such as the Mongols of the Yüan and the Manchus of the Qing dynasty.

Confucian civil servants often found it hard to gain acceptance for their ideological principles, especially among the military, but an imperial decree of the eleventh century permanently subordinated the armed forces to the civil power. This principle still stands. 'The Party commands the rifles' is its updated version.

In foreign policy, however, Confucian scholar-officials pursued the 'long rein' policy, which left local rulers in power but took them under Chinese suzerainty and made allies of them. In many cases, as the imperial court was well aware, this relationship implied no real subordination to China.

The Son of Heaven presented his foreign regents with a warrant of appointment and an official seal, as well as some rank or other in the Chinese nobility. Their envoys, who saluted him with the kowtow, brought tributary gifts of local origin and received imperial gifts in return.

Although garrisons were sometimes stationed in suzerain states, for example at Turfan and Lhasa, Chinese military commanders seldom concerned themselves with internal affairs. Local princes would have counted it a great misfortune to be deprived of their suzerain status or have their tributary gifts refused by the emperor, for the gifts they acquired in return were always far more sumptuous and valuable. This was how the Chinese purchased peaceful neighbours. The price was high, but the emperors of the Sung dynasty calculated that an army would have cost still more. In time, however, these unequal transactions became too heavy a charge on the imperial exchequer.

The tributary states could be quite brazen in their demands – as, for instance, when one of them requested the Emperor's favourite concubine. The Emperor duly dispatched her to the wilds of Manchuria because he could not afford to become embroiled in a war with the Khan. This episode provides the theme for a celebrated drama of the Yüan dynasty.

Imperial civil servants strove to extend the tributary system, which was really an attempt to establish peaceful relations with foreign countries by commercial and economic means, to the 'outer territories' as well. The Chinese were flexible when it came to tokens of submission. In 1793, for instance, when the British envoy Lord Macartney refused to kowtow to the Emperor, they pronounced it sufficient that he should bend the knee on entering the imperial presence.

The following list, which dates from 1808, records the names of countries paying tribute and the routes by which they did so:

Holland	Pays tribute at indefinite intervals. Earlier agreements provided for the payment of tribute every five years.	Via Canton
Portugal The Pope England	Irregular tributary payments.	Via Macao

Gerhard Schröder objected that the conquest of Tibet did not quite fit my exposition of Chinese foreign policy, and he was right. What is wrong, however, is the oft-repeated statement that China's invasion in 1959 constituted a treacherous attack on a country that had always been independent. When the issue was brought before the UN Security Council, the Nationalist Chinese, who at that time occupied China's seat, defended the communist leaders' action in Tibet and blocked their formal condemnation. Tibet not only belonged to China from the middle of the eighteenth century onwards, after its conquest by Kangxi, the foremost member of the Manchurian Qing dynasty, but had done so in a certain sense since the time of the thirteenth-century Mongol emperors. The Tibetans proclaimed their independence when the Qing dynasty fell in 1911, but continued to maintain close relations with China.

In occupying Tibet and firmly reintegrating it, the Chinese communist leaders were undoubtedly motivated by a fear that this weak but territorially extensive country on their southern flank would be unable to maintain its independence of other powers, and that the latter might use it as an operational base against China. They justified their action by invoking the title that had been valid until 1911. Although their fear that the country might fall prey to outside influence was far from groundless, it can hardly be denied that, in Tibet, the Chinese are holding sway over a people who would rather be independent.

But they did not take possession of Tibet in order to exploit it. It has never occurred to the Chinese, throughout their long history, to conquer a country for the sake of its wealth and mineral resources, or to annex territory as distant from China as Macao from Portugal, the Philippines from Spain, Indonesia from Holland, Indo-China from France, the Cameroons from Germany, or India from Great Britain.

Black Dragon River

Heilongjiang means 'Black Dragon River'. Otherwise known as the Amur, the river forms China's northern boundary. Heilongjiang Province is larger than Sweden and twice the size of West Germany. Nearly nine hundred miles separate the frontier town of Manchouli in the west from the Ussuri River border in the east.

From Harbin, the provincial capital, we had taken the night train and travelled even further north. After discussing economic problems with our Chinese companions till midnight, we retired to our 'hard class' couchettes and slept. At 5 a.m. we got out at Bei-An. Bei-An means 'Northern Peace' – quite an apt name for a town little more than a hundred miles from the Sino-Soviet frontier, which runs along the middle of Black Dragon River.

It was cold and dank. Our jeeps bounced along rutted tracks for four interminable hours. The countryside, with its vast, open fields and belts of deciduous forest, was deserted. We passed only three villages throughout the drive, which rattled our teeth and chilled us to the bone. At 9 a.m. we reached our destination, State Farm No. 3. There were five in our party besides myself: Armin Gutowski from Hamburg, one of Germany's 'Five Economic Wise Men', now in China as adviser to the Chinese Central Economic Planning Authorities; his assistant; and three members of Peking's State Planning Commission.

The manager of State Farm No. 3, who came out to greet us in the pouring rain, mentioned that we were not the first foreigners to visit his establishment. A Soviet agricultural delegation had been there before us. We raised our eyebrows. A Soviet delegation? Yes, said the manager, in 1956.

After breakfasting in the staff canteen on soya-bean sprouts, green beans, and rice, we began our conducted tour.

The area under cultivation was so vast that it took some time to grasp its full extent. We drove past fields of grain like giant ribbons, two kilometres long but only two hundred and fifty metres wide, and each separated from its neighbours by alternating double rows of spruce and poplar. The trees were there to prevent the wind from carrying away topsoil and flattening the wheat or rye. My German companions were dubious. Did it help? Yes, it did. 'We began by planting the rows at intervals of five hundred metres,' the manager told us, 'but that was too far apart. Two hundred and fifty is close enough.'

It was still raining, and we found the wind too cold for comfort in our lightweight Peking suits. July or no, the thermometer stood at only fifty degrees – a midsummer temperature in Heilongjiang Province, which enjoys an average of one hundred and six frost-free days a year. Although the farm grew strains of wheat capable of ripening in that brief time, it was not uncommon for early and unexpected frosts to wipe out an entire crop.

We spent over an hour traversing the state farm's patchwork quilt of long, narrow fields, with their unvarying alternation of spruce and poplar, spruce and poplar.

Where agricultural machinery was concerned, the state farm received a preferential treatment not extended to its workers, who lived in crude mud huts. New huts were under construction, but they were no less primitive. The manager, who had been here for twenty-five years, complained of labour shortages, especially at harvest time. Seven thousand young people had been assigned to the farm during the Cultural Revolution, but six thousand of them had returned to their home towns, most of them illegally, and would never come back.

We could well understand why. We should have been just as reluctant to exchange our homes for these northern wilds. The Chinese like living cheek by jowl in settled, mature communities of varied occupational complexion. They must have found it bleak up here, cobbled together into an artificial society and living in these lonely villages, with their rows of primitive mud huts, in a climate averaging only one hundred and six frost-free days a year.

Was it conceivable that population pressure would some day prompt the Chinese to expand at Soviet expense? Would they really spill over into territory where the soil remained frozen all year round – a region that began not much more than a hundred miles to the north, at some points even inside their own border? Would they really risk a showdown with the Soviet Union for the sake of such territory, when they had not yet succeeded in populating the northern and western extremities of their own domain?

The Chinese have always kept their gaze directed inwards. The inhabitants of the Middle Kingdom are a centripetal people. An existence on the edge of the world, the fringes of society, does not appeal to them.

To the Chinese, borderlands still mean places of exile remote from the protective family circle – places where life is poor and government bad, where 'heaven is high and the emperor far'.

A Talk
with Helmut Schmidt

October

I presented the Chancellor with the dwarf pine I had brought from Peking to decorate his office during his forthcoming talks with Hua Guofeng. He asked me what to expect.

'This is Hua's first trip to the West,' I said. 'Everything will be new to him. He says he wants to learn from us. Most of all, he wants to know how we managed to rebuild our industry so quickly after the war. After seeing films of the war damage here, he wants you to explain the reasons for our economic miracle.'

Helmut Schmidt laughed. 'No fear! I don't intend to say too much – I'm always being accused of lecturing people as it is.'

'But he genuinely wants to know. That's why the Chinese are sending so many of their most senior politicians and provincial administrators abroad – to learn.'

'All right, I'll play it by ear. Have you seen and talked to him often?'

'Quite often, yes. The first time we met, he'd been in power for six months. In those days he stuck closely to his prepared brief when talking politics; now he's more relaxed. Hua has learned a lot. He never builds intellectual castles in the air. His arguments are straightforward – you may even find some of them unsubtle. Hua's a practical politician, not a theoretician. Adenauer used simple language too.'

'I doubt if anyone can appreciate what Adenauer achieved till he's sitting in this chair.'

'Hua does his best to establish a consensus,' I went on. 'In one sense, he's more Chinese than Deng Xiaoping, who isn't afraid of showdowns and doesn't always try to avoid them. The ship of state nearly foundered after Mao's death. Hua steered it back into calmer waters, but not with the aid of any grand navigational manoeuvre. He did it with a series of minor, almost imperceptible course corrections.'

'Clever!'

'I sold him short at first, and I can well imagine that many of Deng's circle do the same. For one thing, they criticize his lack of education – he's a country boy, after all. Educated people are universally contemptuous of his handwriting, and that they regard as an important guide to character assessment. According to rumour, he always has to practise before inscribing books for presentation.

'His manner is modest and unassuming. That makes him popular with the man in the street. Discounting any of Mao's old henchmen in their ranks, senior politicians view him with less enthusiasm. Many of them feel he's too hamstrung by Mao's ideas. They think he's inflexible – an obstacle on the road to modernization.'

On that note, we turned to other matters.

East Meets West

24 October

Before the Chinese delegation arrived, a spokesman for the Federal Government stated in a radio interview that we would not let Hua talk us into siding with China against the Soviet Union. Were we trying to assure the Russians of our good behaviour, or what? Although the Chinese construed this remark as an attempt to gag them in advance, they betrayed no sign of their annoyance during the visit.

The first plenary session in the Federal Chancellor's office opened. Hua presented a summary of China's economic position and development plans. After that, he and the Chancellor withdrew for a private talk through interpreters.

They met again on the following afternoon for a second long exchange of views at Schloss Gymnich. This the Chancellor found so interesting that he resumed it after dinner, at which Hua played host, and did not emerge until 1 a.m. He then asked me to accompany him back to Bonn. The drive was devoted to an account of his recent conversation. Never a man to lavish undue praise, the Chancellor owned to being highly impressed by Hua's political stature, balanced judgements, and ability to summarize the international situation in a half-hour exposé. He had detected no efforts on Hua's part to get us to side with China against the Russians.

At breakfast, Hua inquired what time I had got to bed. Just before 3 a.m., I said, and asked him the same question. It turned out that he had done likewise, after working on some telegrams to and from Peking.

At Trier, Hua visited the Karl-Marx-Haus and inscribed the visitors' book as follows: 'China owes her liberation to the ideas of Karl Marx and Chinese practice.' The last two words were symptomatic of the Chinese leaders' new-found self-assurance. No one referred to Mao Zedong throughout the visit.

Aboard the Special Train

'When your technicians were helping us to build the steel plant at Wuhan,' said Hua, 'they complained of poor morale among our Chinese workers. Our people argued that working conditions at Wuhan were worse than in Germany, but your technicians replied, "When we rebuilt our factories on the ruins left by the war, our working conditions were far worse than yours in China." That was a fair retort. We should like to have many more of our personnel trained by you. Not only students but workers too. Above all, works managers, so that they can study your managerial methods.'

We had breakfasted and were now sitting over tea in the special train that was taking us from Stuttgart to Munich. When I expressed confidence that productivity would improve if Chinese workers were given greater material incentives, Hua agreed and said that their wages would soon be substantially increased.

I recalled our post-war currency reform, an overnight measure which left people with only forty marks in ready cash and compelled them either to work or starve. I also recalled how the market had been flooded with consumer goods once Ludwig Erhard did away with rationing. Hua listened intently and asked a number of questions.

The landscape gliding past our windows was like something out of a child's picturebook. The leaves had begun to turn red and gold. The fields were well tended, the roads uncluttered, the houses neat. Bedclothes were draped over windowsills and balconies to air. I talked of home-ownership and the credit facilities available to those who preferred to buy rather than rent. Hua listened, and asked for details. Then he abruptly changed the subject.

'When did you first visit China?'

Vice-Foreign Minister Zhang Wenjin, who had just joined us, answered for me. 'Thirty-six years ago, wasn't it?'

'Even longer ago than that,' I amended. 'It was in 1936.'

'You must have been very young.'

'Yes, twenty-one.'

'What made you go there?'

'The spirit of adventure. China seemed so strange and different – so mysterious.'

'Mysterious?' Hua looked puzzled.

'Many of my fellow countrymen still think your country mysterious.'

He continued to look puzzled, but he let it ride. 'How did you manage to get there?'

Should I tell him, I wondered, or would it be wiser to reply in general terms? I had often sensed, when describing the vagrant life of my younger years to veteran revolutionaries, that their response was far from wholeheartedly approving. They tended to be faintly embarrassed by my story, as if it weren't quite in keeping with my status. Reminding myself that Hua had come to Germany to learn, I decided to tell him.

'I was an exchange student in the United States,' I said. 'When my grant ran out, I earned myself some money by taking odd jobs. America was still suffering from the effects of the Depression, so it wasn't easy to find work, but I lived very frugally and eventually saved enough money to get to China on a Japanese immigrant ship, travelling steerage.'

'Good, good!' Hua exclaimed. 'Very good! And then?'

'Then I spent six months roaming around Japan and China. Finally, when my money ran out in Shanghai, I signed up on a freighter as ship's boy. That's the lowest form of life at sea – so low, the captain doesn't even notice you from his exalted position on the bridge. After one or two detours, I got home and completed my studies.'

'Good, good!' Hua said again. 'Our students in Germany should work too.'

One of our junior ministers, who was accompanying the party, mentioned that he himself had spent three years as a metal-worker after the war.

Hua pronounced this equally commendable. 'Your people didn't give up hope after the war,' he said. 'They cleared away the rubble and rebuilt their country. In view of all the prosperity I've seen during my visit, I'm bound to ask you a question: Does the same spirit live on in your younger generation? Do they possess the drive and energy to build on such a scale?'

Hua Guofeng in Munich

The national anthems were played outside the station. The visitors relaxed as soon as the strains of our own had died away, and my nearest Chinese neighbour casually inquired Munich's height above sea level. I put a finger to my lips because the band had struck up again.

'That,' I said, when the bandsmen had lowered their instruments, 'was the Bavarian national anthem.'

'Do all your provinces have anthems of their own?'

'No, only Bavaria, as far as I know.'

The Premiers of the Bavarian Free State and the People's Republic of China inspected a guard of honour. The Chinese Head of Protocol asked if it was drawn from the Bavarian National Guard.

'No,' I told him, 'the Bavarian police.'

'Police?' he echoed, and I could tell, from his furrowed brow, that he was dredging his memory for some prior occasion on which heads of government had inspected a platoon of policemen.

I had noticed during previous official visits that Chinese in Munich were puzzled by the provincial government's rather strenuous attempts to emphasize Bavaria's sovereignty and special status within the Federal Republic.

The Chinese themselves have always hankered after unity and honoured those who achieved it. 'There is no way of fulfilling the wishes of the people,' declared Shang Yang, 'other than by unifying them.' Qin Shihuang, the First Emperor, is accounted great because he welded the civilized world into a single state. Mao is accounted great because he reunited a divided China into one state and nation.

Chinese provinces and regions are allowed to retain their individuality as long as it goes hand in hand with a strong desire for national unity, but individuality is never carried to extremes. The authorities, who have no wish to cultivate provincialism, are more concerned to reinforce people's sense of belonging to a totality. That is why they encourage the use of *putunghua*, or Modern Standard Chinese, rather than dialects that hamper communication between north and south, sometimes rendering it impossible within one and the same province. Local patriotism is condemned as narrow-minded provincialism. Jokes about other provinces or cities have a long tradition in China; today they are scoffed at – officially, that is.

Whether acting under orders from above or on his own initiative, the Bavarian Head of Protocol was clearly at pains to impress on the Chinese that they were now in the Free State of Bavaria, and that their companions from the Federal capital were redundant. He even omitted to provide transportation for the junior minister in our party, who had to hitch a ride in a police car.

The Bavarian Head of Protocol had further distinguished himself, when drawing up the table plan for lunch, by forgetting that Chinese speak Chinese. No places had been set aside for the interpreters, all of whom were seated at the lower end of the festive board, possibly to prevent them from eavesdropping on what passed between the Premier of the Bavarian Free State and his confrère, the Premier of the People's Republic. Our two Foreign Office interpreters had been segregated with especial care.

It emerged during the hors d'oeuvres that the Bavarian Premier's knowledge of Chinese was limited. Although he had read out a few words of Chinese when greeting his guests at the station, Hua's Pekingese interpreter had failed to translate them, mistaking them for Bavarian. Since Hua Guofeng spoke no language other than Chinese and could not, unlike Franz Josef Strauss, communicate in Latin or ancient Greek, conversation languished. The Head of Protocol, who was summoned, saw at once where the difficulty lay. As soon as two chairs had been hurriedly placed behind the Premiers and equipped with a brace of interpreters, talk could commence. All the other German guests sitting beside Chinese visitors continued to flounder because the rest of the interpreters remained segregated at the foot of the table, chatting blithely to each other.

Renewed problems of communication arose during a visit to the Siemens Building, where a Siemens telephone system was to be demonstrated for the visitors' benefit. The number of the Chinese Embassy in Berne, they were informed, had been specially pre-programmed. Would Premier Hua Guofeng be gracious enough to press that button? He would be through to Switzerland within seconds, and a loudspeaker would enable all present to listen in. The button was pressed, but all we heard was the engaged signal. A second attempt proved equally abortive. No one had thought to warn the embassy because the call was meant to be a pleasant surprise.

But never mind, the number of the Chinese Trade Representative Office in London had also been pre-programmed. Hua got through at once, but the duty operator refused to believe that his Premier was on the line. Indeed, he found the notion so improbable that he suspected a hoax. When he persisted in his disbelief, Hua hung up.

The highlight of the evening's programme was a performance of Richard Strauss's *Salome*. For Hua Guofeng and most of his party, it was their first experience of Western opera. I had pleaded for *The Magic Flute*, which was also being presented in Munich that season, because its plot came closer to the Chinese conception of opera, but the Bavarian Protocol Department informed us that *Salome* had been selected and that was that. Which it was.

Since the action unfolded on an almost unlit stage, most of our travel-weary visitors seized the chance to shut their eyes. Nobody followed the plot, which may have been fortunate. One senior dignitary asked me later if the theme was Israeli in origin. He only inquired, he said, because China maintained no diplomatic relations with Israel.

Differences of Approach

We sat side by side on the sofa in his small but elegant hotel suite. Hua laid his hand on my arm and said a lot of pleasant things. He spoke as one old friend to another, but without any unseemly familiarity.

We reviewed his visit. Hua's talks with Helmut Schmidt had made a deep impression on him, and he asked me to convey his thanks to the Chancellor. He had been agreeably surprised at the warmth of his public reception in Germany. It was his earnest desire that China and the Federal Republic should continue their collaboration, not only in this century and the next, but long after that. 'It must not,' he stressed, 'be a short-term arrangement.'

Half an hour later, after expressing my own thanks, I said *au revoir*. I had to leave Munich before him so as to catch a flight from Athens to Peking.

Foreign Minister Huang Hua came to my room before I left. He, too, struck a cordial, personal note. Franz and I were on good terms with Huang and his wife, He Liliang, and often spoke of other than political matters. Today, however, we spent nearly two hours discussing developments in South-East Asia and Africa. It was, as ever, a frank exchange in which each of us respected and strove to understand the other's point of view, even when it differed from our own.

No disappointment or ill feeling ever marred my relations with Huang and his aides. On the contrary, they often helped me to cut through red tape and render humanitarian assistance. Bureaucracy was kept within bounds at the Chinese Foreign Ministry. The same could not be said of other branches of central government, particularly in the economic sphere, where departmental powers and regulations combined to form a sometimes impenetrable bureaucratic jungle.

Although the Chinese occasionally overestimated their resources on the economic front and were unable to fulfil their undertakings because of conflicts of opinion within the leadership, the Foreign Ministry invariably proved reliable.

I had often found in Bucharest that our Romanian opposite numbers tried to hoodwink us, reneged on firm agreements, invented difficulties, exerted pressure, and employed a whole box of tricks which served no real purpose at all. Like the Russians, the Romanians regarded any partner in negotiations as an opponent to be coerced into concessions and driven into a corner by stratagem and subterfuge. Any chance of negotiating in a straightforward, open manner was thus ruled out from the start.

The Chinese, by contrast, began by stating their position and the reasons for it. They came quickly to the nub of a problem, enabling both parties to see whether and to what extent agreement prevailed between them. They negotiated on the crux of the matter, not with an eye to limited tactical gains. Their line of argument usually disclosed how far they would be willing to go, though the interpretation of their clues, which tended to be discreet, was an acquired art. Henry Kissinger, whose memoirs draw a brilliant and apt comparison between the Russian and Chinese negotiating techniques, regretted that these clues were sometimes too subtle for American ears to detect, but he, too, regarded Peking's style of negotiation as pleasant and productive.

Personal experiences should not, of course, be generalized. With people who enjoy their confidence, or with whom they know themselves to be in fundamental agreement, the Chinese negotiate differently than with those whom they distrust. Russian or Vietnamese experience of dealing with them would not tally with our own, and it is to be assumed that, in negotiating with hostile partners, the Chinese employ the selfsame tactical ruses to which they themselves are subjected. Their brilliant command of these has often been attested by Western diplomats in days gone by.

She Who Awaits the Dawn

November

Swissair, which transported its passengers from Zurich to Peking in nineteen hours, offered the pleasantest and most comfortable means of travel between Europe and the Far East. I was at the airport to meet Lothar Späth, the Premier of Baden-Württemberg, who had come to Peking with a large party of prominent industrialists for talks on closer collaboration between the Chinese and the medium-sized firms in which his province abounds.

We sat or stood around in the airport's reception hall, sipping tea and waiting for baggage clearance. One of the first pieces of luggage to appear was marked 'Georg Moser, Rottenburg'. I glanced inquiringly at Lothar Späth. *Bishop* Moser of Rottenburg? How many medium-sized industrial firms were owned by his diocese? Späth replied that the Bishop had not come for secular reasons. In that case, why? To minister to the spiritual needs of the delegation? No, not that either. Herr Moser wished to form an up-to-date picture of the state of the Catholic Church in China. He also proposed to celebrate Mass in Peking's Catholic Cathedral and visit his fellow cleric, the Bishop of Shanghai.

'The one who's been in prison for decades?' I said, and went on to point out that, if Späth submitted and endorsed such requests in his capacity as head of the delegation, it would hardly assist his trade talks – quite the opposite.

I also had a word with Bishop Moser, who felt that the Chinese might be interested in talking to him because he had recently conferred with the Vatican about their country. I said that, although the Chinese were only moderately interested in the Vatican's ideas, he would undoubtedly be able to discuss them with some Party official responsible for questions relating to religious communities, for instance at the Academy of Social Sciences. His best plan, I said, would be to approach the delegation's Chinese escorts in a personal and private capacity. He could then ask them to arrange a discussion with the Academy on the current state of the Church. I advised him against approaching Chinese clerics direct. This would only embarrass them, because they already had to contend with the suspicion that they received instructions from the Vatican.

Like the Buddhists and Moslems, the Christian Churches in China had lately been granted a few concessions. Nonetheless, government and Party leaders continued to nurse a strong and not unjustified suspicion that ecclesiastical authorities abroad were seeking to exert an influence on Christian communities inside China. They were particularly wary of the Vatican, and for reasons of long standing.

Emperor Kangxi had been well disposed towards Jesuit missionaries during the seventeenth century. They continued to occupy a respected and important position at his court until 1705, when the Vatican instructed them to forbid Chinese Christians to revere Confucius and engage in ancestor worship. Emperor Kangxi found it intolerable that the Jesuits, whom he looked upon as his own civil servants, should take orders from Rome, and that the Vatican should have presumed to pass judgement on ancient Chinese customs and usages. Like Kangxi, China's present rulers dispute the authority of a foreign Church to dictate to Chinese priests or their parishioners.

It is understandable that, at a time when the Catholic Church is losing ground in its traditional spheres of influence, the Catholic press should nurture hopes that the Vatican will gain a foothold in China. These hopes are nonetheless unfounded. Whispered allusions to an underground Church loyal to the Vatican, which can sometimes be heard in ecclesiastical circles, should be treated with the utmost scepticism. Given China's long tradition of secret societies, it is not inconceivable that such small communities exist. Even if they do, however, it would be self-delusive to pin any hopes on them.

During the last century and the first half of our own, the Christian Churches gazed with fascination at China's huge reservoir of heathen souls and vied with each other, by means that were sometimes fair but occasionally foul, to convert and redeem them. They founded schools, universities, and socially exemplary institutions; but despite heavy financial expenditure, strong political backing from the colonial powers, and, last but not least, selfless efforts on the part of many missionaries working under arduous conditions, their harvest of converts remained disappointingly small.

Present-day China affords no scope for missionary activity directed from abroad. The Government would regard this as outside interference and proscribe it, but it would also be greeted with suspicion by the general public. The number of Christians in China has never been precisely ascertained. Being eager to outdo each other, the various denominations and sects always erred on the generous side when enumerating the souls they had saved. Even if all impediments to public worship and religious observance were removed overnight, Christians, Catholics as well as Protestants, would be found to represent no more than half of one per cent of the Chinese population.

Father Ladani is a Jesuit priest who has lived in Hong Kong since the early 1950s, when he first began to publish his *China News Analysis*. He once told me, in 1955, that Christianity might stand a chance in China if communism disappeared because, after years of shallow materialism, the Chinese were thirsting for a religion capable of endowing individual existence with meaning.

My inclination was to doubt and dispute this theory, though I was unsure of my ground. I am little more sure today. What makes it so hard to judge is that, while basic religious ideas have existed in China from time immemorial, and while popular Taoist and Buddhist beliefs are not yet dead there, at least in rural areas, Taoism's serenity through inaction and Buddhism's extinction of self in nirvana have no counterparts in Christianity. Although one still encounters a popular belief in the punishment of sins, meaning infractions of the moral and religious code, heaven and hell are created in the image of the old Chinese world and conform to that pattern. The Chinese have never conceived of God as utterly different from man, nor have they ever devoted thought to encounters with a personal god, to absolute dependence on him, to *religio*, atonement, or the redemption of sins by divine grace.

The Chinese have never agonized over the lack of divine justice, either. The most they have done is express mild surprise like Sima Qian, who, after listing a series of historical injustices, summed up his attitude as follows: 'I am now entirely bewildered. Is the so-called path of heaven just, or is it unjust?'

I therefore doubt if Father Ladani's prediction will ever be fulfilled, though he is certainly right in one respect: many young and thoughtful Chinese are distressed by the emptiness of their lives. I once gave a lecture to students at Peking's Institute of Foreign Languages and invited questions afterwards. The only question to be asked and taken up by several members of my audience was: What are German children taught in religious instruction classes? One could sense that the students were seeking an answer on their own behalf. In the old days, individuals sought refuge from the world's disappointments, evils, and injustices in the bosom of the family. Today, where families have been split up, this source of security is lacking.

Some time ago, the magazine *China Youth* published a letter from a girl who signed herself Pan Xiao, a pseudonym meaning 'She Who Awaits the Dawn'. She wrote:

> I am twenty-three years old, so I have just begun to experience life. But its charms and mysteries hold no fascination for me. When I was very young, I was filled with fine hopes and dreams about life in the new China. My parents and one of my grandfathers were members of the Communist Party. I was confident that I would be true to communism and a member of the Party . . . I was passionately intent on self-abandonment and intoxicated with the idea. I wrote long paragraphs in my diary full of revolutionary ardour, and modelled my words and deeds on revolutionary heroes.

Pan Xiao went on to describe how bewildered she had been by the violence of the Cultural Revolution. She had had to leave school because her mother, with whom she no longer lived, stopped sending her money. She was refused membership of the Youth League for having criticized a Party official. She then fell in love with the son of a veteran functionary who was persecuted by the radicals.

> I did my best to allay the concern he felt for his father. It never occurred to me that he would turn his back on me and desert me when his father was rehabilitated after the downfall of the Gang of Four . . .
>
> In search of the meaning of life, I observed the people and society around me. I started reading books: Hegel, Darwin, Owen, Balzac . . . Literature was my one consolation.
>
> It is said that our age is making progress, and that things are improving. I cannot perceive these immense strides, nor can I see the common foundation that supports us and will, so we are told, repay all our efforts. Why does the road we travel grow steadily narrower? I am in despair. I once visited a Catholic church and attended Mass. I have considered cutting off my hair and becoming a Buddhist nun. I have contemplated suicide . . .
>
> If you have the courage to publish this letter, all the young people in China will learn how I think and feel. I believe that they think and feel as I do . . .

This letter attracted seventy thousand replies, three hundred of which the magazine published. Winding up the correspondence, *China Youth*'s editors tacitly admitted that many of the writers shared Pan Xiao's despair. However, the younger generation were progressing from superstition to faith in science, from personal sorrow to involvement in the historic task of reconstruction, from sighs and lamentations to rigorous ordeals and hard work. 'The search for the meaning of life is never-ending,' the editorial concluded – never-ending, it should have added, in a world devoid of faith.

I had set out to find the New Man, that revolutionary bundle of energy who had left the Old Man and his weaknesses so far behind and beneath him. Was Pan Xiao all that remained of the New Man – a girl who had recognized the illusory nature of revolution, socialism, and progress, and who now, empty and despairing, groped for the answer to a question she couldn't even formulate?

I can hear myself being interrupted and called to order at this point by the editors of *China Youth*. What of the laundry-basket full of letters commending duty, helpfulness, revolutionary consciousness, vigilance, sincerity, Party loyalty, diligence, and scientific method? They leave me as unconvinced as Pan Xiao herself, who longs for the dawn. The void within her lies at a level too deep for her despair to be cured by revolutionary bombast or admonitory fingers raised in a spirit of social responsibility. The remedy lies only in some answer of transcendental character, though its exact nature is open to speculation. Pan Xiao has read Hegel, Balzac, Darwin, Owen . . . One can well understand why Hegel proved unhelpful. So, of course, did the others. Her attention might be drawn to Socrates, or to Jesus as he appears in the Gospels, but one would hesitate to recommend any Christian thinkers who experienced her own spiritual emptiness and wrote about it – Kierkegaard or St Augustine, for example – because too much of what they wrote would escape her comprehension.

My own feeling is that a religious answer derived from Buddhism or Taoism would be better suited to Pan Xiao and her fellow Chinese than a Christian response. The number of Chinese who still approximate to the Buddhist or Taoist outlook is many times greater than the tiny minority of Christians or semi-Christians, not to mention the millions of Moslems concentrated mainly in western China. During the first half of the present century, China had syncretistic sects and cults with millions of adherents. If religious life were ever allowed to develop freely again, cults of this kind would probably attract more members than the established Churches of the West, whose answers to the problems of our age might fail to carry conviction with many Chinese as well as many Westerners.

But this is to speculate vaguely on possibilities that do not exist at the present time, when the political authority of the state and Party remains strong enough to keep such developments in check. Meanwhile, authority will continue to supply people like Pan Xiao with non-answers that do not, and cannot, satisfy them.

1980

1980

Hearsay and Scandals

In the summer of 1979, the National People's Congress debated a draft law prescribing severe penalties for defamation. Simultaneously, at the end of June, Democracy Wall sprouted a poster fifty feet long and inscribed in big, bold characters. This accused Wang Dongxing of having embezzled seven million yüan, or two million pounds sterling, belonging to Party Headquarters.

Wang Dongxing, as we have already mentioned, had begun his career as Mao's personal bodyguard. In charge of Guards Regiment 8341 when Mao died, he ranged himself on Hua's side and was rewarded with a seat on the Politburo Standing Committee. This made him one of the five most senior men in the Chinese political hierarchy.

On the right of the sensational, boldly written denunciation hung another wall-poster giving details: Wang Dongxing had used the seven million yüan from public funds to build private houses for himself and members of his family in Zhongnanhai Park. At 1276 yüan per square metre, the construction costs had been double those of the luxurious Peking Hotel or the Great Hall of the People. A thousand workers' families could have been housed for the same sum. Wang had fraudulently obtained the money on the pretext that his house had been damaged by tunnelling work and needed renovation. Far from carrying out any repairs when the funds were approved, he had constructed everything from scratch in the most sumptuous style and even demolished a house built by Mao because it happened to be in his way.

Responsibility for these charges was assumed by the editors of *Peking Spring*, an underground magazine.

I discussed them on the terrace after dinner with my old friend Lao Yang, while Franz chatted with his wife. They were a serious-minded, dependable couple, he a scientist and she a civil servant.

'I don't understand,' I said. 'Wang Dongxing has overall command of Guards Regiment 8341. Aren't any of his men prepared to go to Democracy Wall and tear the poster down?'

'It's already been up for a week,' said Lao Yang, 'so he must be in trouble. Who knows if he's still in command of the regiment? Even if he is, his men must realize that his position's shaky. They won't stick their necks out for his sake.'

'Anyway,' put in Lao's wife, who had been listening, 'they say the regiment's going to be disbanded. It's a long-standing disgrace – a bunch of officials' sons who've found themselves a soft number. As for what that poster says about Wang living in luxury, you can bet it's true. Have you ever seen the inside of the guards' barracks?'

I laughed. 'You must be joking!'

'Naturally. They'd never take *you* on a guided tour of that place, but *I've* been there. It's between Sun Yat-sen Park and Zhongnanhai – you can see it from Tian An Men Square. They spent years on the building. Everything inside is ultra-luxurious, at least by our standards.'

'Still,' I said, 'one of our interpreters reports that some sceptical comments have been scrawled on the poster.'

Lao shrugged. 'Maybe Wang Dongxing still has a few friends left with the courage to scribble a word or two – it's not as spectacular as tearing down a whole great poster – but I don't share their doubts. The charges are too detailed to be a complete fabrication. Wang must go – he doesn't belong in the Politburo.'

'Why,' I said, 'is he in someone's way? He never seems to court the limelight. Remember him at the inauguration of the Mao Memorial Hall, scurrying around like a protocol chief and tugging Hua and old Ye Jianying by the sleeve to make them face the camera? I toured an exhibition with him once. He made a completely colourless impression. He didn't strike me as particularly intelligent, either.'

'Wang's what he always was – a bodyguard – but it doesn't pay to underestimate the man. He knows the weaknesses of the great. He carries their files in his head.'

'Compiled when he was Vice-Minister of Security, you mean?'

'Not only then. He used to be Mao's major-domo, so to speak. Nothing went on at the Chairman's court without his knowledge. Great men are lonely. They need someone they can trust implicitly – someone who'll act on ideas they haven't uttered and never would. Wang could read Mao's mind. That made him useful.'

'Tell them about Zhang Yufeng,' Lao's wife said eagerly, but he shook his head.

'Yufeng?' I repeated. 'Written *yü* meaning jade and *feng* meaning phoenix? Jade Phoenix? A lady, in other words?'

'Yes, but people don't like talking about her.'

'Well they ought to,' said Lao's wife. 'Besides, everyone knows the story by now.'

'Not everyone,' said Lao, 'though many people do.' He made a grimace of resignation. 'Very well. Rumour has it that Wang used to keep Mao supplied with pretty girls.'

'At his home in Zhongnanhai?'

'No,' said Lao's wife, 'in his sleeping car.'

'I see,' I said. 'And one of them was a girl called Jade Phoenix?'

'Precisely,' said Lao's wife. 'Go on, tell them!'

Lao surrendered. 'Wang was responsible for Mao's security to the very end. One of his duties was to select the girls who waited on him when he travelled by train. They had to be security-screened and entirely trustworthy. But the girls Wang picked were pretty as well – after all, he knew the Great Chairman's taste. Zhang Yufeng was not only pretty but intelligent and well educated.'

'Pretty?' Lao's wife broke in. 'We saw a photo of her once, with Mao leaning on her arm. She was a dainty little thing, but pretty? I don't know about that.'

'Anyway,' said Lao, who didn't seem to share her doubts, 'the Chairman obviously took to her. Wang must have guessed what was in his mind, because he had her transferred to Zhongnanhai and installed there as Mao's private secretary. From then on, Zhang Yufeng never left his side. She handled all his secret papers – all his notes and drafts and the minutes of his conferences. She was very indebted and grateful to Wang, of course, especially when he also found a place for her sister in Mao's household. Her class origins weren't unimpeachable, but Mao apparently said he didn't care. If no one else would have her, he said, she could move in with him.'

'But the Chairman was so old and frail,' I said. 'I find it very hard to believe.'

'Maybe he was an exceptional man from more angles than one,' said Lao's wife. 'Besides, the Zhang Yufeng affair went back a long way. That photo I mentioned appeared in October 1966, if I remember rightly – the *People's Daily* printed it. Mao, Zhou Enlai, Lin Biao, and our other big leaders were attending a Red Guard parade in Tian An Men Square. They left the platform and mingled with the crowds. That's when we first saw the girl and wondered how she came to be in such exalted company. So did everyone else.'

'How did you discover her name?'

'It didn't take long to leak out via senior officials or their families.'

'But we didn't hear the full story till much later on,' said Lao's wife, 'when a friend of ours referred to the Zhongnanhai cess-pit and we asked him what he meant.' She paused. 'Tell them about the child.'

'There isn't much to tell,' Lao said. 'Zhang Yufeng had a child by Mao.'

'Really?'

Lao must have sensed my disbelief. 'It's no rumour. I heard it about six months before Mao died, from a woman doctor employed at a military hospital outside Peking. That's where the girl had her baby – I could even quote you the number of the hospital. The doctor was furious at our leaders' double standards – the discrepancy between the principles they preach to us and their own moral code.'

When I made no comment, Lao went on. 'It's true,' he insisted. No one would have mentioned such a thing for fun in those days. It was too serious – too dangerous.'

'Do many people know?'

'Many people know about Zhang Yufeng and her role in Mao's household, though they only discuss the subject among friends. The child is another matter. Relatively few people know about that.'

'What was Jiang Qing's attitude to Zhang Yufeng?'

'I don't know for sure, but I can guess.'

'She was the last person to talk,' Lao's wife broke in. 'Mao was still married to He Zizhen when she came to Yenan and set her cap at him. That was a scandal even the Politburo couldn't ignore. Besides, she repaid the old man in kind.'

'You mean her alleged affair with the Minister of Sport?'

'Zhuang Zedong was just a table-tennis player, even if he did win the world championship. He owed his ministerial status to Jiang Qing. But why do you say "alleged"? He admitted the whole thing under interrogation.'

'Admitted what, precisely?'

'That she seduced him one night. She forced herself on him, he said – he had no choice. Zhuang wept when they questioned him, and his wife testified that Jiang Qing often used to summon him by phone for late-night "consultations". Ironical, isn't it, when you think of her eight model operas! The creatures on stage were as sexless as the characters in Party-approved literature – not a hint of passion among them. But Jiang Qing herself? She fell for Qian Haoliang, the Peking Opera star who played the lead in *The Red Lantern*, and made him a Vice-Minister of Culture. What's more, she made him drop his family name and call himself plain Hao Liang. He was *years* younger than her. So was Liu Qingtang, a dancer who played the company commander in another of her model operas, *The Red Women's Battalion*. She made Liu a Vice-Minister of Culture too – there were four or five of them. While Mao lay dying, she and her cronies drove out to Dazhai for a party. When she raised a glass of *maotai* and toasted her favourite, Hao Liang, he knelt at her feet and sang the aria "Thank you, Mother!" from *The Red Lantern*. I ask you!'

'Unseemly behaviour,' I said.

'Unseemly isn't the word,' said Lao's wife. 'That's the sort of thing that went on in the old days, at the imperial court. Jiang Qing had no sense of shame. Look what happened to Yang Chunxia, the pretty young actress who played the lead in *Azalea Mountain*. Jiang Qing procured the poor girl for Wang Hungwen, her up-and-coming Shanghai lieutenant. Not so long ago, when Yang Chunxia was marching in a demonstration, the crowd spat at her. She couldn't appear in public for a long time after the Gang of Four were arrested, though she's back on the stage again now. It wasn't her fault.'

'Cliques, cabals, favouritism, blackmail,' said Leo, '—all those things existed at Mao's court just as they did in imperial times. Where Jiang Qing was concerned, her husband's concubine represented a political problem as well as an object of jealousy. Whenever she wanted to find out what had been said at one of Mao's private audiences, from which she was generally excluded, she had to apply to Zhang Yufeng. She was so anxious to get at the confidential files that she tried to win her over after the Chairman's death. So did Mao's nephew. They probably assumed the existence of documents that might help them to seize power.'

'A political testament?' I said.

'Perhaps.'

'Or did they actually know that such a thing existed?'

'Perhaps,' Lao repeated. 'At all events, Zhang Yufeng was scared. Jiang Qing went so far as to offer her money, but Zhang Yufeng can't have rated the widow's chances highly because she reported everything to her friend and patron, Wang Dongxing. Wang, who also saw which way the wind was blowing, went and told Ye Jianying, who in turn told Hua Guofeng. So you see, Wang Dongxing owed his intimate knowledge of what went on around Mao to Zhang Yufeng. He always called her Xiao Zhang, or Little Zhang, even during Politburo sessions. Wang knew what the Chairman was saying and thinking. He may have been colourless and not very bright, but he was dangerous. It's time people like him were removed from the Politburo. They don't reflect well on it.'

'What's the girl doing these days?'

'No idea – working somewhere, I expect. She committed no crime, after all. On the contrary, she did us all a favour. But for her, Jiang Qing might have got at those confidential files.'

'And the child?'

'I don't know if it was a boy or a girl, but I hope it never discovers its father's identity. No child deserves to grow up encumbered by a name as great as Mao's.' Lao paused. 'But we really shouldn't have told you all the lurid details.'

His wife disagreed. 'No, I'm glad we did. We usually keep these things to ourselves, but it's good that you should have heard them before you go home. It may help you to understand what we think of a household where such things could happen. We may find them shocking, but they're all part of the Great Chairman's image.'

'True,' said Lao. 'They were scandalous goings-on, but one naturally can't judge Mao from that angle alone. He still remains one of the greatest men in the history of our country.'

'Of course,' I said. 'And, quite apart from his historic achievements, the conversations published *neibu* during the Cultural Revolution reveal him as a great and independent thinker.'

'Independence,' Lao's wife observed acidly, 'was a luxury only he could afford.'

'Mao's was a complex personality,' said Lao, '—too complex to be analysed so soon. The picture may become clearer later on, when his correspondence and conversations are published in a more objective climate of opinion.'

'He was very self-critical,' I said, 'and he wasn't above admitting his mistakes. That's why I don't propose to attach too much weight to what you've just told us. All it proves is that Mao was a human being with human foibles, not a saint.'

'Very polite of you,' said Lao's wife, who took a sterner view of the matter, 'and very generous. To assess the man correctly, I think we ought to consult his victims' opinions, too. We might also bear in mind that there were some who didn't suffer from the same failings. Deng Xiaoping, Hua Guofeng, Zhou Enlai – they and their wives and families all lived in harmony. Wang Guangmei was Liu Shaoqi's fourth wife, but she was good with the children from his previous marriages and held the family together. It was only Mao's home that was never at peace, always in turmoil.'

Intellectuals

While addressing some Peking students a year before, I'd mentioned that many of our own young girls learned foreign languages by taking *au pair* jobs abroad. They lived like members of the family that employed them. As a rule, they helped in the household for five hours each morning, laying the breakfast table, getting the children washed and dressed, dusting rooms, and so on. In the afternoons they could attend language courses or, by special permission, sit in on university lectures. They were also entitled to free weekends and an adequate supply of pocket money. All else apart, I said, they learned more about their host country and its inhabitants by living in a home environment than they could ever have done in a lecture room.

During the general discussion that followed my talk, everyone wanted to know how to set about obtaining an *au pair* job. Many students, male as well as female, claimed experience of housework and said they didn't mind it. Some could cook, others had regularly bathed their younger brothers and sisters.

I said that Germany played host to *au pair* girls from Scandinavia, France, Britain, and Holland. There were no obstacles that I could see to the admission of Chinese *au pair* girls, but it would, of course, be necessary to get the scheme approved by the Chinese authorities.

From one moment to the next, lively curiosity gave way to silence. The spate of questions dried up.

I later discussed the *au pair* system with the Deputy Minister of Education, pointing out that it might well be the cheapest way of teaching Chinese girls a foreign language. All it would cost the Government was the price of a return flight to Europe. We could start with a dozen students and see how the experiment worked out. The Deputy Minister pronounced my proposal extremely interesting. I submitted it in writing but heard no more. On making inquiries, I was told that it was still under consideration. I also mentioned it to Deputy Premier Fang Yi, the Politburo member responsible for education and research, who likewise pronounced it worthy of consideration.

All further inquiries as to whether a decision had been reached were politely parried. I recalled that Zhou Enlai and Deng Xiaoping had worked and studied in France during the 1920s. Very true, I was told – a valid point. Finally, when the Chinese authorities persisted in their lack of interest, I let the matter drop.

The students themselves had been highly enthusiastic, but officialdom must have deemed it unfitting that a Chinese girl should do housework in a German home. What! Finance her studies by working as a maid-servant – suffer herself to be ordered around and made to perform menial tasks which some foreign housewife probably thought beneath her dignity? Never! She was a student, not a cleaning woman – not an *ayi*.

Intellectuals had now been rehabilitated. Even the elevator girl in one of the foreign diplomats' and journalists' apartment houses let her little fingernail grow, not only because she thought it elegant, but because it signified that she did no manual labour. There is a fundamental belief in China that manual labour shames and degrades those who perform it.

> Great folk have the tasks that befit them just as humble folk have theirs. The former labour with their minds, the latter with their muscles. Those who labour with their minds rule the latter; those who labour with their muscles are ruled by the former.

Thus wrote Mencius in the fourth century BC, and his attitude has survived all the vicissitudes of Chinese history. Two-and-a-half thousand years later, another great Chinese wrote:

> At school I assumed the habits of a student. I did not think it fitting to do even a modicum of hard work, such as carrying my bag in the presence of a crowd of students who were incapable of shouldering a burden or lifting some heavy object. I then had the feeling that the only clean, pure people in the world were intellectuals, while workers, peasants, and soldiers were dirty by comparison. I could wear the clothes of other intellectuals because I thought them clean, but it disgusted me to wear the clothes of workers, peasants, and soldiers because I had the feeling they were dirty.

Who was this great Chinese with an aversion to workers, peasants, and soldiers? Mao Zedong. The passage above comes from a speech he made in 1942.

China was ruled for over two thousand years by philosophers, men of letters, and Grade A examinees who thought as Mao did. Interruptions occurred in time of civil war, invasion, or rebellion, or on the very rare occasions when an emperor spurned his scholar-advisers, or when eunuchs seized power at court; but the scholars always triumphed in the end. If the China of old could not be governed without them, can they be dispensed with by the dictatorship of the proletariat?

Scholars constantly nurtured the prestige of their class. They held aloof from the masses – *odi profanum vulgus* – and wore gorgeous official robes. Notice boards mounted on posts outside their homes proclaimed what level they had attained in the public examination scale. They paid lower taxes and enjoyed greater privileges, for example in courts of law.

Modest though Confucius was, he maintained the ancient equivalent of a carriage and pair. 'Now that I have held public office, it is no longer seemly for me to travel on foot.' His successor, Mencius, lived in greater style. 'His column of wagons numbered several dozen, and his retinue amounted to several hundred people. Thus did they travel from one prince to the next, living on what the courts provided.' It should be added that, even in those days, some of Mencius' fellow philosophers were a trifle dubious about his ostentation.

Many scholars after Mencius' day became wealthy, especially if they were civil servants. Others remained poor, but even poor scholars who had passed their examinations enjoyed public esteem. Of those who held government posts, many took bribes from rich merchants and granted them preferential treatment in return. The only things they never surrendered were the privileges of their class, for those were inalienable. They formed a close-knit group of men who had inherited their monopoly of breeding and refinement. Their ideology was Confucianism, which taught mutual consideration, social responsibility, and a sense of duty binding upon rulers and subjects alike. It also taught respect for authority, age, and education – above all, therefore, respect for the scholar class.

A Chinese author of the eighteenth century, who had failed his provincial examination, made scholars the subject of a mordantly satirical novel in which he pilloried their narrow-mindedness, arrogance, pedantry, venality, avarice, and hypocrisy. His characters were undoubtedly drawn from life.

Although scholar-officials jealously guarded the privileges of their class, however, they did admit members of merchant and peasant families who could demonstrate their gifts in the examination room – a Chinese institution adopted by ourselves. By passing the higher examinations, a man qualified for appointment to a post in the civil service. He also had to submit to the code of the scholar class.

His catechism consisted of the Confucian classics. He displayed his erudition by firing off quotations and literary allusions incomprehensible to the uneducated, and by his ability to construct poems out of existing set pieces. This curriculum was often criticized because it 'compels a man in the prime of life, when he should be studying the principles of politics and administration, to closet himself in a room and devote all his time and energy to composing poems and rhyming couplets'. Thus wrote Wang Anshi, a political reformer of the eleventh century, but the literary canon defied all its critics and their numerous attempts at reform.

Except in times of crisis, China's standard of government was not only good – until the eighteenth century – but generally better than the contemporary standard in European countries. Discussion of administrative methods and reforms attained a level unmatched by Europe until centuries later. The same went for debates on fundamental economic, financial, and political issues, on the relative merits of an expansionist or defensive policy, and on projected agricultural and financial reforms.

Although China's scholar–civil servants never discovered the philosopher's stone, this should be blamed on human inadequacy rather than the men themselves. They voiced their opposition to the emperor, his policy or behaviour, in a manner that was frequently courageous, sometimes courteous, and sometimes so inordinately brusque that their advice cost them their lives. There were occasions when they even seemed to invite this fate for honour and posthumous glory's sake.

During the last century, albeit not for the first time in history, symptoms of decline set in. This process may have been associated with the decline of the Qing dynasty, but it also stemmed from the exposure of China, which had always claimed to be the hub of civilization, to the scientific and technological superiority of the Western world.

China's scholars, however, continued to treat the West with the same arrogant condescension evinced by the West for the Chinese. It was not until the century drew to a close that Chinese reformers gained ground.

Realizing that their country had much to learn from the West, many of them studied abroad in the next few decades and, on returning home, became champions of modernization. The growth of their national awareness was commensurate with the humiliations inflicted on China by the colonial powers. 'Each is responsible for all that occurs under heaven,' runs an old Confucian maxim. As soon as they saw that the campaign against Japanese occupation was being waged more vigorously by Mao than by Chiang Kai-shek, many intellectuals fought their way through to Yenan and joined him there. Distinguished writers whose works had portrayed the intolerable social conditions prevailing in their country, particularly in rural areas, flocked to his banner, united by the hope that he would cleanse public life and establish a just social order.

Once he had created a new, unified state, he was additionally joined by many intellectuals who had hitherto remained aloof.

But it was not long before intellectuals got to see the other side of the coin. The very speech in which Mao had described his youthful belief that intellectuals alone were clean and pure went on to state that, once he became a revolutionary, he realized that 'compared to workers and peasants, non-socialist intellectuals were impure, and that peasants and

344

workers were fundamentally the purest of all. Their hands might be dirty and their shoes caked with cow dung, but they were really cleaner than bourgeois and petit bourgeois intellectuals. This is known as change of outlook – the transition from one class to another.'

Indeed? From one class to another? Was Mao, the peasant's son, representing himself as a scholar who had joined the proletarian class? The truth was that scholars had wanted no truck with a parvenu peasant whose almost unintelligible Hunan dialect remained with him all his life. He once attended a lecture given by Hu Shi, the distinguished philosopher and literary reformer, at Peking University. On learning that Mao was only a junior librarian, not a registered student, Hu Shih declined to answer a question he put. This arrogant rebuff rankled with Mao and wounded his pride so deeply that he never forgot it. He later repaid the intellectuals a hundredfold, but his sense of inferiority lingered.

'As for the professors,' he recalled in 1958, 'we were scared of them when we came to the cities. We did not despise them; we trembled before them. Confronted by men of such great erudition, we felt like nonentities.'

Mao never had a good word to say for intellectuals, even though he felt himself to be one at heart – rightly so – and allowed an artist to paint a monumental portrait of him as a young man attired in a flowing grey academic robe.

To Mao, intellectuals were an endless source of trouble. One of his first major clashes with them occurred in 1954–5, when the eminent literary critic Hu Feng, who disagreed with Mao's views on the role of the writer in Chinese society, said so both publicly and privately, in correspondence with friends.

Thanks to the treachery of one of his correspondents, Hu's letters fell into the hands of the Party. In 1955, they were published by the *People's Daily*, together with a brief commentary by Mao, who described Hu's views as criminal. Enemies without rifles, he wrote, could be more dangerous than any armed foe. Hu Feng was put on trial and sentenced to fourteen years' imprisonment. Released during the Cultural Revolution, he was tried once more and this time sentenced to imprisonment for life. Released yet again several years after the Gang of Four's arrest, he was rehabilitated and given an honorary post in the Writers' Association, but by then his mind had given way.

'Let a hundred flowers bloom and a hundred schools compete . . .' In broadcasting this slogan during 1956 and 1957, Mao seemed to be making his peace with the intellectuals. However, he had clearly underestimated the strength of the opposition that had grown up among them. Taking advantage of their new-found freedom of speech, they unleashed a wave of criticism that shook the Party to its foundations. It was a fierce, far-reaching, and fearless onslaught on the Party, its system, the achievements of its leaders, and Mao himself.

The intellectuals paid dearly for this criticism, not only when the Hundred Flowers slogan was revoked and critics were persecuted, proscribed, and degraded as 'right-wing elements', but in the closing years of Mao's life. They bore the brunt of the so-called Cultural Revolution, and no one knows exactly how many of them were murdered or took their own lives.

Only non-intellectuals could be true revolutionaries, it was said. University teachers were suspected of being counter-revolutionary on principle. University graduates fared little better. Only freshmen could lay claim to purity and innocence. The less a student knew, the better, and one youthful opponent of the examination system was widely acclaimed as a hero for handing in a blank sheet of paper. Intellectuals were branded as national parasites and members of 'the stinking ninth category'.

But Mao and the ultra-leftists failed to destroy the intellectuals as a class. On the contrary, they reinforced their class consciousness and welded them together more firmly. Even in the throes of persecution, intellectuals continued to forgather and debate political issues. Alienated from the Party by the Hundred Flowers campaign and the Cultural Revolution, they remain sceptical of the assurances that have since been given them. At the outset of the Cultural Revolution, Mao declared that socialism was most readily accepted by technicians and scientists, in that order, but that those devoted to the humanities were the least amenable of all. He stated on another occasion that the proletariat must produce its own intelligentsia. He failed to reconcile the intelligentsia and the socialist system. In China, as in other socialist countries, intellectuals tend to be unenthusiastic conformists – fellow travellers as opposed to prime movers.

A hundred years ago, Chinese political reformers belonging to the so-called Yangwu movement planned to acquire technological and scientific know-how from the West without disrupting China's Confucian scale of values and social system. The movement soon came to grief because its aims were irreconcilable.

Today, the same difficulty besets those who advocate modernization but insist that nothing must be allowed to impair the Marxist-Leninist scale of values and social order, both of which have their origins in the nineteenth century. Theirs is the problem of the swimmer who hates getting wet.

Some voices in the Party can be heard to sponsor scientific and technological training while simultaneously demanding that the humanities be strictly controlled and forced into the Marxist-Leninist mould. One needs no crystal ball to predict that this policy, too, will fail, because the arts and sciences require parallel development and mutual enrichment.

The Party is making manifold efforts to woo intellectuals. It realizes that China cannot be modernized without their full co-operation, because few old revolutionaries are equal to new and unfamiliar tasks. Being patriotic, China's intellectuals do not withhold their co-operation, but they keep their distance and remain wary.

Yet political awareness and a sense of political responsibility are the very hallmarks of the Chinese intelligentsia, not the proletariat, wherever that elusive class may be found in the People's Republic. Chinese intellectuals still preserve the belief that each is responsible for 'all-under-heaven'. They are concerned for the welfare of all, not just of their particular class. To them, the state is not an alien thing to be shunned or opposed on principle, after the manner of many West European intellectuals, but a challenge they feel competent to meet. Instead of regarding the politician's trade as suspect, they consider it appropriate to themselves because it makes the highest possible demands on people; not on their intelligence alone, but on their sense of responsibility, their capacity for acting sensibly, dealing with others, influencing them, and caring for them. No material concessions, no privileges or honours, will persuade intellectuals to co-operate wholeheartedly in attaining the Party's political and economic objectives if they are denied a share in defining those objectives and mapping out the routes that lead to them. After all, it was *they* who ruled the empire for two thousand years, not revolutionaries or conquerors.

'You can conquer an empire on horseback but not govern it,' advisers told Liu Bang, the peasant who became the first Emperor of the Han dynasty. The modern equivalent of the same advice might be, 'You can establish a proletarian dictatorship with revolutionaries' fists, but you cannot govern and modernize a country without intellectuals' brains.'

The human spirit cannot be tamed. Its outward manifestations can be curbed, however, and there must be some Party functionaries eager to renew the campaign against scholars and writers who give vent to criticism. Mao himself set the pattern in this respect. Critics whose arguments he found potent and dangerous were simply proclaimed enemies of the people, classified as counter-revolutionaries, and 'subjected to struggle'.

'It is a crime to permit counter-revolutionaries to say all they please,' Mao declared. 'It is, on the other hand, legitimate to employ dictatorship against them. That is precisely our system.'

Brute force is the most convenient way of dealing with criticism, at least in the short term. Although it would be wiser and more profitable for the Party to debate with its critics, older functionaries find it hard to grasp that revolutionary spirit alone is not enough, and that China can solve her problems only in alliance with the intelligentsia. Many of them persist in their fear of intellectuals because the latter fail to reverence Party decisions and the founding fathers of Marxism, and because scientists prefer to acknowledge the dictatorship of facts rather than that of the Party.

In 1978, the Deng-inspired article on theory and practice stated that theories were not eternal or immutable truths, and that Marxism-Leninism should not be 'worshipped like a religious dogma'. Nine months later, Deng himself proclaimed that Marxism-Leninism-Maozedongideas were inviolable. It seems clear that socialism cannot dispense with dogmas and believers.

Intellectuals, or at least the scientists among them, are not the strongest of believers. The majority of scientific advances occur when existing theories or articles of faith are questioned and replaced with new ones.

Why Chinese Children Don't Suck Their Thumbs

Otto was back in Peking with Hildegard, his constant companion. We sat in the library and talked, as usual, of this and that.

'Why don't Chinese children suck their thumbs?' demanded Otto.

'Not that again!' Hildegard turned to us with a look of martyrdom. 'He's been asking everyone the same question, ever since we took off from Shanghai this morning.'

'Sure,' said Otto, 'and nobody knows the answer.'

'Because it's a silly question,' Hildegard said crisply. 'Of course Chinese children suck their thumbs. *You* wouldn't know because their parents don't take them to bars and restaurants.'

'They take them to theatres and the opera.'

'Yes, and the youngsters sit there transfixed, but they suck their thumbs on the way home. All children go through an oral phase. It's universal – scientists proved that years ago.'

'You call psychology a science?' asked Otto.

Franz had a positive contribution to make. She'd once seen a Chinese baby sucking its thumb, albeit rather half-heartedly, while dozing in a day nursery at Changsha. Not only its thumb, she added, but the tip of its blanket as well.

'I believe you,' said Otto, 'but that's not the point. It's natural for a baby to do it, but Chinese babies kick the habit very young. Today, while we were waiting for our flight to be called, there were two Chinese children – maybe four and five years old – sitting on the bench beside us with their mother. The girl was cuddling a rag doll, the boy kept his hands in his lap. They didn't move a muscle, but they took in everything that was going on around them. Then along came two couples, one German and one American, with a pair of kids apiece. The parents parked themselves on the benches behind us, but the four youngsters went racing around like dervishes.'

'Little pests,' said Hildegard, who likes children as a rule.

'It wasn't till they'd knocked a bonsai pine off its stand and an attendant came to sweep up the bits that their parents called them to heel. Sit down and shut up a minute, they were told. So they did – for a minute. One of the German kids stuck its thumb in its mouth. One of the American kids followed suit, and there they both sat, lost to the world and sucking away happily. The other two whined and fidgeted. How come Chinese children sit still when ours can't?'

I recalled that a team of American child psychologists had been struck by the same phenomenon when they toured China a few years back. They'd published their findings in a book. [1]

Otto asked how they had explained the behavioural differences between Chinese and Western children.

'They couldn't. All they established was that Chinese babies behave like American babies for the first few months. Then, very early on, a change sets in. They're quieter and not so restless. They adapt to society quicker. They're less aggressive and hit each other less often than our children do. They don't go smashing up each other's toys. The Americans only once saw a child pushed over deliberately. On that occasion, one kindergarten teacher consoled the victim while another sent the culprit to pat the dust off his pants and clean him up.'

Hildegard wanted to know if Chinese parents beat their children.

'Of course they do, sometimes,' Otto said, 'but the Party frowns on corporal punishment. Parents are urged to rear their offspring in the spirit of Mao. If they're naughty, they must be told that the Great Chairman would have condemned their behaviour, or that Lei Feng, the communist paragon, wouldn't have acted that way. Once upon a time, it wasn't unheard-of for parents to beat a disobedient child to death. Party

[1] William Kessen, *Childhood in China* (Yale University Press, 1976).

propaganda has certainly done some good. Children are beaten less often, but ingrained habits can't be stamped out overnight.'

'What if a child really acts up?' asked Hildegard. 'What does a Chinese kindergarten teacher do if her pupils behave like those Western kids at Shanghai airport?'

'She makes them play communal games. Buses, for instance, with everyone taking a different part – driver, conductor, passengers, et cetera – or kitchens, with one child playing cook, another slicing vegetables, others washing up. It's an early lesson in the virtues of communal co-operation.'

Franz said she'd always been amazed at the peace that reigned in Chinese classrooms. 'The pupils never fidget, never whisper or interrupt their teacher. They sit up straight for an hour at a time with their arms neatly folded behind their backs. If a child puts his hand up to ask a question and forgets to fold his arms again, the teacher corrects him as he passes by – without a word. It isn't that the youngsters look regimented or cowed. They're attentive, that's all.'

'The Americans remarked on that too,' I said. 'They were also struck by what went on in playgrounds. If children got a bit too rowdy, a teacher would step in and calm them down, but not by telling them off or dishing out punishments. My own visits to schools in this country have never left me with the impression that teachers make children feel they're imposing their will on them. Instead, they encourage them not to harm their class-mates' interests or break the rules of the school community. That gives them an early awareness of the need to fit in and show consideration for others. We used to learn that ourselves in the old days. From many points of view, my classmates taught me more and knocked more sense into me than any teacher ever did. You don't learn social behaviour by attending lectures on the subject, you learn it in a community.'

Otto approved. 'In the old China,' he said, 'when the individual was subordinated to the clan or extended family, he must have received an even tougher education in community spirit.'

Franz said, 'You surprise me, Otto. All this high-flown bunkum about restricting your actions to what is socially correct and in keeping with the unwritten laws of society! Paragons like Lei Feng – are *they* the aim of Chinese education? The newspapers have held him up as an example until his very name has become an emetic: Lei Feng, the model soldier who not only oozed nobility and civic duty from every pore but kept a sus-piciously detailed record of his good deeds in his diary. He's the spit and image of those Confucian model sons whom earlier generations were urged to emulate. Well, Lei Feng and his predecessors all came out of a test tube. Look around at Chinese society today, and you're sometimes hard put to it to detect any community spirit at all.'

'Not all paragons are test-tube babies,' I objected mildly.

'And Chinese come in all shapes and sizes,' said Otto. 'They can be lone-wolfish, arrogant, boorish, tactless – anything you like. The essential point is that Chinese society condemns those qualities and doesn't condone them. Children who race around airport lounges and knock over bonsai pines make their parents lose face. Anyone who behaves badly brings disgrace on his family because they've failed to raise him properly. Even very little children are taught social conformity. "What would other children think of you? Would they poke fun at you?" '

Hildegard, who seemed dubious, recalled the Cultural Revolution. Hadn't children denounced their parents – hadn't they hounded and even murdered their teachers?

'That's the other side of the Chinese character,' Otto said. Some revolutions liquidate priests, others kill off feudal overlords or big land-owners. The Red Guards turned on their teachers, who'd tried to impress on them that it was good form to obey social conventions. Under the Red Guard code, failure to attack teachers would have been shameful.'

'A couple of years ago,' I said, 'we talked to two Chinese women who'd just been attending the National Women's Congress. The delegates passed a resolution to the effect that schools must tighten up their discipline and children be taught to respect their parents and teachers.'

'Yes,' said Franz, 'but you should hear what our friend Mrs Gu says about her son. He's rebellious, moody, spoilt, and hard to please. Sometimes, she says, he's quite insufferable.'

'Her son's an only child,' I explained to Hildegard.

'She asked me to get her a Western book on child psychology,' said Franz.

Otto squawked as if he'd been stuck with a pin. 'God forbid!' he said. 'If there's more community spirit in this country than there is back home, for all your eloquent exceptions, and if the Chinese have always re-discovered their old values in spite of rebellions, invasions, and Cultural Revolutions – it's only because they've never been afflicted with child psychologists.'

'Perhaps,' I said, 'but I suspect that Chinese education and Chinese society will undergo a whole lot of changes if the one-child family really takes hold. When it comes to educational theory, the Chinese may be compelled to take a leaf out of our book.'

Otto, the old Confucian, groaned. 'An apocalyptic vision,' was all he said.

The Temple of Heaven

Confronted by perfection, the eye cannot but rejoice that all is just as it is. Any inclination to change some part of it would at once be corrected by the eye, because any change would entail a loss of perfection.

The Forbidden City is not perfect in that sense. Goethe would have called it incommensurable or incalculable. Impossible to take in all at once, it can be apprehended only as a composite of separate views. The Temple of Heaven, on the other hand, presents its full perfection to the beholder at a glance.

It was my last day in Peking and my last in the Foreign Service. Sometimes in previous years, when at odds with the world, I had refreshed my soul with a visit to the Temple of Heaven. The very sight of it was like an infusion of serenity and tranquillity.

I always approached it from the south – the prescribed route. Its beauty is lost on those who approach it from the north, via the grove of ancient thujas beneath its perimeter wall. The route to take is that used by the emperor when going there at the New Year Festival to entreat the confidence of Heaven, which mattered as much to him as the confidence of his people.

Even in the bustle and excitement of our very last day, I had set aside time for a final visit. Lao Zhou, who drove me to the temple precinct, had grown no slimmer in the past few years. He looked more than ever like a Buddha, if only in physical circumference.

'Take care,' Sister Anna had adjured me forty-four years ago, when I was lodging free of charge at the German hospital. 'You'll be passing through the Tianqiao quarter. It's always swarming with riff-raff – beggars, thieves, jugglers, acrobats. I'd better call a rickshaw.' Rather than spend my precious money on a rickshaw, I persuaded her to tell me the way and walked there instead.

Part of the balustrade around the Altar of Heaven had been missing in those days, and grass sprouted from between the blue pantiles of the temple itself, as it did from so many temple and palace roofs in Peking. The window panes of the Temple of Heaven were smashed and the doors nailed up, but it was possible to peer in and see dusty planks, scaffolding poles, and building materials. The beams supporting the lowest roof, which were rotten, sagged a little. The paint was peeling off them, and the gilded boss surmounting the topmost roof stood slightly askew.

Yongle, the great Ming Emperor who transferred his imperial seat from Nanking to Peking, not only laid out the Forbidden City and built himself a magnificent tomb, but commissioned the Temple and Altar of Heaven as well. The thujas in the grounds below date from his reign, or over five hundred years ago, but the temple is not exactly as it was – not, at any rate, by our strict Western standards. Struck by lightning at the end of the last century, it was burned to the ground. This highly inauspicious sign said little for the virtues of the reigning Son of Heaven.

Something still worse had occurred in 1820, when Heaven, not content with admonitory omens, took the bull by the horns and struck down Emperor Jiaqing himself with a thunderbolt. Nothing could explain *that* away, for it proved that Heaven had ceased to think him worthy of imperial office.

When the Temple of Heaven burned down, however, the imperial authorities did their best to dispel any such unwelcome suspicions. Doubtless at the instance of Empress Dowager Cixi, the story was put about that a centipede had scaled the temple's gilded boss in an audacious attempt to reach Heaven. Enraged by its effrontery, Heaven had unleashed a thunderbolt which not only dispatched the megalomaniac insect but destroyed the temple as well.

Everyone realized that the Emperor's ministers had concocted this story because they needed some natural and convincing explanation that would dissuade people from interpreting the fire as a pointer to the Emperor's vices and an evil omen for the empire as a whole. Nevertheless, the Temple of Heaven was promptly rebuilt, column by column and timber by timber, exactly as it had been in the reign of Emperor Yongle. In Chinese terms, therefore, it was and still is the same temple.

On my first visit, I had had the thuja grove and temple all to myself. No jugglers, beggars, thieves, acrobats, or other riff-raff had pestered me on my way through Tianqiao, the district of the Bridge of Heaven. All I saw was a silent throng, and, as I drew nearer, a story-teller perched on a stool in their midst. The people around him were listening enthralled. He saw me coming; they did not. Whether or not he had just been spinning them some grisly yarn about a long-nosed demon with yellow hair and grey eyes, he suddenly pointed in my direction. Everyone swung round, and it would have been hard to say who was more scared: his audience, who found themselves confronted by a real, live, yellow-haired demon, or I myself, whom they stared at fixedly in a far from amiable fashion. As for the story-teller on his stool, he slapped his thigh and laughed till the tears ran down his cheeks.

Today I was driven to the temple by Lao Zhou. The story-tellers, jugglers, and acrobats were no more. Admission was by ticket, and a children's carousel had been installed in the thuja grove.

Now as then, I began by visiting the *Altar* of Heaven. Three concentric marble balustrades enclose the altar terrace, which itself is circular and approached by four flights of white marble steps that narrow as they ascend. The terrace is open to the sky, and its round marble expanse is echoed by the curvature of the horizon that divides the earth – the plain of Peking – from the lofty heavens above. Only to the west and north-west is the skyline broken by the Fragrant Hills, whose distant contours emerge softly from the haze. But that I could only remember, not see in reality. As I stood on the altar terrace now, my view was obscured by a nearby mound of rubble taken from the erstwhile city wall, and Peking's skyline was pierced on all sides by a bristling array of factory chimneys.

I made my way to the centre of the terrace. This was where, at the Winter Solstice, the Emperor made solemn sacrifice and offered up simple, time-honoured oblations of beef broth, boiled grain, fish, cakes, preserved vegetables, incense, and silk as blue as the sky above.

The Son of Heaven was escorted on these occasions by his household – no more than a thousand-odd men including dignitaries, eunuchs, and bodyguards. The women of the palace stayed at home because their presence would have been offensive to Heaven. The *profanum vulgus*, too, were excluded. They remained outside the sanctuary and were never permitted to see the altar or temple.

I stood on the innermost marble slab where the Emperor used to kneel at sacrifice and render an account of the foregoing year to Heaven.

China being the Middle Kingdom, the Chinese regarded this stone as the centre of the world in the same way as Jews regarded the Temple at Jerusalem, Greeks the Omphalos at Delphi, Romans the Lapis Niger in the Forum, and Christians – for many centuries – St Peter's at Rome.

We tend to smile at their common belief that the centre of the world was theirs, but our smile is a trifle wistful. We ourselves, who lost our focal point a long time ago, have no real idea of where we are going or even of where we want to go. We take things as they come, consoling ourselves with the thought that all has gone well enough so far.

When the Emperor of China knelt on this stone and prayed, he felt himself to be alone with Heaven despite the presence of so many courtiers and officiants. I felt the same each time I stood there, though I never, of course, presumed to communicate with Heaven.

Celestial communication was the Emperor's prerogative, which is why the Chinese were so shocked when Christians came to the Middle Kingdom and proclaimed that anyone could pray to Heaven. This time, I stationed myself on the central slab and said something quite inoffensive like 'Here I stand at the centre of the world. Can you hear me?'

The words seemed to issue from the ground and soar skywards. As ever, I had an odd sense of being utterly alone and inaudible to another living soul.

Tourist guides encourage their charges to try this acoustic phenomenon for themselves. Many visitors laugh when they stand on the stone and call out some piece of nonsense, but most of them are quick to descend and rejoin their friends, looking sheepish and faintly uneasy.

It is, of course, one of those acoustic tricks beloved of the Chinese. Scientists would have little difficulty in explaining it, but not to the likes of one who, like me, enjoys surrendering to its spell. After all, where else in the world can you be alone with Heaven, and where else can your voice scale its heights from the bowels of the earth?

I left the stone and threaded my way through a party of tourists. Their guide was just explaining the numerical symbolism of the stone slabs and balustrades, lecturing them on *yin* and *yang* and the significance of the square and circle, those symbols of earth and sky. It was all going in one ear and out the other.

Still following the route trodden by the emperors of old, and ignoring the big mound of rubble thrown up on my left by a barbarous municipal administration, I headed for the Temple of Heaven itself. Elevated and paved with marble, the processional route is quite long, and one eminent art historian has described this complex as the most spacious sacrificial precinct ever built by man.

My view of the temple was still obscured by the lofty gatehouse. A little patience, a few more steps through the gloomy gateway and out into the rectangular courtyard, and the temple stood before me once more in all its perfection.

Like the altar, the temple is enclosed by three concentric marble balustrades and its terrace approached by way of four flights of steps, one at each of the cardinal points. In the centre of the terrace stands the temple itself, the Hall of Annual Prayer.

It is a circular building with an outer wall segmented by engaged timber columns. These support the lowest of the three circular roofs. Superimposed on this, above an intervening drum, is a second roof of smaller diameter. Then comes another drum and the third or topmost roof, whose diameter is smaller still. At the very summit stands the gilded boss by way of which, according to the imperial court, the sacrilegious centipede aspired to reach the firmament.

The three white marble balustrades and three blue roofs progressively diminish in diameter as they ascend from one level to the next, but the upper drum is taller than the lower and the topmost roof taller and far more perceptibly curved than the two below it. Try altering these proportions in your mind's eye, and the building doesn't work – everything falls apart. Just as the Parthenon and the Taj Mahal defy alteration, so the upper drum *must* be taller or the third and topmost roof would become aridly repetitive. Instead of soaring skyward, it would weigh the whole building down. Its greater elevation and more pronounced curvature renders it light – not excessively light, not airy or frivolous, but natural and graceful.

The triad of marble balustrades and the triad of roofs overhead must be seen and 'heard' together. The balustrades and steps ascend to the terrace, at whose centre the temple stands like some precious solitaire presented to the sky.

Mounted in front of the upper drum on the temple's south side, immediately above the entrance, is a large plaque with a gilded frame. This disrupts the roofs' harmonic progression, but try removing *that* disruptive feature in your mind's eye and the melody becomes cloying. Besides, the plaque must be there for tradition and sanctity's sake. Inscribed in gold on a blue ground are the characters that signify 'Hall of the Annual Prayer', also translatable as 'Hall of the Harvest Prayer'.

It goes without saying that the roofs of such a building could not tolerate turrets, statuary, mythical beasts, or similar furbelows. These are suitably accommodated on ancillary buildings in the temple courtyard.

The walls, columns, and roof supports are all made of timber. The ground-floor wall is painted reddish brown and the drums are adorned with gold and green designs. The glazed roof tiles are a deep blue that sometimes, depending on the quality of the light, becomes faintly tinged with violet. As for the white marble balustrades, they dazzle the eye in the midday sun. That is how I should like to describe them now, for that is how I so often saw them.

But not, alas, today. Yesterday's dust storm had deposited a dull yellow film on the Prussian blue tiles, and the marble, too, was yellowish and far from dazzling. Thus the temple would remain till spring or early summer, when the first rains washed it clean once more. Then, perhaps, I would return.

I paused for one more look. Could the temple really be so small? All the guide books put its height at a mere hundred feet, which would enable it to fit with ease into the cathedral naves at Cologne and Strasbourg, not to mention Chartres. And yet, despite the absence of columns like thunderous chords from some celestial organ, of mighty arches, lofty vaults, and soaring pilasters, it gives an impression of grandeur.

But it leaves the beholder room to breathe and contemplate. The sight of it is uplifting rather than oppressive and overwhelming. Its lines are austere and majestic – deliberately aloof, yet serene and beautiful.

The Temple of Heaven is at peace with itself, as though symbolizing the Emperor's divine duty to keep Heaven and earth in harmony through the exercise of personal virtue.

It was time to go – nearly one o'clock – and Lao Zhou might faint at the wheel unless we hurried back to the embassy, where his lunch was waiting.

In the gateway I turned and looked back. It stood there just as it had stood so many years ago, when I saw it for the very first time. It still rejoiced my eyes, and my eyes were no less receptive to its beauty.

All right, time to go!

Aerial Survey

1 February

Our plane had taken off from Peking's new airport runway. The country-side below us was brown. The city receded into the ochreous haze that had shrouded the plain since the last sandstorm. Still climbing, we banked before reaching the Western Hills and headed south-east.

Less than four years ago, I had presented my credentials. That night we stood on the embassy terrace with a party of Chinese and German guests. It was the Moon Festival, the fifteenth day of the eighth month of the old lunar calendar. The moon shone bright and full. 'Autumn is on the way,' said one of our Chinese visitors. He sounded depressed.

Meteorites had fallen from the sky. Earthquakes had killed hundreds of thousands of people. The Chinese leaders were divided and their Chairman had long since lost his grip on the reins. China stood on the brink of economic collapse. Intimidated by the Cultural Revolution, her inhabitants were fearful of the radicals and their commitment to the Chairman's avowed belief that revolution should be a never-ending process.

It was then, while we were standing on the terrace and gazing at the autumn moon, that Chairman Mao Zedong had breathed his last in Zhongnanhai Park.

Four weeks later, the radicals were arrested by Hua Guofeng. He did not take long to stabilize the leadership and readmit Deng Xiaoping to its ranks. The country remained calm. Ordinary Chinese welcomed the new course, which slowly but unmistakably diverged from Mao's and steered for objectives that promised a freer and easier existence – one that might even be free from arbitrary rule.

Stabilization, coupled with the apparently effortless introduction of change, must be accounted a major political achievement. Credit for it belongs primarily to Hua Guofeng and Deng Xiaoping, but it also testifies to the political maturity and common sense of the Chinese people.

They embarked on the new course in a spirit of optimism, encouraged by their revived hopes and new-found, though limited, freedoms to believe that all could be achieved with ease. They planned to turn China into a modern industrial state within twenty years, but they overestimated their resources yet again. Their goal will be attained only by another Long March, not another Great Leap Forward.

We had climbed above the haze and were heading for Shanghai.

And China – where is China heading? The country now has a thousand million inhabitants. Its population is increasing by fourteen million annually. The measures undertaken to curb this increase are harsh and impinge on every young couple. The birth-rate is slowly declining, but the transition to smaller families will bring about many changes in the Chinese outlook on life.

The Chinese are expecting fewer material hardships and a higher standard of living. They are frugal and modest in their demands, especially in the rural areas where eighty per cent of them live. They work hard, but only when hard work pays. They are not prepared to toil for the benefit of future generations, least of all when denied the chance to 'survive' as progenitors of large families.

The numbers of unemployed will rise still further. Social tensions, too, will increase as modernization progresses, as will regional tensions between developed and less developed areas.

Where China's planning authorities are concerned, the introduction of free market economy principles into their vast country's centrally controlled, planned economy is proving an exceptional problem. Given the lack of precedents to learn from, mistakes will be unavoidable. China's economic problems cannot be solved by the simple adoption of our own form of mixed economy. Her planners must proceed step by step, experimenting as they go. Their first task will be to rectify the errors of the past. It will take China perhaps a decade to establish a stable basis for industrialization. The prospects thereafter are good, provided her leaders consent to be guided by computerized facts and figures, however unpalatable. If those conditions are fulfilled, China will be able to construct a modern, efficient economy quite different from the ossified Soviet system, with its built-in wastage of labour and resources.

In terms of raw materials, China is one of the world's richest and most self-sufficient countries. Stocks and reserves of coal, her principal energy source, are immense. Her hydroelectric potential is almost untapped, and her oil reserves are also large – sufficient, at all events, to cover national requirements, though they still remain to be exploited.

Setbacks are inevitable on the road to a modern, developed economy, and setbacks necessitate corrections. The large and powerful class composed of middle-ranking officials may see these as confirmation of their sceptical approach to new ideas. Their inertia and immobility may even be such as to bog down economic reforms half-way.

Political development is under a similar threat. The article proclaiming practice the sole gauge of theoretical correctness was published in the summer of 1978. Theories, it announced, are not eternal truths, and there would be no more political or economic dogmatism. Since 1978, however, special sanctuaries have been re-established for socialism, proletarian dictatorship, Party primacy, and Marxism-Leninism-Maozedongideas. This is a grave sign of weakness. The leadership of the Party fears discussion of these 'four basic principles', though their discussion is essential to China's modernization. The country cannot be industrialized unless it opens its doors to the West, but access to the West will reinforce Chinese intellectuals' demands for greater freedom and wider political participation. Young people, in particular, will grow more restive. Their unrest can already be felt, and China's leaders will not for ever be able to ignore the demands of the intelligentsia and the younger generation.

Some members of the leadership are aware of this, but the Party as a whole is hesitant. Poised on the springboard, it dreads to take the plunge. It timidly clings to the four basic principles for fear that their abandonment may terminate its leading role. In reality, the Party could modernize China and create a thriving economy, *and* remain in power, if it regained public confidence by reforming itself from top to bottom. That, however, would entail removing many veteran functionaries from their cosy niches on grounds of incompetence, corruption, or simple superannuation. 'Heaven did not create the people for the ruler's sake,' declared Xunzi, one of China's greatest philosophers, 'but the ruler for the sake of the people.' There seem to be Party functionaries who have forgotten this.

They are afraid to debate the best means of modernizing the country because some simple soul might blurt out what everyone already knows: that the emperor's new clothes are non-existent and that the socialist experiment has been a universal failure. Why? Because socialism's grand design cannot be tailored to man's shortcomings, and because it is incapable of creating a New Man in its own image.

There are undoubtedly some among the leadership who advocate a return to time-honoured methods of repression because they feel that the path of radical reform presents too many dangers. It would always be possible to suppress political debate and maintain sanctuaries for unworkable ideas, but that, in turn, would mean abandoning any idea of participating in the scientific, technological, economic, and cultural development of the world.

Deng Xiaoping stated that the Party had forfeited public confidence and must regain it. That, in fact, is the central problem.

Confucius was once asked by his pupil Zigong to enumerate the principal functions of government. He listed them as follows: keeping people adequately fed, maintaining armed forces of adequate strength, and sustaining public confidence. What, asked Zigong, could a government most readily dispense with? Armed forces first, replied the Master, and then food, for everyone had to die sooner or later. If people did not trust their rulers, however, government was impossible.

'But Master,' the pupil went on, 'you've forgotten socialism, the dictatorship of the proletariat, the leading role of the Party, and Marxism-Leninism-Maozedongideas.'

'Not at all,' the Master replied with a smile. 'The four basic principles can be dispensed with most readily of all. Aren't they less important than national security and subsistence, and aren't there many nations in the world better off than our own despite their failure to apply the four basic principles?'

The first of the three foregoing paragraphs is a free translation from the *Analects* (XII, 7).

In domestic and economic policy, the People's Republic of China has always veered from one extreme to the other. Its leadership has never remained stable for very long. 'Line' and power struggles have been the rule rather than the exception. China is unlikely to become a stable country with a predictable long-term policy if her leaders continue to vacillate between extremes, and if positions of responsibility continue to be reshuffled by an oligarchy conferring in secret.

The Chinese leaders are chary of submitting practical problems or political appointments to public debate and decision. Not even the Party is allowed to debate them. The Central Committee, the Party Congress, and the National People's Congress, have nothing to do but rubber-stamp decisions already taken by senior members of the Politburo.

How can the Communist Party regain the people's trust when it doesn't trust the people an inch? They might, after all, voice opposition to socialism or, worse still, to the leading role of the Party itself – to the positions of power which many regard as hereditary fiefdoms, to the entrenchment of vested interests, to habitual abuses of power, to corruption in unsupervised corners of the country and crannies of the government edifice. To many functionaries, the preservation of all these things is far more important than the modernization of their country.

Hence the fear of true democracy and a multi-party system. Any democracy in which the people really have some say is maligned as a 'bourgeois' democracy. And yet, provided one or two basic socialist tenets – for example, state control of the means of production – were written into the Constitution, more than one party could exist even under China's present political system. There might, for instance, be a progressive socialist party committed to Deng Xiaoping's ideas, and a conservative, 'left-wing' socialist party loyal to the words and deeds of Mao Zedong. Chinese politicians would consider these notions utterly unrealistic, but only because they are unused to them or because, even with a socialist two-party system, free elections might pluck them from office.

Although the Chinese leaders have sanctioned a few democratic procedures in factories, local districts, and small municipalities, they doubtless feel that further democratization would be too risky. Freedom of speech would have to be permitted, and that might result in attacks on Party Headquarters and senior politicians. They may also fear that electoral campaigns and elections would have a destabilizing effect, heedless of the fact that the present system itself inhibits stability and promotes the power struggles and intrigues that have always been so disastrously endemic to Chinese history, both before and since the advent of the Communist Party. The system encourages extreme views of which the general public, if consulted, would assuredly disapprove. It also precludes a rational division of administrative authority because many politicians, who look upon their sphere of responsibility as a personal domain, devote more attention to interdepartmental disputes than they do to their official duties.

We had reached cruising height. Tea and pastries were being served. The plane droned steadily along. The sun was dazzling, the sky deep blue and, at this altitude, cloudless. *Tian xia* – 'that which is under heaven', or China, the Middle Kingdom – lay hidden in the murk far below.

Many things had improved in the past four years. Life in China was easier. The Party leaders posed as the people's 'father and mother', like the mandarins of old. Functionaries looked after the people in the belief that they knew what was good and bad for them, just as they also knew what was good for themselves. People enjoyed more legal security than before. Newspapers had become more readable and even printed indignant items of correspondence. Courageous journalists sometimes wrote courageous articles. Television programmes were more entertaining. TV news broadcasts included reports from foreign services. The Chinese could laugh and love again – both within limits, of course. They ventured cautiously out of their shells, spoke again and hoped again, but they still remained on their guard.

Although they had yet to recover from their experience of the Cultural Revolution, its horrors had ceased to weigh as heavily on the individual victim when he rose every morning. The recollection was not quite as painful, except perhaps at night. The Chinese people still lacked assurance. Many of them were haunted by a fear of fresh disasters to come. They were afraid.

Of what? They didn't know. Of what lay in store – of the future.

'If horses fear the reins of their harness, their master cannot ride in safety. If common folk fear the government, their ruler cannot be sure of his position. If horses fear the reins of their harness, the sole recourse is to soothe them. If common folk fear the government, the sole recourse is to pacify them.'

Thus wrote Xunzi over two thousand years ago.

If the Party wants to regain the people's trust, it must first allay their fears. But the Party itself is in doubt – still unsure of its way, still groping in the dark. Does it, in turn, fear the people?

'The ruler is the boat, the common folk the water. Water can support a boat, but it can also capsize it.'

Xunzi again.

The surface of the water is still comparatively calm. Although the Chinese people are waiting patiently, their patience is not inexhaustible. Young people, in particular, have already formed a consensus critical of the entire system. Their patience has dwindled since the Cultural Revolution. They are no longer prepared to adopt their elders' views sight unseen. Modern China, unlike the China of old, possesses a younger generation whose ideas and desires differ from those of their seniors.

The trauma of the Cultural Revolution has left the Chinese unresponsive to visionary ideas, political pipe-dreams, and woolly verbiage. Their ideas are realistic, but they hesitate to voice them. They are waiting for the Government to say which ideas are white and which black. Meanwhile, they reserve their innermost thoughts for their families or closest friends. Would they also entrust them to the ballot box?

They may have to learn to, but the Chinese learn fast. We can rest assured that, once relieved of fear and political pressure, the Chinese people would know how to use their democratic freedom and speedily dispose of the abuses that have grown up during decades of unbridled rule by a single political party.

But that is precisely the Party's nightmare. Having once shown the people a picture of a free, progressive society whose sole guide to action would be practice, not impracticable dogmas, it is now resurrecting the communist classics from Marx to Mao.

In short, the Party is doing what has always been done throughout China's history by those who feared the new and extolled the virtues of the old. Confucius spoke of the golden age of the Zhou dynasty, Xunzi of the Three Wise Emperors, and the Confucians obstructed progress for two thousand years by quoting from the Master and his works.

The authorities are now reviving traditional Chinese painting and discouraging artists from experimenting with new forms. Writers, too, are warned against conducting 'formalistic experiments' and attacked if they fail to present a rosy picture of life today – attacked if, instead of describing its alleviations, they write of the fear deep inside people, their uncertainty and confusion, and the dishonesty rampant in public life. The Party presumes to know the difference between black and white, healthy and unhealthy, in art and literature. It knows nothing of the kind, of course, and all that it has so far enunciated in the way of advice and criticism is arrant nonsense.

Writers' advice on political matters is generally not much better. When they write of people and of everyday life, however, politicians would do well to heed them.

In very early times, Chinese of both sexes used to while away the winter months by singing together. If they had complaints to make, they expressed them in song. In the first month of the year, before the spring ploughing, the government employed a number of old men and women to tour the country. They would stand at the roadside, ringing bells with wooden clappers, and record the poems and ditties composed by common folk. Once these had been arranged according to style and rhythm by the Grand Master of Music, they were submitted to the Emperor. 'And so, without leaving his palace, the Emperor heard all the views and complaints of his people.' We owe this information to *Liji*, a record of rites and customs compiled over two thousand years ago.

If writers of today announce that the emperor is naked – that something painted white by the Party is black beneath, or dead, or a stench in the nostrils – the Party castigates them for being 'pessimistic'. Where are the positive things in your writings? Constructive criticism? Hope? Love of socialism? Literature is supposed to 'edify'. Such was the Confucian view, and such is that of the Party's authorized literary critics. This is why they ascribe greater literary merit to exemplary tales about the 'dutiful children' of long ago, or to the diaries of the paragon Lei Feng, than to pornographic slices of life like the novel *Kin Ping Meh*. Writers are expected to give the people courage, even if their political leaders lack the courage to embark on radical measures.

Not all their leaders, of course. Deng Xiaoping can scarcely be accused of cowardice, but he has had to contend with a whole class of functionaries and their vested interests. Besides, where freedom of speech and the arts are concerned, his views differ little from theirs. He spent some years in France as a young man, but that was long ago. Deng was moulded by the Communist Party and reared in its blinkered attitudes. He cannot shake them off at this late stage.

Nevertheless, many people believe in the possibility of far-reaching change, not as a consequence of revolutionary decisions, but in the old and imperceptible Chinese manner; not steady change devoid of ups and downs and vacillations, but a general advance in the right direction. This is possible, perhaps, but not certain. For the time being, things will probably maintain their slow uphill progress, but will that progress be sufficient to prevent many new-found hopes from fading? Will the tensions latent in the Chinese people, and especially in the younger generation, gain strength and erupt once more?

We were flying over a bend in the Yangtze, visible through the haze as a luminous ribbon of red and gold. Far below, we could just make out its associated network of canals and dikes.

Will China's leaders become more self-assured? Will they allow her people to develop their gifts in a modern world, on the road to modern nationhood?

Calls for guaranteed human rights can now be heard in China, as elsewhere. The cry will grow louder. On the other hand, the Chinese have a stronger awareness of human obligations. Although self-interest and personal advantage are among their primary incentives, as they are with us, these are considerably more restricted by a sense of social responsibility and the readiness of the individual to subordinate himself and his personal desires to the welfare of the community – of the family, neigh-bourhood, or unit. He may not always do this voluntarily, but the burden of social obligations weighs less heavily on his shoulders. He, too, aspires to own private property, but he is readier to share it with others.

In China, self-fulfilment never occurs in a social vacuum. The individual 'fulfils' himself or develops his personality only in the service of society and as a member of some community. There is little or no support in China, even among individualistic artists, for the extreme liberalism that ignores the needs of others, for universal permissiveness, for a refusal to adapt to society and 'drop out'. It was different in earlier times, when even emperors 'dropped out' and became hermits, but that was not Confucian – not the general rule. In theory, if not always in practice, the common weal still ranks higher in China than individual freedom.[1]

Many of these old and traditional ideas render the Chinese more modern-minded and better equipped to meet the future than ourselves, for restrictions on individual freedom and regard for social obligations are unavoidable in a cramped and increasingly integrated world.

All things considered, the Chinese have a chance of persevering in their new Long March and attaining their goal. A chance, but no more than that.

Beneath us lay a stretch of water. It could only be Lake Tai, with its attendant cities Wuxi and Suzhou. Ahead and to our right loomed the dome of haze that hung over Shanghai. We did not land there, but flew on east towards the sea.

In their encounter with the spirit of the West, its science and technology, will the Chinese throw their traditional values overboard? Will they embrace and adopt everything, good and bad, that emanates from the West? This is a long-standing Chinese fear – a century old or more – but I find it exaggerated. Even if China's leaders flung her doors wide enough to admit everything without exception – even if the city down there in the haze were reinhabited by its old soul or a close relative – the spirit of China herself has never dwelt in cities, always in the countryside. There, even in an age of technology and world-wide cultural assimilation, it would survive for a long time to come.

A few traditions may wither. Traditions have always withered through-out history, but China is rich in them. The West would do well to heed this wealth and acquire as much of it as possible, before it is hidden

[1] The Chinese language did not even have a word for 'freedom' until Western missionaries of the late nineteenth century chose the archaic word *ziyou* (literally 'let yourself go') to convey the notion of liberty. But *ziyou* always had a negative, faintly anarchistic ring to Chinese ears.

beneath a layer of jetsam from all over the world. Many Western nations could learn a great deal, especially about the questions of personal and social coexistence that plague us so sorely.

We were flying over the Yangtze estuary, so wide that it looked like a bay. The river water could still be distinguished, far out to sea, as a spreading yellow stain. Behind us, China merged with the horizon.

I was taking my leave and hanging up my official hat. I found it easier than I expected. I was indulging in a luxury I'd always denied myself and peering through the prophet's telescope. Even then, however, I failed to discern which route the Chinese would take.

The only certainty is that an industrialized and politically united China inhabited by over a thousand million people would affect the world to a degree that far exceeds our present imaginings. China might become a power which, even in the course of development, would change the face of the world and redirect its commercial traffic. The combined strength of China, Japan, South Korea, Taiwan, Hong Kong, and the rapidly emerging ASEAN states, might be such as to transfer the world's economic and political centre of gravity to the Pacific and the Far East, many thousands of miles from Western Europe, whose interminable debates at Brussels and Strasbourg would prove that it had lost the capacity for grand designs. Meanwhile, the Soviet Union would continue its listless labours on an edifice whose ground-plan, laid out a generation ago, is far too big, and whose foundations are far too weak to support it.

It is far from certain that China will take the steep, uphill road, but we cannot discount the possibility. Visions of the power accruing to an industrialized and politically powerful China are not invariably welcome, even to those who deride the Yellow Peril syndrome. Moscow, one suspects, must find such visions peculiarly distasteful.

No inexperienced prophet can make any hard-and-fast predictions about the direction of Chinese policy in the far distant future. He can, however, draw certain inferences from China's past history and traditional ideas.

China has never possessed a missionary idea like Islam or Christendom or, in the secular sphere, Panslavism. The Chinese never objected if barbarians across their borders aspired to cure their crudity by partaking of the Chinese ethos. If that was what they wanted, however, they had to move to the Middle Kingdom and acquire refinement there. It was not thought necessary to conquer foreign countries and introduce them to the blessings of civilization by force of arms. The Chinese are the only civilized nation to have condemned wars of conquest for over two thousand years, although some of their emperors could not resist the temptation to make war on their neighbours.

Prophecies require no vindication, just as historical precedents yield no incontrovertible proof. We also know that people in the mass can be so captivated by some novel idea, however absurd, or so swayed by some magnetic personality that a nation will be induced, for a limited period, to act at variance with its history and traditional principles. However, this reservation applies to any speculative pronouncement that ventures far into the future.

I believe that, thanks to the experiences they underwent during the latter decades of Mao's life, the Chinese people have acquired long-term immunity against Utopian ideas and the concept of permanent revolution. They want peace and quiet in their vicinity, and, within their own borders, stability, security under the law, and the chance to construct a politically and economically modern state.

Acknowledgements

Acknowledgements

This book was not written for the benefit of sinologists. I have therefore refrained from overloading it with footnotes and bibliographical references. Instead, I shall confine myself to a few general remarks on the English-language books I consulted most often.

Excerpts from classical Chinese texts (Confucius, Mencius, *The Book of Songs*, *The Book of Documents*, *The Doctrine of the Mean*) are based on James Legge's *The Chinese Classics*, a bilingual work in five volumes (Oxford University Press, 1893; reprinted Hong Kong, 1970). Quotations from Confucius are restricted to the *Analects* (*Lun Yü*), the most reliable source of his teachings.

Excerpts from works by, or attributed to, the philosophers Xunzi, Han Feizi, and Shang Yang have been freely adapted from the English versions by H. H. Dubs, W. K. Liao, and J. J. L. Duyvendak. In the case of Sima Qian, my quotations are based on *Selections from Records of the Historian*, translated by Yang Hsien-yi and Gladys Yang (Peking, 1979).

General works frequently consulted:

Fung Yu-Lan, *A History of Chinese Philosophy*, translated by Derk Bodde (Princeton, 1952), Vol. I.

Kung-chuan Hsiao, *A History of Chinese Political Thought*, translated by F. W. Mote (Princeton, 1979), Vol. I.

J. O. P. Bland and E. Backhouse, *Annals and Memoirs of the Court of Peking* (London, 1914).

John A. Harrison, *The Chinese Empire* (New York/London, 1972).

On China's attitude to the outside world:

John K. Fairbank (ed.), 'The Chinese World Order', *Harvard East Asian Series, No. 32* (Cambridge (Mass.), 1968).

Ssu-yü and John K. Fairbank, *China's Response to the West: A Documentary Survey* (Cambridge (Mass.), 1979).

On China's recent history:

Edgar Snow, *Red Star over China*, revised and enlarged edition (New York, 1978).

Stuart Schramm, *Mao Tse-tung* (London, 1977).

John Bryan Starr, *Continuing the Revolution: The Political Thought of Mao* (Princeton, 1979).

Chi Hsin (pseudonym), *Teng Hsiao-ping: A Political Biography* (Hong Kong, 1978).

Raymond Lotta (ed.), *And Mao Makes 5: Mao Tsetung's Last Great Battle* (documentary compilation) (Chicago, 1978).

Index

Index

Drozdyenko, Vassily, Soviet Ambassador to Romania, 164

and adviser to the Chinese Central Planning Authorities, 318

Eisenhower, Dwight D., 186

Fack, Fritz Ullrich, co-editor of *Frankfurter Allgemeine*, 307
Fang Yi, Deputy Premier, 248, 341
Fenn, Nick, British Chargé d'Affaires, 83, 84
Fengshui, science of wind and water, 58–9
Filbinger, Hans, Premier of Baden-Württemburg, 132, 134
Fischer-Dieskau, Thomas, economic counsellor, 239
Forbidden City, the, 51, 67–9, 88, 89, 352
Frank, Paul, Undersecretary of State in Bonn, 19–20
Fraser, John, American journalist and author, 293–5, 300

Gang of Four, the, 50, 82, 83–4, 85–6, 91, 94, 95, 99–102, 103, 107, 108, 109, 111, 117, 118–9, 123–5, 126, 131, 133, 134, 135, 138, 166, 176, 213, 214–15, 228, 234, 249, 260, 281, 289, 290, 292, 308, 339 *and see* Jiang Qing, Zhang Chunqiao, Wang Hungwen, Yao Wenyuan
Gao Chang, abandoned city in Xinjiang Province, 312–3
Genscher, Hans Dietrich, Foreign Minister in Bonn, 32
George III, King, 81
Gerson, J. H. C., British Embassy foreign policy specialist, 84
Golmud (Go-erh-mu), industrial town in Tibet, 270
Gong Peng, first wife of Qiao Guanhua, 118
Grass, Günter, 227–8, 298
Gromyko, Andrei A., 117
Guilin, in Guangxi Province, 92–3, 96
Gu Mu, Vice-Premier, 307
Gutowski, Armin, German economist

Hata Men, Peking, 38–40
Hauswedell, Peter Christian, internal affairs adviser, 175, 177–8, 224, 294
Hegel, G. W. F., 13, 38, 70, 215
He Long, Marshal, 236
He Zizhen, second wife of Mao Zedong, 65, 99, 102, 338
Hitler, Adolf, 93, 279
Höfer, Hans Jürgen, dpa correspondent, 47, 48, 75, 88–90
Hong Kong, 18, 19, 21, 179–80, 308
Hua Guofeng, 71–3, 76, 78, 82, 85, 91, 94, 99–101, 106, 117, 125–6, 129, 131, 132–4, 135, 177–8, 183, 186, 210, 225, 261, 268, 282, 287, 289, 290, 296, 310, 320–6, 339, 340, 357–8
Huang Hua, Foreign Minister, 117, 326
Huang Yungyü, painter, 283
Hu Feng, literary critic, 345
Humin, Otto, 58–64, 68–70, 76, 203–9, 348–51
Hung Xiuquan, leader of Taiping Rebellion, 96–7
Hu Shih, philosopher and literary reformer, 345
Hwa, village near Canton and site of beginning of Taiping Rebellion, 96–7

Ichun, town in Jiangxi Province, 146, 151

Jade Phoenix *see* Zhang Yufeng
Jiang Nanxiang, Minister of Education, 232
Jiang Qing, 50, 51, 54, 65, 70, 71–3, 76, 82, 84, 85–87, 99–106, 108, 111, 117, 118, 123, 151, 154–5, 184, 205, 212, 264, 267, 310, 338–9 *and see* Gang of Four, the

Kang Sheng, Party leader, 150, 151
Kangxi, Emperor, 143–4, 227, 317, 329

Robert C. Christopher
The Japanese Mind £2.95
the Goliath explained

A thought-provoking book that lays bare Japan's remarkable life since the Second World War. A distinguished American journalist explains all those aspects Westerners find hard to understand — the racial and cultural homogeneity, the emphasis on group effort, the passionate desire for achievement. He examines corporate giants and backyard businesses, the role of the robot, women at work, education, entertainment and the family.

'A brilliant account of how Japan works and thinks' RONALD STEEL

'One of the most comprehensive studies to appear' NEWSWEEK

Roland Huntford
Scott and Amundsen £3.95
the race to the South Pole

'This huge and gripping book's primary aim is to re-examine every detail of the great race for the South Pole between British and Norwegian teams that took place in 1911–12. But in the course of retelling the saga, Roland Huntford demolishes a legend. Amundsen reached the Pole on December 15 and returned safely. Scott reached it on January 17 but never came back ... In death Scott became immortal. Now his reputation and character are torn to shreds' SUNDAY TELEGRAPH

'For more than sixty years the story of Scott of the Antarctic has been one of our great national legends. Mr Huntford has at last shown Scott plain ... The plaster saint has been smashed for ever' CHRISTOPHER BOOKER, SPECTATOR

'A masterly achievement' GENERAL SIR JOHN HACKETT, OBSERVER

Larry Gurwin
The Calvi Affair £2.95
death of a banker

The discovery of the hanging body of banker Roberto Calvi under Blackfriars Bridge in June 1982 made headline news. The mystery was heightened by the collapse of his Banco Ambrosiano, revealing a twisted net of intrigue. Journalist Gurwin has produced a thrilling account of Calvi's financial and political wheelings and dealings, his involvement with the notorious masonic lodge P2 and links with the Vatican Bank.

'Takes a hard look at those who played Mephistopheles and Lucifer to Calvi's overweening ambition ... leaves the reader in little doubt that Calvi was murdered' FINANCIAL TIMES

Fiction

☐ **The Chains of Fate**	Pamela Belle	£2.95p
☐ **Options**	Freda Bright	£1.50p
☐ **The Thirty-nine Steps**	John Buchan	£1.50p
☐ **Secret of Blackoaks**	Ashley Carter	£1.50p
☐ **Hercule Poirot's Christmas**	Agatha Christie	£1.50p
☐ **Dupe**	Liza Cody	£1.25p
☐ **Lovers and Gamblers**	Jackie Collins	£2.50p
☐ **Sphinx**	Robin Cook	£1.25p
☐ **My Cousin Rachel**	Daphne du Maurier	£1.95p
☐ **Flashman and the Redskins**	George Macdonald Fraser	£1.95p
☐ **The Moneychangers**	Arthur Hailey	£2.50p
☐ **Secrets**	Unity Hall	£1.75p
☐ **Black Sheep**	Georgette Heyer	£1.75p
☐ **The Eagle Has Landed**	Jack Higgins	£1.95p
☐ **Sins of the Fathers**	Susan Howatch	£3.50p
☐ **Smiley's People**	John le Carré	£1.95p
☐ **To Kill a Mockingbird**	Harper Lee	£1.95p
☐ **Ghosts**	Ed McBain	£1.75p
☐ **The Silent People**	Walter Macken	£1.95p
☐ **Gone with the Wind**	Margaret Mitchell	£3.50p
☐ **Blood Oath**	David Morrell	£1.75p
☐ **The Night of Morningstar**	Peter O'Donnell	£1.75p
☐ **Wilt**	Tom Sharpe	£1.75p
☐ **Rage of Angels**	Sidney Sheldon	£1.95p
☐ **The Unborn**	David Shobin	£1.50p
☐ **A Town Like Alice**	Nevile Shute	£1.75p
☐ **Gorky Park**	Martin Cruz Smith	£1.95p
☐ **A Falcon Flies**	Wilbur Smith	£2.50p
☐ **The Grapes of Wrath**	John Steinbeck	£2.50p
☐ **The Deep Well at Noon**	Jessica Stirling	£2.50p
☐ **The Ironmaster**	Jean Stubbs	£1.75p
☐ **The Music Makers**	E. V. Thompson	£1.95p

Non-fiction

☐ **The First Christian**	Karen Armstrong	£2.50p
☐ **Pregnancy**	Gordon Bourne	£3.50p
☐ **The Law is an Ass**	Gyles Brandreth	£1.75p
☐ **The 35mm Photographer's Handbook**	Julian Calder and John Garrett	£5.95p
☐ **London at its Best**	Hunter Davies	£2.95p
☐ **Back from the Brink**	Michael Edwardes	£2.95p

☐	**Travellers' Britain**	⎫ Arthur Eperon	£2.95p
☐	**Travellers' Italy**	⎭	£2.95p
☐	**The Complete Calorie Counter**	Eileen Fowler	80p
☐	**The Diary of Anne Frank**	Anne Frank	£1.75p
☐	**And the Walls Came Tumbling Down**	Jack Fishman	£1.95p
☐	**Linda Goodman's Sun Signs**	Linda Goodman	£2.50p
☐	**Scott and Amundsen**	Roland Huntford	£3.95p
☐	**Victoria RI**	Elizabeth Longford	£4.95p
☐	**Symptoms**	Sigmund Stephen Miller	£2.50p
☐	**Book of Worries**	Robert Morley	£1.50p
☐	**Airport International**	Brian Moynahan	£1.75p
☐	**Pan Book of Card Games**	Hubert Phillips	£1.95p
☐	**Keep Taking the Tabloids**	Fritz Spiegl	£1.75p
☐	**An Unfinished History of the World**	Hugh Thomas	£3.95p
☐	**The Baby and Child Book**	Penny and Andrew Stanway	£4.95p
☐	**The Third Wave**	Alvin Toffler	£2.95p
☐	**Pauper's Paris**	Miles Turner	£2.50p
☐	**The Psychic Detectives**	Colin Wilson	£2.50p
☐	**The Flier's Handbook**		£5.95p

All these books are available at your local bookshop or newsagent, or can be ordered direct from the publisher. Indicate the number of copies required and fill in the form below 11

....

Name_____
(Block letters please)

Address_____

_____

Send to CS Department, Pan Books Ltd, PO Box 40, Basingstoke, Hants
Please enclose remittance to the value of the cover price plus:
35p for the first book plus 15p per copy for each additional book ordered
to a maximum charge of £1.25 to cover postage and packing
Applicable only in the UK

While every effort is made to keep prices low, it is sometimes
necessary to increase prices at short notice. Pan Books reserve
the right to show on covers and charge new retail prices which
may differ from those advertised in the text or elsewhere